Introduction to Emergency Management and Disaster Science

A definitive resource, the *Introduction to Emergency Management and Disaster Science* presents the essentials to better understand and manage disasters. The third edition of this popular text has been revised and updated to provide a substantively enriched and evidence-based guide for students and emerging professionals. The new emphasis on disaster science places it at the forefront of a rapidly evolving field. This third edition offers important updates, including:

- Newly commissioned insights from former students and professional colleagues involved with emergency management practice and disaster science; international policies, programs, and practices; and socially vulnerable populations.
- Significantly enriched content and coverage of new disasters and recent research, particularly the worldwide implications of climate change and pandemics.
- Pedagogical features like chapter objectives, key terms and definitions, discussion points, and resources.
- The only textbook authored by three winners of the Blanchard Award for excellence in emergency management instruction.
- Online Support Material containing instructional videos with practical information and learning objectives for the next generation of emergency managers and disaster scientists.

The *Introduction to Emergency Management and Disaster Science* is a must-have textbook for graduate and undergraduate students and is also an excellent source of information for researchers and professionals.

Brenda D. Phillips, PhD, is Dean of the College of Liberal Arts and Sciences and Professor of Sociology at Indiana University South Bend.

David M. Neal, PhD, is a Visiting Scholar and Affiliated Scholar with Indiana University South Bend, and an Affiliated Researcher with the Risk and Crisis Research Centre at Mid Sweden University.

Gary R. Webb, PhD, is Professor and Chair of Emergency Management and Disaster Science at the University of North Texas.

Acknowledgments

Brenda would like to thank her husband, David M. Neal, her parents, Frank and Mary Jane Phillips, and her pets (Scarlet, Sloopy, and Jesse) who persevered with her writing this third edition during quarantine in the COVID-19 pandemic. Thanks also go out to the emergency managers and utility workers who got the power back on during a derecho and ice storm during the same time period. She also would like to thank the next generation of emergency managers, disaster scientists, and students who will face similar threats and hazards and will dedicate themselves to doing all they can to save lives of people and animals alike. She remains grateful to the health care workers, first responders, emergency managers, and scientists who battled the pandemic first-hand and gave us a life-saving, pandemic-ending vaccine. Deep thanks go out to former student, Dr. Gary R. Webb, for his dedicated help in completing this third edition.

Dave would like to thank his spouse, Brenda D. Phillips, for her total support for my efforts. Just before we started this edition, Dave was stricken with Guillain-Barré Syndrome (GBS) and was paralyzed for a while. Her long hours providing support at the hospital certainly helped his progress. Once home, she really helped him get back to normal. While he is mostly recovered now, she also assisted him to move his chapters along. His furry assistants, Scarlet, Sloopy, and Jesse, all aided with mental health duties during GBS, the pandemic, and writing. His colleague and friend, Gary R. Webb, also provided additional help as part of this journey. He would also like to acknowledge his thousands of students in his many emergency management/disaster science classes who are now professionals in their respective fields. Their feedback through the decades certainly helped guide his thinking on these respective fields and many topics in this textbook. And finally, a grateful thanks for those on the frontline throughout the world with our pandemic response. Although the pandemic losses were large, they would have been much worse without their efforts. Their efforts were and are amazing.

Gary would like to thank his wife, Lisa Dalton, and son, Spencer Webb, for serving as constant reminders of what is most important in life and for always helping to keep things in perspective, and Goldie, our dog, for enduring all those Zoom meetings throughout the COVID-19 pandemic. Thanks also to the faculty and staff in EMDS for everything they do to advance disaster science and prepare the next generation of emergency management professionals; to our many alumni who have worked so hard to keep our communities safe through an unimaginable number of catastrophic events in recent months and years; and to our students for instilling hope and confidence that we can achieve a safer and more resilient future.

The authors would also like to thank everyone who contributed to this volume at our publisher, including Natalja Mortensen, Charlie Baker, and Assunta Petrone.

Introduction to Emergency Management and Disaster Science

3rd Edition

Brenda D. Phillips,
David M. Neal,
Gary R. Webb

Routledge
Taylor & Francis Group

NEW YORK AND LONDON

Cover images: © Getty Images

First published 2022
by Routledge
605 Third Avenue, New York, NY 10158

and by Routledge
2 Park Square, Milton Park, Abingdon, Oxon, OX14 4RN

Routledge is an imprint of the Taylor & Francis Group, an informa business

First edition published by CRC Press 2012
Second edition published by CRC Press 2017

Library of Congress Cataloging-in-Publication Data
A catalog record for this title has been requested

ISBN: 978-0-367-89900-4 (hbk)
ISBN: 978-0-367-89899-1 (pbk)
ISBN: 978-1-003-02191-9 (ebk)

DOI: 10.4324/9781003021919

Typeset in Sabon
by codeMantra

Emergency managers and disaster scientists lost Dr. Dennis Mileti, the world's top disaster researcher and consultant in warnings, in the COVID-19 pandemic. We dedicate this third edition to his memory as well as to the mentors and colleagues we miss: E.L. Quarantelli, Russell R. Dynes, Joseph B. Perry, Bill Anderson, Clyde W. Franklin, Eve Coles, and Mary Fran Myers.

Contents

List of Boxes and Figures *xviii*
About the Authors *xx*
Preface *xxii*
Acknowledgments *xxiii*

PART 1
The Disciplines of Emergency Management and Disaster Science 1

1 History and Current Status of Emergency Management and Disaster Science 3

2 Emergency Management Careers 23

3 Key Concepts, Definitions, and Perspectives 60

4 Advancing Emergency Management through Disaster Science 84

PART 2
Comprehensive Emergency Management 113

5 Preparedness 115

6 Planning 135

7 Response 160

8   Recovery   195

9   Mitigation   221

PART 3
Working and Volunteering in Emergency Management   251

10   Public and Private Sectors   253

11   International Humanitarian Disaster Management   283
      Jenny Mincin

12   The Next Generation of Emergency Managers and Disaster
      Scientists   309

Index   *333*

Detailed Contents

List of Boxes and Figures   *xviii*

About the Authors   *xx*

Preface   *xxii*

Acknowledgments   *xxiii*

PART 1

The Disciplines of Emergency Management and Disaster Science   **1**

**1   History and Current Status of Emergency Management and
       Disaster Science**   **3**

Chapter Objectives   *3*

Key Terms   *3*

1.1   *Introduction*   4

          1.1.1   Emergency Management   4

          1.1.2   Current and Future Challenges   5

1.2   *The Evolution of Emergency Management in the U.S.*   6

          1.2.1   The Era of Civil Defense   6

          1.2.2   Professionalization of Emergency Management   7

                   1.2.2.1   Leadership Challenges and Changes   8

                   1.2.2.2   Disasters Change Things   9

                   1.2.2.3   Structural Changes   11

          1.2.3   The Emergence of Emergency Management Degree Programs   14

          1.2.4   The Evolution of Disaster Science   15

                   1.2.4.1   What Is Disaster Science   15

                   1.2.4.2   A Brief History of Disaster Science   16

                   1.2.4.3   Research Centers in the United States   17

                   1.2.4.4   Disaster Science in International Context   18

Summary   *18*

Discussion Questions   *19*

Summary Questions   *19*

References   *20*

Resources   *22*

2	**Emergency Management Careers**	**23**
	Chapter Objectives	23
	Key Terms	23
2.1	*Introduction*	24
	2.1.1 The Profession of Emergency Management	24
	2.1.1.1 Competencies and Expected Behaviors	25
	2.1.1.2 Body of Knowledge	27
	2.1.1.3 Lifelong Learning	28
	2.1.1.4 Ethical Standards and Code of Conduct	29
	2.1.1.5 Career Paths	30
2.2	*Working in the Profession of Emergency Management*	31
	2.2.1 Government Sector Emergency Management	31
	2.2.2 Private Sector Emergency Management	32
	2.2.3 Voluntary Sector Emergency Management	33
	2.2.4 International Emergency Management and Humanitarian Aid	33
	2.2.5 Military Careers and Emergency Management	36
	2.2.6 Specialized Professional Opportunities for Emergency Managers	37
2.3	*Hazards That Can Become Disasters*	38
	2.3.1 High Wind Events	40
	2.3.2 Hurricanes, Cyclones, and Typhoons	41
	2.3.3 Earthquakes	42
	2.3.4 Floods	42
	2.3.5 Volcanoes	43
	2.3.6 Chemical Hazards	44
	2.3.7 Biological Hazards	45
	2.3.8 Radiological and Nuclear Hazards	46
	2.3.9 Terrorism	46
	2.3.10 Computer Crimes and Cyberterrorism	47
	2.3.11 Space Weather	48
	2.3.12 Crowds and Collective Behavior	49
	2.3.13 Climate Change	49
	2.3.14 The Complexity of Hazards that Become Disasters	54
	Summary	55
	Discussion Questions	55
	Summary Questions	55
	References	55
	Resources	59

3   Key Concepts, Definitions, and Perspectives   60

Chapter Objectives   60
Key Terms   60
3.1   *Introduction*   61
3.2   *Defining Disaster*   61
    3.2.1   A Continuum of Disaster   62
        3.2.1.1   Emergency   62
        3.2.1.2   Disaster   63
        3.2.1.3   Catastrophe   63
    3.2.2   Political Definitions of Disaster   64
    3.2.3   Slow versus Fast-Moving Views of Disaster   66
3.3   *The National Governor's Association Report in the U.S.*   67
    3.3.1   The Disaster Life Cycle   68
    3.3.2   All-Hazards Approach   69
3.4   *Major Perspectives in Disaster Science*   70
    3.4.1   The Hazards Tradition   70
    3.4.2   The Disaster Tradition   71
    3.4.3   The Risk Perspective   72
    3.4.4   The Crisis Approach   73
    3.4.5   Major Perspectives Summary   74
3.5   *Cross-Cutting Themes in Disaster Science*   74
    3.5.1   Social Vulnerability   74
    3.5.2   Resilience   76
    3.5.3   Summary of Cross-Cutting Themes   77
3.6   *Embracing a Multidisciplinary Approach*   77
3.7   *The View from Emergency Management Higher Education*   78
Summary   79
Discussion Questions   80
Summary Questions   80
References   80
Resources   83

4   Advancing Emergency Management through Disaster Science   84

Chapter Objectives   84
Key Terms   84
4.1   *Introduction*   84
4.2   *Disaster Science as a Multidisciplinary Field*   85
4.3   *The Importance of Disaster Science to Emergency Management*   91
4.4   *Research Process*   95
4.5   *Types of Research*   96
    4.5.1   Basic and Applied Research   96
    4.5.2   Primary and Secondary Research   97
    4.5.3   Cross Sectional and Longitudinal Research   97
    4.5.4   Individual and Aggregate Research   98
    4.5.5   Quantitative and Qualitative Research   98

4.6	Research Methods		99
	4.6.1	Surveys	99
	4.6.2	Interviews	100
	4.6.3	Observations	102
	4.6.4	Archives	103
	4.6.5	Spatial Tools	104
4.7	Ethics		105
4.8	Research Challenges		106
Summary			107
Discussion Questions			108
Summary Questions			108
References			108
Resources			112

PART 2
Comprehensive Emergency Management 113

5 Preparedness 115

Chapter Objectives			115
Key Terms			115
5.1	Introduction		115
5.2	Prioritizing Preparedness		116
5.3	Defining Preparedness		120
5.4	Types and Levels of Preparedness Activities		121
	5.4.1	Individuals and Households	121
	5.4.2	Organizations	122
	5.4.3	Communities	124
5.5	Factors Influencing Levels of Preparedness		125
	5.5.1	Previous Disaster Experience	125
	5.5.2	Risk Perception	126
5.6	Preparedness Initiatives at State, National, and International Levels		127
	5.6.1	Examples of State-Level Preparedness Initiatives	127
	5.6.2	Examples of National-Level Preparedness Initiatives	127
	5.6.3	Examples of International Preparedness Initiatives	128
5.7	Working and Volunteering in Preparedness		129
Summary			130
Discussion Questions			131
Summary Questions			131
References			131
Resources			134

6   Planning   **135**

Chapter Objectives   *135*
Key Terms   *135*
6.1   Introduction   *135*
6.2   *Principles of Planning*   *136*
6.3   *Types of Planning*   *142*
    6.3.1   Planning Across the Life Cycle of Emergency Management   *142*
    6.3.2   Business Continuity Planning   *143*
6.4   *Levels of Planning*   *143*
    6.4.1   Individual- and Household-Level Planning   *144*
    6.4.2   Community-Based Planning   *145*
    6.4.3   State and National Planning Guidance in the U.S.   *147*
6.5   *Working and Volunteering in Planning*   *154*
Summary   *155*
Discussion Questions   *155*
Summary Questions   *156*
References   *156*
Resources   *159*

7   Response   **160**

Chapter Objectives   *160*
Key Terms   *160*
7.1   Introduction   *160*
    7.1.1   Ignoring Other Phases of Disaster   *161*
    7.1.2   Envisioning Chaos   *162*
    7.1.3   Assuming Need for Command and Control   *162*
7.2   *Getting Started: Definitions and Activities*   *162*
    7.2.1   Defining Response   *163*
    7.2.2   Typical Response Activities   *163*
7.3   *Disaster Warnings*   *165*
    7.3.1   Warning Process   *165*
    7.3.2   Taking Protective Action   *166*
        7.3.2.1   Evacuation and Temporary Sheltering   *167*
        7.3.2.2   Factors Affecting Evacuation and Public
                Shelter Usage   *168*
    7.3.3   Characteristics of Effective Disaster Warnings   *169*
7.4   *Disaster Response: Myths and Realities*   *171*
    7.4.1   Myth-Based View of Disaster Response   *172*
    7.4.2   Research-Based View of Disaster Response   *176*
    7.4.3   Sources and Limitations of Community Resilience   *180*
7.5   *Disaster Response in an International Context*   *181*
7.6   *Disaster Response and Principles of Effective Emergency Management*   *183*
    7.6.1   Comprehensive Emergency Management   *183*
    7.6.2   Integrated Emergency Management   *184*
    7.6.3   Flexibility in Emergency Management   *185*

7.7	*The Future of Response*	*186*
7.8	*Working and Volunteering in Response*	*188*
Summary		*189*
Discussion Questions		*190*
Summary Questions		*190*
References		*190*
Resources		*194*

8   Recovery   **195**

Chapter Objectives		*195*
Key Terms		*195*
8.1	*Introduction*	*196*
	8.1.1 Defining Recovery	196
	8.1.2 Recovery Is a Process	197
8.2	*Damage Assessment*	*197*
	8.2.1 Preliminary Damage Assessment	198
	8.2.2 Needs Assessment	200
8.3	*Recovery Functions*	*201*
	8.3.1 Shelter and Housing	201
	8.3.2 Businesses	203
	8.3.3 Infrastructure and Lifelines	206
	8.3.4 Psychological Impacts	207
	8.3.5 Environmental Concerns	209
	8.3.6 Historic and Cultural Resources	210
8.4	*People-Centered Recovery*	*211*
	8.4.1 Kinds of Recovery Planning	212
8.5	*Working and Volunteering in Recovery*	*215*
Summary		*216*
Discussion Questions		*216*
Summary Questions		*217*
References		*217*
Resources		*220*

9   Mitigation   **221**

Chapter Objectives		*221*
Key Terms		*221*
9.1	*Introduction*	*222*
9.2	*What Are the Risks?*	*222*
	9.2.1 Threat and Hazard Identification	222
	9.2.2 Capability Assessment	223
	9.2.3 Risk Assessment	224
	9.2.3.1 Social Vulnerability Assessment	226
	9.2.3.2 Loss Estimation	227

9.3   What Is Mitigation?   228
        9.3.1   Structural Mitigation   233
        9.3.2   Nonstructural Mitigation   239
9.4   Mitigation Planning with Stakeholders   241
        9.4.1   Resilience   241
        9.4.2   Mitigation Planning Basics   241
        9.4.3   Inclusive Mitigation Planning   242
        9.4.4   Strategies for Community Engagement   244
9.5   Careers and Volunteering in Mitigation and Resilience   245
Summary   247
Discussion Questions   248
Summary Questions   248
References   248
Resources (last accessed January 7, 2021)   250

PART 3
Working and Volunteering in Emergency Management   251

10   Public and Private Sectors   253

Chapter Objectives   253
Key Terms   253
10.1   Introduction   253
10.2   The Public Sector   254
        10.2.1   Local Government   254
                  10.2.1.1   Elected Officials and the Emergency
                             Management Offices   254
                  10.2.1.2   Local Departments   255
        10.2.2   State Government   256
                  10.2.2.1   Role of the Governor   256
                  10.2.2.2   Emergency Management and Homeland
                             Security Offices   256
        10.2.3   Accrediting State and Local Governments   258
        10.2.4   Federal Government   259
                  10.2.4.1   The Executive Branch   259
                  10.2.4.2   Congress   261
10.3   The Private Sector   262
        10.3.1   The Importance of the Private Sector   262
        10.3.2   The Impacts of Disasters on the Private Sector   264
                  10.3.2.1   Direct Impacts   264
                  10.3.2.2   Indirect Impacts   265
                  10.3.2.3   Remote Impacts   265
        10.3.3   The Private Sector and the Life Cycle of Emergency
                  Management   267
                  10.3.3.1   Preparedness   267
                  10.3.3.2   Response   269

	10.3.3.3	Recovery	271
	10.3.3.4	Mitigation	272
10.4	Public and Private Partnerships		273
10.5	Working and Volunteering in the Private Sector		275
Summary			277
Discussion Questions			278
Summary Questions			278
References			278
Resources			282

11   International Humanitarian Disaster Management   283

Jenny Mincin

Chapter Objectives			283
Key Terms			283
11.1	Introduction		284
	11.1.1	UN High Commissioner on Refugees	284
	11.1.2	Coordination	286
	11.1.3	Climate Change and Disaster Response	286
11.2	International Emergency Management System		287
	11.2.1	UN Cluster System	288
	11.2.2	Sphere	289
	11.2.3	U.S. Agency for International Development	289
11.3	How to Work in International Contexts		290
	11.3.1	Cultural Awareness and Integrating Context	290
	11.3.2	Community Integration and Resiliency Models in International Emergency Management	293
	11.3.3	Guidance for Helping as Non-Aid Workers	295
11.4	Working with Refugees in Camps, Urban Environments, and Resettlement Programs		296
	11.4.1	Refugee Camps	297
	11.4.2	Urban Refugees	299
	11.4.3	Refugee Resettlement	299
	11.4.4	A Moment in the Life of a Refugee and Asylee Fleeing	300
11.5	Disaster Risk Reduction at the International Level		301
11.6	Working and Volunteering in an International Setting		301
	11.6.1	International Aid Workers: Lives on the Line	303
Summary			303
Discussion Questions			304
Summary Questions			304
References			305
Resources			308

**12   The Next Generation of Emergency Managers and
Disaster Scientists**   **309**

Chapter Objectives   *309*
Key Terms   *309*
12.1   *Introduction*   *309*
12.2   *Reflecting Our Communities*   *310*
         12.2.1   Race, Ethnicity, and the Profession of Emergency Management   312
         12.2.2   Gender   313
         12.2.3   Indigenous People   313
         12.2.4   An Accessible Workplace for All   315
         12.2.5   LGBTQ+   316
         12.2.6   Guidance for Everyone: Mentors and Networking   317
         12.2.7   Fellowships and Scholarships   317
         12.2.8   Internships and Practical Experience   320
12.3   *Continuing Your Education*   *320*
         12.3.1   Undergraduate Degree Programs   320
         12.3.2   Graduate Programs   321
         12.3.3   Online Degree Programs   324
         12.3.4   Continuing Education   324
                   12.3.4.1   Training   324
                   12.3.4.2   Exercises and Drills   325
                   12.3.4.3   Conferences, Workshops   325
                   12.3.4.4   Professional and Scientific Journals   325
12.4   *Finding Your First Employer*   *327*
Summary   *329*
Discussion Questions   *329*
Summary Questions   *329*
References   *330*
Resources (Accessed May 18, 2021)   *332*

Index   *333*

Boxes and Figures

Boxes

1.1	Other Important Federal Disaster Organizations	10
1.2	Current Emergency Support Functions	12
2.1	Becoming a Certified Emergency Manager	29
2.2	Working in the Voluntary and Public Sectors (Jessica Bettinger)	34
2.3	Working in Crowd Settings (Dr. Barb Russo)	50
3.1	The Process of Naming a Presidential Declaration of Disaster	65
4.1	Converge: NHERI	86
4.2	Social Science Extreme Events Research	89
4.3	The Value of Research for Emergency Management	92
4.4	Academic Journals in Emergency Management and Disaster Science	96
5.1	Lessons Unlearned: Understanding Social Vulnerability to Improve Preparedness	117
5.2	Preparedness and the Whole Community	119
5.3	Preparedness Recommendations	123
6.1	Lessons Unlearned: Dusting Off the Plan	138
6.2	Make a Household Disaster Preparedness Plan	146
6.3	Hazard-Specific Planning: Pandemics	150
7.1	Disaster Myths and the COVID-19 Pandemic	173
7.2	Lessons Unlearned: Dealing with Disaster Donations	177
8.1	FEMA National Recovery Framework	199
8.2	Lessons Unlearned, Equity Issues in Shelter and Housing	204
9.1	Threat and Hazard Information Sources	223
9.2	Threat and Hazard Identification and Risk Assessment	224
9.3	Lessons Unlearned, from Champions of Disaster Mitigation	234
9.4	Assessing Building Vulnerability to Terrorism	238
9.5	Mitigation and Resilience Career Examples (Verbatim from Sources)	246
10.1	Resuming Operations during the COVID-19 Pandemic	266
10.2	Lessons Unlearned: Improving Business Disaster Preparedness	268
11.1	Eleanor Roosevelt and the Universal Declaration of Human Rights	285
11.2	Integration and Empowerment: Women and Girls and People with Disabilities	292

11.3	Hiring Former Refugees	294
11.4	Myanmar Coup and Ongoing Instability	298
12.1	What Cultural Competency Can Do	311
12.2	Bridging Research and Practice: The Life of Mary Fran Myers	314
12.3	Bill Anderson Fellow: An Applied Linguist in Emergency Management	318
12.4	Pursuing Graduate Studies	322
12.5	An Interdisciplinary Journey in Hazards and Disasters Research	326
12.6	Becoming a Certified Emergency Manager	328

Figures

3.1	Major Perspectives in Disaster Science	70
3.2	Cross-Cutting Themes in Disaster Science	74
4.1	Steps in the Research Process	95
4.2	Methods of Data Collection	99
5.1	Types of Preparedness Activities	121
5.2	Priorities for Action in the Sendai Framework for Disaster Risk Reduction, 2015–2030	129
6.1	Steps in the Planning Process	149
6.2	The Planning and Preparedness Cycle	149
6.3	The Incident Command System	153
7.1	Warning Process	166
7.2	Types of Organized Responses to Disasters	180
7.3	Characteristics of Future Disasters	187
7.4	Understanding Future Risks	188
10.1	The EU Civil Protection Mechanism	262
10.2	Billion-Dollar Weather Disasters in the U.S. in 2020	263
10.3	Business Continuity Planning Process	270
10.4	Community Lifelines	274

About the Authors

Brenda D. Phillips, PhD, is Dean of the College of Liberal Arts and Sciences and Professor of Sociology at Indiana University South Bend. She is the author of *Mennonite Disaster Service, Qualitative Disaster Research, Disaster Recovery*, and *Disaster Volunteers*, a co- author of *Business Continuity Planning*, and an editor of *Social Vulnerability to Disasters*. Professor Phillips has conducted research on disaster recovery since 1982, beginning as a student of E.L. Quarantelli at The Ohio State University's Disaster Research Center. Her published research can be found in a variety of journals, including the *International Journal of Mass Emergencies and Disasters, Disaster Prevention, Disasters, Humanity and Society, the Journal of Emergency Management, Natural Hazards Review*, and *Environmental Hazards*. She has been funded multiple times by the National Science Foundation to study disasters and vulnerable populations. Dr. Phillips has been invited to teach, consult, or lecture in New Zealand, Australia, Germany, India, Costa Rica, Mexico, Canada, Peru, and the People's Republic of China. Her volunteer activities have included serving on Local Emergency Planning Committees, county- level safety committees, and multicounty health care coalitions for disaster preparedness, as well as serving as a subject matter expert for the U.S. Federal Emergency Management Agency, the National Council on Disability, and the Office of the Federal Coordinator of Meteorology. She holds considerable expertise in business continuity planning and has helped complete over 60 academic continuity plans. In 2012, she received the Blanchard Award for Excellence in Emergency Management Education. In 2013, she was inducted into the International Network of Women in Emergency Management and Homeland Security's Hall of Fame.

David M. Neal, PhD, recently retired as Professor Emeritus in Fire and Emergency Management from Oklahoma State University and is now a Visiting Scholar and Affiliated Scholar with Indiana University South Bend, and an Affiliated Researcher with the Risk and Crisis Research Centre at MidSweden University. He has conducted disaster research since 1978 and taught his first disaster class in 1979. He has also received funding for his research from the National Science Foundation, Department of Homeland Security, Federal Emergency Management Agency, National Aeronautics and Space Administration, the American National Red Cross, and the Alabama Consortium on Higher Education, among others. His academic publications can be found in such journals as *International Journal of Mass Emergencies and Disasters*,

Natural Hazards, Journal of Emergency Management, Disaster Prevention and Management, International Journal of Risk Reduction, Sociological Focus, and *Sociologiska Forsking*, among others. He has given a number of invited international presentations in England, Canada, Russia, Germany, Costa Rica, India, and Sweden. He has taught in emergency and disaster management degree programs since 1989 (University of North Texas, Jacksonville State University, Oklahoma State University). As a faculty member or consultant, he helped establish or enhance a number of early degree programs related to emergency management or fire administration, including on-line degree programs. In 2015, he received the Blanchard Award for Excellence in Emergency Management Education.

Gary R. Webb, PhD, is Professor and Chair of Emergency Management and Disaster Science at the University of North Texas, Denton, Texas. Previously, he was a faculty member in the sociology department at Oklahoma State University, where he received the Regents Distinguished Teaching Award. His research has been supported by various agencies, including the U.S. National Science Foundation, and it has appeared in a variety of professional journals, including the *International Journal of Mass Emergencies and Disasters, International Journal of Emergency Management, Journal of Contingencies and Crisis Management, Natural Hazards Review*, and the *International Journal of Disaster Risk Science*. His research has also been featured in national media outlets, including the *New York Times, Los Angeles Times*, and National Public Radio. He has delivered invited presentations on hazards, disasters, and emergency management in Denmark, France, Sweden, South Korea, Taiwan, the Netherlands, and Turkey. In 2021, Dr. Webb received the Blanchard Award for Excellence in Emergency Management Education.

Dr. Jenny Mincin is an Assistant Professor in Health and Human Services at State University of New York Empire State College. She has over twenty-five years of experience in the government, non-governmental, and academic sectors both nationally and internationally and is a specialist in disaster human services and humanitarian crisis work, refugees and immigrants, and vulnerable and special needs populations. Jenny has worked for the City of New York, International Rescue Committee, and the Federal Emergency Management Agency among others. She continues to work with Church World Services supporting research and program development for refugees and asylees. In addition to teaching and researching fulltime at SUNY Empire State College, she oversees the Certificate in Crisis Prevention and Intervention program and serves as an Advisory Board Member for the Rockefeller Institute Center for Policy and Law and the SUNY Empire/New York State Women's Corporate Leadership Academy. She was the recipient of SUNY Empire State College's Scholars Across the College program for academic year 2017–2018 and has received three innovation in research awards. Jenny received her PhD in Social Welfare Policy and a Masters of Philosophy in Social Welfare Policy from Hunter College School of Social Work, CUNY Graduate Center. She also has an MPA from Columbia University School of International and Public Affairs and received her BA from Barnard College/Columbia University in Religion and Environmental Science.

Preface

Disasters never have been equal opportunity events. People who are poor and who have been historically marginalized suffer terribly in disasters. We can change that.

This third edition aims to inform and inspire the next generation of emergency managers to be the change that people at risk need. To do so, we must immerse ourselves in the science of disasters to learn all we can that reduces risk for those most socially vulnerable. Accordingly, readers will find content on socially vulnerable people embedded in every single chapter, not set off as a separate chapter to study in a certain week but as an integrated and essential part of every single action that an emergency manager takes. Yes, it will take that level of commitment and dedication to make the difference we need to save lives.

Effort and meaning well will not be enough. Science must serve as the basis for decisions and actions taken in the practice of life safety. We expect students and practitioners to learn lessons in the book – not to follow in the tradition of lessons *un*learned – and stop repeating the errors of the past. Learn the science, practice its application, and then you can take the essential actions needed to address the disproportionate impacts of disasters.

Toward that end, this third edition integrates emergency management with the discipline of disaster science at a new level of effort. The text now follows a more traditional path through an introductory course with essential content – concepts, theories, and methods – followed by an organized section on the heart of evidence-based best practices in planning, preparedness, response, recovery, and mitigation, and completed by looking at the places in which emergency managers work: the public and private sectors and the international, humanitarian sector. A concluding section lays out why active representation of a more diverse set of emergency managers will expedite our chances of reducing those unequal impacts.

We have not and never will give up on the messages in this book: reduce the disproportionate impacts of disasters, read the science, build an evidence-based practice. We do so not only out of a conviction that disaster science can and does make a difference, but that we must. You are invited to join us on this journey to make the world a safer place. Do not ever give up.

PART **1**

The Disciplines of Emergency Management and Disaster Science

History and Current Status of Emergency Management and Disaster Science

---

CHAPTER OBJECTIVES

Upon completing this chapter, readers should be able to:

- Describe the development of Civil Defense and Emergency Management (EM) in the U.S.
- Discuss the central role of the Federal Emergency Management Agency in the U.S. since 1979.
- Review the origins and roles of the Department of Homeland Security in U.S. emergency management (EM) since 2004.
- Give examples of how EM functions in other countries.
- Explain the value and role of disaster science for the practice of EM role of disaster science for the practice of EM.
- Show how using disaster science enhances EM.

KEY TERMS

- Civil Defense
- Cold War
- Department of Homeland Security
- Disaster Research

- Disaster Science
- Dual Disaster Track
- Emergency Management
- Emergency Manager

DOI: 10.4324/9781003021919-2

- Emergency Support Function
- Federal Emergency Management
  Agency

- Federal Response Plan
- National Response Framework

1.1 INTRODUCTION

Catastrophic hurricanes and cyclones. Destructive tornadoes. Deadly pandemics. Extensive flooding. Choking droughts. Massive wildfires. Extreme worldwide temperatures. Cyberattacks. Near miss asteroids. Cross-national protests. Contagious, deadly pandemics. Devastating earthquakes. Invading killer hornets. Potentially devastating space weather. Are these events potential plot lines for new movies? Perhaps, because these and other events are occurring now, and we will see more in the future. If you like excitement and new challenges, the profession of emergency management (EM) and studying how people behave in such events may suit you.

Dealing with disasters is not new. Disaster science pioneer Russell Dynes (2003) observed that Noah was the first emergency manager, and he faced the same problems and issues that emergency managers face today. Although Noah received news about a major flood from an impeccable source, only a few heeded Noah's warning and helped him to prepare. Today, we face similar and perhaps more problems than Noah. People continue to live in disaster-prone areas (e.g., earthquakes, hurricanes) and often do not or cannot take steps that lessen the impact of such events. Indeed, annual deaths and economic losses from disasters continue to increase worldwide. Emergency managers work to address such losses, enhance life safety, protect property, and make jurisdictions, homes, and workplaces safer places (Waugh 2000).

Professional EM presents many challenges, but through careful study in its related discipline of disaster science, you can make a difference. To assist emergency managers, a long line of research on disasters provides insights for emergency managers to make informed decisions before, during, and after events. The science of disasters (i.e., research on how people and organizations behave) serves as a basis for this textbook. To start you on a journey toward becoming an emergency manager, this chapter describes how the field has evolved in the U.S. and worldwide.

1.1.1 Emergency Management

More than 60 years ago, the field of EM was known as civil defense. Typically, people held part-time positions in local government, often focused on nuclear disasters (including war) and to a lesser extent on other disasters (e.g., tornadoes, floods, hurricanes, and explosions). Since then, the profession has expanded among local, state, and federal governments, and also in the private, volunteer, and international relief sectors. Emergency managers now prepare for, respond to, recover from, and reduce risks to (mitigate) a wide range of events, including floods, hurricanes, tornados, tsunamis, earthquakes, volcanoes, explosions, hazardous waste accidents or sites, and terrorist attacks. In addition, emergency managers assist with newer types of threats such as cyberattacks, pandemics, and climate change. For those who like the unknown and the challenging, and who want to make a difference with their lives, EM offers a promising and meaningful career path. Your journey begins with acquiring an understanding of what emergency managers face in today's work and into the future.

1.1.2 Current and Future Challenges

Nearly 30 years ago, disaster researcher E.L. Quarantelli (1991) warned that the world would face more disasters, larger disasters, and new and different types of disasters. His predictions have come true. First, we have created new technologies with unknown consequences. For example, while rapidly evolving computers and the internet connect us, such technologies have vulnerabilities. Cyberterrorism provides one example, which can shut down health care or government, disrupt elections, stop gasoline pipeline delivery, or damage electrical grids used to power hospitals, businesses, and medical devices. Space weather has also emerged as a new hazard which, under the right conditions, could disrupt navigational systems, cell phone functioning, and the electrical grid.

Second, social scientists have continued to find that human behavior continues to transform hazards into disasters (Quarantelli 1991; Mileti 1999). For example, people build along coastal areas or waterways, which are prone to hurricanes and floods. Or, people live and work close to hazards, which may include chemical facilities or transportation arteries where major accidents occur. Further, as uninhabited places become more densely populated, risks increase. A rural cornfield in Iowa could devastate a farmer's planting, but without loss of life. Yet, a subdivision built in "tornado alley" becomes a potential tragedy. The popular Atlantic and Gulf coastal areas in the U.S. have seen increased density too, including residents, "snowbirds," and tourists. Hurricanes, increased flooding from climate change, and electrical grid disruptions means more people may be affected in those areas. Clearly, people serve as an active human agent in transforming a hazard into a disaster, because a hazard alone cannot become a disaster without people to transform its potential or to bear the consequences (Mileti 1999).

Worldwide, disaster impacts have increased. From 2000 to 2020, the UN documented 7,348 major disaster events that caused 1,230,000 deaths and affected 4,200,000,000 people. Asian nations, including India, the Philippines, and Indonesia, ranked among the top ten affected (Reuters 2020). The year 2020 is especially noteworthy of large-scale events. In just that year, record-breaking wildfires (especially the western regions), multiple tropical storms, and hurricanes plagued the U.S. Some events, such as Category 5 Hurricane Iota (the strongest category), created close to catastrophic conditions in Central America (NOAA 2020). In Africa, record-breaking rains created massive floods, which have destroyed crops (leading to famine) and killed hundreds (Smith 2020). During 2020 in East Central Africa, some countries confronted simultaneously extreme rain, mudslides, flooding, locusts, and COVID-19 which collectively caused massive evacuations, population displacements, severe illness, and significant loss of life (McCoy 2020).

Occasionally, catastrophic events occur, such as the COVID-19 pandemic. In addition to the large numbers of people that acquired the disease, suffered, and died from it, mitigation efforts to curtail the pandemic changed daily activities and undermined economies. Restaurants, museums, sporting venues, movie theaters, and malls all closed for weeks to months with considerable loss of revenue. Schools and universities ended semesters early and hedged their bets by moving classes online. As the virus surged in devastating waves, hospitals became overwhelmed with patients. Countries created travel bans to reduce high infection and death rates. Between March and December 2020, over 60,258,185 people had the virus, with 1,418,614 dying worldwide (COVID Dashboard 2020; DHS 2020). In the U.S., millions caught the virus with 700,000+ dead as this book went to press. Furthermore, research shows that about 10% of those with the virus became "long haulers." These individuals will suffer from lasting effects from the virus, including coughing, fatigue, body aches, joint pain, shortness of breath, loss of taste and smell, insomnia, headaches, heart issues, or brain fog (UC Davis Health 2020).

What do emergency managers do about such challenges? The remainder of this chapter looks at how the profession has developed, especially as it has responded to major challenges like terror attacks and other major disasters. The challenge before us is to remain mindful of Quarantelli's prediction and to always be looking ahead to what we may have not expected.

1.2 THE EVOLUTION OF EMERGENCY MANAGEMENT IN THE U.S.

Almost 70 years ago, the profession of EM did not exist. Within the U.S., for example, disaster offices were scattered across units that dealt with nuclear war, floods, hurricanes, and similar hazards. Local governments had offices of civil defense to help protect the nation against a possible nuclear attack from the Soviet Union. Typically, civil defense positions were part time, low paying, and required little if any training or education. The Red Cross and Salvation Army were the most common volunteer organizations available to assist disaster victims. Businesses typically did not have disaster planners. Only a few organizations throughout the world provided international disaster relief. No universities offered a major or minor in EM, nor were any individual courses available. A lot has changed since then.

EM has slowly risen to become a full-fledged profession. Today, those in the U.S. Federal Emergency Management Agency (FEMA), as a part of the Department of Homeland Security (DHS), coordinate most of our national disaster efforts. All states and most local governments have emergency managers and agencies. Major businesses hire individuals to manage risks and conduct disaster planning. A large number of volunteer organizations assist survivors. Worldwide, a wide range of organizations offer disaster relief within and across national borders. Many professionals in the field today have earned college degrees, and about 150 universities in the U.S. alone offer bachelor, master, or doctoral degrees in EM. This section provides an overview of this extraordinary growth and describes some of the key organizations today that play major roles in EM. Four phases generally characterize growth in the field: (1) the era of civil defense, (2) the professionalization of EM, (3) the evolution of homeland security, and (4) the emergence of higher education (Webb 2016).

1.2.1 The Era of Civil Defense

Throughout much of the last century, the federal government coordinated the protection of U.S. citizens from foreign attack through the idea of civil defense. For example, during World War II, civil defense authorities trained civilians to spot enemy aircraft, ships, and submarines. Cities practiced evening blackouts, turning out lights so that enemy bombers could not find their targets. Civil defense became even more prominent in the early 1950s with the arrival of the Cold War when the (former) Soviet Union and the U.S. became bitter ideological enemies. With each having nuclear weapons, attention turned to the possibility of devastating war. During the Cold War, the U.S. created various offices of civil defense (i.e., Federal Civil Defense Agency 1953–1958; Office of Civil Defense Mobilization 1958–1961; and the Office of Civil Defense 1968–1979) to lead and coordinate efforts. Well-known activities supported by Civil Defense included "duck and cover" protective actions and encouraging citizens to build nuclear bomb shelters in their homes. In addition, some public buildings were designated as "Civil Defense Shelters" where those under attack would take protective action (Sylves 2008; FEMA Task Force 2010). Today, you can still find historic Civil Defense Shelter Signs on public buildings.

Major events began to transform the field from civil defense to EM. In 1950, following severe flooding in the upper Midwest, Congress passed the Disaster Relief Act. This legislation allowed the federal government and the President to become involved in future disaster relief efforts without additional congressional approval. Although the Disaster Relief Act provided only a narrow scope of disaster assistance, it created a foundation for Congress to later expand the role of the federal government in disaster (Kreps 1990; Sylves 2008). Subsequent large disasters (e.g., Hurricane Camille, 1969; San Fernando Earthquake, 1971; Hurricane Agnes, 1972) broadened the federal government's role during disaster and increased the number of responding voluntary organizations (Kreps 1990). The Disaster Relief Act of 1974 and the Stafford Act of 1988 gave the federal government a means to deliver assistance directly to communities and disaster victims. Most importantly, these acts described how a Presidential Declaration could be made and what kinds of aid can be delivered (Sylves 2008).

Thus, between 1950 and 1979, the federal government supported two separate crisis management tracks. One focused on civil defense (i.e., nuclear war), while the other concentrated on natural disasters (and some technological disasters). Although these unintended dual tracks made sense at the time, they also created problems. First, duplication of tasks developed between the civil defense and natural disaster efforts and increased costs. Second, since these disaster offices were not centralized, problems of communication and inefficiency developed (National Governor's Association 1979). In addition, in both civil defense and peacetime-focused organizations, occasional reorganization seemed to be the norm. For many, the dual tracks (rather than having one centralized federal agency) and constant reorganization hurt the nation's ability to deal with disasters (Kreps 1990). In response, President Jimmy Carter centralized most of the nation's disaster efforts under one organization in 1979 by creating the FEMA, an effort that fueled the professionalization of EM.

1.2.2 Professionalization of Emergency Management

Several themes characterize how EM has moved from the dual tracks into a more comprehensive and coordinated career field. Transformative events have included leadership appointments, structural changes, disaster events, and the rise of degree programs based on disaster science.

1.2.2.1 Leadership Challenges and Changes

Presidents nominate FEMA Directors, whose leadership influences the agency and what is emphasized. Perhaps not surprisingly, some FEMA Directors have been critiqued as political appointees lacking relevant experience with FEMA's reputation suffering as well (Daniels and Clark-Daniels 2000). It was not until 1992 that James Lee Witt became the first FEMA Director with EM experience. Witt arrived at FEMA well-grounded in disaster terminology and issues while also understanding the roles of the local, state, and federal government during disasters. President Clinton also made FEMA a cabinet-level position, which gave the FEMA director access to the White House (Daniels and Clark-Daniels 2000). During his tenure as FEMA director, Witt and his associate director Kay Goss (the first woman in such a high-level position) emphasized mitigation (see Chapter 9), or efforts to reduce disaster impacts and costs. One key program was Project Impact, a citizen-based, community-wide effort that involved nearly 200 communities and over 1,000 businesses (Witt and Morgan 2002). For example, residents in Chesapeake, Virginia, installed storm shutters in their homes and local governments invested funds to mitigate damage to public buildings. Under Witt, FEMA streamlined a rather bureaucratic aid process by creating a National Tele-Registration Center (NTC) located in Denton, Texas. As another first, FEMA developed a strategic plan, which gave the organization a better sense of direction and purpose (Witt and Morgan 2002).

In 2001, President Bush named one of his top political aides, Joe Allbaugh, as the new FEMA director, though he lacked a background in EM (Holderman 2005, p. A17). Ironically, the same day that the administration eliminated Project Impact, a magnitude 6.8 earthquake rattled the Seattle area which absorbed the shock reasonably well due to Project Impact mitigation efforts. Critics became convinced that EM and mitigation were no longer top federal priorities (Holderman 2005, p. A17). Upon taking office eight years later, President Obama named Craig Fugate as the new director of FEMA. As a fire fighter and paramedic, county emergency manager, and director of the Florida Division of Emergency Management, Fugate quelled concerns about lack of experience in agency leadership. In speaking to the FEMA Higher Education Conference in 2009, Fugate became the first FEMA director to support the value of disaster research and encouraged emergency managers to listen to social scientists. During the Trump Administration (2017–2021), FEMA had three Acting Directors and one Director who served for 16 months. As this book went to press, President Joe Biden had appointed the first woman to serve as FEMA director. Deanne Criswell, an experienced emergency manager with local and FEMA career experience, had most recently served as the director of New York City's Emergency Management Department where she had expressed concern over climate change raising the area's sea level.

Despite these top-level appointments, it is important to note that career personnel have always kept FEMA operational and focused on its mission. Without leadership at their levels, FEMA's mission could have been seriously compromised. Nonetheless, FEMA has borne its share of criticism, especially during major disasters.

1.2.2.2 Disasters Change Things

In 1969, Hurricane Camille struck the U.S. Gulf Coast, causing catastrophic damage. Overwhelmed local governments required help beyond the traditional outreach from the Red Cross and Salvation Army in caring for displaced residents who required assistance to rebuild and recover. In one of the largest movements to influence disaster relief efforts, dozens of faith-based and civic groups sent help. Into the formal mix of federal agencies, a new effort emerged called the National Voluntary Organization Active in Disasters (NVOAD). Today, NVOAD has become the backbone of much mass care and recovery efforts when disasters strike. Big disasters change things.

Across its 40 years of existence, FEMA has also been transformed by the "big ones" (The White House 2006; U.S. Congress 2006). For example, in 1992 Hurricane Andrew damaged or destroyed about 125,000 Florida residences, killed at least 61 people, and caused $27 billion in economic losses (or close to $51 billion in 2021; NOAA 2011). Reconnaissance for the damage came in slowly, however, and FEMA again faced criticism for its response. The disaster also led to significant changes in the nation's brand new federal response plan (FRP) and contributed to President Bush losing a second term in office.

In contrast to the focused southern Florida location of Andrew, FEMA again faced significant challenges in 1989 when Hurricane Hugo slammed the Atlantic coast and a major earthquake (Loma Prieta) struck northern California with deadly consequences and significant collapses of buildings, bridges, and infrastructure. This time, FEMA's resources had to be split in two different directions which stretched its personnel. Today, FEMA mobilizes on-call personnel that nearly doubles its size when such events happen. Multiple agencies support FEMA when disaster happens.

Striking the U.S. Gulf Coast on August 29, 2005, Hurricane Katrina damaged levees in New Orleans and sent a massive storm surge 6–12 miles inland across Mississippi. The storm is believed to have killed close to 1,800 people and injured thousands. Storm surge and high winds caused some of the largest economic and infrastructural damage in U.S. disaster history, costing well over $100 billion in damage. Again, the federal government faced criticism for a response limited in its scope as people tried to survive on rooftops and overpasses (Waugh 2006). Criticism rose in particular over extremely vulnerable populations who lacked the means to evacuate – and died, with a higher percentage from racial and ethnic minorities in comparison to whites. Lawsuits arose over inaccessible trailers for people with disabilities. FEMA's director was relieved of his position and a military general was put in charge to expedite the response (for more details, visit https://www.nhc.noaa.gov/archive/2005/KATRINA.shtml).

But undoubtedly the largest change that occurred in FEMA's history came after September 11, 2001. The terrorist attack claimed thousands of lives, including hundreds of police and firefighters. Reports laid blame at federal agencies which had failed to share information about possible attacks or concerns. In response, the Department of Homeland Security (DHS) emerged and encapsulated FEMA under its organizational structure (more on this soon). A new focus on terrorism soon emerged,

BOX 1.1

OTHER IMPORTANT FEDERAL DISASTER ORGANIZATIONS

Although FEMA has the primary federal EM function for disasters, three other entities also have lead roles under specific circumstances. For events that affect tribal reservations, special laws and processes exist for Native Americans. During any nuclear emergency (e.g., nuclear explosion, radiological incident), the Department of Energy (DOE) coordinates the Federal response. Finally, issues related to health and disease during a disaster, or epidemics, or pandemics, the Center for Disease Control and Prevention (CDC) assists with managing the event.

Federally recognized Tribal Nations have a unique relationship with FEMA. By law, Tribal governments are sovereign nations and must be treated as such. As a result, for disaster issues, they can interact directly with FEMA without going through state or local governments. FEMA must consult with tribal leaders and officials on policies, programs, and projects that may affect the related nations. Such consideration must involve cultural and religious interests, sacred, historical, and cultural sites as well as locations of concern, infrastructure, and economic interests. Such interactions require sensitivity and communication between FEMA and tribal leaders (FEMA 2020).

Since the development of nuclear weapons and power, the DOE coordinates radiological or nuclear events in the U.S. through the National Nuclear Security Administration (NNSA) Office of Emergency Operations (OEO). Although most people may not have heard of the NNSA, they play an active role in readiness. Team members travel about 100 times a year to major professional sports (e.g., the Superbowl), political activities (e.g., political conventions, Presidential Inaugurations), and other large gatherings to detect potential radiological or nuclear devices and respond if an explosion occurs. Both NNSA and OEO also coordinate planning, training, and responding to radiological and nuclear events, and insuring the continuation of the U.S.' government if a major event occurs. They also assist other countries. On March 11, 2011, an earthquake and subsequent tsunami created a disaster at the Fukushima nuclear power plant. Quickly sending representatives to Fukushima, Japan, to gather information, NNSA scientists engaged in predictive modeling, monitoring radiation levels, sampling the soil, air, and water followed by laboratory analysis. These rapid activities assisted Japan with understanding the events, and also enhanced US-Japanese civil nuclear cooperation (DOE 2016).

The CDC takes an active role with health issues related to emergencies and disasters. Generally CDC investigates and provides advice on disaster-generated issues including unsafe water, mold exposure, environmental contamination, or cleanup injuries. One recent example of CDC's activities occurred during the summer and fall 2015 with Ebola. Initially, the deadly outbreak occurred in West Africa, with over 27,000 people contracting the disease and over 11,000 deaths. In the U.S., CDC confirmed four patients exhibited the disease in the U.S. and seven others arrived in the U.S. and were then diagnosed. One patient died (CDC 2015b, 2015c). In 2020, CDC played a key role in tracing and providing guidance on COVID-19 (CDC 2019).

with critics charging that attention had pulled away from the most common disaster in the U.S. and worldwide: flooding. More recently, a Government Accountability Report (GAO 2018) found that FEMA faced challenges again from Hurricane Maria's 2017 impact on Puerto Rico, which followed other heavy storms on mainland U.S. The hurricane killed almost 3,000 people and decimated much of the island's electrical infrastructure, housing, businesses, and healthcare with lingering, debilitating conditions surrounding survivors for some time (CDC 2019; Arnold 2019).

Clearly, disasters cause stress for responding organizations, especially during large events or ones that spread resources and personnel out geographically. In response, FEMA has changed, often through legislated mandates that transformed the agency.

1.2.2.3 Structural Changes

Structural changes, often forged through leadership decisions and major events, have also changed EM. To improve the overall effectiveness of EM in the U.S., President Carter initiated Reorganization Plan #3 in 1978 to centralize EM functions in FEMA (NGA 1979, 3). The reorganization brought together nearly a dozen offices like the Defense Civil Preparedness Agency (formerly in the Department of Defense), the Federal Preparedness Agency (from the General Services Administration) and the Dam Safety Coordination Program (Executive Office of the President for more, see Box 1.1).

During the 1980s, FEMA personnel worked to develop the agency amid criticisms of inefficiency and ineffective leadership. In 1989, "dual disasters" (on two coasts: Hurricane Hugo and the Loma Prieta/California Earthquake) challenged FEMA to manage large-scale disasters dispersed across the nation. As a consequence, FEMA created the FRP, which details how a large-scale disaster response should be managed through Emergency Support Functions (ESFs; like transportation, mass care, or public health), and which Federal or volunteer agency should coordinate the ESF (FEMA 1992; Neal 1993). At the time of the FRP's creation, each ESF was coordinated by a federal agency (except ESF #6, Mass Care, which was then headed by the Red Cross). A federal agency tasked with a specific function would coordinate the overall effort with assistance from other agencies.

Soon after the federal government completed the final version of the FRP in August 1991, Hurricane Andrew struck Dade County and Miami, Florida. Government officials shipped hundreds of copies of the FRP to provide help and direction with the overall response (Neal 1993). However, observers generally graded the overall response as an abysmal failure. Federal assistance arrived slowly to disaster areas, in some cases taking over ten days due to poor initial reconnaissance and damage assessment. Congressional hearings following Hurricane Andrew questioned why FEMA directors and those in top management possessed little if any background in disaster management (NAPA 1993, pp. 1–3; Neal 1993). Changes resulted and the document became refined since then, until its current version as the National Response Framework (NRF). Today, the NRF retains the ESF structure and has been used to organize state and local response plans (FEMA 2020 see Box 1.2).

The terrorist attacks of September 11, 2001, highlighted additional challenges that emergency managers needed to address. Potential indicators of a terror attack had not been shared across federal agencies that could have been useful for stopping a terrorist attack (9/11 Commission Report 2004). After much public debate and through a

BOX 1.2

CURRENT EMERGENCY SUPPORT FUNCTIONS

ESF's lay out by how the U.S. Federal government organizes disaster aid to states. ESF's have changed over the last 30 years. As of January 2021, the current ESFs are (https://www.fema.gov/emergency-managers/national-preparedness/frameworks/response):

- **ESF #1: Transportation**. The Department of Transportation coordinates transportation and related infrastructure operations but is not responsible for the actual movement of goods, equipment, animals, or people.
- **ESF #2: Communications**. The DHS coordinates communication tasks. These activities may include providing emergency communications, helping to reestablish existing communication systems, forging new, and preparing for future events through planning, and training, exercises.
- **ESF #3: Public Works and Engineering**. The Department of Defense, through the U.S. Army Corps of Engineers, coordinates pre- and post-disaster assessments of infrastructure, contracting real estate, giving post-disaster repair to key infrastructure sites, and related tasks.
- **ESF #4: Firefighting**. The Forest Service, through the Department of Agriculture, and the U.S. Fire Administration coordinate all Federal activities related to fire in wildland, rural, and urban settings.
- **ESF #5: Information and Planning**. FEMA handles collecting, analyzing, processing, and disseminating information about actual or potential events.
- **ESF #6: Mass Care, Emergency Assistance, Temporary Housing, and Human Services**. FEMA coordinates activities related to feeding, sheltering, housing, and other social needs. In short, these activities focus in assisting specially the social needs of the survivors. In real situations, many voluntary agencies provide support, particularly the American Red Cross.
- **ESF #7: Logistics**. The General Services Administration provides support and assistance in delivering crucial resources as efficiently as possible.
- **ESF #8: Public Health and Medical Services**. The Department of Health and Human Services (DHHS) coordinates providing medical care, assisting local communities with medical care, and monitoring the safety of medical supplies, food, and agriculture products.
- **ESF 9: Search and Rescue**. DHS and FEMA coordinate and use a number of federal agencies, including FEMA, The Coast Guard, Department of the Interior/National Park Service, and the Department of Defense to successfully find those who survived the disaster.
- **ESF 10: Oil and Hazardous Materials Response**. The Environmental Protection Agency coordinates planning, preparedness, training, exercises in addition to response to oil and hazmat events. When bodies of water become involved, the Coast Guard's role increases.
- **ESF 11: Agriculture and Natural Resources**. The Department of Agriculture organizes and coordinates activities related to food, farmland, livestock, and related

areas, including technical expertise related to the safety of the nation's meat, poultry, and egg products. In addition, with the Department of Interior, they work to preserve natural and cultural resources and historic properties.

- **ESF #12: Energy**. The DOE coordinates activities including producing, storing, refining, transporting, generating, and transmitting energy, among other activities during times of disaster.
- **ESF #13: Public Safety and Security**. The Bureau of Alcohol, Tobacco, Firearms and Explosives focuses on Federal public safety and assistance to other U.S. jurisdiction in times of disaster or terrorist attack.
- **ESF #14: Cross-Sector Business and Infrastructure**. The Cybersecurity and Infrastructure Security Agency coordinates and stabilizes supply chains and related infrastructure.
- **ESF #15: External Affairs**. DHS coordinates the delivery of accurate, coordinated, timely, and accessible information to governments, the media, businesses, and local residents with attention to various languages and literacy levels.

Source: FEMA 2019.

number of steps, President Bush and the U.S. Congress made what has become the most significant change to FEMA when they authorized and financed the DHS in 2003, with Tom Ridge serving as its first Director (DHS 2008). In order to protect the homeland in a unified fashion, DHS would focus on border and transportation security, emergency preparedness and response, chemical, biological, radiological, and nuclear countermeasures, and information analysis and infrastructure protection (DHS 2002, p. 3). To pursue these tasks, DHS integrated 22 federal agencies under its organizational umbrella. FEMA also lost its cabinet-level status.

Critics again pointed fingers after Katrina, charging FEMA, DHS, state and local governments with a slow response that claimed lives. In subsequent investigations by the U.S. Congress and the White House, concerns generated a context for change. As written in the U.S. Congressional investigation report, *A Failure of Initiative* (United States Congress 2006, p. 1):

> The Select Committee identified failures at all levels of government that significantly undermined and detracted from the heroic efforts of first responders, private individuals and organizations, faith-based groups, and others. The institutional and individual failures we have identified became all the more clear when compared to the heroic efforts of those who acted decisively. Those who didn't flinch, who took matters into their own hands when bureaucratic inertia was causing death, injury, and suffering. Those whose exceptional initiative saved time and money and lives.

Congress also passed the Post Katrina Emergency Management Reform Act (PKEMPRA). New attention emerged concerning those at highest risk, including people with disabilities, medical conditions, and inadequate resources that would influence one's ability to prepare, evacuate, and survive. States commenced extensive efforts to revise evacuation and shelter plans. Drills and exercises increased to build stronger relationships between involved agencies, particularly across state lines. New partnerships emerged between federal, state, and local levels of government and voluntary organizations. Those efforts paid off in 2008 when Hurricane Ike slammed into Texas. Well in advance, a prepositioning of assets and a massive evacuation moved thousands of people to safety. Shelters functioned much better with heightened attention to medically fragile populations, low-income families, pets, and livestock.

Today, EM continues as one of many functions assigned to DHS (DHS 2019). Other tasks include U.S. Customs and Border Protection, U.S Citizenship and Immigration Services, U.S. Coast Guard, U.S. Immigration and Customs Enforcement, U.S. Secret Service, and Transportation Security Administration. DHS has the second largest department in the federal government, with only the Department of Defense having more employees. As of 2020, FEMA employs about 20,000 personnel and during disaster may increase up to 50,000 full- and part-time employees. Many of these employees serve as reservists, ready to travel to a disaster site to help those in need following an event. FEMA's offices include its main location in Washington, D.C., ten regional offices throughout the U.S., the Center for Domestic Preparedness and Noble Training Center in Anniston, Alabama, the National Emergency Training Center in Emmitsburg, Maryland, and other sites. The evolution of the field has meant that those seeking a career need to be well prepared to take on the work.

1.2.3 The Emergence of Emergency Management Degree Programs

Another trend that has influenced the field of EM has been the development of degree programs based on a scientific body of knowledge. As noted earlier, local governments often selected the first set of local EM's based heavily on their military experience. Although no records exist about their level of education, we believe that most had a high school diploma. We do know that by 1992, about 25% of local EM's had a high school degree and about another 25% had no high school degree (Sample 1992). During the early 1990s, what is now the International Association of Emergency Managers (IAEM) created the Certified Emergency Manager (CEM) program (IAEM 2020). The idea behind the CEM was to enhance professionalism and legitimacy. To obtain the EM, the committee decided that years of experience in the field, training hours, and a bachelor degree were all necessary.

The University of North Texas offered the nation's first bachelor degree, with hundreds of degree programs following across the nation and worldwide (e.g., see https://training.fema.gov/hiedu/collegelist/). Following the National Governor's Association 1979 report and FEMA directorate structure, many programs first used a core set of courses focused on preparedness, response, mitigation, and recovery. FEMA played an important role in bringing academics and practitioners together to flesh out curriculum, course design, and programs through its FEMA Higher Education initiative. Similarly, established disaster research centers worldwide contributed careful and rigorous research studies that have informed course content (more on this soon).

Because of such efforts, students can now pursue a certificate, minor, bachelor, master, or doctoral degrees worldwide. Most recently, Departments of Emergency Management and Disaster Science have begun to emerge (the University of North Texas) as has a College of Emergency Preparedness, Homeland Security, and Cybersecurity at the State University of New York-Albany. Homeland Security degree programs have also developed, in part due to the impact of the 9/11 terror attacks and federal funding. Over the last 10–15 years, degree programs have developed in Sweden, South Africa, South Korea, England, Australia, New Zealand, India, and Australia, among others. Overall, in just about 40 years, the field has grown from one undergraduate degree program at the University of North Texas to hundreds of undergraduate and graduate degree programs available globally.

Degrees in EM have evolved considerably with increasing complexity and specializations. While two decades ago an EM graduate might pursue a career as a local emergency manager, it is now possible to pursue specialties focused on resilience, climate change, or socially vulnerable populations, or planning specific to schools, businesses, or health care, or cybersecurity. Students with more global interests might pursue international aid and humanitarian assistance or public health and pandemics, and find themselves not only working in government but alongside nongovernmental organizations. Degrees also provide a firm foundation to move into consulting and private practice or within a business focused on risk reduction and business continuity.

Much like the medical profession that saves lives, emergency managers must learn the evidence-based practices involved in designing an effective plan, writing a warning message that people will respond to, or organizing a recovery effort that reduces future risk (Meyers 1993). Faculty members who research disasters have dedicated their lives to making a difference. It is our goal that this volume encapsulates what they have worked so hard to produce and that it enables you to become an effective and dedicated practitioner. Your instructor is part of that community and remains dedicated to sending you on to a career path that saves lives through science. This volume is based on that body of knowledge, as an introduction to the field.

1.2.4 The Evolution of Disaster Science

Disaster science is the academic field of study that informs the profession of EM. Like EM, the origins of disaster science can be traced to the middle part of the 20th century, and thus the two have evolved along parallel paths. It is essential for students to know that every profession is influenced by an underlying specialized body of scientific knowledge. In fact, those specialized bodies of knowledge are what distinguish professions from each other, and a key part of becoming a professional in any field is developing a mastery of that knowledge. Thus, whether a person wants to become a lawyer, a physician, a teacher, a social worker, or an emergency manager, they will first need to spend time pursuing an education that will prepare them for their future careers. For aspiring emergency managers that means they will need to learn about disaster science.

1.2.4.1 What Is Disaster Science

Disaster science is *the multidisciplinary study of the human dimensions of hazards and disasters*. Keep three points in mind as you move through this text. First, disaster science draws from the insights of multiple academic disciplines, especially the social sciences, natural sciences, engineering, and computer science. As such, researchers from all of these areas have made important contributions to our understanding of how disasters impact human societies. Second, disaster science encompasses a wide range of hazards and disasters, including those emanating from the natural environment, such as earthquakes, tornadoes, and hurricanes; those arising from technology, such as oil spills, chemical plant explosions, and widespread power outages; and those considered to be human-induced, such as terrorism and riots. Finally, disaster science is an *applied* field of study that can strongly benefit society. While many researchers in other fields are more focused on conducting basic research to refine and improve theories and concepts, disaster science, with its focus on the human dimensions of hazards and disasters, can dramatically improve EM practice and contribute to a safer and more resilient future.

1.2.4.2 A Brief History of Disaster Science

Many students are surprised when they learn that there is a "science of disasters." They also tend to be surprised when they learn when and why the field emerged in the first place. While a few early isolated studies were pursued, systematic efforts of social scientists to examine the human dimensions of hazards and disasters began in earnest in the early 1950s.

The impetus for establishing a field of study devoted specifically to the human dimensions of hazards and disasters came from the U.S. military. During World War II, the U.S. military conducted extensive studies of its bombing campaigns against Germany and Japan (Fritz 1961). Surprisingly, those studies revealed that the bombings did not have severely debilitating effects. Both Germany and Japan demonstrated strong resilience and an impressive capacity to rebound in the wake of such massive destruction. Based on these observations, the central question for the military became, what would happen if a major U.S. city was unexpectedly attacked by an enemy? Would civil society remain intact or would social order break down into chaos?

To answer these questions, the military issued research grants to social scientists to study how people respond to disasters. Initially, studies were conducted by social scientists at the University of Chicago's National Opinion Research Center (NORC), the University of Oklahoma, and the University of Texas. Subsequent studies were conducted by researchers affiliated with the National Academy of Sciences Disaster Research Group. These early researchers studied human responses to tornadoes, airplane crashes, and chemical plant explosions (Quarantelli 1987). For their purposes, the type of event was not important as long as it happened quickly and unexpectedly, replicating an event that resembled bombing attacks. As Charles Fritz (1961, p. 653), one of the pioneers of disaster research, wrote:

> The impetus for systematic studies of human behavior in disaster developed primarily from two interrelated practical needs: first, to secure more adequate protection of the nation from the destructive and disruptive consequences of potential atomic, biological, and chemical attack; and second, to produce the maximal amount of disruption to the enemy in the event of a war.

For the most part, these early studies that focused on the impacts of disasters on individuals and families reached the same conclusion as the military's investigations during World War II. They generally concluded that survivors of natural and technological disasters in the U.S. exhibited the same kind of resilience and recuperative capacity as residents of the cities bombed in Germany and Japan. These studies laid a foundation for the rise of dedicated research centers.

1.2.4.3 Research Centers in the United States

Scholars from different academic areas have founded research centers, resulting in a broad scope of relevant research. Although not a formal "disaster" or "hazard" research center, the NORC at the University of Chicago initiated the first major series of disaster studies. Funded by the Department of Defense, they wanted to understand human behavior (specifically soldiers') during time of nuclear and chemical war. The research team established "quick response" research, traveling to a disaster site quickly to obtain an unvarnished look at what occurs. This line of research showed that commonly assumed behaviors of panic, mass hysteria, looting, and similar behaviors were generally false. Rather, disasters seemed to bring out the best in people, including neighbors and family serving as informal first responders. Charles Fritz managed this research project, and one of the graduate students on the project was E.L. Quarantelli (1987).

In the early 1960s, sociologists E.L. Quarantelli, Russell Dynes, and J. Eugene Haas formed the first academic center, the Disaster Research Center (DRC) at The Ohio State University (now located at the University of Delaware). DRC researchers initially devoted their attention to local organizations (police and fire departments), voluntary associations (Red Cross), and other groups that focused on the response period of disaster. Today, DRC draws upon a multidisciplinary approach to study a wide range of events across all phases of disaster.

During the mid-1970s, geographer Gilbert White, along with others, formed the Natural Hazard Research and Applications Information Center (NHRAIC) at the University of Colorado Boulder. Their initial research focused upon hazard mitigation as a reflection of White's geography background (White 1936). In addition, the center established an annual, well-attended workshop, "quick response" disaster research funding, and a resource and information center for academics, professionals, policy makers, and others. The annual workshop continues to give academics, EM professionals, and government officials who fund research a chance to discuss new and emerging research and policy trends in the field. The Hazards Center is now led by Dr. Lori Peek.

In 1988, Texas A&M University established the Hazards Reduction & Recovery Center with sociologist Dennis Wenger serving as its first director. Drawing upon various disciplines (e.g., architecture, planning, sociology, policy analysis, economy, engineering), it uses an interdisciplinary perspective for its research. Today, HRRC members devote much of their attention to land use planning and coastal issues. Geographer Susan Cutter created the Hazards & Vulnerability Research Institute (HVRI; see HVRI 2015) in the mid-1990s at the University of South Carolina. Although having a strong focus on geographical issues, members also engage in interdisciplinary research from both the natural and social sciences. The HVRI has developed a strong reputation especially regarding its work on vulnerability and resiliency. Other centers in the U.S., such as the Center for Disaster and Risk Analysis at Colorado State University, the Center for Disaster Research and Education at Millersville University, and the Stephenson

Disaster Management Institute at Louisiana State University have joined the research community in establishing useful research findings.

1.2.4.4 Disaster Science in International Context

Researchers outside the U.S. have conducted studies of the impacts of disasters in some of the least developed countries in the world. For example, researchers have studied cyclones in Bangladesh, flooding and landslides in Honduras, earthquakes in India and Pakistan, and the tsunami of 2004 that devastated several Asian countries. Disasters in the least developed countries of the world often produce death tolls in the tens or hundreds of thousands, completely devastate entire towns and villages, and severely disrupt community life for months or years. International research has yielded valuable findings in how to reduce disaster risks, respond in sometimes difficult to reach areas and across national boundaries, and best practices for stakeholder-driven recovery.

Second, the increased involvement of scholars around the world has broadened horizons in disaster science. As explained above, the field has its origins in the U.S. military's concerns about how well American cities would survive in the event of an enemy attack. In contrast, researchers from various European countries, including Sweden, the Netherlands, and France, take a broader view of disasters and use the term *crisis* instead of *disaster* because it connotes a broader range of threats. For example, creeping threats develop over a period of months or years, and often go unforeseen until it is too late. European researchers also devote attention to the cascading effects of crises and disasters, such as power failures that cross state or national lines and threaten transportation, medical care, and communications. Thus, in addition to studying conventional types of disasters, European researchers have broadened disaster science to include financial crises, food contamination outbreaks, and transportation system failures. Research centers now exist worldwide in Europe (e.g., the Netherlands, Sweden, Great Britain), Africa, Asia (e.g., India, Japan, Thailand), and Australia. For example, recently, scholars created the African Center for Disaster Studies located at North-West University in Potchefstroom, South Africa, and Sweden has developed a number of centers at its universities over the last 20 years (Neal 2012).

Finally, as the field of disaster science has grown to include scholars from many countries outside the U.S., researchers have increased efforts to reach, expand, and strengthen the sense of community among those working in the field. Perhaps the strongest contribution to that effort was the creation of the International Research Committee on Disasters (IRCD) in the 1980s. Although the IRCD is a research committee within the International Sociological Association (ISA), its membership includes scholars from a range of scientific disciplines and practitioners of EM worldwide.

***

SUMMARY

Following World War II and during the start of the Cold War, EM evolved along two different paths in the U.S. One path oriented practitioners toward civil defense, aimed at protecting the U.S. from nuclear war with the Soviet Union. The other path focused primarily on natural disasters. In 1979, in an effort to improve the nation's disaster capabilities, President Carter consolidated most EM tasks and functions into FEMA, which has evolved considerably over time in terms of leadership, response to events, and professionalization. Although FEMA continues to be the nation's lead emergency disaster organization, others also have key roles under specific circumstances. The Cold War also played a key role with initiating disaster research and related centers. Original disaster research by NORC at the University of Chicago and the formation of the DRC at The Ohio State University led the way for other centers to form worldwide. Today, disaster science helps policy makers and others understand human behavior before, during, and after disaster, and how we can better prepare for, recover from, and mitigate impacts. Disaster science also provided the knowledge base for college degrees in EM and other related disciplines including international and humanitarian work.

Discussion Questions

1. Can you think of any recent examples of citizens, government officials, or others ignoring warnings about possible disasters from credible sources? What are the possible disasters and from whom do these warnings come from? Consider tornados, pandemics, and terrorist threats in your discussion.
2. What advantages do you see of putting FEMA under the direction of DHS? Should FEMA become an independent agency? Why or why not?
3. Discuss and provide examples why disaster science and interdisciplinary research can inform the practice of EM today.
4. Think about why disaster research should take place in as many different countries as possible rather than just in the U.S. Provide some good illustrations for your answers.
5. Disasters promote change in EM and can shift attention away from other hazards. What do you predict will happen after COVID-19 for the practice of EM?
6. In 2011, a strong earthquake struck Japan causing a tsunami that also killed many, destroyed cities, and compromised a nuclear power plant, spreading radiation. In 2020, the COVID-19 virus struck, killing and injuring tens of millions worldwide. More recently, cyberattacks have undermined abilities to safeguard private information and shut down governmental and health care operations (Collier et al. 2020). Peering into the future, what types of new or different disasters could realistically strike over the next decade?

Summary Questions

1. What have been the key turning points in the history of FEMA in the U.S.?
2. How has the field of EM professionalized over the years?
3. What has propelled the evolution and development of disaster science?
4. Define key terms using the list at the start of this chapter, particularly EM and disaster science.

REFERENCES

Arnold, Carrie. 2019. "Death, Statistics and a Disaster Zone: The Struggle to Count the Dead after Hurricane Maria." *Nature* 566(7742): 22–26. Retrieved November 29, 2020 https://www.nature.com/articles/d41586-019-00442-0.

Centers for Disease Control and Prevention (CDC). 2019. "2014–2016 Ebola Outbreak in West Africa." Retrieved August 3, 2020 https://www.cdc.gov/vhf/ebola/history/2014-2016-outbreak/index.html.

Collier, Kevin, Den Dilanian, and Tom Winter. 2020. "More Hospitals Hit by Ransomware as Feds Warn about Cyberattacks." Retrieved November 29, 2020 https://www.nbcnews.com/tech/tech-news/more-hospitals-hit-ransomware-feds-warn-about-cyberattacks-n124529.

COVID Dashboard. 2020. "COVID Dashboard." Retrieved November 25, 2020 https://www.arcgis.com/apps/opsdashboard/index.html#/bda7594740fd40299423467b48e9ecf6.

Daniels, Steven R. and Carolyn L. Clark-Daniels. 2000. *Transforming Government: The Renewal and Revitalization of the Federal Emergency Management Agency.* 2000 Presidential Transition Series, Birmingham: University of Alabama.

Department of Energy (DOE). 2016. "Fukushima: Five Years Later." Retrieved July 7, 2020 https://www.energy.gov/nnsa/articles/fukushima-five-years-later.

Department of Homeland Security (DHS). 2002. "The Department of Homeland Security." Available at http://www.dhs.gov/xlibrary/assets/book.pdf, last accessed February 15, 2011.

Department of Homeland Security (DHS). 2008. "Brief Documentary History of the Department of Homeland Security: 2001–2008". Retrieved February 15, 2011 http://www.dhs.gov/xlibrary/assets/brief_documentary_history_of_dhs_2001_2008.pdf.

Department of Homeland Security (DHS). 2019. "Department of Homeland Security Organizational Chart." Retrieved September 2, 2020 https://www.dhs.gov/sites/default/files/publications/19_1205_dhs-organizational-chart.pdf.

Department of Homeland Security (DHS). 2020. "Coordinating the Federal Response." Retrieved July 15, 2020 https://www.dhs.gov/cononavirus/federal-response.

Dynes, Russell R. 2003. "Noah and Disaster Planning." *Journal of Contingencies and Crisis Management* 11(4): 170–177.

Federal Emergency Management Agency (FEMA). 1992. *Federal Response Plan.* Washington, DC: U.S. Government Printing Office.

Federal Emergency Management Agency (FEMA) Task Force. 2010. *Perspective on Preparedness: Taking Stock since 9/11.* Retrieved February 9, 2011 http://www.fema.gov/pdf/preparednesstaskforce/perspective_on_preparedness.pdf.

Federal Emergency Management Agency (FEMA). 2020. "FEMA Tribal Policy." Retrieved December 1, 2020 https://www.ready.gov/sites/default/files/2020-07/fema_tribal-policy.pdf.

Fritz, Charles E. 1961. "Disaster." Pp. 51–694 in *Contemporary Social Problems*, eds. R.K. Merton and R. A. Nisbet. New York: Harcourt Brace Jovanovich.

Government Accountability Office (GAO). 2018. "2017 Hurricanes and Wildfires: Initial Observations on the Federal Response and Key Recovery Challenges." Retrieved July 2, 2020 https://www.gao.gov/products/GAO-18-472.

Hazards & Vulnerability Research Institute (HVRI). 2015. "Hazards & Vulnerability Research Institute." Retrieved June 13, 2015 http://artsandsciences.sc.edu/geog/hvri/front-page.

Holderman, Eric. 2005. "Destroying FEMA." *The Washington Post.* Retrieved February 15, 2011 http://www.radixonline.org/resources/destroying_fema.doc.

International Association of Emergency Managers (IAEM). 2020. "History of the IAEM Certification Program." Retrieved November 29, 2020 https://www.fema.gov/about/website-information.

Kreps, Gary. 1990. "The Federal Emergency Management System in the United States: Past and Present." *International Journal of Mass Emergencies and Disasters* 8(3): 275–300.

McCoy, Stephen. 2020. "East Africa: Millions Face Triple Disasters of Floods, Locusts and COVID-19." Retrieved November 24, 2020 https://www.wsws.org/en/articles/2020/05/27/-eafr-m27.html.

Meyers, Mary Fran. 1993. "Bridging the Gap between Research and Practice." *International Journal of Mass Emergencies and Disasters* 11(1): 41–54.

Mileti, Dennis. 1999. *Disasters by Design*. Washington D.C.: Joseph Henry Press.

National Academy of Public Administration (NAPA). 1993. *Coping with Catastrophe: Building an Emergency Management System to Meet People's Needs in Natural and Manmade Disasters*. Washington, DC: National Academy of Public Administration.

National Commission on Terrorist Attacks upon the United States. 2004. "The 9/11 Commission report: final report of the National Commission on Terrorist Attacks upon the United States." Retrieved September 20, 2021 from http://www.gpoaccess.gov/911/index.html.

National Governor's Association (NGA). 1979. *1978 Emergency Preparedness Project: Final Report*. Washington, DC: Defense Civil Preparedness Agency.

National Oceanic and Atmospheric Administration (NOAA). 2011. "Extreme Events: Hurricane and Tropical Storm." Retrieved February 9, 2011 http://www.economics.noaa.gov/?goal=weather&file=events/hurricane&view=costs.

National Oceanic and Atmospheric Administration (NOAA). 2020. "2020 Atlantic Hurricane Season Takes Infamous Top Spot for Busiest on Record." Retrieved November 29, 2020 https://www.noaa.gov/news/2020-atlantic-hurricane-season-takes-infamous-top-spot-for-busiest-on-record.

Neal, David M. 1993. "Emergency Response Philosophy of the Federal Response Plan: Implications in the Case of a Catastrophic Disaster." *Proceedings of the 1993 National Earthquake Conference*: 511–518. Memphis, Tennessee.

Neal, David M. 2012. "The Survivability of Swedish Emergency Management Related Research Centers and Academic Programs: A Preliminary Sociology of Knowledge Analysis." *Sociologiska Forsking* 49(3): 227–42.

Quarantelli, Enrico L. 1987. "Disaster Studies: An Analysis of the Social Historical Factors Affecting the Development of Research in the Area." *International Journal of Mass Emergencies and Disasters* 5(3): 285–310.

Quarantelli, Enrico L. 1991. "Different Types of Disasters and Planning Implications." Preliminary Paper 169, Disaster Research Center, University of Delaware.

Reuters. 2020. "Natural Disasters Soar in Last 20 Years, Asia Hardest Hit: UN." Retrieved November 24, 2020 https://www.bangkokpost.com/world/2000979/natural-disasters-soar-in-last-20-years-asia-hardest-hit-un.

Sample, James. 1991. "Survey of Emergency Management Professionals on Standards/Certification Development." Final Report to the National Coordinating Council on Emergency Management. Washington, D. C.: International City Management Association.

Smith, Elliot. 2020. "Record Flooding Hammers the African Sahel, the Latest in a Series of Shocks." Retrieved November 24, 2020 https://www.cnbc.com/2020/09/10/record-flooding-hammers-the-african-sahel-the-latest-in-a-series-of-shocks.html.

Sylves, Richard. 2008. *Disaster Policy and Politics: Emergency Management and Homeland Security*. Washington, DC: CQ Press.

UC Davis Health. 2020. "Long Haulers: Why Some People Experience Long-term Coronavirus Symptoms." Retrieved November 29, 2020 https://health.ucdavis.edu/coronavirus/covid-19-information/covid-19-long-haulers.html.

United States Congress. 2006. *A Failure of Initiative*. Washington, DC: U.S. Congress. Retrieved January 7, 2012 http://www.gpoaccess.gov/serialset/creports/katrina.html.

Waugh, William. 2000. *Living with Hazards, Dealing with Disasters: Introduction to Emergency Management*. Armonk, NY: M.E. Sharpe.

Waugh, William. 2006. *Shelter from the Storm: Repairing the National Emergency Management System after Katrina*. The ANNALS of the American Academy of Political and Social Science Series.

Webb, Gary R. 2016. "Emergency Management and Local Services during Disasters." Pp. 329–335 in *Guide to Urban Politics and Policy*, eds. Christine Palus and Richardson Dilworth. Los Angeles: Sage.

White, Gilbert F. 1936. "The Limit of Economic Justification for Flood Protection." *The Journal of Land & Public Policy Economics* 12(2): 13–148.

White House, The. 2006. *The Federal Response to Hurricane Katrina: Lessons Learned.* Washington, DC: The White House. Retrieved January 7, 2001 http://georgewbush-whitehouse.archives.gov/reports/katrina-lessons-learned/letter.html.

Witt, James Lee and James Morgan. 2002. *Stronger in the Broken Places.* New York: Times Books.

RESOURCES

A number of websites provide good information on topics related to EM, disasters, and hazards. Since this is the first chapter of the text, consider these resources as starting points or overviews. As we explore other topics throughout the text, we will provide resources with deeper information.

- Websites sponsored by the U.S. provide a lot of good and relevant information on disasters. Both FEMA and DHS websites are excellent starting points for general information. FEMA can be found at www.fema.gov and DHS can be located at www.dhs.gov.
- Other federal agencies noted in this chapter include DOE (www.energy.gov) and CDC (www.cdc.gov).
- The National Emergency Management Association (NEMA) represents the state EM directors' perspective on EM. Their link is www.nemaweb.org.
- Although discussed in more detail in later chapters, the IAEM represents the interests of local emergency managers. They also created the Certificate in Emergency Management (CEM), an important symbol of professionalization in the field. This group also supports student participation in many ways. You can find information on IAEM at www.ieam.org.
- Volunteer organizations play an important role in disaster management. Such organizations as the American Red Cross (www.redcross.org) and Salvation Army (www.salvationarmyusa.org) are well known. However, many other organizations are active in both the U.S. and internationally. These include in the U.S. National Volunteer Organizations Active in Disaster (www.nvoad.org), an umbrella organization for many volunteer organizations. Internationally, the International Red Cross and Red Crescent (www.icrc.org) illustrate just one of many examples.
- The number of disaster-related research centers has grown significantly since the establishment of the DRC in 1963. Here, we provide links to the centers mentioned in this introductory chapter: The DRC (https://www.drc.udel.edu), The Natural Hazards Center (https://hazards.colorado.edu), The Hazard Reduction and Recovery Center (https://hrrc.arch.tamu.edu), HVRI (https://artsandsciences.sc.edu/geog/hvri/), Risk and Crisis Research Centre (https://www.miun.se/en/RCR/).
- Legislation that has transformed FEMA can be found at https://www.fema.gov/disasters/authorities.
- For more on FEMA, visit these sites published in late 2020 and check for updates:
    - "About Us." Available at https://www.fema.gov/about.
    - "U.S. Department of Homeland Security / FEMA." Available at https://www.fema.gov/sites/default/files/2020-08/FEMA_Org-Chart_July-30-2020.pdf.
    - "National Response Framework." Available at https://www.fema.gov/emergency-managers/national-preparedness/frameworks/response.
    - "U.S. Department of Homeland Security / FEMA." Available at https://www.fema.gov/sites/default/files/2020-08/FEMA_Org_Chart_Aug-12-2020.pdf.

CHAPTER 2

Emergency Management Careers

CHAPTER OBJECTIVES

Upon completing this chapter, readers should be able to:

- Describe the work of an emergency manager in various sectors and specializations.
- Outline the characteristics of a professional emergency manager.
- Explain and adopt ethical principles and the code of conduct for the practice of emergency management (EM).
- Identify the career paths that emergency managers typically pursue.
- Explain how human behavior transforms hazards into disasters.
- Explain and give examples of hazards that exist and the roles that emergency managers play in reducing their impacts.

KEY TERMS

- Certified Emergency Manager
- Climate Change
- Compounding Natural Disaster
- Core Competencies
- Cyberterrorism
- Disaster
- Emergency Manager
- Hazards
- International Association of Emergency Managers
- Local Emergency Planning Committee

- Mitigation
- NaTech
- Nongovernmental Organization
- Preparedness
- Private Sector
- Professionalization
- Recovery
- Response
- Space Weather
- Terrorism
- Voluntary Organization

DOI: 10.4324/9781003021919-3

2.1 INTRODUCTION

People enjoy living where hazards exist. We settle along coastlines (hurricanes), next to rivers (floods), cold weather areas (blizzards), mountains (earthquakes, volcanoes), extreme climate locales (heat waves, polar vortexes, wildfires, and droughts), and areas with sudden and violent weather changes (derechos, tornadoes, and hail). In short, we do not avoid areas of risk – sometimes intentionally and sometimes because it is where we must live and work. Consequently, we need to be wise as to how the human and built environments interact with the natural environment because our presence may convert a hazard into a disaster (Quarantelli 1996, 2001; Mileti 1999). In addition, other hazards include hazardous materials spills, transportation accidents, infrastructure failures, terrorism, pandemics, and space weather – just to mention a few challenges that emergency managers will address during their careers.

The job of the emergency manager is to understand that complex intersection of the human and built environments vis-à-vis various threats, from a tornado that tears through a neighborhood to an act of terrorism that can bring down a tall building. Emergency managers do so in a variety of professional careers in the public or private sectors, the military, humanitarian agencies, and consulting. Emergency managers can be generalists, with a career that spans all phases in EM or a specialist who concentrates on historically marginalized people that shoulder heavier disaster impacts. You may opt to be field-based, where you work with disaster-impacted communities and/or rise upward to manage a large agency. The profession of EM has never been more diverse or interesting than it is now.

Career paths and job opportunities will always exist in EM. To learn more, this chapter describes the emergency managers in the public and private sectors as well as international and humanitarian settings. You will also find out about a military route where you may take on tasks like preparing for a chemical attack, handling emergency communications, or managing an emergency operations center (EOC). Perhaps your interests lie more in an international direction, like organizing relief operations after a devastating earthquake or supporting refugees. EM represents an incredible opportunity to make the world a safer and more humane place despite the wide array of hazards that can become disasters. We start your journey to becoming a professional emergency manager by discussing what characterizes a profession and invite you to consider a career in this profession.

2.1.1 The Profession of Emergency Management

What characterizes a *profession*? To start, a liberal arts education like a student acquires in general education courses enables future professionals to gain critical thinking, problem solving, communicating, and collaboration skills which employers seek (Anders 2017). To become a professional in a specific field, you must also acquire a specialized body of knowledge, related skills, and relevant attitudes. Professionals follow a code of conduct, behave with integrity, embrace ethical principles, and work effectively with others, both within and across a diverse set of organizations and communities

(Schwartz, Kotwicki, and McDonald 2009; Riley and Kumar 2012; Birden 2014). They commit to lifelong learning to remain current and avoid malpractice.

Professionals belong to a specific and recognized occupational group like physicians, pilots, or teachers who enjoy various levels of prestige, income, and respect (Friedson 2008). To move the profession forward and to experience upward mobility, they form organizations that enable additional professional development and advocate for the profession, including income, standards, ethics, competencies, and respect. To illustrate, the International Association of Emergency Management states: *The mission of IAEM is to advance the profession by promoting the principles of emergency management; and, to serve its members by providing information, networking and development opportunities.* Accordingly, this section examines some of the central hallmarks of becoming a professional: core competencies, the knowledge base, capabilities and behaviors, lifelong learning, and ethical standards that will propel you into an array of career pathways (IAEM 2005).

2.1.1.1 *Competencies and Expected Behaviors*

Professionals demonstrate certain competencies and behave according to codes of conduct. For EM, core competencies have evolved over time through the Federal Emergency Management Agency (FEMA) Higher Education Project based on the expertise of both academics and practitioners. Most recently, the FEMA Higher Education Project (2017, p. 1) described desirable qualities for students pursuing the EM career path:

> The next generation of emergency management professionals must be self-programmable, values-based, flexible, able to adapt to changing cultural models along the life cycle, capable of bending without breaking, and possess the ability to remain inner-directed while evolving with the surrounding society.

To meet these expectations, specific core competencies were identified, which will be discussed further in this and future chapters:

- *EM Competencies that Build the Individual*:
  - *Operate within the EM Framework, Principles, and Body of Knowledge*, which means that an EM works within an understanding of how preparedness, planning, response, recovery, and mitigation form the core of one's activities to create safer communities. An emergency manager's efforts "must be comprehensive, progressive, risk-driven, integrated, collaborative, coordinated, flexible, and professional" (FEMA 2017, p. 8).
  - *Possess Critical Thinking*, the hallmark of a liberal education, which enables an EM to identify and analyze problems so that they can synthesize insights and work toward a solution with others in a rigorous manner.
  - *Abide by Professional Ethics*, which governs personal conduct in a professional setting, including working with others and serving the public.
  - *Value Continual Learning*, so that a knowledge base continues to evolve, develop, and grow to serve one's workplace and community best. Emergency managers must remain interested in their discipline and its knowledge base.

- *EM Competencies that Build the Practitioner*: As indicated earlier, professionals must acquire a body of knowledge, which for emergency managers emanates from disaster science and results in:
  - *Scientific Literacy*, leading EM professionals to demonstrate an ability to understand and apply evidence-based knowledge from the natural, social, fiscal, and applied sciences.
  - *Geographic Literacy*, so that an EM sees the connections between hazards, vulnerability, and risk and can use tools to illustrate such complexities.
  - *Sociocultural Literacy*, which enables an EM to identify human vulnerability and to understand how human behavior influences reactions to disasters. Sociocultural literacy promotes empathy of a diverse society and enables EM's to build trust across historic divisions that have placed people at risk.
  - *Technological Literacy*, because the tools that EM's use continually develop greater levels of sophistication and application. An emergency manager must master the ability to not only use those tools but to continually learn and adapt as new versions and tools emerge.
  - *Systems Literacy*, the work of EM plays out not only within an organizational structure but within and across other organizations. Consequently, an EM must understand the ways in which hazards, vulnerability, and risk intersect with the human, built, and natural environment.
- *EM Competencies that Build Relationships*:
  - *Disaster Risk Management*, which serves as the primary goal of EM, involves practitioners in reducing the impacts of disasters through hazards identification and risk management.
  - *Community Engagement*, because an emergency manager must lead and engage with those affected by disasters and reduce their risks through collaboration and teamwork (Feldman-Jenson, Jenseen, and Maxwell Smith 2017). Emergency managers should empower those whose voices have been absent and commit to reducing impacts for those at highest risk.
  - *Governance and Civics*, so that an EM can work with an array of stakeholders and organizations, reflective of relevant workplace policies and practices.
  - *Leadership*, so that an emergency manager will engage in effective decision-making, management, communication and improvement with others (Feldman-Jenson, Jenseen, and Maxwell Smith 2017).

In addition to these core competencies, the International Association of Emergency Managers (IAEM) has outlined a Professional Code of Conduct (see https://www.iaem.org/certification/intro/code-of-conduct/a/main, last accessed August 14, 2020). The IAEM Code of Conduct expects members to engage in high quality work and to demonstrate competency around the Principles of Emergency Management (see https://www.iaem.org/About/Principles-of-EM, last accessed May 25, 2021). Emergency managers should be professionally responsible, operate independently, and be loyal to the people of their community. As professionals, emergency managers should treat everyone with respect and fairness and be objective in their work decisions. Such objectivity requires making evidence-based decisions about requests and decisions, including financial stewardship. To maintain currency in one's ability to make evidence-based decisions, an emergency manager never stops learning.

2.1.1.2 Body of Knowledge

Becoming a professional requires that an individual master a *body of knowledge* suitable to succeed at specific work. A surgeon, for example, needs to learn anatomy and physiology, circulatory and respiratory systems, surgical procedures, emergency procedures, and teamwork. Their life-saving careers require detailed knowledge that can be acted upon quickly, accurately, and effectively. Your life may depend on how well they have studied and practiced their craft. A medical knowledge base is acquired through a focused and concentrated course of study that culminates in a degree. University professors in medical schools confirm that the physician has acquired the knowledge base, holds competency, and can practice medicine safely. Physicians then continue lifelong learning through practical experience including hospital rotations, medical rounds, and residencies before joining a medical practice, working independently in a health care setting, or adding a specialization through additional study. Physicians never stop learning.

EM professionals acquire a body of knowledge through the study of disaster science coupled with practical experience. For example, disaster science provides an evidence-based way to craft a warning message. Being able to design a warning requires knowing what to say, how to say it, and how to reach populations at risk. Warning messages also require an understanding of disseminating messages through various media, across languages, and in consideration of how people interpret messages based on their culture. Lives depend on wording a message effectively to inform people of risk and to motivate self-protection. Students working to become professionals in EM acquire this body of knowledge and experience through degree plans that offer specific courses, internships, and capstone course experiences.

Courses of study to prepare emergency managers have been in place since the mid-1980s and can now be pursued worldwide. Today, the FEMA Higher Education Program lists hundreds of programs in many nations, spanning both the general field of EM and its relatives, including homeland security, cybersecurity, humanitarian interventions, and public health. Students can secure a certificate and/or a degree at associate, bachelor, master, and doctoral levels. The field has also influenced other disciplines, with cross-fertilization from disaster science into engineering, public health, meteorology, transportation, and logistics.

The body of knowledge that embraces the general work of an emergency manager typically includes foundational courses in subjects like preparedness, planning, response, mitigation, and recovery (the core of this book). Additional depth of knowledge will come from higher-level courses, such as a required course in why some people bear disproportionate risks in a disaster. Understanding social vulnerability, an integrated theme throughout this book, will necessitate learning both social and natural sciences which should inform your choice of electives. You may also begin a specialization in your field. For example, you might want to consider courses on pandemic planning, terrorism, or cybersecurity. Courses often incorporate technologies that EM's will use from virtual emergency operating centers to geographic information system (GIS) to hazard assessment software, starting you on a journey toward technological literacy.

The body of knowledge will include other courses. A theory course will broaden your critical thinking abilities to view and understand a problem from different angles (see Chapter 3). Most bachelor- and graduate-level programs also expect students to understand research methods so that they may continue to acquire applicable scientific insights as a part of lifelong learning (see Chapter 4). Courses in leadership and management may also be part of your course of study. An interest in humanitarian work might include courses in cultures, languages, and nonprofit organizations.

To tie disaster science to practice, students will likely pursue an internship, practicum, and/or capstone project. Graduate students seeking a master or doctoral degree will acquire additional depth of knowledge, usually in a specialized area (like warnings), and then learn how to conduct research to build further the scientific foundation of EM. This book starts, but never ends, your journey to acquire the body of knowledge essential for becoming an employed professional. To continue in the profession of EM also requires a commitment to continually improving your knowledge base.

2.1.1.3 *Lifelong Learning*

Just like physicians, EM professionals commit to lifelong learning. Physicians continue to read academic journals, attend professional conferences, and learn new techniques. They must stay current in their field, whether they treat infectious diseases or conduct surgery. Their patients and workplaces will expect them to *know* the latest science and techniques, to be able to assess its value accurately, and to use knowledge and techniques to save lives. Workplaces will expect their emergency manager to lead them with knowledge and strategies that reduce risks, decrease losses, and enable resilience.

You are at the start of this journey by taking an introductory class in EM. Immerse yourself in that journey and learn so that you will be able to base your work on the best disaster science. Know that the science will grow and evolve, and that professionals commit to lifelong learning to stay current and to serve communities and workplaces. The importance of staying current is easily reflected in students who pursue cybersecurity. In addition to such specialists, even generalist emergency managers must understand cyberthreats, how criminal and espionage can threaten a community and its EM system, and ways to deter cyberattacks (Knapp, Maurer, and Plachkinova 2017).

Another pathway for lifelong learning comes from pursuing credentials suitable to the field. Newcomers to the field often start with training, which involves a student in a short and focused course. FEMA, for example, offers free online independent study courses in task-oriented subjects like incident command, pandemic planning, or pet preparedness (see https://training.fema.gov/is/, last accessed August 25, 2020). Such short, self-directed studies produce baseline insights into a subject, which can be pursued further at weeklong seminars offered by FEMA (https://training.fema.gov/emicourses/) and through additional study of disaster science. Pet, livestock, and exotic (zoo) animal preparedness, for example, relies on a body of knowledge that shows how EMs can spur evacuation, save the lives of highly vulnerable people, and reduce injuries and trauma for people and animals alike (Heath et al. 2001; Chadwin 2017; Douglas et al. 2019).

BOX 2.1

BECOMING A CERTIFIED EMERGENCY MANAGER

By the late 1980s and early 1990s, members of the NCCEM (today the IAEM) in the U.S. became concerned about the perception of emergency managers and their profession. Overall, they felt that others in local, state, and federal government did not take the profession of EM seriously. Second, NCCEM members wanted to increase their salaries as incomes often fell close to the lowest paid positions in local government. As a result, NCCEM established a committee during the early 1990s to move EM toward becoming a true profession. The main goal was to establish a foundation to offer qualified individuals the title of "Certified Emergency Manager". Committee members believed that having a CEM would increase status and pay while simultaneously raising standards along with respect from colleagues. To assist with the creation of the CEM, NCCEM surveyed local emergency managers to understand the type of people in the profession. A key finding was that half of those surveyed had a high school education or less. Education is one of the three ways to measure socioeconomic status along with occupation and income. The three measures often interact – along with a low education comes low pay. People with lower pay typically experience a lower socioeconomic status and less respect from peers.

In addition, the profession lacked diversity. Many local coordinators were white males, over 50 years of age, with many having a background in the military. Given the diversity of the nation along with the very real threat of disaster vulnerability among women, racial and ethnic minorities, and people with disabilities, it was hoped that professionalization would attract a more diverse set of emergency managers reflective of the larger population.

Today, IAEM offers a CEM or AEM credential. The CEM requires a four-year baccalaureate degree along with experience and additional application materials and testing. The AEM requires contact hours, an essay, and an exam among other materials. For detailed information, visit https://www.iaem.org/Certification/Getting-Started, last accessed August 28, 2020.

Pandemic planning basics can be covered briefly in a few hours of training but will require additional knowledge to produce a comprehensive plan integrated across an array of health care and community organizations, particularly for high-risk (O'Sullivan and Phillips 2019).

The IAEM offers a pathway to become a certified emergency manager (CEM). Their efforts first began in the early 1990s when the National Coordinating Council on Emergency Management (NCCEM) launched discussions around the required knowledge base and competencies for professionals. Today, an aspiring emergency manager can work toward an Associate Emergency Manager (AEM) and a CEM. IAEM also produces guidelines for expected behaviors, which we turn to next (see Box 2.1).

2.1.1.4 Ethical Standards and Code of Conduct

The International Association of Emergency Management has outlined three core ethical principles: respect, commitment, and professionalism. IAEM's ethical code situates professionalism in education, safety, and protection of life and property. Professional emergency managers must commit to being honest and trustworthy in their relationships and to providing the best service possible to their organizations.

A professional code of conduct further affirms that emergency managers should produce quality work, be professionally independent, respect human dignity, and follow legal requirements that affect their work. EM's should remain objective, honest, and reliable and demonstrate competence in their duties. As professionals, EM's should maintain confidentiality as appropriate, and hold a level of professional responsibility that includes alerting others to any negative consequences of their actions (Ramsay and Renda-Tanali 2018). Members must treat others with courtesy and fairness, be cooperative, respect all coworkers, follow laws and regulations, and serve as good financial stewards.

Because the ethical principles and code of conduct are embedded in the IAEM certifications, members are not allowed to abuse their membership or engage in a conflict of interest. CEMs may be subject to sanctions from IAEM for violating the ethical principles and/or code of conduct (see https://www.iaem.org/CEM-Code-of-Ethics, last accessed August 26, 2020).

2.1.1.5 *Career Paths*

Students seeking career paths, especially those new to the profession or lacking practical experience, typically follow several routes to a successful career pathway. While still an undergraduate, faculty can assist students with securing an internship that offers a means to integrate knowledge with practice. Given that most local jurisdictions have some type of EM agency, students should be able to find a practical setting that allows them to shadow and support a working professional. Students might also want to pursue multiple internships that increase the range of settings they can learn from, even working their way up from a local agency to a state, provincial, or national internship.

Students may also volunteer in local efforts to acquire experience. Citizen Corps (in the U.S.) includes Community Emergency Response Teams (CERTs), Volunteers in Police Service (VIPS), Fire Corps, Neighborhood Watch, and Medical Reserve Corps volunteer opportunities. Several universities have CERTs on their campuses, making it easier to join and learn. Students may also want to start or join a Red Cross Club on their campus or volunteer in their community. The Red Cross offers training to its volunteers as well as opportunities to serve locally, from installing fire alarms to deploying with an emergency response team in the field. Voluntary organizations (e.g., see www.nvoad.org) may also yield chances to travel to affected disasters and move through a range of roles needed in a disaster recovery, from repairing and rebuilding homes to case management or supervising volunteer teams.

Disasters also require paid workers and students may be able to secure a semester of employment to learn hands-on. FEMA, for example, hires temporary employees when major disasters occur, such as people who staff disaster field offices for response, recovery, and mitigation work. A temporary disaster-located opportunity may also be an ideal entry-level point for a recent graduate, whose knowledge base and newly acquired practical experience may raise their resume to the attention of a hiring manager seeking permanent employees.

2.2 WORKING IN THE PROFESSION OF EMERGENCY MANAGEMENT

Within the field of EM, many work locations and career opportunities can be pursued. Emergency managers may find work in several traditional sectors: government or public work, voluntary organizations (paid or service work), international, non-governmental organization (NGO), and humanitarian work, the military, and private companies. Careers can also be pursued in highly specialized areas, such as resilience or mitigation. This section provides a brief overview of both traditional and specialized opportunities for you to consider.

2.2.1 Government Sector Emergency Management

A traditional pathway for a new emergency manager is to work in the public sector, for example, as a local emergency manager or in a state- or national-level agency. Local emergency managers may be hired full-time or part-time, depending on the jurisdiction's needs and budget, or may be jointly appointed, such as a fire or police chief who also shoulders EM. Such a traditional position typically tasks the emergency manager with handling common activities around preparing and planning for an emergency, being part of a disaster response, leading through a recovery, and organizing efforts that mitigate future disasters. This textbook organizes around these core activities as foundational to the body of knowledge any emergency manager needs to acquire.

Preparedness includes efforts to educate the public, to plan with responding partners and to encourage readiness across communities. Emergency managers will develop plans for a crisis and prepare their staff and partners in learning, drilling, and testing the plan. By conducting tabletop and full-scale field exercises, emergency managers prepare partners and communities for an event. The *response* phase of disasters involves an emergency manager in activating and coordinating plans to warn, evacuate, shelter, and rescue people at risk in a disaster. They will work with a wide set of partners: public works, police, fire, emergency medical services (EMS), search and rescue teams, waste management for debris removal, voluntary organizations, and medical teams. They will serve as a liaison from their affected community to broader public organizations such as a state, provincial, regional, or national EM agency. *Recovery* involves many partners to assess and determine local needs, clean up, repair, and rebuild, in an effort that may take years. Ideally, an EM agency will have conducted *mitigation* planning pre-disaster, but it often unfolds after a disaster motivates public support. Mitigation actions might include a seawall, dam, or levee to hold back flood waters or a building retrofitted for earthquakes or terrorist attacks. Emergency managers may also work with partners to rezone floodplains as nonbuilding areas, create building codes to reduce future impacts, or establish barrier islands and sand dunes that break storm surge. The remainder of this book will walk you through these phases in detail, providing evidence-based best practices for each.

2.2.2 Private Sector Emergency Management

Careers inside the private sector might include working in the oil and gas industries, with insurance companies or banks, or for major corporations, utilities, health care, or education. Emergency managers who work inside businesses or as consultants can help with crafting business continuity plans that increase the chance of a business surviving a disaster (Phillips and Landahl 2021). Thus, emergency managers help their workplaces preserve their financial bottom line to pay employees, produce goods, and meet external demands for their products and services. Businesses also hire emergency managers to maintain internal safety measures, reduce losses, and liaise with external partners. They focus on internal safety to keep a workforce alive and healthy by following state and national regulations for human, occupational, and environmental safety.

A classic example of emergency managers working inside a company comes from September 11, when terrorists attacked the World Trade Center buildings in New York City. Morgan-Stanley had prepared, through the efforts of their Vice President of Security, by planning, learning, and practicing evacuation. In an event that claimed over 3,000 lives in New York City, Morgan-Stanley lost 7 out of over 2,700 employees (Coutu 2002). Nearly 20 years later, essential workers bravely faced the COVID-19 outbreak. Emergency managers working in health care and educational settings operationalized pandemic plans, monitored safety protocols, secured resources, including personal protective equipment, updated plans that required expansion, supported efforts that added special COVID-19 units or sites, and educated fellow employees and the surrounding public. They liaised with public health authorities and government officials, often invisible to the public.

How did your educational setting meet its mission during the coronavirus pandemic that began in 2020? School systems usually worked closely with local and state public health agencies and emergency managers to identify positive cases and how to protect students, staff, and teachers. Some schools started online while others opened in person. Others transitioned online when positive cases rose. Many universities relied on internal medical and EM professionals, alongside public health professionals, to acquire and understand emerging science on the pandemic coupled with evidence-based best practices to keep their students and employees safe. Experts inside universities crafted guidance documents that referenced the science and outlined parameters for how to reopen as safely as possible (see https://www.iu.edu/covid/faq/index.html, last accessed May 25, 2021). EM professionals launched those protocols, such as wearing masks, reducing classroom capacity, establishing cleaning protocols, conducting arrival and surveillance testing, initiating contact tracing for outbreaks, and recommending when to transition online to reduce contagion. Keeping everyone as safe as possible required mastering key bodies of knowledge, remaining current, monitoring cases, updating protocols, and acting in concert with evidence-based best practices.

2.2.3 Voluntary Sector Emergency Management

Many voluntary organizations hire paid staff and recruit large cadres of volunteers to focus on "people" needs, especially during the recovery phase of a disaster. Voluntary organizations alleviate survivor stress by providing food, sheltering, housing, debris removal, repairs, transportation, reconstruction, and medical, dental, or mental health services. Recovery for many citizens, particularly those at low incomes, would not be possible at all without the contributions of such faith-based, voluntary, and community organizations (Phillips and Jenkins 2009).

For example, The Red Cross and the American Psychological Association provide certified disaster mental health workers to help traumatized survivors. Lutheran Disaster Services trains and sends chaplains to help. Church of the Brethren offers certified disaster childcare workers (Peek, Sutton, and Gump 2008). The Southern Baptist Men cook food for victims, first responders, and voluntary workers. The Red Cross opens and staffs shelters and delivers food to neighborhoods through emergency response vehicles. The Medical Reserve Corps coordinates volunteers with medical experience. Mennonite Disaster Service coordinates short- and long-term volunteer teams to repair and rebuild homes. Catholic Charities often funds specific needs, such as for people with disabilities. The United Methodist Committee on Relief trains case managers to assist survivors through the confusing morass of relief and rebuilding.

Careers in voluntary organizations can range from managing a nonprofit or nongovernmental agency as its executive or managing field-based operations. A career might involve an EM professional in educating the public about risks or could tap their talents to produce hurricane evacuation and sheltering plans. Opportunities include working in a local voluntary organization or moving into the national level or into international, humanitarian work (see Box 2.2).

2.2.4 International Emergency Management and Humanitarian Aid

Many nations, especially ones historically impoverished, rely upon international disaster relief organizations to provide food, water, shelter, equipment, personnel, and other resources for disasters. Careers can be found in managing international agencies, organizing supply chains and logistics to deliver humanitarian resources, conducting field-based assessments, repairing and rebuilding homes and livelihoods, and being hands-on with helping those directly harmed by a disaster in refugee encampments, medical tents, and with rebuilding.

As one example, NGOs played a crucial role with the initial response and recovery activities after the 2004 Indian Ocean Tsunami struck 13 nations. Over 400 different NGOs in Nagapattinam, India, helped devastated fisherpeople with survival needs such as food, shelter, and medical care. Local NGOs worked with international organizations to assist responders and survivors, including over 1,000 new orphans. Various NGOs obtained materials for burying over 10,000 dead, provided potable drinking water, offered immunizations to stop the spread of disease such as cholera, and donated new fishing boats to help jump-start the local economy (Phillips et al. 2008).

BOX 2.2

WORKING IN THE VOLUNTARY AND PUBLIC SECTORS (JESSICA BETTINGER)

Jessica Bettinger

Jessica Bettinger earned her undergraduate degrees in Political Science and Sociology with a minor in Emergency Management from Oklahoma State University (OSU). She graduated with honors and was selected as a Top Ten Senior and honorary College of Arts & Sciences Outstanding Student for the undergraduate commencement. Jessica continued onto graduate school at OSU as a Department of Homeland Security Fellow researching various topics related to fire and EM and completed her thesis, "The Influence of Gender on Disaster Volunteers: An Exploratory Study of Mennonite Disaster Service." During her fellowship, Jessica interned with the FEMA National Preparedness Assessment Division (NPAD) at their headquarters in Washington D.C. In this position, Jessica assessed whole community preparedness through qualitative and quantitative techniques, developed preparedness policy, and identified resilience strategies. Additionally, Jessica volunteered with the Stillwater American Red Cross chapter focusing on disaster preparedness and response efforts. Jessica supported Disaster Action Team (DAT) coordination efforts and participated in local, regional, and statewide exercised to further develop DAT capacity. The combined experiences of the DHS Fellowship, FEMA internship, and American Red Cross volunteer work laid the groundwork for a career in emergency management.

Shortly after earning her Masters, Jessica began working with National Voluntary Organizations Active in Disaster (NVOAD) in Washington D.C. as a program manager for a disaster data sharing initiative through a cooperative agreement with the Centers for Disease Control (CDC). In this role, Jessica primarily focused on stakeholder engagement with internal and external project stakeholders on project design and implementation. She collaborated with partners to complete project goals and objectives, maintain a functional project structure, and successfully engage voluntary agencies in large-scale disaster data sharing efforts. Jessica's aptitude for engaging with VOAD partners led to her role as Member Services Manager where she was responsible for the organization's communications and member engagement. This included over 60 NVOAD members, including American Red Cross, The Salvation Army, Southern Baptist Convention, and Mennonite Disaster Service; partners such as American Aid Logistics Network (ALAN), the Center for Disaster Philanthropy (CDP), AirBnB, and 56 state/territory VOADs. In this role, Jessica supported coordination efforts for a multitude of domestic disasters, monitoring national disaster and voluntary organization trends and connecting unmet needs to available resources. A significant part of ensuring the success of large-scale coordination efforts revolved around building relationships with members and creating opportunities for members to build relationships with one another. Jessica served as the primary coordinator for two major NVOAD events: the annual NVOAD Conference and the Fall Members Meeting. In addition, she managed external relations via website and social media feeds, highlighting best practices, resources, and other pertinent information for VOAD members. Last, Jessica worked with external partners and served as the National VOAD liaison on the IAEM Community Service and Faith-Based Organizations and the FEMA National Response Coordination Center (NRCC). Jessica's time with NVOAD built a strong foundational network of voluntary and government contacts and she was recognized for her dedication and service to the VOAD Movement.

In 2016, Jessica served at The Salvation Army as their National Community Relations Department Emergency Disaster Services/Government Relations Specialist, further developing relationships with fellow voluntary agencies and federal partners. In this position, Jessica deployed to Texas in support of the 2016 floods and supported the Point of Distribution (POD) center, mass feeding, and distribution with Southern Baptist Disaster Relief and interagency coordination efforts.

Building on her experience working with government agencies, Jessica transitioned to FEMA's Office of Response and Recovery Individual Assistance (IA) division, Mass Care and Emergency Assistance (Emergency Support Function 6). Through IA programs, FEMA provides direct assistance to individuals and households as well as state, local, tribal, and territorial (SLTT) governments to support individual survivors. In 2017, Jessica served as a Mass Care Specialist (ESF 6) in the NRCC in support of Hurricanes Harvey, Irma, and Maria response and recovery efforts. Jessica coordinated with FEMA regional counterparts, other federal agencies, and voluntary agencies to ensure resources were delivered to the right place at the right time in support of mass care activities, including feeding, sheltering, and distribution of emergency supplies. Jessica's work in the NRCC directly impacted disaster survivors, and in subsequent weeks, Jessica deployed to Puerto Rico to directly support distribution of emergency supply efforts in Puerto Rico. Following her Puerto Rico deployment, Jessica deployed to DR-4407-CA for a mass care mission in Chico, California. While deployed to California, Jessica played a key federal role by leading partner agency coordination and managing the daily operations of Multi-Agency Shelter Transition Teams. These teams worked with shelter populations to transition them to more permanent housing and link them with other agency and community resources. She also coordinated with other local NGO's and private sector entities that were providing disaster survivors with casework and transportation, ensuring survivors had equitable access to these services.

Jessica currently works in FEMA's Office of Response and Recovery Public Assistance (PA) division. Programs include: the PA program that reimburses costs for debris removal, life-saving emergency protective measures, and restoring public infrastructure; the Community Disaster Loan program that provides operational funding to help local governments that have incurred a significant loss in revenue as a result of a major disaster; and the Fire Management Assistance Grant program that reimburses costs for mitigation, management, and control of fires on publicly or privately owned forests or grasslands. Within the division, Jessica works in the Program Management Office (PMO). The PMO leads Division efforts for project planning, communications and outreach, and budget formulation and execution. In this role, Jessica ensures division programs are aligned with agency strategic priorities and coordinates with division branches to ensure efficient delivery of division resources. Additionally, Jessica facilitates the division's readiness plan, ensuring program areas are building and sustaining capabilities for current and future disaster recovery efforts.

After the 2015 Nepal 7.8 magnitude earthquake, nongovernmental and governmental agencies provided vital help. The U.S. Agency for International Development (USAID) Disaster Assistance Response Team, agencies from the UN, and NGOs worked collaboratively to provide shelter, water, sanitation, and hygiene. Oxfam, for example, conducted damage and needs assessments. The Government of Canada's humanitarian team supported sheltering. The UN Humanitarian Air Service sent helicopters while the UN World Food Program delivered emergency rations (USAID 2015).

People living in developed nations tend to fare far better when disaster strikes because of the amount of resources, trained personnel, and number of available volunteers. However, as we will learn in this text, great disparities still exist. Even in a nation as powerful as the U.S., we have not saved people with disabilities, senior citizens, historically marginalized people, and single parents lacking transportation when disasters have struck (Anderson 2008). Disasters are not equal opportunity events for people in developing nations or living in economically marginalized conditions. The purpose of this text, though, is to address such conditions and describe evidence-based ways to relieve suffering, build more disaster resilient communities, and inspire you to become a positive part of that process.

2.2.5 Military Careers and Emergency Management

The military provides another route into and for EM. Members of the military have been engaged in a range of disaster roles from pre-staging emergency supplies to search and rescue to rebuilding critical infrastructure. In the U.S., the military has turned out for a range of disasters, most recently in Puerto Rico after Hurricane María. Members of the military provided medical, engineering, and logistical support, established mortuaries, and restored utilities. In China, the military serves as a primary resource during floods, earthquakes, and pandemics and extends their assistance for rescue work to international settings. The Canadian Armed Forces also render assistance in the event of a disaster and did so in a 1998 ice storm. Troops deployed to launch rescues, support vulnerable populations, including the elderly, and clear trees down on transportation arteries. Multiple nations sent military teams to Haiti after the 2010 earthquake, from a U.S. naval hospital to specialized Israeli units that saved victims buried in rubble. Military units in many nations can provide rapidly assembled teams capable of working efficiently and effectively in many settings and in a range of roles from support to full management, thus offering valuable experience while serving.

The military in many nations also provides educational benefits. While serving, troops can pursue an associate or bachelor degree in EM through online degree programs. Once a stint in the military has been completed, the newly degreed emergency manager will bring both evidence-best practices and practical experience into a workplace. The military can also provide an internal career path. By working through the ranks to become an emergency manager, a service member may prepare troops for chemical attacks, manage an EOC, coordinate base security, handle cyberthreats, or coordinate humanitarian rescue and relief operations and emerge with a skill set of interest to the public and private sectors.

2.2.6 Specialized Professional Opportunities for Emergency Managers

The profession of EM has grown dramatically over the last 30 years. In addition to the traditional and general career opportunities just outlined, specialized professional opportunities have emerged as well. Students may wish to pursue additional coursework, minors, or certificates to position themselves for careers in areas like:

- *Critical Infrastructure and Lifelines.* Students with interests in engineering, transportation, and utilities may want to secure additional courses in the sciences. Seismologists, transportation and structural engineers, and planners all collaborate in designing safe spaces and arteries that enable people to live in safety and the economy to thrive. The derecho storm of 2020 linked EM efforts with utility companies restoring massive downed power lines. People and places without power resorted to emergency measures, including nursing homes and hospitals which required preplanning and preparedness efforts by emergency managers.
- *Cybersecurity.* Cyberthreats represent significant hazards that can undermine the ability of a hospital to deliver patient care or a city to provide basic services. Espionage and cyberwarfare can also compromise a nation's security. Expertise in computing systems and cybersecurity can enable an emergency manager to move into computing sectors in departments of defense, elections systems, or health care and banking security.
- *Accessibility.* After Hurricane Katrina in the U.S., FEMA launched specialist positions in disability support. They did so to reduce the impacts of disasters, empower people at risk to prepare and be present at community-wide planning tables, and reduce life loss. Specialists may focus on making shelters accessible, work with disability advocacy organizations, raise awareness among people with accessibility needs, and teach emergency managers how to decrease risks within their own communities.

- *Livestock, Service Animals, Pets.* Hurricane Katrina also raised awareness about animals, resulting in agencies and specialists who focus on how disasters affect animals. Livestock may be imperiled during a flood or high wind event, both during the event or from ingesting debris. Zoos and animal sanctuaries, both of which may include "exotic" animals, will require specialized attention. Service animals, highly trained and expensive (and loved), should never be left behind during an evacuation to maintain the mobility and accessibility of the humans they support. Pets require advance planning to protect and shelter them when hazards emerge, an effort that also increases human compliance with warning and evacuation messages. Specialists might work in a state agricultural department or a nonprofit agency focused on animals.

- *Refugees and Humanitarian Crises.* In recent years, EM students with interests in serving humankind have gravitated toward caring for refugees. In a later chapter, you will learn more about opportunities to make a difference for people fleeing war, famine, drought, and other crises. Careers may involve an EM professional in direct on-the-ground care in relief camps, in working with refugees seeking asylum, or through resettling survivors in a new and safer home.

- *Public Health.* As witnessed in the COVID-19 pandemic, the first of its kind in over 100 years, emergency managers also work in public health. Their expertise in warning and educating the public serves communities during infectious disease outbreaks and may support vaccine clinics, called points of distribution (POD). Emergency managers also serve onsite with health care agencies, nursing home sectors, and hospitals. Professionals might also manage public health agencies, with work that would span educating and warning the public, securing personal protective equipment, and managing outbreaks.

- *Resilience Specialists* may work with businesses to promote rebounding after a disaster impacts a company or at a community level, engaging with neighborhoods to build an ability to bounce back from a disaster. Specialists will need a background in planning, preparedness, mitigation, and risk assessment along with abilities to collaborate with a diverse set of stakeholders. The goal is to reduce risks by building an understanding of and how to resist and reduce disaster impacts. Within a company, resilience might involve supporting medical workers facing health threats or working in information technology (IT) to improve the robustness of computer systems. At a community level, a specialist might create a neighborhood safety and watch network, help neighbors build a response plan, and provide education around preparedness.

No matter what path you choose, opportunities abound to make the world a safer place. Your journey continues next with learning about the hazards that you might face as a professional emergency manager.

2.3 HAZARDS THAT CAN BECOME DISASTERS

People settle into dangerous areas because they want to or because they must. The 2004 Indian Ocean tsunami, for example, resulted in hundreds of thousands of deaths. Many people died in heavily populated tourist locations along beaches and on tropical islands. Others perished because their livelihoods required living or working near the ocean. Thus, while hazards may exist naturally in an area, it is because people live and work in harm's way that hazards become disasters. We call this human agency, meaning that human behavior influences risk.

What complicates human agency, which may assume intentional behavior like building a vacation home in a hurricane-prone location, is the nature of human societies. To illustrate, many women drowned in the tsunami because gender-specific clothing became entangled in the water-borne debris. Women had not been taught how to swim, a potential protective action, yet were expected to work along a shoreline. The gendered structure of human society placed them at risk and approximately 80% of the 300,000 who died were women and children. It is the intersection of the human, built, and natural environments that endangers people, and it is the task of an EM student to understand and address that intersection (Mileti 1999).

Furthermore, disasters can become extremely complex and interconnected. A natural disaster, like the 2011 Japanese earthquake and tsunami, compromised the Fukushima-Daiichi nuclear power plant. Similarly, negligence can put people at risk, such as when industries fail to provide appropriate security around potential spills, explosions, fires, or accidents. Similarly, when agencies or governments fail to act in the face of a threat, people experience harm. For example, the government of Burma refused external aid after Cyclone Nargis, causing thousands of people to die from exposure, injuries, hunger, and thirst. Similar criticisms erupted when the COVID-19 pandemic unfolded in 2020. It is human agency that transforms a natural hazard into a disaster that impacts people, places, animals, economies, and environments.

Because people choose to or must live and work where hazards exist, EM has developed to protect lives and property. While this next section on hazards may seem daunting, know that emergency managers have a knowledge base and tools to address risks. For example, some hazards can be anticipated because they are seasonal. In the U.S., the "tornado alley" season commences on March 1 in Oklahoma, Texas, Arkansas, Kansas, and Nebraska. Hurricane season, from June 1 through the end of November alerts coastal residents in the Americas and Caribbean to prepare. Cyclone season occurs from November 1 through April 30 in the South Pacific. In the U.S., Californians are urged to reduce wildfire fuel from May through November, while Australians prepare for the onset of such events in August. Depending on where an emergency manager works, ice storms, blizzards, and spring rains that generate river and flash flooding can be anticipated. Emergency managers must be attuned to those risks to alert their region when hazards threaten the community's well-being.

Other disasters do not offer advance warning. Earthquakes can happen at any time, although locations of seismic risk can be identified. Earthquake-prone areas such as the Hayward fault in northern California or the Indian subcontinent carry significant threats to residents. Volcanoes erupt without much warning, though some do give out early signals of an impending event. Similarly, terrorist attacks and active attackers happen without much warning, though intelligence may surface potential threats. Cyberattacks happen on a daily basis, and while such threats can and should be anticipated, crimes that target workplaces may be less predictable.

Finally, disasters overlap and turn into compounding events. When COVID-19 erupted worldwide in 2020, affected nations still had to address floods, hurricanes, earthquakes, wildfires, drought, terror attacks, and cybersecurity threats. Emergency managers must juggle these overlapping hazards and how they affect human populations, workplaces, utilities, lifelines, and transportation sectors. By the end of this book, readers will have learned how emergency managers tackle such challenges.

2.3.1 High Wind Events

Severe weather can produce thunderstorms, straight line winds (including derechos), downbursts, and tornadoes. What an emergency manager will need to know is how to reduce the impacts of a high wind event through mitigation efforts like roof design and safe rooms. Emergency managers will also need to issue an effective warning that motivates the public on how and when to take protective action. Emergency managers may also be involved in the immediate response effort when severe weather impacts a community and then throughout the short- and long-term recovery periods. Several high wind events illustrate both the impacts and the work for an emergency manager, particularly tornadoes and derechos.

Tornadoes appear as rapid-onset events, varying in width, length on the ground, and wind speed or intensity, most commonly occurring in the late spring. The U.S. faces an average of 1,200 tornadoes per year, which are ranked on the Enhanced Fujita (EF) scale from EF1 to EF5 (with EF5 the worst). Buildings provide varying degrees of protection for inhabitants. For example, think about the potential impact of an EF1 tornado approaching where you live. If you live in a brick house with a safe room or basement shelter area, you will be safer than if you live in a mobile home (NOAA 2009a). However, if an EF5 impacts the area, catastrophic damage and significant loss of life may occur despite the best levels of protection.

An EF5 tornado struck Joplin, Missouri, on May 22, 2011, with 200 mph winds generating a one-mile wide and 22.1 miles long path of destruction through the heart of the city (National Weather Service 2011). The EF5 tornado ripped apart wood-construction homes, destroyed a hospital, splintered businesses, and killed 158 people. A nursing home that lay in the path lost 18 residents and staff. Canada also experiences tornadoes, though typically with less damage and fewer deaths. For example, in July 2000, an EF3 tornado affected a rural community in Ontario with damage to a single farm.

Another extreme wind event is called a derecho, which is a straight line windstorm that pushes through a large area over several days. The derecho may also produce tornadoes, hail, and heavy thunderstorms. In August 2020, a derecho began in Iowa in the U.S., generating hurricane-force gusts up to 140 mph. The line of thunderstorms caused significant damage as it pushed through Iowa, Illinois, Indiana, Michigan, and Ohio. Massive power outages resulted across Iowa lasting for up to one month, along with trees down on homes and businesses. It became difficult to use cell phones, preserve food, and keep businesses functioning. The derecho occurred while the COVID-19 pandemic was escalating dramatically in the U.S. The combination of the epidemic and the derecho damage made it difficult for responding agencies to aid people safely, open shelters, and restore utilities. The pandemic had disrupted supply chains and caused shortages to some food production, cleaning supplies, and some protective equipment. The derecho caused additional, major crop damage on top of the pandemic's consequences.

2.3.2 Hurricanes, Cyclones, and Typhoons

Hurricanes, cyclones, and typhoons are also high wind events but with additional impacts, including heavy rainfall, storm surges, tornadoes, and flooding. The main difference between the three names is where they occur. Hurricanes can be found in the North Atlantic and Northeast Pacific, with typhoons in the Northwest Pacific Ocean, and cyclones in the South Pacific and Indian Ocean.

In the U.S., hurricanes occur during predictable time periods from May through October, with a peak in August and September. The Saffir-Simpson scale measures hurricanes based upon sustained wind speed, with a tropical storm transitioning into a Category 1 hurricane when it reaches 75 mph (Schott et al. 2010). The scale, however, does not capture such factors as the speed of a hurricane as it moves over land, the amount and intensity of rainfall, or the impacts of floods, tornadoes, and storm surge. Nor does it consider such factors as the type, quality, and age of buildings in the path of the hurricane.

Hurricane María, one of the strongest Category 5 hurricanes to impact U.S. citizens, devastated Puerto Rico in September 2017. The storm produced a surge up to nine feet in height, and one area of Puerto Rico reported 38 inches of rainfall (NOAA 2019). Officially, 69 people died in the hurricane on Puerto Rico, though death estimates remain challenging in such situations. A study by George Washington University (2018) found that 2,975 deaths could be attributed to the hurricane. Deaths were higher among people who were low income (especially older men). The storm also took down 80% of the power poles on the island, which meant that medical care could not be delivered well or at all in many locations. The hurricane also compromised health care for storm-related injuries and regular care for dialysis, cancer treatment, and diabetes. Death rates went up in the year following the storm, indirectly increasing because of the storm's impact on the infrastructure.

Typhoon Haiyan devastated the Philippines in 2013 (locally called Super Typhoon Yolanda). At least 6,300 people died in historic storm surge, winds sustained at 170 knots, and heavy rainfall. Nearly 30,000 sustained injuries, many serious, and thousands remain missing (Lagmay et al. 2015). The category 5 storm crippled the nation's infrastructure and business sectors, nearly wiped out some islands, and created a massive humanitarian crisis that challenged NGOs. Helping required people and organizations experienced in cultural competencies to aid people with appropriate relief and recovery strategies (Haupt and Knox 2019; Knox and Haupt 2015; Knox, Emrich and Haupt 2019). Emergency managers, first responders, and aid workers needed to be able to communicate in multiple languages and to navigate destroyed governmental systems. Those seeking to help also needed to manage the complexities of culture and faith as people grieved for family members, livelihoods, homes, and businesses taken by the storm. As students will learn throughout this volume, working abroad requires that students acquire evidence-based best practices for cross-cultural interaction (Edwards et al. 2012). Social science, language, and diversity classes can help.

2.3.3 Earthquakes

Rather than a seasonal projection, seismologists describe earthquakes via probabilities and rank them using either the Mercalli or Richter scales. The San Andreas Fault line in California generated a massive 7.8 Richter Scale San Francisco earthquake in 1906 that caused significant devastation. The probability of this level of earthquake happening again is about 2% or about every 200 years (USGS 2020). However, a magnitude 7 or higher event on the nearby Hayward fault carries a higher probability and is expected by the year 2032 (USGS 2020). While the U.S. remains braced for another major earthquake, the worst and most recent events have devastated developing nations.

Five of the ten most fatal earthquakes have happened in the last 50 years. The 1976, Tangshan, China, earthquake of Richter magnitude 7.1 killed 255,000 people. The Haiti earthquake, measuring as a magnitude 7.0, killed at least 222,570 and injured another 300,000 in 2010. A 2005 earthquake in Pakistan took the lives of 86,000 with a 7.6 event. Nepal suffered from a 7.8 earthquake in 2015, claiming over 7,000 lives (USAID 2015). Earthquakes take lives in part because of their magnitude but also because of the intersection with the human and built environment. Seismic codes in California have increased life and property safety in recent decades, which will reduce the impacts of an earthquake. However, in another nation lacking such codes or the financial means to physically protect their people means that a significant number of people could perish even with a smaller magnitude earthquake.

Another element of earthquakes comes from their related effects. The 2004 Indian Ocean tsunami started with a 9.1 magnitude shake that occurred far offshore from the 13 nations where people died. Similarly, the 2011 Sendai offshore earthquake from Japan sent a massive tsunami onshore that claimed lives, devastated towns, and crippled a nuclear power plant. In the U.S., the most powerful earthquake happened in 1965 near Anchorage, Alaska (Anderson 1969). Thirty blocks of Anchorage were devastated, including businesses, homes, schools, utilities, and transportation arteries. The 9.2 magnitude quake generated a tsunami that reached 67 meters in Valdez, Alaska, and damaged coastal areas in Alaska, the western U.S., and Hawaii. The shaking lasted nearly five minutes, caused 131 deaths, and over $2 billion in property loss in 1964 dollars (about $16 billion today). Emergency managers carry a responsibility to inform the public of such risks and to help prepare individuals, neighborhoods, businesses, schools, and agencies on how to reduce impacts and take protective action.

2.3.4 Floods

Annually, floods represent the most common natural hazard worldwide. Globally, flooding impacts about 520 million people, with 25,000 deaths, and $50–$60 billion in economic damages every year (United Nations 2007). Over the last 30 years, flood losses averaged $7.96 billion in the U.S. with about 82 fatalities a year, many from becoming trapped in vehicles (NOAA 2015). Two main kinds of flooding occur, river flooding and flash flooding.

River flooding happens when a stream overflows its banks. Major storms can cause significant levels of precipitation as can ice melt in certain areas. Dams and levees have been put in place to hold back water, direct its course, or protect areas along a river or lake. One of the worst floods is believed to have happened in China in 1931 (Kawasaki et al. 2018). Heavy snow melt, coupled with extensive rain, swelled the Yangtze River. Flooding damaged both housing and farmland. A dike failure pushed a high wall of water into the city of Wuhan, where tens of thousands perished rapidly. Massive displacements resulted, which coincided with an outbreak in multiple diseases, including cholera that claimed even more lives. Damage to croplands, along with drought the previous year, resulted in famine. Estimates vary, but at least 500,000 people died.

Flash floods occur when water rises rapidly over a short time period due to heavy rainfall. In 2020, East African nations experienced significant flooding under heavy rainfall. The storms also caused mudslides and landslides in multiple nations, particularly Rwanda and Kenya. Flooding claimed 453 lives and affected over 700,000 people, some of whom became displaced. Heavy precipitation also damaged croplands, though the rain proved beneficial in some areas historically experiencing drought (Relief Web 2020).

Sea level rise, which is related to increased temperatures as a result of climate change, will be increasingly impacting coast lines in the U.S. and other nations. Typically, meteorologists calculate the probabilities of a flood occurring in 100-year intervals. Sea level rise has changed those intervals, making the possibility of flooding occur more frequently. Some coastal cities, like Boston and Atlantic City, may see an even more significantly occurring flood threat (Kirshen et al. 2008).

Emergency managers will undoubtedly address flooding at some point in their careers due to its common occurrence. Work related to flooding will task EMs to work with public works offices to establish barricades, local media and weather services to issue alerts, area schools and businesses to plan for flooding, and residents and businesses to move through a recovery process. International relief might involve logistics work to fly in needed supplies, including food and potable water. Humanitarian aid might also include opening relief encampments for internally displaced persons and supporting sites with medical care. Given that climate change appears to be worsening flood risks, EM specialists will need to engage in resilience planning and community education too.

2.3.5 Volcanoes

Volcanoes can remain inactive for centuries and then erupt. In addition to ash, volcanoes also emit lethal gases, lava flow, and rocks that fly as dangerously as missiles. The 1980 eruption of Mt. St. Helens in the U.S. caused over $1 billion in damage, stranded about 10,000 people, isolated communities, and stopped all forms of transportation in the area. About 900 million tons of white ash caused much of the damage and disruption (USGS 2005). Mount Kilauea in Hawaii has been active for several decades, with the most severe effects in 2018. Lava flow destroyed several towns, claimed homes and businesses, and reached an environmentally sensitive beach.

Volcanoes exist worldwide. While eruptions may not occur very frequently, the impacts can be catastrophic, as the residents of Pompeii, Italy, learned when Mount Vesuvius erupted in AD 79. Nearly 20 feet of ash buried the city, trapping residents and entombing the community forever. In 1700, the Tseax Cone in British Columbia, Canada, erupted and killed 2,000 people. Indonesia's Krakatoa violently erupted in 1883, killing an estimated 36,000 people in an explosive sound heard over 2,000 miles away in Australia. The Nyiragongo volcano exploded in 2002, claiming 200 lives. In 2018, the Volcán de Fuego vented, taking 190 lives in Guatemala.

Other losses also occur. For example, Mount Eyjafjallajökull in Iceland erupted in 2010. The resulting ash cloud disrupted airline travel worldwide, resulting in weeks-long delays for business travelers and tourists who could not fly home. Airline industries suffered economic losses as they waited for the cloud to dissipate and make airline travel safe again. Thus, despite the relatively irregular timing of volcanic activity, emergency managers need to be aware of threats both locally and at a distance. Despite its infrequent occurrence, emergency managers should be involved in preparing communities for volcanic eruptions through education and preparedness efforts, including evacuation planning, training, and exercising.

2.3.6 Chemical Hazards

In December 1985, a pesticide plant in Bhopal, India, spewed at least 40 tons of the lethal chemical gas methyl isocyanate, which killed over 2,000 individuals immediately and injured at least another 170,000. The long-term lethal and chronic impacts claimed another 10,000 lives soon after the release, and another 15,000 to 20,000 died over the next two decades (Broughton 2005). Tragically, a few months later, another methyl isocyanate leak occurred at a chemical plant in Institute, West Virginia, operated by the same company. Although the accident did not take lives, the chemical did injure over 100 residents (EPA 2000).

In 1986, the U.S. Congress passed the Emergency Planning and Community Right to Know Act (EPCRA). Communities formed Local Emergency Planning Committees (LEPCs), usually led by emergency managers, to enhance communication and planning among local organizations involved in a hazardous materials response. In addition, EPA regulations now require workplaces to keep records about onsite chemicals so that first responders and emergency managers could better handle an accident.

Yet, accidents still occur. On April 17, 2013, an explosion occurred at the West Fertilizer Company in Texas, destroying the plant and damaging numerous homes. The event began when a fire caused an explosion of a stored chemical called ammonium nitrate. Fifteen people, including ten firefighters, died in the event. The surrounding area sustained considerable damage and several schools had to be demolished. Much of the town was affected. According to the U.S. Chemical Safety Board, the event was "preventable. It should never have occurred" (Chemical Safety Board 2014). In 2020, a massive explosion occurred portside in Beirut, again with ammonium nitrate as the chemical. The explosion took 181 lives and injured well over 5,000 people. A significant number of businesses were lost as well, resulting in billions of dollars (USD) in damage. In addition, the explosion compromised homes for hundreds of thousands of people. Once again, the explosion was avoidable as it occurred due to a history of unsafe handling of a chemical hazard. An emergency manager working inside any of the places described in this section would bear responsibility for insuring the safety not only of the plant itself but the surrounding community. They would be deeply involved in planning for a potential accident, with detailed steps outlining what employees and work teams should do to reduce damage, save lives, and contain a chemical release.

2.3.7 Biological Hazards

Some biological hazards develop naturally, such as the Irish potato blight and infectious diseases. The potato played an important nutritional role for Ireland, but a blight struck much of the 1845 crop and the 1846 crop failed. By the end of the 1840s, about 1,500,000 had died of starvation, while another 1,000,000 immigrated (Barton 1970). Roles for emergency managers today might include assisting with recovery resources, coordinating logistical deliveries of food supplies, or supporting refugees displaced by famine.

In contrast, the Bubonic Plague or "Black Death" is spread by rats. The disease struck Europe, Northern Africa, and the Near East beginning in the mid-1300s, and killed up to 33% of the affected populations. The U.S. reports an average of seven plague cases a year, usually bubonic. Biological sources have also been weaponized for bioterror throughout history, including the plague (Wheelis 2002; Riedel 2005). Epidemics have always been a problem, especially spread through travelers. Multiple diseases spread through parts of North and South America between the 1500s and the 1700s when Europeans brought measles, mumps, and smallpox that decimated local Native Americans, sometimes with intent. In the Caribbean islands and Mexico, outbreaks killed at least a third of the local population (Wilson 1995). During the end of World War I (1917–1919), influenza spread worldwide, killing up to 100 million (Taubenberger and Morens 2006). Military movements spread the flu and deeply affected involved troops. In 2014, multiple nations dealt with the possibility of a global threat from Ebola, which is transmitted through direct contact with an infected person's bodily fluids (U.S. Centers for Disease Control and Prevention, visit http://www.cdc.gov/vhf/ebola/). The most affected countries were in West Africa, particularly Sierra Leone, Liberia, and Guinea, although Nigeria, Senegal, Spain, the U.S., Mali, and the U.K. had confirmed cases.

COVID-19 began in late 2019 and spread worldwide through travel. Emergency managers, public health agencies, health care workers, social service providers, and governments pivoted to address a virus with a far deadlier risk than influenza. New Zealand quarantined its residents quickly, with minimal deaths. Other nations, like the U.S., shut down but reopened within months. Summertime social gatherings led to a rapid uptick in cases in the U.S., with nearly 200,000 dead between March and October 2020, followed by another major surge that led to over 600,000 deaths by May 2021. Pandemic planning represents a crucial activity for disaster managers to conduct, particularly in a situation like COVID-19. An interdisciplinary, all-hands approach is required to educate, protect, and respond to a deeply endangered public with highly vulnerable people, particularly those with preexisting conditions that increase their susceptibility to become ill or to die. Emergency managers worked in health care settings, public health agencies, and both governmental and NGOs tasked with securing and delivering personal protective equipment, supporting testing and contact tracing, setting up field hospitals, and educating the public about the mitigation value of wearing a mask, socially distancing, washing hands frequently and thoroughly, and receiving a vaccine.

2.3.8 Radiological and Nuclear Hazards

Of all technological hazards, those involving nuclear or radiological threats carry a significant amount of fear, as the hazard is largely invisible to those who might be exposed. In 1986, a meltdown and explosion occurred at the Chernobyl nuclear power plant in the Ukraine. People living in the immediate area were not evacuated for 36 hours. Radiation from the explosion traveled through the air into Scandinavia and parts of Europe. Hundreds of thousands of people were exposed to radiation, including 350,000 immediate area residents and 200,000 emergency workers. An 18-mile radius around the facility remains closed and will not be opened for perhaps thousands of years (U.S. NRC 2009).

In 2011, an earthquake triggered a tsunami off the Japanese coast. The consequences included significant damage at the Fukushima Daiichi nuclear power plant. Massive evacuations ensued with questions lingering about long-term consequences for increased cancer and leukemia risks. Eight years later, efforts began to dismantle the nuclear reactors. The effort will likely last years, with related problems occurring. Flooding has reportedly carried off bags of contaminated soil, the majority of which have been retrieved. Handling the damage has cost billions (USD) or trillions in Japanese yen. Emergency managers involved in nuclear plant sites would be involved internally in planning for potential risks not only from nuclear accidents or explosions but from area hazards that could impact a plant, including earthquakes, typhoons, and floods. They would also work with the LEPC to coordinate response efforts and educate the public about what to do in the event of an incident.

2.3.9 Terrorism

Terrorism is defined as an intentional or purposeful, goal-oriented act that uses extraordinary violence (Waugh 2007). Terrorists seek out symbolic targets with the goal of causing not only death and destruction but fear and economic impacts (Waugh 2007). International terrorist attacks have occurred both in the U.S. and worldwide: a mall in Nairobi, Kenya; a café in Sydney, Australia; a Tunisian art museum; a magazine workplace in Paris; the Pentagon and New York City in the U.S; and at the Boston Marathon. Attacks have ranged from piloting planes into buildings to the use of intentional explosive devices (IEDs) and violent assaults on workplaces and museums. Terrorism also includes domestic threats, such as the attack on the Murrah Federal Building in Oklahoma City that claimed 168 lives in 1995. Terror groups also exist based on hatred of others, including those who target people because of their race, ethnicity, or gender.

Terrorists have historically used resources at their disposal, proving adaptable to new resources and strategies. Generally, explosions appear to be the preferred method. Chemicals are relatively easy to obtain and bomb-making information is available on the Internet. Common household materials like pressure cookers contained explosives used in the Boston Marathon bombing and were hidden in attackers' backpacks. Radiological threats or "dirty bombs" also concern homeland security professionals. The explosion would spread radiation and contaminate both people and property (National Academy of Sciences 2004). An initial blast could kill hundreds of thousands while contaminating the ground in the area of the blast. Fallout (debris made radioactive by the explosion and falling to the ground) could further contaminate additional property and also poison and perhaps kill more people (National Academy of Sciences 2005). However, while not impossible, the steps involved in getting the needed material, manufacturing a bomb, and transporting it to the proper location would be difficult. Chemical weapons could also be used. In 1995, domestic terrorists deployed Sarin, a colorless and odorless chemical agent that attacks the nervous system, in a Japanese subway. Twelve people died and another 1,000 sustained injuries. Biological attacks, such as anthrax, have also been used. Following the attacks of September 11, an unknown person sent anthrax through the U.S. mail. This attack directly exposed 11 people, killing five (DHS 2009).

More recently, terrorism has played out in active attacks using modified weapons to kill a large number of people. Guns have served as a particularly lethal means, such as the 2017 Las Vegas concert attack. A shooter, using the 32nd floor of a hotel, opened fire on ground-level concertgoers. Fatalities numbered 59, with over 400 wounded and nearly 900 injured. Despite the horror, people demonstrated courage and resilience as they sheltered each other, tended to injuries, transported the wounded, and comforted the traumatized. As this book will reveal in future chapters, the worst of times typically reveals the best of human behavior.

Based on recent attacks, it is clear that terrorists will continue to adapt available resources to their targets. Emergency managers and homeland security professionals must prove to be similarly flexible in discerning and responding to new and emerging threats, such as those described next. Detection, prevention, and deterrence will prove to be the most useful tools for an emergency manager or homeland security specialist. Educating the public on how to report threats and how to respond will pay dividends when an attack ensues, whether in a small office or a large open-air venue.

2.3.10 Computer Crimes and Cyberterrorism

Cybersecurity represents a very promising field for any EM student, so readers should be encouraged to add computer science courses into their electives or consider a minor or a certificate. Cyberthreats could include criminal attacks such as ransomware, espionage or governmental interference in another nation, criminal penetration that can occur through phishing schemes, and malicious efforts to disrupt software and technology.

In 2018, hackers penetrated the City of Atlanta's government system and demanded payment to restore systems. The ransomware effort succeeded because the city had not upgraded its technology, leaving dated systems open to a successful attack. The SamSam ransomware compromised a range of agencies, including bill paying, court information, and police operations. The international airport in Atlanta lost its internet capabilities, which made business travel and communications challenging. In 2021, Colonial Pipeline paid a reported $4+ million when hackers shut down operations that temporarily stopped fuel flow. Consumers across a number of U.S. states were affected in a matter that required the White House to respond.

Emergency managers participate by first keeping their own agencies and workplaces safe from and resilient to cybersecurity threats. They can join in and support educational efforts to reduce cybersecurity penetrations, such as ransom demands at a hospital or university that compromise patient care. Full-time careers also exist, from increasing the resiliency and recovery capacities of internal computer systems to analyzing cyberthreats in workplaces or governmental systems. You can also start mitigating your own risks by adhering to best practices for personal cybersecurity such as using and changing a complex password frequently, updating virus software, being alert to clickable links that look suspicious, backing up your files, and checking accounts regularly (see also https://www.fema.gov/media-library-data/1558564285012-6f81784140c5b5116240a804610eaf12/Cyberattack_InfoSheet_061418.pdf, last accessed August 27, 2020).

2.3.11 Space Weather

Concerns related to events that occur outside our atmosphere called "space weather" include asteroids, geomagnetic storms, solar flares, coronal mass ejections (CMEs), and more. In the U.S., the National Weather Service Space Weather Prediction Center (https://www.swpc.noaa.gov/, last accessed August 26, 2020), includes an Emergency Management Dashboard. Forecasts can notify EMs of alerts, watches, and warnings about possible space weather and expected effects. For example, solar flares can produce radio blackouts that impede communications. Solar energetic particles can affect satellites and initiate electrical failures. CMEs can cause geomagnetic storms on earth that disrupt power and alter Geographic Positioning Systems (GPS) signals. In 1972, a solar storm caused severe technology disruptions. With global dependence significantly higher today, the impacts could be considerable.

Think how much of our life today includes the use of satellites, such as GPS, television, voice and data communications, and weather data. Impacts could be felt on navigation systems for commercial jets, marine traffic, and military aircraft. National security could be compromised with remote sensing satellites out of commission. Some flares could be strong enough to penetrate the Earth's atmosphere. As a result, electronics could be damaged or destroyed. As you notice space weather alerts on social and traditional media, consider how such an event could affect how we eat, travel, work, communicate, interact, and live.

Power disruptions also cause concern. Experts worry that a geomagnetic storm could destabilize the power grid on the U.S. northeast coast due, in part, to needed upgrades. A power loss in the winter could threaten a significant number of lives, including people who rely on heat, oxygen, and medical equipment to survive. In March 1989, for example, a storm caused a nine-hour outage on the Quebec, Canada, power grid. Though power returned relatively quickly, it did cause disruptions to radios, satellites, and utilities. Emergency managers need to learn more about space weather so they can educate the public, prepare businesses and homes for potential impacts, and issue appropriate warnings when needed – especially to people at highest risk during a power loss or for businesses that rely on navigation like airports, waterways, and transit systems.

2.3.12 Crowds and Collective Behavior

Disaster science comes from multiple disciplines, with a strong core emanating from collective behavior research in the social sciences. Collective behavior includes a range of mass gatherings, including crowds, social and political unrest, social movements, and disasters. For an emergency manager, crowds may represent one of the biggest concerns no matter how they originate (see Box 2.3). Crowd events could be intentional such as an annual Thanksgiving parade, accidental like people gathering at a multi-vehicle crash, or organized like a march in a nation's capital. Intentional events like sports venues, for example, may include massive crowds as university and professional stadiums hold well over 100,000 people. Imagine what might happen should a terror attack or severe weather event happen. A considerable amount of planning has gone into place for such settings, such as the Super Bowl or in states where tornado outbreaks occur. Months of planning result in carefully screening entering crowds, nonpublic entrances and vendors, flyovers, and other ways in which someone could cause intentional harm to a wide number of people. The Las Vegas concert represents one such venue, as did the Bataclan café and concert club in Paris. Terrorists opened fire and detonated suicide vests there in 2015, killing 90 people and injuring over 200. In 1989, concertgoers in Cincinnati, Ohio, pressed forward when doors opened for open seating. The pressure of the crowd compressed people together, leading to 11 people suffocating to death (Johnson 1987). At a Hillsborough, England, soccer match, overcrowding led to 96 deaths and nearly 800 injuries. Even in peaceful settings, tragedies can occur with crowds. The annual Islamic pilgrimage to Mecca, called the Hajj, has caused compression crushes as well. In 2015, 717 people died. A similar event killed 45 in northern Israel in 2021.

Other kinds of crowds can lead to concerns. Tourists often increase population density simply by walking or traveling in highly popular locations. Terrorists used a popular street in Nice, France, to kill 86 people and injure over 400 by driving a truck down a heavily populated street. At a peaceful protest against racism in Charlottesville, Virginia, an individual drove a car into protestors, killing one person and injuring others. Emergency managers, partnering with first responders, work to reduce such kinds of opportunities and impacts for those with criminal intent. Similar crowd settings now require blockades with large vehicles to stop such intrusions, such as at large marathons. Emergency managers may also work with first responders to monitor situations by operating onsite, remote, or virtual emergency operating centers such as when major sporting events occur, from university football games to the Olympics.

2.3.13 Climate Change

Climate change, which is influenced by human agency and natural processes, produces several trends that concern emergency managers. Climate change refers to changes in average conditions, like ocean and land temperatures, which typically accrue over years or decades. Emissions from greenhouse gases are largely responsible for the changes. Global warming, for example, has slowly been rising as human habitation has increased and with unprecedented frequency since the 1950s (NASA 2020). Changes in land and ocean temperatures produce polar ice loss, rising sea

BOX 2.3

WORKING IN CROWD SETTINGS (DR. BARB RUSSO)

Dr. Barb Russo

One of the most challenging tasks faced by an emergency manager is crowd management. Simply put, crowd management involves the plans and measures put in place to control crowd behavior. The goal, of course, is to provide safety to those attending events attracting a significant crowd.

While serving as the campus emergency manager for the University of Mississippi, I had an opportunity to experience crowd management and control in various settings. It is important to understand that each event attracts its own crowd type and as such, the management strategies and tactics must vary to ensure appropriate actions are taken to protect attendees and participants alike.

Ideally in crowd management, one needs people to be able to move steadily throughout the venue and event. Ingress and egress routes must be maintained so that evacuation routes remain accessible by emergency service providers. Finally, medical-related incidents and criminal acts should be kept to a minimum to protect all those in attendance. This is generally supported with a police or security presence along with EMS on site.

You may be wondering: how in the world can you achieve this during a Southeastern Conference (SEC) football game when 100,000 people descend upon your campus? I had that same question and many sleepless nights during football season during my time at Ole Miss, but I can tell you crowd management can successfully be completed by following a three-step process regardless of the type of event.

The first step is the strategic phase in which the emergency manager sits down with the key stakeholders to discuss some of the basic assumptions and needs, objectives of the event, and gathers additional information about the event such as whether it will be indoors or outdoors, number of attendees, and so on. This may very well be the most important step of the entire process and I have a perfect example to demonstrate why. At Ole Miss, Student Affairs hosts a spring concert every year at the university. One year, the performer was country singer Brad Paisley who performed in the university's new arena. A couple of years later, the university had planned on bringing in rap artist Gucci Mane for an outdoor concert open to the public in The Grove. The Paisley concert went off without a hitch and surprisingly was poorly attended. When word got out that Gucci Mane was coming to campus, social media blew up and we had students planning to travel to campus from as far away as Texas and Alabama to see this show. On top of that, Gucci Mane had recently had some issues with performances on other university campuses, which included smoking marijuana during his performance – something Ole Miss was not prepared to manage.

This is an excellent example to demonstrate that no two events are alike – even though both were concerts. As emergency managers, we are looking at the event profile – what type of event is it, who is it for (students or the general public as well), and the character of the performer, all of these are important considerations. We must then look at the attendees – are they students, families as well as age demographics – to determine anticipated risks and behaviors. We would not have staffed the Paisley concert the way we would have staffed the Gucci Mane concert. At the end of the day, bad weather forced the Gucci Mane concert to be cancelled, but preparations had been made for an increased police presence and limited the concert to ticketed students only. We were extremely concerned about the possibility of external issues becoming a factor on campus.

The second step in crowd management is the tactical phase, which involves drawing up the actual plans. For every major event an Event Action Plan (EAP) is drawn – a complex plan developed by the emergency manager often in concert with other public safety partners. An example of this tactical phase occurs every Monday during football season ahead of home games. Together with the university police department, we would coordinate all our staffing for the coming Saturday's game which included the police department's plan for staging its officers and K-9s (more than 100 officers), EMS (more than 24 personnel and three ambulances), and representatives from several public safety agencies who would assume seats in the stadium EOC throughout the game. They included the County and City Emergency Managers, Department of Transportation, Highway Patrol, City of Oxford Fire Department, FBI, Oxford Police Department, and Lafayette County Sheriff's Department.

Once seated in the EOC on game day, the third step in crowd management kicks in – the operational phase. During the operational phase the plans are put into motion. If there were to be an incident in the stadium, such as a fire, the Oxford Fire Department representative would immediately dispatch the necessary resources and we would begin our evacuation plan for the stadium. While many erroneously believe that mass panic would ensue and people would be stampeding over one another to evacuate, this would hardly be the case. In the event of a fire, we would only evacuate the portion of the stadium impacted to avoid any such situation. This is why crowd control and management are so important and that a one size fits all approach is not taken for this process.

While at Ole Miss, I had an opportunity to plan for numerous large-scale events ranging from football games to commencement, each with its own unique crowd management plan. While the task can often seem overwhelming, managing the process through the three steps presented will get any emergency manager through this daunting task.

levels, an increase in severe weather events, and impacts to vegetation. Even a slight increase in global temperatures can intensify evaporation, leading to increased moisture in the atmosphere that produces heavier rainfall. Concerns for emergency managers include coastal and island flooding potential and extreme weather events that require adaptations (Pelling 2011). Predictions suggest that New York, England, and Wales could face storm surge or coastal flooding costing a significant amount economically (Kirshen et al. 2008; Gornitz et al. 2020). Dryer and warmer lands also lead to droughts and wildfires. While climate change is a natural process, it is the human-generated rapidity of the change in the last half century that calls emergency managers to address related hazards.

2.3.13.1 *Heat Waves and Drought*

Increasing temperatures produce both heat waves and drought. Heat waves, in particular, have been increasing and accelerating. A 1936 heat wave in the U.S. produced what became known as the Dust Bowl. In 1995, the city of Chicago lost 778 to a heat wave, primarily African Americans and lower-income elderly. A heat wave in 2019 killed 1,500 people just in France. A European heat wave of 2020 raised temperatures into the 90s (Fahrenheit, upper 30s Celsius) across numerous nations. Despite the dangers of COVID-19, people went to beaches and outdoor areas to escape the heat. Emergency managers would be particularly concerned with high-risk populations for both heat and infectious diseases, including elderly, people who are homeless, and low-income families without means to cool their homes or businesses.

Heat waves also produce drought, which the U.S. Drought Monitor (www.climate.gov) categorizes in several levels, with D4 being the highest level. Over 70% of Oklahoma experienced D4-level drought from 2010 to 2015, with serious impacts to tourism, agriculture, business capacity, and utilities (National Integrated Drought Information System 2020). In short, D4 means that a community cannot supply water sufficient for its social and economic needs. Australia typically experiences the worst drought, with multiple long-term events that have affected farmers, agricultural production, reservoir capacity, and livestock and increased fuel for bushfires. From 1895 to 1903, one of the worst droughts decreased the nation's 100 million sheep by half and dropped wheat production dramatically, undermining traditional food sources (e.g., see Australian Bureau of Statistics, https://www.abs.gov.au/ausstats/). Emergency managers can play a role by helping communities become more resilient to drought through planning, risk assessment, and mitigation efforts, including directly addressing human-induced climate change that increases temperatures.

2.3.13.2 Wildfires and Fire Weather

Wildfires, which are called bushfires in Australia, can occur naturally (e.g., lightning strikes or downed power lines) or from human actions (tossing a cigarette, not minding a campfire, or by criminal intent). Large wildfires can generate their own weather when the intense heat creates pyrocumulonimbus clouds that fuel thunderstorms and fire tornadoes. Wildfires and bushfires have been increasing in recent decades with heavy impacts in the U.S., Australia, and Canada. What used to be an occasional hazard now seems to be turning into an annual threat. Emergency managers play a role in educating the public, planning with partners, warning the public, orchestrating evacuations, supporting shelters, assisting with response, coordinating recovery, and implementing mitigation measures.

United States To illustrate this increasing hazard, seven of the ten most expensive wildfires in the U.S. have occurred in the last two decades or during the lifetime of a traditionally aged, first year college student. Because people and businesses reside in or adjacent to wooded areas, the "wildland-urban interface" (WUI) can be rapidly overcome by wildfire (National Integrated Fire Agency 2007). The Oakland Hills (CA) fires of 1991 killed 25 people, burned over 3,800 residences, and made about 6,000 victims homeless in just four short hours (Hoffman 1998). In July 2013, 19 firefighters lost their lives battling a blaze in Arizona. Known as the Yarnell fire, the tragedy demonstrated a national need to reduce wildfire risks and protect firefighters' lives. In 2018, the Camp Fire in California took 85 lives and devastated entire communities. A grand jury report blamed downed power lines from Pacific Gas and Electric for the fire (Butte County 2020).

Canada Canada has created a Fire Weather Index (https://cwfis.cfs.nrcan.gc.ca/report, last accessed August 26, 2020). Concerns about increasing wildfire threat have also led to a body of knowledge produced by wildland fire researchers across North America (e.g., see https://www.canadawildfire.org/) and by social scientists (e.g., see Plush and Cox 2019). In 2017, nearly 200 wildfires affected British Columbia, requiring that 40,000 people evacuate. Caused by dry lightning and human-induced climate change, the fires consumed homes and closed transportation routes. This massive number of fires followed the 2016 Fort McMurray fire that launched the largest evacuation in the history of Alberta (Slick 2019). Military units helped nearly 90,000 people leave their homes. As many as 4,000 homes were lost to the event, in a fire that smoldered for nearly a year.

Australia In 2009, hot weather conditions (113 degrees Fahrenheit), drought, and high winds created an Australian firestorm. This event killed at least 200 people, destroyed over 750 homes, and burned over 815,000 acres of land. Australian wildfires in the last 30 years have been worsening, in a trend like that experienced in the U.S. (Lite

2009). In 2015, bushfires burned through South Australia, part of a warming pattern increasing average temperatures coupled with decreasing rainfall. One of Australia's worst bushfires happened in 2019–2020, consuming 3,000 homes and 33 people. The worst damage happened to Australia's unique wildlife, with an estimated loss of 143 million mammals, 2.45 billion reptiles, 180 million birds, and 51 million frogs (World Wildlife Fund 2020).

2.3.14 The Complexity of Hazards that Become Disasters

Typically, when we consider a hazard or disaster, we think of one type of disaster agent or event. Natech events take matters one step further. The word "Natech" is devised from the first two letters of "natural" disaster and the first four letters of "technological" disaster (Cruz et al. 2004). For example, a hurricane, flood, or other naturally occurring event may spawn a technological disaster such as a chemical release. In 1999, an earthquake in Kocaeli, Turkey, killed over 17,000 and injured at least 40,000. At least 21 major hazardous materials releases occurred, including large amounts of crude oil that spilled into Izmit Bay. Other chemicals were released into the atmosphere and contaminated the ground (Cruz et al. 2004). When a natech or a "compounding natural disaster" happens, effective response between an array of partners can save lives and property.

The idea of compounding natural disasters is somewhat similar to a natech and Perrow's (1984) idea of a "normal accident." Let's consider Southern California. Areas around Los Angles often have droughts and as a result, the mountains become quite dry. Whether through a natural cause (lightning) or human behavior (campfire or arson), a fire will burn hundreds of acres of land. The fire undermines mountainside vegetation which helps hold the soil. Hard, heavy rains could then cause massive mudslides since little holds the soil to the mountain. Or an earthquake could shake the area, also causing a landslide. Consider the case when rivers freeze during the winter. As spring approaches and parts of the river thaw, ice breaks and creates a dam, stopping the flow of the water and creating flooding behind the ice jam. From the perspective of an emergency manager, one event leads into the next.

The year 2020 challenged emergency managers with compounding disasters in the U.S. COVID-19 complicated everything and not only health care settings. When Hurricane Laura slammed Category 4 winds into the Louisiana coast, emergency managers had to address evacuation and sheltering protocols that protected evacuees, volunteers, and coworkers from the storm and the pandemic. Wildfires erupted in California, stretching thin the ranks of wildland firefighters and responding organizations and requiring assistance from Australian firefighting teams. Social and political movements developed to address serious matters of racism and injustice. Heat waves and a major derecho beleaguered first responders and emergency managers as they battled one disaster after another. Concerns arose around the national election about potential cyberattacks and acts of terrorism. As we noted earlier in this chapter, the work of emergency managers is necessary to protect and serve the public. Careers in an array of areas will certainly continue to provide opportunities to make the world a safer place.

***

SUMMARY

This chapter provided an overview of the array of careers that a student might want to pursue within EM. Those opportunities include working in the public, private, humanitarian, voluntary, and military sectors. Careers can be sought as a generalist or a specialist across a wide span of possible pathways. Emergency managers are expected to master an evidence-based body of knowledge to pursue the profession, along with following specific principles, ethics, and codes of conduct. Professionals should also be lifelong learners to continue to provide the best service possible to their workplaces and communities, including learning about strategies to address a range of hazards that, through acts of human agency, can become disasters.

Discussion Questions

1. If a supervisor asks an emergency manager to violate a policy, rule, or regulation that governs their profession, what should the emergency manager do?
2. What value is there in mastering a body of evidence-based disaster science for the practice of EM?
3. Which hazard do you believe presents the most significant hazard that an emergency manager would face in your community?
4. Why would an emergency manager need to pursue lifelong learning?

Summary Questions

1. Provide an overview of ethical principles that an emergency manager should embrace and demonstrate in their work.
2. Describe the kinds of impacts that an emergency manager might anticipate in their communities from three different kinds of hazards.
3. What are the most common general as well as the more specialized career opportunities that exist for emergency managers today?

REFERENCES

Anders, George. 2017. *You Can Do Anything: The Surprising Power of a "Useless" Liberal Arts Education.* New York: Little, Brown, and Company.

Anderson, William A. 1969. *Disaster and Organizational Change: A Study of the Long-Term Consequences in Anchorage of the 1964 Alaska Earthquake.* Columbus: The Ohio State University Disaster Research Center.

Anderson, William A. 2008. "Mobilization of the Black Community following Hurricane Katrina: From Disaster Assistance to Advocacy of Social Change and Equity." *International Journal of Mass Emergencies and Disasters* 26(3): 197–217.

Barton, Allen. 1970. *Communities in Disaster.* New York: Anchor Books.

Birden, Hudson, et al. 2014. "Defining Professionalism in Medical Education: A Systematic Review." *Medical Teacher* 36(1): 47–61.

Broughton, Edward. 2005. "The Bhopal Disaster and Its Aftermath: A Review." *Environmental Health: A Global Access Science Journal* 4(6). Available at http://www.ehjournal.net/content/pdf/1476-069X-4-6.pdf, last accessed February 27, 2011.

Butte County. 2020. *The Camp Fire Public Report.* Butte County, CA: Butte County District Attorney.

Chadwin, Robin. 2017. "Evacuation of Pets during Disasters: A Public Health Intervention to Increase Resilience." *American Journal of Public Health* 107(9): 1413–1417.

Chemical Safety Board. 2014. *Statement by CSB Chairperson Rafael Moure-Eraso and Supervisory Investigator Johnnie Banks News Conference,* Dallas, TX, West Fertilizer Accident. Available at http://www.csb.gov/assets/1/16/Statement_-_News_Conference_%28Final%29. pdf, last accessed April 24, 2014.

Coutu, Diane L. 2002. "How Resilience Works." *Harvard Business Review on Point.* Available at https://hbr.org/2002/05/how-resilience-works, last accessed August 29, 2020.

Cruz, Ana Maria, Laura J. Steinbert, Anna Lisa Vetere Arellano, Jean-Pierre Nordvik, and Francesco Pisano. 2004. *State of the Art in Natech Risk Management.* Italy: European Union.

DHS. 2009. "Biological Attack: The Danger." Available at http://www.dhs.gov/files/publications/gc_1245183510280.shtm, last accessed January 31, 2011.

Douglas, Rachel, et al. 2019. "Evacuating People and Their Pets: Older Floridians' Need for and Proximity to Pet-Friendly Shelters." *The Journals of Gerontology: Series B* 74(6): 1032–1040.

Edwards, Frances L., Kristen A. Norman-Major, and Susan. T. Gooden. 2012. "Cultural Competency in Disasters." *Cultural Competency for Public Administrators,* 197–218.

Feldman-Jensen, Shirley, Steven Jensen and Sandy Maxwell Smith. 2017. *The Next Generation of Core Competencies for Emergency Management Professionals.* Washington D.C.: FEMA.

Friedson, Eliot. 2008. "The Characteristics of a Profession." Pp. 247–257 in *The Sociology of Healthcare: A Reader for Health Professionals,* eds. Sarah Earle and Gayle Letherby. New York: MacMillan.

George Washington University. 2018. *Ascertainment of the Estimated Excess Mortality from Hurricane Maria in Puerto Rico.* Washington, DC: Milken Institute School of Public Health, George Washington University.

Gornitz, Vivien, et al. 2020. "Enhancing New York City's Resilience to Sea Level Rise and Increased Coastal Flooding." *Urban Climate* 33: 100654.

Haupt, Brittany and Claire Connolly Knox. 2018. "Measuring Cultural Competence in Emergency Management and Homeland Security Higher Education Programs." *Journal of Public Affairs Education* 24(4): 538–556.

Heath, Sebastian E., et al. 2001. "Human and Pet-related Risk Factors for Household Evacuation Failure during a Natural Disaster." *American Journal of Epidemiology* 153(7): 659–665.

Hoffman, Susanna M. 1998. "Eve and Adam among the Embers: Gender Patterns after the Berkeley Firestorm." Pp. 55–62 in *The Gendered Terrain of Disaster,* eds. Elaine Enarson and Betty Hearn Morrow. Westport, CT: Praeger.

International Association of Emergency Managers. 2007. *Principles of Emergency Management Supplement.* Available at https://www.iaem.org/About/Principles-of-EM, last accessed August 28, 2020.

Johnson, Norris R. 1987. "Panic at "The Who Concert Stampede": An Empirical Assessment." *Social Problems* 34(4): 362–373.

Kawasaki, Akiyuki, et al. 2018. "Reconstruction of the 1931 Yangtze River Flood for Exploring a New Economic History." *AGUFM* 2018: GC31A-08.

Kirshen, Paul, et al. 2008. "Coastal Flooding in the Northeastern United States Due to Climate Change." *Mitigation and Adaptation Strategies for Global Change* 13(5–6): 437–451.

Knapp, Kenneth J., Christopher Maurer, and Miloslava Plachkinova. 2017. "Maintaining a Cybersecurity Curriculum: Professional Certifications as Valuable Guidance." *Journal of Information Systems Education* 28(2): 101.

Knox, Claire C. Christopher T. Emrich, and Brittany Haupt. 2019. "Advancing Emergency Management Higher Education: Importance of Cultural Competence Scholarship." *Journal of emergency management (Weston, Mass.)* 17(2): 111–117.

Knox, Claire C. and Brittany Haupt. 2015. "Incorporating Cultural Competency Skills in Emergency Management Education." *Disaster Prevention and Management* 24(5): 619–634.

Lagmay, Alfredo Mahar Francisco, et al. 2015. "Devastating Storm Surges of Typhoon Haiyan." *International Journal of Disaster Risk Reduction* 11: 1–12.

Lite, Jordan, 2009. "Death Toll Climbs in Aussie Wildfires," *Scientific American*. Available at http://www.scientificamerican.com/blog/post.cfm?id=death-toll-climbs-in-aussie-wildfir-2009-02-09, last accessed February 4, 2011.

Mileti, Dennis. 1999. *Disasters by Design*. Washington, DC: Joseph Henry Press.

NASA. 2020. "Overview: Weather, Global Warming and Climate Change." Available at https://climate.nasa.gov/resources/global-warming-vs-climate-change/, last accessed August 24, 2020.

National Academy of Sciences. 2004. "Radiological Attack: Dirty Bombs and Other Devices." Available at http://www.dhs.gov/xlibrary/assets/prep_radiological_fact_sheet.pdf, last accessed January 31, 2011.

National Academy of Sciences, 2005. "Nuclear Attack." Available at http://www.dhs.gov/xlibrary/assets/prep_nuclear_fact_sheet.pdf, last accessed January 31, 2011.

National Integrated Drought Information System. 2020. "Drought in Oklahoma." https://www.drought.gov/drought/states/oklahoma, last accessed August 26, 2020.

National Integrated Fire Agency. 2007. "Fire Information – Wildland Fire Statistics." Available at http://www.nifc.gov/fire_info/fire_stats.htm, last accessed February 6, 2011.

National Weather Service. 2011. "Storm Event Reports, May 22, 2011." Available at http://www.crh.noaa.gov/sgf/?n=event_2011may22_reports, last accessed April 24, 2014.

NOAA. 2009. "The Enhanced Fujita Scale." Available at http://www.spc.noaa.gov/efscale/, last accessed January 25, 2011.

NOAA. 2015. *Hydrologic Information Center – Flood Loss Data*. Washington, DC: NOAA. Available at http://www.nws.noaa.gov/hic/, last accessed May 6, 2015.

NOAA. 2019. *National Hurricane Center Tropical Cyclone Report Hurricane María*. Available at https://www.nhc.noaa.gov/data/tcr/AL152017_Maria.pdf, last accessed August 27, 2020.

O'Sullivan, Tracey L. and Karen P. Phillips. 2019. "From SARS to Pandemic Influenza: The Framing of High-Risk Populations." *Natural Hazards* 98(1): 103–117.

Peek, Lori, Jeannette Sutton, and Judy Gump. 2008. "Caring for Children in the Aftermath of Disaster: The Church of the Brethren Children's Disaster Services Program." *Children, Youth and Environments* 18(1): 408–421.

Pelling, Mark. 2011. *Adaptation to Climate Change*. London: Routledge.

Perrow, Charles. 1984. *Normal Accidents*. New York: Basic Books.

Phillips, Brenda, Dave Neal, Tom Wikle, Aswin Subanthore and Shireen Hyrapiet. 2008. "Mass Fatality Management after the Indian Ocean Tsunami." *Disaster Prevention and Management* 17/5: 681–697.

Phillips, Brenda and Pam Jenkins. 2009. "The Roles of Faith-based Organizations after Hurricane Katrina." Pp. 215–238 in *Meeting the Needs of Children, Families, and Communities Post-Disaster: Lessons Learned from Hurricane Katrina and Its Aftermath*, eds. R. P. Kilmer, V. Gil-Rivas, R. G. Tedeschi, and L.G. Calhoun. Washington, DC: American Psychological Association.

Phillips, Brenda and Mark Landahl. 2021. *Business Continuity Planning*. New York: Elsevier Press.

Plush, Tamara and Robin Cox. 2019. "Hey, Hey, Hey—Listen to What I Gotta Say: Songs Elevate Youth Voice in Alberta Wildfire Disaster Recovery." *Engaged Scholar Journal: Community-Engaged Research, Teaching, and Learning* 5(2): 181–194.

Quarantelli, E. L. 1996. "The Future Is Not the Past Repeated: Projecting Disasters in the 21st Century from Current Trends." *Journal of Contingencies and Crisis Management* 4(4): 228–240.

Quarantelli, E. L. 2001. "Another Selective Look at Future Social Crises: Some Aspects of Which We Can Already See in the Present." *Journal of Contingencies and Crisis Management* 9(4): 233–237.

Ramsay, James D., and Irmak Renda-Tanali. 2018. "Development of Competency-Based Education Standards for Homeland Security Academic Programs." *Journal of Homeland Security and Emergency Management*, 15(3): 1–27.

Relief Web. 2020. "Special Report: East Africa 2020 Flood Impacts on Agriculture." Available at https://reliefweb.int/report/somalia/special-report-east-africa-2020-flood-impacts-agriculture-updated-may-19th-2020, last accessed August 27, 2020.

Riedel, Stefan. 2005. "Plague: From Natural Disease to Bioterrorism." *Baylor University Medical Center Proceedings*, Vol. 18, No. 2. Taylor & Francis.

Riley, Sarah and Namita Kumar. 2012. "Teaching Medical Professionalism." *Clinical Medicine* 12(1): 9.

Schott, Timothy, et al. 2010. "Saffir-Simpson Hurricane Wind Scale," NOAA, National Weather Service. Available at http://www.nhc.noaa.gov/sshws.shtml, last accessed January 25, 2011.

Schwartz, Ann C., Raymond J. Kotwicki, and William M. McDonald. 2009. "Developing a Modern Standard to Define and Assess Professionalism in Trainees." *Academic Psychiatry* 33(6): 442–450.

Slick, Jean. 2019. "Experiencing Fire: A Phenomenological Study of YouTube Videos of the 2016 Fort McMurray Fire." *Natural Hazards* 98(1): 181–212.

Taubenberger, Jeffery K. and David M. Morens. 2006. "1918 Influenza: The Mother of All Pandemics." *Emerging Infectious Diseases*. Available at http://www.cdc.gov/ncidod/eid/vol12no01/05-0979.htm, last accessed February 6, 2011.

U.S. Agency for International Development. 2010a. *Pakistan Floods, Fact Sheet #8*. At http://www.usaid.gov/our_work/humanitarian_assistance/disaster_assistance/countries/pakistan/template/fs_sr/fy2010/pakistan_fl_fs08_08-25-2010.pdf, last accessed August 25, 2010.

U.S. Agency for International Development. 2010b. *Haiti Earthquake, Fact Sheet #63*, July 16, 2010. Available at http://www.usaid.gov/our_work/humanitarian_assistance/disaster_assistance/countries/haiti/template/fs_sr/fy2010/haiti_eq_fs63_07-16-2010.pdf, last accessed August 25, 2010.

U.S. Agency for International Development. 2015. *Nepal Earthquake Fact Sheet #9*, May 6, 2015. Available at http://www.usaid.gov/sites/default/files/documents/1866/05.06.15-USAID-DCHANepalEarthquakeFactSheet9.pdf, last accessed May 8, 2015.

United Nations. 2007. *International Flood Initative*. Available at http://unesdoc.unesco.org/images/0015/001512/151208e.pdf, last accessed January 27, 2011.

United States Nuclear Regulatory Commission (U.S. NRC). 2009. "Backgrounder on Chernobyl Nuclear Power Plant Accident." Available at http://www.nrc.gov/reading-rm/doc-collections/fact-sheets/chernobyl-bg.html, last accessed February 27, 2011.

USGS. 2020. "When will it happen again?" Available at https://earthquake.usgs.gov/earthquakes/events/1906calif/18april/whenagain.php, last accessed August 26, 2020.

Waugh, William L, Jr. 2007. "Terrorism as Disaster." Pp. 388–404 in *Handbook of Disaster Research*, eds. H. Rodriguez, E. L. Quarantelli, and Russell R. Dynes. New York: Springer.

Wheelis, Mark. 2002. "Biological Warfare at the 1386 Siege of Caffa." *Historical Review* 8(9): 971–975.

Wilson, Mary E. 1995. "Travel and the Emergence of Infectious Diseases." EID 1/2. Available at http://www.cdc.gov/ncidod/eid/vol1no2/wilson.htm, last accessed February 27, 2011.

World Wildlife Fund. 2020. *Australia's 2019–2020 Bushfires: The Wildlife Toll*. Published report by the World Wildlife Fund.

RESOURCES

- International Association of Emergency Managers, Certified Emergency Management program, https://www.iaem.org/certification/intro.
- International Association of Emergency Managers, Code of Ethics, Code of Conduct, https://www.iaem.org/Certification/Certification-Code-of-Ethics.
- International Disasters Database, EMDAT, https://www.emdat.be/.
- NOAA, databases, articles, histories, current forecasts, https://www.noaa.gov/.
- U.S. Tsunami warning center, https://www.tsunami.gov/.
- Climate Change, https://climate.nasa.gov/.
- Canada Public Health, https://www.canada.ca/en/public-health.html.
- U.S. Department of Homeland Security, https://www.dhs.gov/.
- FEMA Independent Study Center (free courses, earn a certificate), https://training.fema.gov/is/crslist.aspx.
- Emergency Management Competencies, https://training.fema.gov/hiedu/emcompetencies.aspx.

CHAPTER 3

Key Concepts, Definitions, and Perspectives

CHAPTER OBJECTIVES

Upon completing this chapter, readers should be able to:

- Have a general ability to define disaster.
- Distinguish among emergency, disaster, and catastrophe.
- Identify the different research traditions in disaster science and be able to distinguish between them.
- Explain the importance of resilience and social vulnerability in both emergency management and disaster science.
- Outline the value of a multidisciplinary approach for the practice of emergency management (EM).

KEY TERMS

- All-Hazards Approach
- Catastrophe
- Comprehensive Emergency Management
- Crisis
- Crisis Approach
- Disaster
- Disaster Tradition
- Emergency

- Emergent Norm Theory
- Hazard
- Hazards Tradition
- Life Cycle of Disasters
- Resilience
- Risk Perspective
- Social Vulnerability
- Sustainability

DOI: 10.4324/9781003021919-4

3.1 INTRODUCTION

This chapter introduces important concepts, ideas, and perspectives related to both EM and disaster science. First, we sort through various meanings of the word "disaster," focusing on scientific and political definitions. Second, we review the importance of a report by the National Governor's Association (NGA) written over 40 years ago. The ideas from this document, particularly comprehensive disaster management, the all-hazards approach, and the phases of EM, still drive both EM and disaster science today. Next, we provide a brief history of four perspectives that help us study disasters. These include the disaster tradition, the hazards tradition, the risk perspective, and the crisis approach. Finally, we discuss the importance of interdisciplinary research to better understand how people behave before, during, and after disasters.

3.2 DEFINING DISASTER

People attach a number of different meanings to the word *disaster*. Quarantelli and Dynes (1970) suggest the word disaster is a "sponge concept," since it soaks up many different meanings. For example, in general conversations, people may refer to a traffic ticket, missed appointment, or broken leg as a disaster. Within the context of EM, the word disaster may mean the disaster agent (e.g., tornado, flood, hurricane), the damage and the loss of life caused by the agent, the social definition of the event (e.g., moderate versus very bad) by the various parties involved, or the social disruption generated by the event (Dynes 1974). This chapter will help you to understand the concept of disaster and related terms in all of its complexity.

Even those of us who study disaster have different meanings and views on the topic. However, for the purposes of this text, we will draw upon a definition that has guided many researchers through a number of decades. Noted scholar Charles Fritz (1961, p. 655) defined disasters as:

> ...actual or threatened accidental or uncontrollable events that are concentrated in time and space, in which a society, or a relatively self-sufficient subdivision of society undergoes severe danger, and incurs such losses to its members and physical appurtenances that the social structure is disrupted and the fulfillment of all or some of the essential functions of the society, or its subdivision, is prevented.

Notice the main components of this definition. First of all, disasters are social events – unless the event impacts people, it is not a disaster. For example, if a tidal wave totally covered an island not inhabited by people, then the event would not be considered a disaster. Second, the situation must cause social disruption for a specific group of people. For example, if a tornado destroys part of a town of 50,000 people, life may not change much for those not directly affected. For an event to be a disaster, significant disruption to a community must occur. For example, businesses, schools, hospitals, and government offices may be closed from the damage.

Third, the area with the people impacted will need to obtain help from the outside. External help may include search and rescue teams for victims and medical needs, companies with bulldozers and chain saws to assist with clearing debris, or utility specialists to fix power lines. Volunteers and volunteer organizations will also bring in food and water for survivors as well as those assisting with search and rescue, conduct debris removal, and take other actions.

Another important issue within Fritz's definition is considering that the *situation* may not be an actual physical event, but rather the perception that an event could be or is taking place. For example, thousands of people may evacuate when a hurricane warning is issued. Such an event disrupts the lives of the residents, local and state government officials, businesses and volunteer organizations. All these individuals' lives change to varying degrees – even if the hurricane does not strike. But, at least, they get to return and resume their day-to-day lives. In short, Fritz's definition suggests that life as we know it dramatically changes when disaster strikes. Next, let's look at the differences among emergencies, disasters, and catastrophes.

3.2.1 A Continuum of Disaster

People may think of an event in simple terms – either something is or is not a disaster. A car wreck is not a disaster. A tornado is a disaster. A house fire is not a disaster. A large chemical accident is a disaster. Yet, whether an event can be defined as a disaster is not always clear (Fischer 2003). Rather, think how events occur along a continuum where some events occur as day-to-day emergencies, others as disasters (with some larger than others), and on rare occasions, catastrophes.

3.2.1.1 Emergency

Emergencies are part of everyday life in a community. Emergency response situations may include heart attacks, house fires, or car accidents. Emergency response organizations can generally anticipate their emergency response needs on a yearly basis. For example, in the U.S., Independence Day (July 4th) and New Year's are the busiest times of the year for firefighters. The annual July 4th peak in the U.S. is a result of fireworks and, to a lesser degree, outside grilling. Fires around New Year's also involve firecrackers and flammable Christmas trees (U.S. Fire Administration 2019, 2004). Anybody in the medical business knows that weekends generally are busier than weekdays for emergency response organizations. Since these emergency response patterns are predictable, governments and response units can plan accordingly and manage these situations. In addition, except for those primarily directly involved in the emergency, life goes on for everybody else.

Situations do arise where some outside help may be needed. For example, in the case of a large apartment fire, responding fire departments may activate a Memorandum of Understanding (MOU) with nearby fire departments. When a major event occurs, the neighboring fire department will arrive to either aid with the large fire or provide backup if another fire occurs within the city. Thus, although resources may be stretched, local communities can carry on business as usual when the emergency occurs.

3.2.1.2 Disaster

Drawing upon Fritz's definition (1961), noted above, a disaster exceeds the local community's ability to respond to an event even when outside help is drawn upon. For example, response organizations such as fire and police may not be able to respond to all the immediate needs or may not be able to respond at all. The number of immediate victims may outnumber the availability of emergency response capabilities. Debris and damage may inhibit emergency responders from entering the disaster site. In addition, the emergency responders may be victims also. But a disaster is much more than the inability of emergency responders to do their duty. The infrastructure may suffer major damage. Most of the community may not have electrical power. Water (including drinking water and sewage) may not be available. Highways and bridges may either be impassable from excessive debris (e.g., from a tornado), inaccessible (e.g., flooded), or destroyed (e.g., earthquake). Family members may be separated from each other, have no food or water, or find their homes gone. Businesses, schools, and other organizations will close since the buildings will be damaged or destroyed, and people cannot travel to these locations. In short, everyday life as we know it ceases. Priorities change to focus on the event at hand. The community cannot fend for itself. Most importantly, it needs outside help.

3.2.1.3 Catastrophe

Catastrophes are much more than just "larger disasters." Following Hurricane Katrina, Quarantelli (2006) noted that the hurricane's social impact and aftermath included the basic characteristics that distinguish a catastrophe from a disaster. First, in a catastrophe the disaster agent impacts or destroys almost all of an area's buildings and infrastructure. With Hurricane Katrina, over 80% of New Orleans flooded, and much of the area along the Mississippi coast experienced extensive storm surge damage. The floodwaters and wind either directly or indirectly made most of the infrastructure (e.g., electricity, drinking water and sewage, transportation) inoperable. Police, fire, and other local and even regional emergency response organizations were generally unable to operate since the hurricane's aftermath impacted their buildings and staff. Furthermore, outside assistance organizations (Federal, state, volunteer organizations) had difficulty initially helping. Cell phones did not work for most carriers for nearly a week. Transportation was difficult, if not impossible, into the area. When help did arrive, they had trouble finding facilities to use. The sheer magnitude of the event made it difficult to know where to begin.

Second, many local officials could not tend to their jobs after Katrina, even into the initial recovery period. In many cases, these individuals had no place to go to work and/or had lost their homes. This issue also became evident following the Indian Ocean Tsunami in 2004 and the Haitian Earthquake in 2010. With thousands dead, including government officials in some places, response activities became difficult, if not impossible, to coordinate.

Third, during and following a disaster, help generally arrives rather quickly. In fact, a problem following a disaster is that too much help (e.g., people, food, supplies) arrives, a problem known as "convergence." However, with the massive nature of a catastrophe, help may be slow in coming. Specifically, large cities may not be able to help nearby smaller cities and nearby smaller cities cannot help larger cities since the entire region has been impacted. People, food, and other needed supplies initially have no place to go to provide assistance (Quarantelli 2006).

Fourth, catastrophes mean that daily routines of individuals, families, organizations, governments, businesses, schools, and other sites will experience significant disruptions. Consider again the case of Hurricane Katrina, with little if any functioning infrastructure, heavily damaged buildings, over one million residents displaced, the routine of life along the Gulf Coast came to a halt. Reflect also on the 2010 Haiti earthquake, where in addition to massive destruction of buildings and infrastructure, approximately 300,000 people died, many of whom carried out important day-to-day tasks for government, businesses, and households (Quarantelli 2006).

Finally, during a catastrophe, the Federal government's role moves to center since it has the resources to provide direct assistance to the impacted region. Following the earthquake in Haiti, issues about who was in charge surfaced quickly. The death of some politicians and possible lack of leadership in other areas created a major political vacuum. In addition, catastrophes such as Hurricane Katrina cross local, county (or in this case, Parish), and state jurisdictions, so the Federal government can help serve under-resourced areas (Quarantelli 2006).

In short, a catastrophe varies significantly from a disaster. The disaster agent destroys most, if not all, of a region's buildings and infrastructure. The lives of individuals and routines of whole communities become totally disrupted. Outside helpers have difficulty in arriving and even setting up operations. Local, state, and the Federal government must all become increasingly involved to deal with the massive problems generated by a catastrophe.

Now that we have a general understanding of the conceptual continuum from emergency to disaster to catastrophe, we will next discuss some concepts used by both professionals and researchers when trying to understand how emergency managers organize their daily activities to manage disasters.

3.2.2 Political Definitions of Disaster

Politics certainly play a role in whether an event is defined a disaster. Political definitions become important in the U.S., since the amount and type of aid during and following the event is contingent upon how the event is defined (e.g., hurricane, flood, landslide) and whether the event becomes a Presidentially Declared Disaster.

FEMA does not have a set of numerical factors for determining whether an event is a disaster. For example, an event might be declared a disaster if nobody dies or an event might not be declared a disaster if 150 people die. To illustrate, a slow-moving flood may not kill anyone, but it could be declared a disaster. And cases certainly exist where a plane crash kills over 100 people, but the President does not declare a disaster. Rather, for an event to qualify for a disaster declaration, FEMA focuses upon the severity, magnitude, and impact of the event, among other factors (see Box 3.1). FEMA draws upon the criteria listed below as guidelines for a state's governor to use in making a request for a federal disaster declaration (FEMA no date, *verbatim*):

BOX 3.1

THE PROCESS OF ISSUING A PRESIDENTIAL DECLARATION OF DISASTER

Through the last few decades, the Federal Emergency Management Agency (FEMA) has established a process and general criteria for a Presidential Declaration of Disaster (PDD). Authority for such a declaration comes from a number of related sources. In a general sense, article 2 and section 3 of the U.S. Constitution implicitly gives the President the power to take emergency action to insure that all laws are followed and to command the use of the military (as Commander in Chief). The Disaster Relief Act of 1950 and the Disaster Relief Act of 1974 gave the President power to provide relief and assistance to disaster victims. Finally, the Robert T. Stafford Disaster Relief and Emergency Assistance Act (i.e., The Stafford Act; first passed in 1988 and later amended) gave the President further power to declare a disaster more quickly (such as in the case of a terrorist attack). In essence, today, with a Presidential Declaration, the Federal Government through the Executive (i.e., Presidential) branch can provide immediate funds. Through the years, Congress has amended the Stafford Act, including the process and general criteria for the declaration of a disaster (Sylves 2008).

The Stafford Act also spells out the process local and state governments must follow to apply for a declaration and receive Federal resources. Drawing upon the criteria noted above, local and state officials will provide the state's governor with a damage assessment. The state's governor will then submit a formal request to its FEMA regional office (one of ten in the U.S.). The governor's request should demonstrate that state and local governments do not have the resources to manage and recover from the event. Both the regional and national FEMA offices will assess the report, and then make a recommendation to the President (FEMA 2021).

Politics can and at times do enter into the Presidential declaration. In a specific analysis on Presidential disaster declarations issued between May 1953 and January 2007, a distinct pattern emerged (Sylves 2008). First, during this time period, there were 1,674 major disaster declarations. This represents an average of 31 declarations a year or close to 2.5 declarations a month. However, if we look at the time period from January 1993 to September 2005, we see a dramatic rise in disaster declarations. The average increased to 48.2 declarations a year or four a month, with the increase believed to be tied to:

- The public's belief that the Federal Government's role is to provide aid.
- Various politicians' views and use of federalism (or how the state and Federal Governments interact with each other).
- Presidents being more willing to declare disasters.
- Laws allowing more aid to disaster hit communities and victims (Sylves 2008, p. 84).

Interestingly, partisanship does not seem to be part of the political process of major disaster declarations. For example, a request by a Republican governor to a Democratic President will not diminish the chance of an event being declared a disaster. Or, a request by a Republican governor to a Republican President will not enhance the chance of an event being declared a disaster. However, during the same 45-year time period, mentioned earlier, researchers also found that Democratic Presidents accepted a higher proportion of declaration requests than Republican Presidents. In addition, Presidents were more likely to approve a governor's request for natural rather than technological disasters (Sylves and Buzas 2007). The pace of a disaster may influence a decision as well, for example, when an Enhanced Fujita (EF) 5 tornado devastates an area, a Presidential declaration typically occurs more quickly than a slowly developing drought.

- "Amount and type of damage (number of homes destroyed or with major damage).
- Impact on the infrastructure of affected areas or critical facilities.
- Imminent threats to public health and safety.
- Impacts to essential government services and functions.
- Unique capability of the Federal Government.
- Dispersion or concentration of damage.
- Level of insurance coverage in place for homeowners and public facilities.
- Assistance available from other sources (Federal, State, local, voluntary organizations).
- State and local resource commitments from previous, undeclared events, and
- Frequency of disaster events over a recent time period." [end *verbatim*]

3.2.3 Slow versus Fast-Moving Views of Disaster

Generally we think of disasters as events that quickly strike a population such as an explosion, flood, earthquake, tornado, or similar event. The perspective of looking at sudden or quickly moving events is, in part, based upon the research and professional roots of the field. Remember that dealing with nuclear and chemical war with the start of the Cold War drove much of our view of EM in the U.S. To study human behavior in this context, researchers looked at human behavior during sudden or quickly oc-curring disasters like explosions or tornadoes. Even today, much of our knowledge of disaster behavior, especially in developed nations such as the U.S., Canada, Japan, and Western Europe focuses upon the sudden, quick event.

However, not all events occur quickly, suddenly, or without warning, but develop slowly. For example, meteorologists can often predict long-term patterns of drought which can cause crop failure leading to famine, especially in places like Central Africa. In turn, famine may force migration for survival, which may lead to other challenges when internally displaced persons (IDPs) generate competition for resources, con-flict, or human rights violations (Hoffman and Oliver-Smith 2002; for more, see also Chapter 11).

Environmental disasters can also be slow-moving. The neighborhood of Love Canal, part of Niagara Falls, New York, became contaminated due to hazardous waste buried there by the Hooker Chemical Company starting in 1942. During the early and mid-1950s, the property was sold to a developer to build homes. A school soon followed. By the mid to late 1970s, residents started to notice odd odors and health problems, including a higher rate of miscarriages, mental health issues, and physical illnesses. A local newspaper tested the water in the area and found high amounts of hazardous materials. As a result, local residents formed a protest group in order to help with solving their medical issues, selling homes, and closing the neighborhood. In the end, as part of an Environmental Protection Agency program, over 800 families left the neighborhood with most of the homes then being demolished (Levine 1982; Blum 2008).

In this circumstance, the real issue is "when did the disaster start?" For some, it started the second the hazardous waste was improperly disposed of. For others, it began when the property was sold for development. Perhaps, for the residents, the event became defined as a disaster when people started to get sick. By the late 1970s and early 1980s, government officials recognized the event as a disaster. Federal assistance and the Environmental Protection Agency became involved as people moved out of the area to safer locations. But, as a slow- and long-onset event, it was hard to pinpoint the exact time when the "threshold" was met to call the event a disaster (Levine 1982; Blum 2008).

In short, various types of events (e.g., droughts, famines, hazardous chemicals, pandemics) do not become immediate disasters. Rather, their impacts, consequences, and even public definitions of the event becoming a disaster may unfold over months, years, or decades. As a result, emergency managers and others cannot state an exact time when such an event becomes a disaster. These types of events slowly creep upon us, until, perhaps, the attributes of disaster suddenly exist and it becomes too late to mitigate, prepare, or even respond properly. Regardless, it is the job of the emergency manager to take on such challenges, which historically has been characterized as a life cycle of activities usually organized into four phases.

3.3 THE NATIONAL GOVERNOR'S ASSOCIATION REPORT IN THE U.S.

For decades, the U.S. struggled with disasters. The nation had no clear or central vision on how to handle disasters. Consequently, two important steps occurred that continue to impact EM today. First, President Carter established FEMA in 1979 to centralize and streamline EM responsibilities. At the same time, the NGA (1979) issued a major report on how to improve EM. More than 40 years since it was published, ideas from this report continue to drive and define EM and provide important tools for disaster researchers. These concepts, outlined below, are embedded within the idea of Comprehensive Emergency Management (CEM) and an "all-hazards" approach to disaster that spans four phases of EM.

CEM encourages a broad holistic approach to managing disasters. The NGA report on EM defined CEM as a:

> ... state's responsibility and capability for managing all types of emergencies and disasters by coordinating the actions of numerous agencies. The 'comprehensive' aspect of CEM includes all four phases of disaster or emergency activity: mitigation,

preparedness, response, and recovery. It applies to all risks: attack, man-made, and natural, in a federal-state-local partnership.

(NGA 1979, p. 11)

The four phases and all-hazards approach to disasters continue to serve as the foundation for emergency managers and as important concepts for disaster researchers. We review these two concepts below.

3.3.1 The Disaster Life Cycle

Through the years, researchers and professionals have tried to break the disaster process down into specific categories, even beyond the four phases commonly used today. Some have suggested using the terms pre-impact, impact, and postimpact. However, the NGA (1979) report of four phases (mitigation, preparedness, response, recovery) has stayed in place for a long time. Other nations have adopted the same idea. For example, in New Zealand they are known as the four "Rs": readiness, response, recovery, and reduction. Regardless which organization or nation takes on the tasks of EM, four general phases capture the bulk of what typical emergency managers do:

- *Mitigation*: "activities that actually eliminate or reduce the probability of occurrence of a disaster...arms build-up, land-use management, establishing CEM (i.e., comprehensive EM programs) programs, building safety codes" (NGA 1979, p. 13).
- *Preparedness*: "activities [that] are necessary to the extent that mitigation measures have not, or cannot, prevent disasters...develop plans, mounting training exercises, installing warning systems, stockpiling food and medical supplies, mobilizing emergency personnel" (NGA 1979, p. 13).
- *Response*: "activities [that] follow an emergency or disaster. Generally, they are designed to provide emergency assistance for casualties...seek to reduce the probability of secondary damage...and to speed recovery operations" (NGA 1979, pp. 13–14).
- *Recovery*: "activities [that] continue until all systems return to normal or better... short-term recovery activities return vital life-support systems to minimum operating standards. Long-term recovery activities...return life to normal or improved levels" (NGA 1979, p. 14).

Both professional emergency managers and researchers have found these categories useful for their work. For professionals, the phases give a unique way to divide their tasks and focus on their work. For example, in many state EM agencies and in large cities, offices often have specific sections or jobs related to some of the four phases. Historically, FEMA has had divisions organized around the phases, although FEMA's organizational structure today has become even more complex. FEMA also provides federal grants related to these categories. As a result, states and local communities can secure funds for preparedness, response, recovery, or mitigation activities.

Academic degree programs in disasters and textbooks (including this) draw upon the four phases of EM as a way to organize degree programs and courses (Neal 2000).

Researchers also use these concepts to categorize the type of studies they do (Mileti, Drabek, and Haas 1975; Drabek 1986; Mileti 1999).

In short, the life cycle or phases approach helps emergency managers organize their activities, although they do overlap to some degree. The removal of disaster debris from roads (response) may still occur while people return home (recovery). Or, following a flood, people may rebuild their homes (recovery) while government officials strengthen levees to lessen the impact of another flood (mitigation). In addition, certain activities may be hard to distinguish between phases. For example, public education programs for disaster warnings help people know what to do when the alarm is sounded. Yet, the same public education program could be considered mitigation since it can lower the loss of life and injury (Neal 1997).

Furthermore, activities during one disaster phase may concurrently support activities in other phases. Better preparedness should improve response. An effective response means a better recovery. For example, having stricter building codes for earthquakes (i.e., mitigation) means generally that less damage will occur during an earthquake. As a result, less time and money will be needed to repair buildings or the infrastructure (i.e., recovery). In short, all the phases have an important impact on the other phases. Overall, the phases are useful tools to help us manage disasters, but in reality, they nest within other phases and overlap (Neal 1997).

3.3.2 All-Hazards Approach

A second idea central in EM is what was initially called the "all risks" approach, and is today known as the "all-hazards" approach. The National Governor's Report showed that regardless of the event, certain governmental activities have stayed the same across events. During this same time, researchers also advocated an all-hazards approach to disasters, using the phrase "agent generic." Although specific hazards may create specific problems or issues, overall similar issues will arise across disasters.

For example, communication and collaboration must occur across all kinds of disasters. Warnings must be written and disseminated for a tornado or a drought. By working to understand how to warn people at risk, the basic principles of warning should work despite the hazard. In a later chapter, you will learn the basics of how to craft such an effective warning message. Similarly, various organizations must work together to address relief efforts whether a pandemic has unfolded or a terror attack just happened. First responders and emergency managers need to coordinate resources for search and rescue. Voluntary organizations need to organize efforts for the social and psychological impacts of unexpected events. Recovery organizations need to coordinate to use resources well and avoid redundant efforts. Similarly, the process of educating the public follows the same processes across various types of disasters. Or, those more vulnerable to disasters (e.g., the poor, racial and ethnic minorities, women, the elderly, some people with disabilities) are more likely to be affected and to require more extensive assistance.

In short, the overall similarities of how we respond to disasters are much greater than the differences (Dynes 1974; Quarantelli 1982). By realizing the many similarities across hazards, professionals can focus on writing one generic plan (with short, hazard-specific annexes) rather than creating many similar plans. Such functional areas cross the type of hazard, thus managing a disaster – or writing a plan to do so – can and should use similar knowledge and approaches despite the kind of event.

3.4 MAJOR PERSPECTIVES IN DISASTER SCIENCE

Next, we describe the different ways researchers look at and study how people behave before, during, and after disaster. These perspectives can also provide emergency managers different ways to understand events. Words such as hazards, disaster, risk, and crisis represents certain components of EM while also reflecting different but important research traditions (see Figure 3.1).

3.4.1 The Hazards Tradition

In the simplest form, hazards are disasters waiting to happen. People may live or work in the path of floods, tornadoes, hurricanes, or chemical accidents. Researchers from the Hazards Tradition look at interaction among people, nature, and technology, and how these interactions can increase or decrease the chance of a hazard being transformed into a disaster that disrupts community functioning (Mileti 1999; Cutter 2001).

Geographer Gilbert White founded and established the hazards tradition. During his long and distinguished career, he focused on the value of structural mitigation projects (e.g., levees and dams) that decrease flooding along rivers (Kates 2011). In short, he found that structural mitigation may minimize natural hazards annually, but some hazards (and time) may prove structural mitigation insufficient. For example, a 1993 flood punctuated White's concerns. For decades, a system of levees had minimized most flooding along the Mississippi River in the U.S. However, a combination of above-average river levels, wet soil allowing for rain runoff, and excessive spring and summer precipitation overwhelmed the structural mitigation efforts. As a result, hundreds of levees failed, causing massive flooding across nine states and about 150 rivers and tributaries. Around 15 million acres of farmland flooded, with water inundating and destroying 10,000+ homes and invading 75+ towns. The rising waters destroyed bridges, stopped barge traffic and commerce, flooded ten airports, and killed about 50 people (Larson 1996). Structural mitigation has its limits, based on the event, maintenance and upkeep, and the costs of preventing a hazard from becoming a disaster. New Orleans witnessed a similar event when storm surge from Hurricane Katrina devastated the levee system and flooded the city for months. Although the levees have been rebuilt and strengthened, the level of protection remains at a Category 3 storm level of protection. Katrina was a Category 4. Why not rebuild to a higher level? The cost of

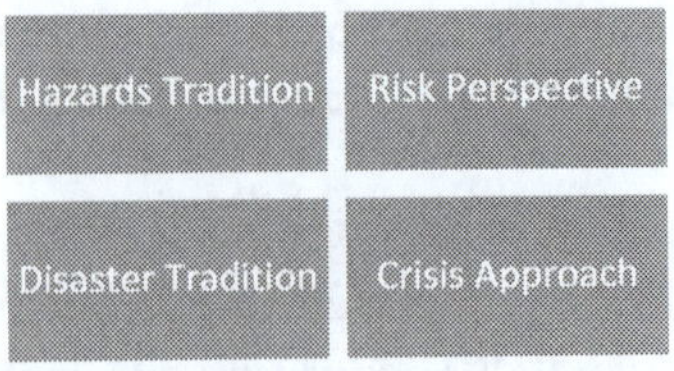

Hazards Tradition	Risk Perspective
Disaster Tradition	Crisis Approach

FIGURE 3.1 Major Perspectives in Disaster Science

protection, political will, and our inability to live in harmony with nature characterize the hazards tradition, along with an emphasis upon non-structural mitigation, including safer land-use decisions..

During the 1970s, White and various colleagues published several key books looking at issues and problems related to a wide range of natural hazards from local, regional, and international perspectives (White 1974; White and Haas 1975). The research led White to establish the Natural Hazards Research and Application Information Center (also known as the Natural Hazards Center) at the University of Colorado Boulder in the mid-1970s (Natural Hazards Center, n.d.). A key purpose behind the new center was to break down barriers, so emergency managers, professionals/policy makers, and researchers could talk about hazard issues.

White's work with his colleagues helped to define the hazards perspective which has evolved into a multidisciplinary approach. Geographers, along with psychologists, sociologists, economists, engineers, and geologists now work together on research and practical applications to mitigate hazards. As part of his legacy, the Natural Hazards Center also has a large resource center and hosts an annual workshop for professionals, researchers, and others interested in the field of hazards (Myers 1993; also visit www.colorado.edu/hazards). The center today continues to be at the forefront of creating and pursuing innovative ideas for both the professional emergency manager and researchers.

3.4.2 The Disaster Tradition

The disaster tradition's initial focus is grounded in disaster response activities, and sociologists did much of the early research. Much of this goes back to civil defense activities during the start of the Cold War between the U.S. and the Soviet Union (from the late 1940s until the fall of the Berlin Wall in November 1989). During the Cold War, each country prepared to respond to potential nuclear and chemical strikes. The U.S. military provided research funding to the University of Chicago to understand how soldiers and civilians would respond to these types of attacks. The National Opinion Research Center (NORC) at the University of Chicago, led by Charles Fritz, initiated much of this research. Obviously researchers could not expose cities and people to nuclear bombs or chemical weapons. So, researchers selected to study events similar to war – disasters. Researchers traveled to disaster sites soon after impact and studied how people and organizations responded. Contrary to popular belief, researchers found that disasters did not cause behaviors such as mass panic, looting, or hysteria. Rather, disasters brought out the best of behaviors – altruism abounded (Quarantelli 1987, 1994).

Drawing upon the "quick response" research of the NORC studies, sociologists Henry Quarantelli, Russell Dynes, and Eugene Haas formed the Disaster Research Center (DRC) in 1963 at The Ohio State University. Dynes and Haas both specialized in organizations, and Quarantelli had been a graduate student at the University of Chicago during the 1950s where he served as a research assistant with NORC. Like NORC, much of DRC's initial funding came from the Department of Defense and focused upon the social aspects of disaster response.

Today, DRC (now located at the University of Delaware) continues to be a leading international research center studying a wide range of events and topics. Since the center started in 1963, it has studied over 600 events not only in the U.S. but throughout the world (e.g., 1964 Alaska earthquake, 1974 Super Outbreak of Tornadoes, 1989 Loma Prieta Earthquake, 2001 Terrorist Attacks, 2004 Indian Ocean Tsunami). In addition to what could be considered more traditional issues related to disaster research, DRC has focused on new, innovative research topics, including handling the dead, sheltering and housing, mental health delivery systems, emergent citizen groups, organizational improvisation, hospitals and medical delivery, crowds and riots, the Ebola crisis, stakeholder decision in creating disaster policies, resiliency, and COVID-19 (see https://www.drc.udel.edu/, last accessed May 26, 2021).

DRC has also made a major contribution by training a large number of graduate students. These former graduate students have gone on to further quick response research, provide a clearer understanding of disaster response, contribute to disaster research beyond the four phases, and establish academic degrees in disaster management. DRC also has the most comprehensive disaster library collection in the world and scholars travel from throughout the world to use the collection and meet with the center's staff (DRC 2015, 2016).

From a practical view, the disaster tradition has helped to provide emergency managers with evidence-based best practices, particularly for responding to disasters. Recent major U.S. planning documents, such as Comprehensive Planning Guide 101 (see resources), explicitly draw upon the disaster tradition to ground its preparedness and response suggestions.

3.4.3 The Risk Perspective

Another perspective used to understand hazards and disaster centers on understanding risk, particularly individual perceptions of risk. In large part, Paul Slovic (the University of Oregon) helped create the study of risk research over 35 years ago (Decision Research 2015a, 2015b; Slovic 1987). Initially, the field of risk analysis grew out of questions of safety around nuclear power. Such issues and concerns intensified after the Three Mile Island (TMI) nuclear accident in the U.S. in 1979 and the Chernobyl (in the former Soviet Union) nuclear power plant explosion in 1986. Today, the concept of risk goes beyond issues of nuclear power to consider a range of risk-related topics.

Originally coming from a (social) psychological perspective, researchers have tried to understand how individuals view and respond to risk. For example, the risk perspective may focus on why people perceive some activities as more risky than others (e.g., flying on a commercial airliner versus driving a car). It may also concern environmental issues, such as how much of a hazardous substance should be allowed into rivers or waste sites. Or, risk can deal with the trade-offs between having offshore oil wells and their potential damage to the environment from a major oil spill versus a need for oil. Not all activities dealing with the risk perspective may deal with hazards and disasters, such as topics related to "risky activities" (e.g., smoking, skydiving) or other situations (e.g., possible exposure to cancer from environmental threats).

Risk is also defined as the probability of an event occurring. We filter risk through various levels of perception and understanding. For example, the "cone of uncertainty" meteorologists use to describe a projected hurricane path can be very challenging to comprehend. Public response depends on understanding the ways in which the hurricane may move; thus the cone projects a wide path that changes daily, if not hourly. Because we cannot know with a high degree of certainty where a hurricane will strike until 24–36 hours before landfall, it is hard to inform the public – who must evacuate most areas 48 hours ahead of impact. People may simply take their chances based on an assumption that "it won't happen to me" or previous experience with hurricanes. Coupled with a low degree of concern with disasters for most people (Lindell and Perry 2001), it can be very hard to communicate a warning message and convince the public of an impending risk. Think, for example, of how likely it will be that an existing hazard might generate a major disaster in your area and then think through how many preparations you have taken to be ready. Did you pay attention to risk information and see its relevance to your personal safety?

Understanding risk can assist us with understanding why people choose to evacuate or not during a hurricane or chemical explosion, or why people may be willing to live next to a potentially hazardous site (e.g., chemical company or nuclear power plant, floodplain). Understanding risk perception makes us more capable of helping the public by designing preparedness campaigns and organizing evacuations.

3.4.4 The Crisis Approach

The end of the Cold War and demise of the Soviet Eastern Bloc created turmoil in Northern Europe. Political and other related crises emerged among these countries and social scientists lacked sufficient analytic tools to describe such events. As a result, researchers, first in the Netherlands and then Sweden, started to focus on how organizations and leaders attempt to manage crises. The usage of the word crisis suggests that researchers look at a much broader range of events, including financial collapses, computer failures, and many others. Organizational decision-making, leadership, and how policies develop during and following the crisis became their focus of analysis.

We can trace the origins of the Crisis Approach to the Leiden University Center of Crisis Research in the Netherlands. Generally, the Crisis Approach focuses upon situations where a society's values and norms are threatened, there is a short period of time to act, and decision makers must deal with a high degree of uncertainty (Rosenthal, Charles, and Hart 1989; Hansen 2003). Unlike previous perspectives, the Crisis Approach has a strong political and administrative view of events. This view should not be a surprise as Uri Rosenthal, founder of the Crisis Perspective, has served both as an academic researcher and a politician in the Netherlands.

A similar perspective grew out of Sweden and their National Defense College (now known as The Swedish Defense University). Led by Professor Bengt Sundelius, scholars focused upon crises such as mad cow disease, political assassinations, kidnappings, environmental issues, a grounded foreign submarine, power blackouts, political refugees, terrorism, and risk communication, among many related similar issues (Swedish Defence University n.d.a.). CrisMart, at that time the social science research arm of the Swedish National Defence College, also conducted research on these topics. Using a case study approach, they have focused on communication and leadership to analyze each situation (Neal 2012). Since January 2018, CrisMart has become part of the Centre for Societal Security within the Swedish National Defence College (Swedish Defence University n.d.b).

The Crisis Approach has become an entrenched and useful perspective to understand crisis events, though the other three perspectives still drive much of the research published in recent journals (Kuipers and Welsh 2017). Nonetheless, the Crisis Approach provides a fresh way to look at disasters. It covers a much broader range of events; focuses upon the decision-making process and leadership before, during, or after the crisis; and utilizes systematic case studies to understand the management and decision-making process that occurs during a crisis. This approach also allows researchers to compare these events over time (Boin 2009).

3.4.5 Major Perspectives Summary

We have identified four different perspectives that help us understand human behavior before, during, and after disaster. Each tradition has its own origins and a unique perspective for understanding disasters. Although initially grounded in the disciplines of geography, sociology, psychology, and political science/public administration, these perspectives today draw upon multiple disciplines to answer important research questions.

3.5 CROSS-CUTTING THEMES IN DISASTER SCIENCE

As the field has grown, broader views on disasters, hazards, risk, and crises have influenced how we see the world around us. These two viewpoints include social vulnerability and resilience (Figure 3.2).

After decades of research, both professionals and scholars know that disasters are social events, and that those with fewer resources (e.g., money, wealth, power) based on social factors (e.g., ethnicity, gender, social class, social/physical disabilities) are at greater risk of experiencing a disaster and will take longer to recover. Conversely, resilience provides a means to understand how members of society rebound after a crisis or disaster occurs. Below, we look at these perspectives in more detail.

3.5.1 Social Vulnerability

Disasters are not equal opportunity events. Rather, specific groups of people are at greater risk to hazards and becoming disaster victims and having more problems while recovering from disasters. Two divergent perspectives provide contrasting approaches to explain what happens in disasters. Called the dominant and the social vulnerability perspectives, each focuses on why disasters occur, what effects they cause, and what can be done by emergency managers (Fordham et al. 2013). The dominant perspective may

FIGURE 3.2 Cross-Cutting Themes in Disaster Science

sound familiar, as it emphasizes the physical hazard itself – an earthquake happens and a home topples as a result. To care for those affected, emergency managers would use a combination of engineering and science to recover. The home would be rebuilt with new seismic bracing standards created within the building code itself. The goal would be to reduce future damage by overcoming the challenge presented by nature.

The dominant perspective has generally fallen out of favor among researchers and many professionals who look at other reasons to explain why the disaster happened. Socioeconomic and political circumstances are considered over the physical hazard itself. For example, if a flood occurs and homes are inundated – why did that occur? Could it be that homes are situated too close to the river or allowed to be built in a floodplain? Such decisions are usually allowed through policy decisions, though history and societal relationships also play a role. In some locations, homes are subject to flooding after generations of segregation based on racial and ethnic discrimination (Cutter and Emrich 2006; Phillips, Stukes, and Jenkins 2012). Subsequent generations may have lacked the financial means to relocate or may have built strong social ties that provided useful resources, keeping people in place. Similarly, places like Haiti or Nepal, which suffered devastating earthquakes in 2010 and 2015, lost hundreds of thousands of people. They died in buildings that collapsed on them, because they could not afford stronger dwellings. Similar outcomes occur after tornadoes strike affordable but less resistant mobile homes, where even an EF1 tornado can destroy a dwelling. In 2004, the Indian Ocean tsunami claimed about 300,000 lives with approximately 80% being women and children. Many perished waiting on the shore for fishermen to return from the sea. Their role? To process and sell the fish as part of a gendered division of labor in places like India and Sri Lanka. Further, demographic changes worldwide are making disasters worse (Quarantelli 1991). For example, many cities developed along rivers and floodplains due to ease of transportation. Yet, coastal areas remain at risk of flooding and storms. Climate change continues to threaten those that live in such flood-prone regions, from wealthier landowners to low-income workers.

The vulnerability perspective then says that the hazard itself is not the problem. Rather, it is the way in which society marginalizes people by age, disability, gender, race, income, and other factors. Overcoming vulnerability requires empowering those historically marginalized to reduce their vulnerability and educating emergency managers on how to empower at-risk stakeholders. Vulnerability reduction also requires that societies address historic patterns of discrimination and marginalization which keep people subject to risk. To illustrate, consider what happened to people with disabilities after Hurricane Katrina. A catastrophic event, the Federal government lacked sufficient resources to provide accessible temporary housing units – which led to a lawsuit that changed things (*FEMA v. Brou*). Movement through the recovery process meant facing even more barriers, particularly a lack of transportation and access to disability resources and services (Stough et al. 2015).

Perhaps this point has been best punctuated during COVID-19. Internationally, issues of social class, ethnicity, gender, disability, age, and income have all impacted the response to COVID-19. These factors include becoming ill, being hospitalized, and dying. People in low-paying jobs were more likely to be exposed and die from COVID-19. Large nations with extreme pockets of poverty, such as Brazil and India, have suffered severe losses coupled with the lack of vaccinations. Children of more vulnerable parents appear to suffer from short- and probably long-term educational impacts. Furthermore, many with higher vulnerability, particularly racial and ethnic minorities, had lower rates of vaccination requiring significant outreach by public health and EM officials (*The Lancet* 2021).

Making people aware of social vulnerability is one step to decreasing its effects. Also, a common approach is to build bridges between those deemed potentially vulnerable, such as people with disabilities, and those in positions of authority, such as emergency managers. By working together, emergency managers and people with disabilities can identify and reduce the potential impacts of disasters. People dependent on mobility devices, for example, may require access to a location with power (such as a fire station) to remain independent. Or, shelter managers will benefit from talking to people with disabilities to design movement pathways, appropriate nutritional options, accessible showers, and advocacy efforts to help people return home (NCD 2009). We will return to this cross-cutting social vulnerability theme throughout the remainder of the text as a means to stem losses, reduce suffering, and make EM more effective.

3.5.2 Resilience

A term we hear with disasters, and even life in general, is resilience. In the most simple and general terms, we can think of resilience meaning the capability to "bounce back" after a tragic event. In the most basic terms from a disaster perspective, a National Academies (2012, p. 1) report defines resilience as "the ability to prepare and plan for, absorb, recover from, and more successfully adapt to adverse events." Here, a specific focus is given before a disaster strikes, since these efforts, through preparedness, planning, and adaptation, assist people in "bouncing back" more effectively. It also allows for policy makers to engage in cost–benefit analysis to determine where specific efforts or programs can create better outcomes. Resilience is an idea that today is firmly entrenched both within the profession of EM and disaster science. It is rooted in the idea of sustainability that we must act accordingly to maintain our planetary well-being for both current and especially for future generations.

Toward that end, the U.S. National Academies of Science, Engineering, and Medicine have created a Resilient America program. The effort embraces science as a means to build an "adaptive and resilient nation" by interacting with all sectors to (verbatim; see https://www.nationalacademies.org/resilient-america/about):

- "increase understanding of *complex risks and extreme events* in a changing environment, and the exposure of communities, infrastructure, and natural systems to these threats;
- investigate and strengthen attributes of *equitable, resilient systems and communities*, their interconnections and interdependencies;
- test, communicate and strengthen implementation of *equitable strategies for adapting to changing risks and robust recovery* from disruptions;
- *share accessible science and data for strengthening resilience and adaptive action*, including policies, tools, best practices, and metrics; and
- *connect and facilitate partnerships* among scientists, data providers, practitioners, and decision makers." [end verbatim]

Other nations, like New Zealand, have also embraced resilience as a way to organize and direct thinking around hazards (https://www.civildefence.govt.nz/cdem-sector/plans-and-strategies/national-disaster-resilience-strategy/). The Ministry of Civil Defence and Emergency Management there centers their strategies that (verbatim):

- "promotes the sustainable management of hazards in a way that contributes to safety and wellbeing;
- encourages wide participation, including communities, in the process to manage risk;
- provides for planning and preparation for emergencies, and for response and recovery;
- requires local authorities to coordinate reduction, readiness, response and recovery activities through regional groups;
- provides a basis for the integration of national and local planning and activity; and
- encourages coordination across a wide range of agencies, recognising that emergencies are multi-agency events affecting all parts of society." [end verbatim]

Yet, resilience and sustainability do not provide all the answers. Aguirre (2002; Aguirre and Best 2014) points out that these concepts may reflect a more "northern" or industrial viewpoint of disasters, while also inhibiting multiple indigenous people's views of an event. Thus, resilience often may engage only key power brokers in government and business, while leaving out the views and perspectives of those potential and actual survivors of the events. Again, the social vulnerability perspective redirects us to consider everyone's definitions and approaches to hazards that become disasters. New Zealand has embraced this by building partnerships and empowering Māori within their strategies.

3.5.3 Summary of Cross-Cutting Themes

Both resilience and social vulnerability have become key perspectives to describe and explain the social dimensions of disasters. Social vulnerability provides the view that those with minimal or no power (e.g., based on ethnicity, gender, social class, income, disabilities) are more likely to become disaster survivors, and will generally take longer to recover from such events (if ever). Resilience provided the idea that individuals, families, groups, and nations can "bounce back" from disasters.

3.6 EMBRACING A MULTIDISCIPLINARY APPROACH

As noted earlier in this chapter, the different disaster perspectives have their individual roots in geography (hazards), sociology (disaster), (social) psychology (risk), and political science/public administration (crisis). These perspectives have and will continue to help build scientific knowledge in today's fields. However, as the field becomes more complex, new approaches will be needed, such as the analysis of big data to observe patterns. Cell phone and Geographic Positioning Systems (GPS) data, for example, have been used to alert people to area risks and examine logistical issues over large spaces during a crisis. It is clear that future disaster science and EM will be necessarily multidisciplinary. We will have to work together to save lives.

For example, by the early 1980s, meteorologists had devised rather sophisticated equipment to detect, show, and predict the strength and paths of tornadoes. Despite setting this equipment up, the number of annual deaths due to tornadoes and severe storms did not decline. People had to be made aware of the hazard, educated about the warning system and how it worked, and given explicit instructions on how to take protective action – if they could. Studies suggested that warning messages had to be repeated in multiple languages and through multiple modes and the message had to be personalized to those at risk. Once meteorologists worked with social scientists in devising a social science-based tornado warning system, coupled with the sophisticated equipment, deaths from tornadoes and severe storms decreased (Quarantelli 1993; for an example, see the CASA project at the University of Massachusetts, http://www.casa.umass.edu/). In recent years, the Office of the Federal Coordinator of Meteorology has established a working group to integrate social science findings into partnerships with those who detect, predict, and deliver meteorological information. The goal: to reduce deaths among those most vulnerable to weather, particularly senior citizens, the poor, people with disabilities, and the traveling public that may be unaware of risks down the road.

Further, whether at the local, state, or national level, those involved in disaster policy must have a wide range of knowledge (Sylves 2008) For example, making policy on earthquake preparedness would include geology (understanding fault lines in an area), planners and geographers (land use), architects (creating specific building codes), geographers (hazards), and sociologists (public education and risk communication programs). Taking a broad array of courses will serve students well as they pursue a degree in higher education. Many EM degree programs offer courses with both social and natural science content.

3.7 THE VIEW FROM EMERGENCY MANAGEMENT HIGHER EDUCATION

The annual FEMA Higher Education Symposium (which started in 1998), and offshoots from these meetings, has provided a foundation for defining EM and what we should teach in the field. Spirited discussion among those who attend have led to some general agreement on what to call "emergency management" and if it constituted a field, a discipline, or a profession (Urby and McEntire 2015). Four common characteristics for a separate field to be named (like sociology or physics) include occupational groups, a body of knowledge, standards of contact, and professional qualifications (Urby and McEntire 2015). We argue in this text that EM has indeed arrived at such a standalone designation.

As the field started, no real consensus existed on what EM was and what should be taught. New programs found it difficult to find qualified faculty members who were knowledgeable with the disaster science literature. Since programs were small, administrators placed programs within other academic units, often meaning the EM program lost part of its identity or needed resources. Faculty had few quality textbooks to select from. Those within the university did not see EM as a sound academic discipline. Many emergency managers saw EM programs as just an exercise in "book learning" with little or no practical application (Neal 2000). That has changed with the development of about 150 degree programs in the U.S. alone, along with programs in Canada, Mexico, New Zealand, India, the U.K., South Africa, Sweden, South Korea, and many other locations.

Today, students graduating from EM programs can use a well-developed body of knowledge to secure a career. They can pursue additional credentials through graduate degrees and/or certifications. You will be meeting some of them as you read this book. Take the time to read their biographical statements and learn about their journey into emergency management and disaster science.

***

SUMMARY

The profession of EM deals with managing disasters. Yet, among scholars and emergency managers, no firm definition of disaster exists. Many today still draw upon Fritz's (1961) definition, defining disasters as a perceived event that occurs rapidly in a specific time and space leading to social disruption. Today, we need to think of disasters in a more sophisticated way – as if it were a variable. During everyday life, emergencies occur (e.g., heart attacks, car accidents, house fires). But such events are part of the daily fabric. Disasters, such as tornadoes, floods, hurricanes, explosions, among many other events, may damage the infrastructure of a community, disrupt people's lives, and undermine workplaces. A catastrophe may cause total damage and create absolute social disruption within a wide geographical area for a long time. Certainly the impact of Hurricane Katrina or the Fukushima earthquake/tsunami/radiological release would fit this category. Emergency managers engage in activities to manage disasters and catastrophes.

The NGA (1979) report made such notions as the four phases of EM and CEM important tools for the profession. These concepts are still important today for anybody engaged in EM. Emergency managers may work across all four phases or may even specialize in one, such as mitigation. Several different research traditions have emerged within the field: hazards, disaster, risk, and crisis. Although each tradition grew from different academic fields (such as geography, sociology, social psychology), researchers have slowly merged these perspectives in part to create a more multidisciplinary approach to the field.

More broadly, two ideas, resilience and social vulnerability, drive how we try to manage these events. Resilience suggests we find ways to "bounce back" from disaster. Such activities can occur before, during, and after a disaster. Social vulnerability describes how certain groups lacking power (e.g., ethnic minorities, women, lower income, those with disabilities) are less likely to be prepared for disasters, more likely to be impacted by disasters, and have more problems recovering from disasters. These two perspectives also stress that disasters are not natural, but rather human generated.

Discussion Questions

1. Discuss why it is important to be able to distinguish between an emergency and a disaster, and a disaster and catastrophe. Why are these differences important for both the emergency manager and the social scientists studying people's behavior?
2. Explain why we may have so many different definitions of disaster. This includes different definitions among both emergency managers and disaster researchers. Why might different people and different organizational representatives see the same event and: (1) define it an emergency rather than a disaster; (2) have one claim the event is one type of a hazard, whereas another may say the event was a totally different type of hazard (e.g., flood versus a technological failure)?
3. The NGA Report (1979) remains a key document today. What are some of the important concepts introduced in this report and how many of these concepts are still used today by both emergency managers and researchers? How have these concepts influenced EM? Being over 40 years old now, should the whole approach in the document be rewritten?
4. What specific insights into disaster behavior to each of the four perspectives (i.e., hazards, disasters, risk, crisis) provide? Do you see these perspectives becoming more separate from each other or blending together?
5. How does the idea of social vulnerability change the way we may look at disasters today? Specifically, think about such issues as preparedness, community outreach, or that communities are *not* homogeneous.
6. Discuss how the idea of resilience can help us manage current and future hazards and disasters. Think about what insights resilience can provide when dealing with any events showing up in the news.

Summary Questions

1. Explain the differences between emergency, disaster, and catastrophe.
2. How does a political definition influence if a disaster is really viewed as a disaster?
3. Distinguish between the hazards, disaster, risk, and crisis perspectives. Identify their origins and the viewpoint they hold.
4. Define and distinguish between the dominant and social vulnerability perspectives.
5. Define and give examples of how resilience activities may enable communities to bounce back.

REFERENCES

Aguirre, Benigno E. 2002. "'Sustainable Development' as Collective Surge." *Social Science Quarterly* 83(1): 101–118.

Aguirre, Benigno E. and Eric Best. 2014. "How Not to Learn: Resilience in the Study of Disaster." Pp. 236–252 in *Learning and Calamities: Practices, Interpretations, Patterns*, eds. Heike Egner, Marén Schorch, and Martin Voss. New York: Routledge.

Blum, Elizabeth D. 2008. *Love Canal Revisited*. Kansas: University of Kansas Press.

Boin, Arjen. 2009. "The New World Crises and Crisis Management: Implications for Policy-making and Research." *New Policy Research* 26(4): 367–377.

Cutter, Susan L. 2001. "The Changing Nature of Risks and Hazards." Pp. 1–12 in *American Hazardscapes*, ed. Susan L. Cutter. Washington, DC: Joseph Henry Press.

Cutter, Susan L. and Christophere T. Emrich. 2006. "Moral Hazard, Social Catastrophe: The Changing Face of Vulnerability along the Hurricane Coasts." *The ANNALS of the American Academy of Political and Social Science* 604(1): 102–112.

Decision Research. 2015a. "Paul Slovic, Ph.D." Available at http://www.decisionresearch.org/researcher/paul-slovic-ph-d/, last accessed June 17, 2015.

Decision Research. 2015b. "About." Available at http://www.decisionresearch.org/about/, last accessed June 17, 2015.

Disaster Research Center (DRC). 2015. "Research." Available at http://drc.udel.edu/research/, last accessed June 16, 2015.

Disaster Research Center (DRC). 2016. "About DRC." Available at http://www.udel.edu/DRC/aboutus/index.html, last accessed February 3, 2016.

Drabek, Thomas. 1986. *Human Systems Response to Disaster: An Inventory of Sociological Findings*. Springer-Verlag, New York.

Dynes, Russell R. 1974. *Organized Behavior in Disaster*. Disaster Research Center, Newark, DE.

FEMA. 2021. *How a Disaster Gets Declared*. https://www.fema.gov/disaster/how-declared, last accessed May 25, 2021.

FEMA. No n.d. *FEMA: Declaration Process Fact Sheet*. Washington D.C.: FEMA.

Fischer, Henry W. 2003. "The Sociology of Disaster: Definitions, Research Questions and Measurements." *International Journal of Mass Emergencies and Disasters* 21(19): 91–108.

Fordham, Maureen, William E. Lovekamp, Deborah S. K. Thomas, and Brenda D. Phillips. 2013. "Understanding Social Vulnerability." Pp. 33–56 in *Social Vulnerability to Disaster*, eds. Deborah S. K. Thomas et al. Boca Raton, FL: CRC Press.

Fritz, Charles E. 1961. "Disaster." Pp. 651–694 in *Contemporary Social Problems*, eds. Robert K. Merton and Robert A. Nisbet. New York: Harcourt Brace Jovanovich.

Hansen, Dan. 2003 (1990). *The Crisis Management of the Murder of Olof Palme*. Stockholm, Sweden: The National Swedish Defense College.

Hoffman, Susanna M. and Anthony Oliver-Smith. 2002. *Catastrophe and Culture: The Anthropology of Disaster*. Sante Fe: School of American Research Press.

Kates, Robert W. 2011. *Gilbert F. White 1911–2006: A Biographical Memoir*. Washington, DC: National Academy of Sciences.

Kuipers, Sanneke and Nicholas H. Welsh. 2017. "Taxonomy of the Crisis and Disaster Literature." *Risk, Hazards & Crisis in Public Policy* 8(4): 272–283.

Lancet, The. 2021. "COVID-19-Break the Cycle of Inequality." *The Lancet* 6(February). Available at https://www.thelancet.com/action/showPdf?pii=S2468-2667%2821%2900011-6, last accessed May 23, 2021.

Larson, Lee W. 1996. *Destructive Water: Water-Caused Natural Disasters - Their Abatement and Control*. Paper presented at IAHS Conference. Retrieved https://www.nwrfc.noaa.gov/floods/papers/oh_2/great.htm, last accessed February 25th, 2021.

Levine, Adeline Gordon. 1982. *Love Canal: Science, Politics and People*. New York: D. C. Heath and Company.

Mileti, Dennis S. 1999. *Disasters by Design*. Washington D.C.: Joseph Henry Press.

Mileti, Dennis S., Thomas E. Drabek, and J. Eugene Haas. 1975. Human Systems in Extreme Environments: A Sociological Perspective. Boulder: University of Colorado.

Myers, Mary Fran. 1993. "Bridging the Gap between Research and Practice: The Natural Hazards Research and Applications Information Center." *International Journal of Mass Emergencies and Disasters* 11/1: 41–54.

National Council on Disability (NCD). 2009. *Effective Emergency Management: Making Improvements for Communities and People with Disabilities*. Washington D.C.: National Council on Disability.

National Governor's Association (NGA). 1979. *1978 Emergency Preparedness Project: Final Report*. Washington, DC: Defense Civil Preparedness Agency.

Natural Hazards Center. n.d. "Gilbert White." Available at http://www.colorado.edu/hazards/gfw/, last accessed February 23, 2011.

Neal, David M., 1997. "Reconsidering the Phases of Disaster." *International Journal of Mass Emergencies and Disasters* 15(2): 239–264.

Neal, David M., 2000. "Developing Degree Programs in Disaster Management," *International Journal of Mass Emergencies and Disasters* 15(3): 417–438.

Neal, David M. 2012. "The Survivability of Swedish Emergency Management Related Research Centers and Academic Programs: A Preliminary Sociology of Knowledge Analysis." *Sociologiska Forsking* 49(3): 227–242.

Phillips, Brenda, Patricia Stukes, and Pam Jenkins. 2012. "Freedom Hill Is Not for Sale and Neither Is the Lower Ninth Ward." *Journal of Black Studies* 43(4): 405–426.

Quarantelli, E. L. 1982. "What Is a Disaster?: An Agent Specific or an All Disaster Spectrum Approach to Socio-behavioral Aspects of Earthquakes." Pp. 453–478 in *Social and Economic Aspects of Earthquakes*, eds. B. Jones and M. Tomazevic. New York: Cornell University, Program I Urban and Regional Studies.

Quarantelli, E. L. 1987. "Disaster Studies: An Analysis of the Social Historical Factors Affecting the Development of Research in the Area." *International Journal of Mass Emergencies and Disasters* 5(3): 285–310.

Quarantelli, E. L. 1991. *More and Worse Disasters in the Future*. Paper presented at the UCLA International conference on the Impact of Natural Disasters. Los Angeles, CA.

Quarantelli, E. L. 1993. "Converting Disaster Scholarship into Effective Disaster Planning and Managing." *International Journal of Mass Emergencies and Disasters* 11(1): 15–39.

Quarantelli, E. L. 1994. "Disaster Studies: The Consequences of the Historical Use of a Sociological Approach in the Development of Research." *International Journal of Mass Emergencies and Disasters* 12(1): 5–23.

Quarantelli, E. L. 2006. "Understanding Katrina: Catastrophes Are Different from Disasters." *Perspectives from the Social Sciences*. Available at http://understandingkatrina.ssrc.org/Quarantelli/, accessed January 3, 2011.

Quarantelli, E. L., and Russell R. Dynes. 1970. "Editors Introduction." *American Behavioral Scientist* 13(3): 325–330.

Rosenthal, Uriel, Michael T. Charles, and Paul Hart, eds. 1989. *Coping with Crises: The Management of Disasters, Riots and Terrorism*. Springfield, IL: Charles C. Thomas.

Slovic, Paul. 1987. "Perception of Risk." *Science* 236(4799): 280–285.

Stough, Laura, Amy N. Sharp, J. Aaron Resch, Curt Decker, and Nachama Wilker. 2015. "Barriers to the Long Term Recovery of Individuals with Disabilities following a Disaster." *Disasters* doi: 10.1111/disa.12161

Sylves, Richard. 2008. *Disaster Policy and Politics: Emergency Management and Homeland Security*. Washington, DC: CQ Press.

Sylves, Richard and Zoltan Buzas. 2007. "Presidential Disaster Declaration Decisions, 1953–2003: What Influences Odds of Approval?" *State and Local Government Review* 39(1): 3–15.

Swedish Defence University. n.d.a. "CRISMART Research Programme." Available at https://www.fhs.se/en/centre-for-societal-security/research/crismart.html, last accessed March 3, 2021.

Swedish Defence University. n.d.b. "Centre for Societal Security." Available at https://www.fhs.se/en/centre-for-societal-security.html, last accessed March 25, 2021.

The National Academies. 2012. *Disaster Resilience: A National Imperative*. Washington, DC: The National Academies Press.

United States Fire Administration. 2019. *Fires in the U.S. 2008-2017*, 20th edition. Washington D.C.: FEMA.

U.S. Fire Administration. 2004. *The Seasonal Incidents of Fire in 2000*. Topical Fire Research Series Issue 6 Volume 3. Washington, D.C.: FEMA.

Urby, Heriberto and David McEntire. 2015. "Field, Discipline, and Profession: Understanding Three Major Labels of Emergency Management." *Journal of Emergency Management* 13(-5): 389–400.

White, Gilbert F. 1974. "Natural Hazards Research: Concepts, Methods, and Policy Implication". Pp. 3–16 in *Natural Hazards: Local, National, and Global*, ed. Gilbert F. White. Toronto: Oxford University Press.

White, Gilbert F. and J. Eugene Haas. 1975. *Assessment of Research on Natural Hazards*. Cambridge, MA: The MIT Press.

RESOURCES

- Those involved in designing and teaching EM courses have also discussed and written extensively on definitions of EM. This link will give you access to many other papers and documents that discuss defining EM and related concepts to the field: https://training.fema.gov/hiedu/emprinciples.aspx, last accessed May 25, 2021.
- CPG 101 (FEMA), https://www.fema.gov/media-library-data/20130726-1828-25045-0014/cpg_101_comprehensive_preparedness_guide_developing_and_maintaining_emergency_operations_plans_2010.pdf, last accessed May 25, 2021.
- To learn more about Disaster Declarations in the U.S., visit https://www.fema.gov/disaster/how-declared, last accessed May 25, 2021.
- The FEMA Higher Education College List can be found at https://www.training.fema.gov/hiedu/collegelist/, last accessed May 25, 2021.

CHAPTER 4

Advancing Emergency Management through Disaster Science

CHAPTER OBJECTIVES

Upon completing this chapter, readers should be able to:

- Define disaster science and describe it as a multidisciplinary field of study.
- Discuss the importance of disaster science to the profession of emergency management (EM).
- Demonstrate scientific literacy by understanding the research process, types of research, and methods used by disaster scientists to gather empirical data.
- Describe ethical guidelines for studying human subjects and discuss the unique challenges involved in conducting research on disasters.

KEY TERMS

- Disaster Science
- Ethics
- Evidence-Based Practice
- Research Methods

- Research Process
- Scientific Literacy
- Types of Research

4.1 INTRODUCTION

Disasters interest people for many reasons. Novelists and filmmakers craft compelling storylines celebrating selfless acts of heroism or, more commonly, images of chaos and pandemonium in the wake of a catastrophe. Members of the mass media flock to the scenes of disasters, often conveying those same images of civil disorder and social breakdown to their viewers, readers, and listeners. In contrast to those who exploit disasters for sales and ratings, emergency managers, first responders, public officials,

DOI: 10.4324/9781003021919-5

and volunteers have a professional interest in disasters and a strong desire to alleviate the suffering of those impacted by them.

Scientists also have a professional interest in disasters, and they share a common vision of reducing the human and financial costs of disasters. Ultimately, the goal of disaster science is to improve our understanding of hazards and disasters while also contributing to a safer and more resilient future. While you may not see them on the front line throwing sandbags or delivering meals, engineers, geologists, and social scientists work hard at testing building construction practices, mapping hazardous areas, observing organizational responses to disasters, evaluating disaster-related policies and programs, and identifying vulnerable populations who are most susceptible to the devastating impacts of disasters. The results of their work may not always produce immediate benefits, but over the long term, the findings of disaster science can contribute significantly to a more resilient society.

4.2 DISASTER SCIENCE AS A MULTIDISCIPLINARY FIELD

As emphasized throughout this text, disaster science is *the multidisciplinary study of the human dimensions of hazards and disasters*. That means that scholars from many different academic disciplines and fields of study contribute to disaster science. From the *natural sciences*, for example, some *geologists* specialize in the study of earthquakes, volcanoes, landslides, and other hazards, and with increased concern around the world about the problem of climate change, we are becoming more aware of the work of *climatologists* and *meteorologists*. Within the field of *engineering*, *structural engineers* seek to design buildings that are safer and more resilient, while *civil engineers* conduct research to improve the performance of transportation systems and other types of critical infrastructure.

But what makes disaster science unique is its emphasis on humans, and that is why the social sciences have played such a prominent role in the development of the field. *Sociologists*, for example, have studied how households, organizations, and communities deal with the major social disruptions caused by disasters (Quarantelli 1994; Kreps 1995). *Geographers* have conducted important research in terms of identifying and mapping various types of hazards in the environment and helping us better understand the spatial distribution of social vulnerability (Cutter 2001; Phillips et al. 2010). *Psychologists* have studied individual risk perception and the impacts of post-traumatic stress disorder (PTSD) among children, emergency workers, and others in the contexts of natural disasters and terrorist attacks (Jenkins 1998; Pfefferbaum, Call, and Sconzo 1999; Norris, Friedman, and Watson 2002a; Norris et al. 2002b; North et al. 2002). *Anthropologists* have sought to understand how cultural beliefs and practices change after disasters (see Oliver-Smith and Hoffman 1999; Hoffman and Oliver-Smith 2002). Scholars from *political science* and *public administration* have made significant contributions to our knowledge of disaster policies and politics and how to manage them more effectively (Birkland 1997, 2007; Platt 1999; Olson 2000; Waugh 2000, 2006; Sylves 2008). And *economists* have conducted extensive research on the financial costs and long-term economic impacts of natural disasters (Dacy and Kunreuther 1969; Wright et al. 1979). As explained in Box 4.1, disaster science is a good example of

BOX 4.1

CONVERGE: NHERI

Lori Peek, Ph.D.
University of Colorado

Convergence research is an approach to knowledge production and action that involves diverse teams working together in novel ways – transcending disciplinary and organizational boundaries – to address vexing social, economic, environmental, and technical challenges in an effort to reduce disaster losses and promote collective well-being (Peek et al. 2020). The National Science Foundation (NSF)-funded CONVERGE facility, which was established in 2018 as the first social science-led component of the Natural Hazards Engineering Research Infrastructure (NHERI), supports and advances research within a convergence framework that includes the following elements:

1. **Identifying Researchers**: The hazards and disaster field is composed of researchers from many different disciplines across multiple scientific and engineering domains who are affiliated with academic, private sector, nonprofit, and government organizations. One approach to finding researchers is to ask them to self-identify with groups or associations that are most aligned with their interests and expertise. This is the idea that has, in part, driven the creation of several NSF-supported Extreme Events Reconnaissance and Research (EER) networks that draw researchers from diverse disciplinary communities together.

2. **Educating and Training Researchers**: Core to the mission of CONVERGE is to accelerate the education of a diverse next generation of hazards and disaster researchers. To that end, the CONVERGE team has developed a series of training modules that cover a wide range of topics, including, for example, social vulnerability and disasters, disaster mental health, cultural competence, and emotionally challenging research. The CONVERGE team has also initiated a series of check sheets that provide best practice recommendations to help inform the scientific rigor and ethical conduct of extreme events research. The training materials and guidance documents being developed by CONVERGE are available for free and online as part of a broader effort to democratize access to foundational and recent research in the field.

3. **Setting a Convergence Research Agenda that is Problem-Focused and Solutions-Based**: Convergence, with its focus on interdisciplinary or transdisciplinary research driven by a desire to solve specific and compelling problems, offers a framework where members of the hazards and disaster research community come together to characterize the mounting threats communities face. A convergence research agenda requires precision, beginning with identifying which type or combination of disaster losses researchers seek to address and the root causes of those losses. Importantly, researchers must also identify specific actions that will reduce

the historical and socio-technical problems, inequalities, and injustices that turn natural hazards into disasters.

4. **Connecting Researchers and Coordinating Functionally and Demographically Diverse Research Teams**: The challenge of connecting researchers across disciplinary divides and coordinating research teams is a difficult and longstanding concern in the hazards and disaster field. The members of the CONVERGE Leadership Corps, including principal investigators with backgrounds in engineering, social sciences, and natural sciences, meet regularly to share information and to generate opportunities for cross-disciplinary collaborations. CONVERGE also partners with other organizations to ensure that scholars from historically underrepresented groups are supported to participate in workshops, mentoring activities, and research experiences.

5. **Supporting and Funding Convergence Research, Data Collection, Data Sharing, and Solutions Implementation**: With the NSF's commitment to cultivating convergence research and its support of the CONVERGE facility, the field now has improved coordinating structures and additional resources to support early stage convergence research. For example, during the global COVID-19 pandemic, CONVERGE convened researchers from dozens of disciplines via successive virtual forums. Spurred by the interest and activity of the research community, CONVERGE then established a global research registry available in five languages and funded 90 distinct COVID-19 Working Groups focused on population groups of special concern, impacts and recovery, compound and cascading hazards, and emergent methodological and ethical issues. To catalyze convergence research, each Working Group was required to include members from a minimum of three different disciplines and to submit a research agenda-setting paper that was published on the CONVERGE website.

The various research activities led by the CONVERGE facility exemplify how teams of researchers can come together to understand and solve complex problems. As new structures and systems are developed to support interdisciplinary and transdisciplinary research, our field – with convergence as our guide – can stem the tide of growing disaster losses and promote collective well-being for all people.

For more information about CONVERGE, please see: https://converge.colorado.edu.
Source: Peek, Lori, Jennifer Tobin, Rachel Adams, Haorui Wu, and Mason Mathews. 2020b. "A Framework for Convergence Research in the Hazards and Disaster Field: The Natural Hazards Engineering Research Infrastructure CONVERGE Facility." *Frontiers in Built Environment*, https://www.frontiersin.org/articles/10.3389/fbuil.2020.00110/full.

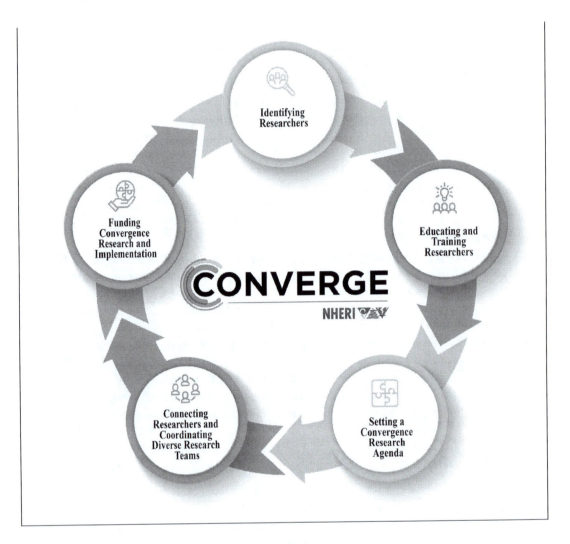

convergence research because it involves so many different disciplines and focuses on such a complex and compelling societal problem (Peek et al. 2020b).

Although researchers from these various disciplines have been studying extreme events since at least the 1950s, the term disaster science is in fact relatively new. For many years, the network of scholars devoted to studying the human dimensions of hazards and disasters has been referred to as the "hazards and disaster research community," but in more recent years the term disaster science has been gaining in popularity. As evidence of this trend, consider a recent survey of more than 1,000 members of the Social Science Extreme Events Research (SSEER) Network (Peek et al. 2020a), a group comprised of researchers around the world that is described in Box 4.2.

When asked to identify their primary academic disciplinary background, a plurality of respondents (32.6%) chose disaster science as their primary affiliation, which was followed by geography (23.2%), sociology (22.4%), public administration/EM (21.9%), and decision-making and risk analysis (21.7%). Importantly, of the 20

BOX 4.2

SOCIAL SCIENCE EXTREME EVENTS RESEARCH

Lori Peek, Ph.D.
University of Colorado

The NSF-funded SSEER network was formed, in part, to respond to the need for more specific information about the status and expertise of the social science hazards and disaster research workforce. Core to the mission of SSEER is to identify and map social scientists involved in hazards and disaster research to highlight their expertise and connect social science researchers to one another, to interdisciplinary teams, and to communities at risk to hazards and affected by disasters. Ultimately, the goals of SSEER are to *amplify* the contributions of social scientists, to *advance* the field through expanding the available social science evidence base, and to *enhance* collective well-being through the development of an annual census of social scientists who study hazards and disasters.

The SSEER research team, which is led by Dr. Lori Peek, began by developing a brief survey questionnaire and issuing a call for social scientists to join the network (https://hazards.colorado.edu/news/director/a-call-to-social-scientists). The survey, which can be completed in about seven minutes, was designed to assess the researcher's disciplinary background, highest level of academic training, and years in the field. The survey asks respondents to identify the research methods they use, phases of disaster management they study, general types of hazards and disasters they study, the names of specific disaster events they have researched, and keywords that highlight their expertise. Respondents are also asked to select their level of involvement in hazards and disaster research, answer a series of demographic questions, provide their work address, and confirm their consent to be geolocated and added to the online SSEER mapping platform (https://converge.colorado.edu/research networks/sseer/researchers-map).

A total of 1,230 researchers joined the SSEER network between July 8, 2018, and December 31, 2020. The SSEER database and map make it possible, for the first time, to not only analyze basic data regarding what social science disaster researchers study but also to visualize where they are located in relation to the disasters they research. As the SSEER network continues to grow and as future iterations of the census are released, the database will also make it possible to provide demographic snapshots as well as longitudinal portraits of the evolution of the social science research community. Furthermore, de-identified data are published and shared with the hazards and disaster community through the DesignSafe platform, allowing other researchers to view and analyze the SSEER data.

As disasters increase in frequency and magnitude, and as more people are exposed to their effects, the social science hazards and disaster research community must be prepared to respond by bringing the full force of our knowledge and expertise to bear. The SSEER network is made up of a diverse, highly skilled group of researchers with the potential to mobilize to apply their knowledge and expertise to help reduce the harm and suffering caused by disasters. It is important to continue to monitor the status of this research workforce so we can see not just who counts themselves among the ranks of social science hazards and disaster researchers, but so we can identify what matters most when investing in the future vitality of this research community.

For more information about the SSEER network, please visit: https://converge.colorado.edu/research-networks/sseer.

Source: Peek, Lori, Heather Champeau, Jessica Austin, Mason Mathews, and Haorui Wu. 2020a. "What Methods Do Social Scientists Use to Study Disasters? An Analysis of the Social Science Extreme Events Research (SSEER) Network." *American Behavioral Scientist* 64(8): 1066–1094.

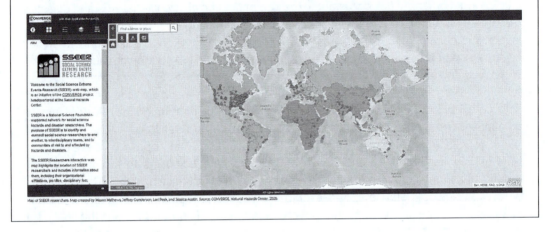

Map of SSEER researchers. Map created by Mason Mathews, Jeffrey Gunderson, Lori Peek, and Jessica Austin. Source: CONVERGE, Natural Hazards Center, 2020.

academic disciplines identified in the study, disaster science was the one most commonly embraced by respondents.

In addition to being used more frequently by individual scholars to describe their own work, the term disaster science is also being incorporated into the names of major academic programs. For example, the Emergency Administration and Planning program, which was established as the nation's first EM bachelor's degree program in 1983 at the University of North Texas, is now housed in the Department of Emergency Management and Disaster Science. The University of Delaware, which is home to the Disaster Research Center (DRC), the world's oldest institute devoted to the social scientific study of disasters, now offers degree programs in Disaster Science and Management. Additionally, there is a School of Disaster Science and Emergency Services at the University of Akron and a Division of Emergency Management and Disaster Science at the University of Nebraska, Omaha.

Clearly, disaster science is an academic field of study that is on the rise (McNutt 2015; Wachtendorf 2019). It spans multiple disciplines, involves an ever-expanding number of individual scholars, and serves as the foundation for a growing number of academic programs. Importantly, disaster science is also closely related to the profession of EM, and it provides valuable knowledge and insights that are integral to the advancement of the profession.

4.3 THE IMPORTANCE OF DISASTER SCIENCE TO EMERGENCY MANAGEMENT

As you will see in this section, disaster science is critically important to the profession of EM. With catastrophic disasters on the rise all across the globe, the stakes are simply too high to continue learning by trial and error after every major event. Instead, it is our firm conviction that the best path to advance the profession and contribute to a safer and more resilient future is through science. And for emergency managers, this means embracing and valuing disaster science as described in Box 4.3.

All professions, including law, medicine, social work, education, criminal justice, and many others, are based on specialized bodies of knowledge. And before entering those professions, aspiring practitioners must first complete a lengthy educational process to acquire and demonstrate mastery of that particular body of knowledge. Before becoming a practicing lawyer, for example, a person must first obtain a bachelor degree, often in disciplines such as English, history, or political science, and then attend law school for three years beyond that. Similarly, medical doctors first obtain a bachelor degree, then attend medical school for four years, and then complete a residency.

Disaster science is important to EM because *it is the specialized body of knowledge that underlies and informs the profession.* Compared to law and medicine, EM is relatively new, and the path to entering the profession is not as rigid and clearly specified, but the educational requirements for becoming an emergency manager have been steadily increasing over the years. In the early 1980s, for example, only one university, the University of North Texas, offered a bachelor degree program in EM, so educational opportunities were extremely limited. Today, however, there are more than 100 undergraduate degree and certificate programs, dozens of master's programs, and a handful of doctoral programs, including those at North Dakota State University, Jacksonville State University, Oklahoma State University, and the University of Delaware. Rather than being intimidated or discouraged by these rising educational expectations, students of EM should instead be encouraged and motivated because in all professions, heightened educational and credentialing requirements translate into enhanced legitimacy, greater occupational prestige, better pay and benefits for practitioners, and ultimately a stronger profession.

Disaster science is also important to EM because *it promotes evidence-based practice.* Although disasters are stressful events that often come as a surprise to us and create a significant amount of confusion and ambiguity, we actually know a great deal about them, particularly in terms of how humans typically respond to such extreme events. Indeed, emergency managers today and the aspiring professionals of the future can draw on more than 70 years of social science research to help them better prepare for, respond to, and recover from all kinds of disasters, including global pandemics (Tierney 2020). And with that knowledge, emergency managers will be equipped to make decisions rooted in science rather than based on intuition, whims, or myths. In fact, one of the greatest impediments to evidence-based EM has been the unfortunate embracement and perpetuation of disaster myths, which are discussed in much greater detail in Chapter 7. It is widely believed that, for example, disasters bring out the worst in people, leading to panic, looting, and widespread social breakdown. On the basis of

BOX 4.3

THE VALUE OF RESEARCH FOR EMERGENCY MANAGEMENT

William Anderson (1937–2013)

Dr. William Anderson, a graduate of The Ohio State University and an alumnus of the DRC, writes here about the value of research for emergency managers. Dr. Anderson, who first studied the 1964 Alaska earthquake, went on to a distinguished career at the U.S. NSF and the National Academy of Sciences. We reprise his first edition feature again in memorial. Please see the last chapter in this book for information about scholarships associated with the William Averette Anderson Fund.

Emergency managers can access and apply findings and principles from decades of disaster research when undertaking such actions as communicating risk information to the public, developing disaster preparedness plans, and undertaking crucial disaster response and recovery activities. Disaster researchers continue to produce new knowledge on such subjects. Thus emergency managers need to periodically update their understanding of advances in the disaster research field as they pursue the goal of making their communities more disaster resilient. Staying abreast of new insights from disaster research can be rather challenging, but it should be a lifetime commitment for career emergency managers.

Many senior emergency managers have set a good example for the next generation by successfully bridging the gap between the EM and disaster research communities throughout their careers. Thus the emerging generation of emergency managers can gain much in the way of their own continued growth by emulating them. There are several ways in which emergency managers have been able to access disaster research information on a career-long basis, enabling them to apply it strategically in their professional work.

Interpersonal Connections

Experience has shown that emergency managers can learn much from disaster researchers through personal contact with them. Many emergency managers have established important long-term ties with disaster researchers at their local universities or those in the immediate region for the purpose of gaining knowledge useful for their decision-making. Emergency managers discover that most disaster researchers are quite eager to discuss and share their expert knowledge with them and also point them toward valuable resources such as publications, courses, workshops, and other learning opportunities. The message here is that making friends with approachable disaster scholars should be a top priority for young EM practitioners.

Continuing Education

Many emergency managers understand the importance of continuing education for those in their profession. Thus many obtain additional education after they have completed college and launched their careers. To help meet the needs of today's EM practitioners, there is quite a variety of learning experiences to choose from that are offered by disaster scholars at local universities as well as those made available online by experts at distant universities, including degree and nondegree courses, full- and short-term courses, and seminars.

Conferences and Workshops

As disasters have drawn more attention in the past several years, there has been a surge in the number of conferences and workshops that bring together disaster scholars, EM practitioners, and disaster reduction policy makers to exchange ideas and experiences through discussions and presentations. The workshops organized by the Disasters Roundtable at the National Academy of Sciences in Washington, D.C. and the Annual Hazards Workshop organized by the Natural Hazards Center at the University of Colorado Boulder are two examples of such activities that involve the active participation of emergency managers, providing them with the opportunity to learn about discoveries in disaster research directly from researchers. Of course, disaster researchers also learn much from emergency managers during such exchanges.

Publications

The above learning strategies involve social interaction, mostly the critical face-to-face variety, between emergency managers and researchers. This is crucial because most emergency managers are seldom inclined to spend much time reading through the technical terminology and explanations of scientific research methodology found in leading scholarly research publications. However, there are publications geared to making disaster research more understandable to EM practitioners, and these do attract a sizable number of them, including the two editions of *Emergency Management: Principles and Practice for Local Government* (Drabek and Hoetmer 1991; Waugh and Tierney 2007) published by ICMA, a leading professional association for local government managers. Newsletters like the *Natural Hazards Observer* and the online publication *Disaster Research*, both published by the Natural Hazards Center, are other sources of written information about developments in the disaster field that are reader friendly to emergency managers.

New Media

In this information technology age, emergency managers can now turn to new media sources for information on disaster research, and many are doing so. This is an area where young emergency managers may eclipse their elders in the field. Important information on disaster research can be accessed through Google searches and some disaster scholars make information available on their blogs. Also, the emergence of web-based social media, such as Facebook, Twitter, and YouTube, offers unparalleled access to disaster research information of value to emergency managers.

In conclusion, acquiring relevant insights from the disaster research field throughout their careers in ways noted here and effectively applying them will help make the next generation of emergency managers the leaders their communities need to combat natural, technological, and human-induced disasters.

William Anderson

these myths, public officials sometimes withhold information from the public out of fear of inciting panic and devote substantial resources to restore order, prevent crime, and control the population. Decades of social science research, on the other hand, confirms that disasters are far more likely to bring out the best in people, not the worst. In the aftermath of devastating events, community members typically rally to the support of their neighbors, mass donations pour into disaster-stricken areas from surrounding communities, and crime rates fall. Thus, an educated and informed emergency manager knows that rather than asserting strong command and control to address problems that largely do not exist, effective disaster response instead requires communication, coordination, and collaboration (Dynes 1994).

A third and final reason that disaster science is important to EM is that *it promotes scientific literacy*. A recent report by the Federal Emergency Management Agency (FEMA) Higher Education Program contends that in order to deal with more frequent, increasingly complex, and financially costly disasters of the future, the next generation of emergency managers will need a new set of core competencies. Among these are geographic literacy, sociocultural literacy, and scientific literacy. Geographic literacy is an ability to understand places and the spatial distribution of hazards, while sociocultural literacy is an ability to understand people and communities. Scientific literacy is "the capacity to objectively and systematically work through complex problems, using the scientific process to identify questions, interpret evidence based findings to inform decision making, and effectively communicate the results to policy makers and the public" (Feldman-Jensesn, Jensen, and Smith 2017: 9). For our purposes, scientific literacy requires familiarity with and understanding of: (1) the research process, (2) different types of research, (3) research methods, and (4) ethics and research challenges.

4.4 RESEARCH PROCESS

As shown in Figure 4.1, the research process involves a systematic series of steps, beginning with the identification of a research problem, such as the factors that determine whether or not people will prepare themselves and their households for disasters. We would then conduct a review of existing literature on the topic by reading studies published in academic journals, such as the ones listed in Box 4.4. From our literature review, we would learn that income and education levels have been found to influence household preparedness levels, and thus we would formulate our hypotheses and predict that those with higher income and education levels are more likely to prepare for disasters than those with lower levels. We would then collect data to test our hypotheses using one of the research methodologies, described later in this chapter, analyze the information, and then disseminate our findings by publishing the results. The research process, as you can see, is an ongoing loop aimed at continually refining our knowledge of disasters and thereby improving the practice of EM.

Using a scientific approach to understand the world around us, in this instance, disasters, is important for three reasons. First, researchers rely on *systematic observations* in which they thoroughly document what they see and hear in the field. In contrast, experience-based knowledge is often based on selective observations and anecdotal accounts of what happened in a disaster. Second, researchers gather *empirical evidence* to support their findings. Rather than relying on rampant rumors or media sensationalism and speculation, researchers report what actually happened and systematically amass evidence to substantiate their findings. Finally, disaster studies are valuable sources of knowledge to emergency managers because researchers collect *perishable information* that is critical to understanding post-disaster events fully. By deploying as rapidly as possible to the scene of a disaster, researchers can paint an accurate picture of the

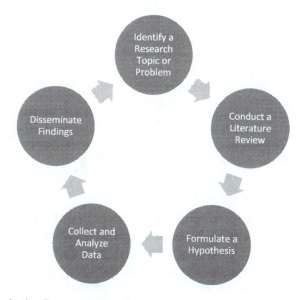

FIGURE 4.1 Steps in the Research Process.

BOX 4.4

ACADEMIC JOURNALS IN EMERGENCY MANAGEMENT AND DISASTER SCIENCE

Australian Journal of Emergency Management
Disaster Management and Response
Disaster Prevention and Management
Disasters
Emergency Management Review
Environmental Hazards
International Journal of Disaster Risk Reduction
International Journal of Disaster Risk Science
International Journal of Emergency Management
International Journal of Mass Emergencies and Disasters
Journal of Contingencies and Crisis Management
Journal of Emergency Management
Journal of Homeland Security and Emergency Management
Natural Hazards
Natural Hazards Review
Prehospital and Disaster Medicine
Risk, Hazards & Crisis in Public Policy

---

response effort – a task that becomes much more difficult as time passes, memories fade, response teams leave, and ad hoc ways of working are replaced by normal routines. Researchers bring a neutral stance to observing events and thus generate more objective, measurable results that can steadily improve EM practice.

4.5 TYPES OF RESEARCH

Having discussed the importance and relevance of disaster science to EM, we now turn to a more in-depth discussion of how research is actually conducted. This discussion will be beneficial to you by providing guidance on how to conduct your own research and also give you a basis upon which to evaluate the quality and usefulness of research conducted by others. Before describing the specific methods typically used to gather data on disasters, we will discuss the different types of research.

4.5.1 Basic and Applied Research

On a general level, research can be characterized as basic or applied. Basic research is conducted to satisfy intellectual curiosity, explore previously uninvestigated topics, or address core theoretical debates in a discipline. While the results of basic research may not have immediate applicability to solving social or technical problems faced by society, it is possible that over time, this kind of research will change the way scientists think about an issue, stimulate new lines of inquiry, and ultimately produce results that can be translated into practical solutions to problems. *Applied research*, on the other hand, begins with a specific problem identified by a user community and seeks to provide practical, data-based guidance for solving the problem. For example, evaluation studies are often conducted in various settings to assess the effectiveness of new policies, programs, or technologies (see Ritchie and MacDonald 2010).

Both types of research are common in the field of disaster science. As Fritz (1961) pointed out, since its inception the field has sought to answer both basic and applied questions. Basic disaster research seeks to better understand how social systems respond to disruptions and refine theories about how society works. A good example of such research is Gary Kreps's work to develop a theory of organizations (Kreps 1989). Like Fritz, he views disasters as strategic sites for answering basic questions about society and sees organizations as central elements of the social structure. He has attempted to conceptually isolate the core properties of organizations and empirically document the timing and sequencing of those properties Kreps's work may sound highly theoretical and abstract at first, but it has important implications for maximizing the efficiency and effectiveness of organizations responding to disasters.

Disaster scientists are perhaps best known for their applied research, which in some form or fashion seeks to improve some aspect of society's readiness for, response to, or recovery from disasters. For example, they have conducted extensive research on preparedness levels, warning systems, evacuation behavior, intergovernmental coordination, and many other topics. They have also performed evaluation studies of disaster-related programs such as FEMA's Project Impact, a community-based mitigation program designed to enhance disaster resilience in the U.S. (Wachtendorf and Kompanik 2000; Wachtendorf 2001). And they have used participatory action research (PAR) to identify strategies to improve emergency preparedness for large-scale evacuations of high-rise buildings (Gershon et al. 2008).

4.5.2 Primary and Secondary Research

Whether you are conducting a study of your own or reading research done by someone else, you will find two main sources of data: primary and secondary. *Primary research* involves the collection of original data obtained through surveys, interviews, or observations to answer a basic or applied research question. As discussed in the next section, there are various ways in which those data can be collected, but the important point is that primary research is based on new data. *Secondary research* is based on data that already exist and were gathered by someone else. As an emergency manager, you will find numerous sources of secondary data useful. For example, the U.S. Census Bureau maintains massive amounts of data that you can use to study the demographics of your community. The data cover age distribution, racial composition, income and education levels, home ownership rates, and many other characteristics. As will be seen in Chapter 5, these factors play a significant role in determining how prepared households and communities are for disasters.

4.5.3 Cross Sectional and Longitudinal Research

Another issue to consider in conducting or reading research is the time frame over which information used in the study was or will be collected. *Cross sectional research* is based on data gathered at one point in time and is often described as offering a snapshot of reality at a particular time. In cross sectional research, the goal is to present a picture of how things look at the time of data collection, not predict how they might look in the future. *Longitudinal research*, however, involves prolonged data collection over time.

The goal of this kind of research is to track changes over time. As an emergency manager, you will find both approaches useful. For example, if you need a benchmark of how prepared your community currently is for a disaster, a cross sectional study would be fine. However, if your community has recently been struck by a disaster and you want to monitor its recovery over time to see whether conditions are improving or getting worse, a longitudinal approach would be more appropriate.

4.5.4 Individual and Aggregate Research

When gathering data on disasters or any topic for that matter, you must decide the level at which you need information. Are you seeking to understand something about individuals or larger social groupings such as households or organizations? *Individual-level research* seeks to describe and explain the attitudes and behaviors of individuals. For example, if you are interested in risk perception levels of people living near a nuclear power plant, you must determine how likely they think an accident is.

If you want to know whether people in your community are suffering negative psychological consequences from a recent disaster or other community emergency, you must ask them about their feelings and experiences with the event. If, on the other hand, you want to know how well the police and fire departments communicated while responding to a recent emergency in your community, you will need *aggregate-level research* to describe and explain characteristics of collectivities, including households, organizations, communities, or entire societies.

4.5.5 Quantitative and Qualitative Research

Another important distinction you will encounter in conducting your own studies or reading works by others is between quantitative and qualitative research. At the most basic level, *quantitative research* is the application of mathematical principles and statistical analyses to the study of social life. Stated another way, quantitative studies seek to describe and explain variation in the numeric properties of some aspect of social life. For example, researchers have developed elaborate scales and indices to precisely measure and quantify levels of risk perception and disaster preparedness. They also employ sophisticated statistical techniques to identify factors that contribute to higher or lower levels of these phenomena (Bourque, Shoaf, and Nguyen 2002).

Qualitative research, on the other hand, seeks to describe and explain the processes involved in some aspect of social life. Whereas quantitative research largely assumes that social life is patterned and predictable, qualitative research assumes that reality is variable, fluid, and less predictable.

While both quantitative and qualitative studies are common in disaster science, qualitative methods are particularly useful in the early aftermath of a disaster. During that period, there is a great deal of ambiguity and a tremendous amount of activity, much of which is unplanned and improvised, as survivors, first responders, governmental agencies, and voluntary organizations converge on a scene and initiate a response. As Phillips

(2002, 2014a, 2014b) points out, because qualitative methods focus on social processes and afford the researcher flexibility, they are well suited for the post-disaster environment. Indeed, there is a long tradition of quick response field studies in disaster science in which researchers are dispatched to the site of a disaster as quickly as possible after impact to gather valuable data that might otherwise perish (Quarantelli 2002; Michaels 2003). Researchers have also employed qualitative methods to conduct longitudinal studies of such topics as the experiences of children and extended families in Hurricane Katrina (Browne 2015; Fothergill and Peek 2015), the role of religious organizations in disaster response and recovery efforts (Phillips 2014c), and community controversies over the practice of hydraulic fracturing or "fracking" in natural gas exploration (Gullion 2015).

4.6 RESEARCH METHODS

There are numerous ways in which disaster scientists gather data (see Figure 4.2), and knowledge of those methods may help you as an emergency manager to measure preparedness levels in your community, monitor the performance of local agencies and departments in responding to a disaster, gauge short- and long-term recovery after a disaster, and assess community support for a proposed mitigation program or policy (Killian 2002; Donner and Diaz 2018; Gaillard 2019; Rivera 2021). In collecting information about disasters, the most important consideration is to select a methodology that will appropriately and adequately provide data on the question or questions you pose. Researchers, analysts, and other professionals certainly develop clear preferences for methods of gathering data. For example, some people are quantitatively inclined and feel best if they can see statistics on the magnitude of a problem. Others are more visually inclined and prefer to see maps and other spatial or visual representations of an issue. Still others are more qualitatively oriented and want to gain in-depth understandings of disasters from the perspective of those experiencing them. Fortunately, researchers, emergency managers, and others interested in gathering disaster data have a broad and diverse range of tools available for such purposes. Indeed, probably the best way of gathering data on any social phenomenon is through *triangulation* – the use of multiple methodologies.

4.6.1 Surveys

If you are interested in learning about a relatively large population of people, the survey is an appropriate choice. Surveys involve the administration of a standardized

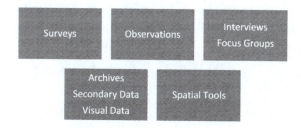

FIGURE 4.2 Methods of Data Collection.

questionnaire to a sample of people to better understand perceptions, attitudes, opinions, preferences, and behaviors prevalent in a larger population. The most common approaches to administering surveys are by phone, mail, face-to-face meetings, and increasingly via the Internet. Questions on surveys are usually closed-ended; respondents are forced to select one response option for each question. These kinds of questions are preferred in survey research because they are easier to quantify and subject to statistical analyses. Surveys have been used extensively in disaster science to study a wide variety of topics. For example, surveys have been administered to measure household preparedness levels, evacuation decision-making, recovery outcomes, and people's willingness to pay for mitigation programs.

In designing a survey questionnaire, it is important to develop questions that are reliable and valid. *Reliability* is best described as a measure of consistency. In other words, reliable questions should elicit common responses in repeated administrations of a survey instrument. In reality, of course, a survey is administered only once to respondents, so it is important to spend a lot of time and effort crafting good questions. Pilot testing of surveys usually results in clear wording that respondents can understand and thus select responses that best fit their perceptions.

Validity is best described as a measure of accuracy. Valid questions should elicit accurate information on the phenomena they seek to address. If you are interested, for example, in understanding people's perceptions of the likelihood of a terrorist attack in their community, you do not want to ask questions that instead measure their fear of terrorism. The two concepts may be similar, but they are not the same. Indeed, to illustrate how they are actually two separate (albeit related) concepts, consider the hypothesis that those with higher levels of fear of terrorism will also perceive a greater likelihood of an attack.

Importantly, surveys typically involve *random sampling* techniques, whereby every person in the study population has an equal chance of being asked to participate. This is much better than convenience sampling in which researchers administer their surveys in a non-randomized manner to people who are most readily available. While random sampling has many advantages, many studies still rely on convenience sampling (Norris 2006). The advantage of random sampling is that it ensures *representativeness* of a sample: the demographic, attitudinal, and behavioral characteristics of the people who complete the questionnaire should closely resemble those of others in the population who were not selected for participation. Thus, findings from properly conducted surveys are *generalizable*: statistics generated from the sample of study participants can be used to estimate and make projections about the attitudes and behaviors of others in the larger population. For example, national political polls that project how tens of millions of people will likely vote in an election are typically based on samples of approximately 1,000 respondents. That is the strength and power of applying mathematical principles and theorems to the study of social life.

4.6.2 Interviews

In some cases, you may be less interested in making generalizations about a very large population and more interested in the experiences of a smaller, more select group of people or organizations. In those cases, you may find interviewing a more appropriate technique for gathering information than surveys. *Interviews* are focused conversations conducted to gain in-depth understanding of the views and experiences of respondents (Rubin and Rubin 2005). They can be conducted one-on-one or as part of a larger focus group (Peek and Fothergill 2009; Rivera 2019). Although interviews are similar to surveys, in that they seek to obtain respondent answers to particular questions, they are different in several important ways.

First, while surveys ask standardized questions of all respondents, interviews are typically conducted with the assistance of an interview guide. Interview guides provide researchers with a list of topics to cover and some topical questions to ask but allow flexibility in the order in which they are covered. In contrast to the closed-ended questions common in surveys, interviews typically rely on open-ended questions designed to elicit thoughtful, detailed, and in-depth responses from interview subjects. For example, you might ask the head of a local agency or department, "What are the most important challenges your agency has faced in the days since the disaster?" In-depth interviewing allows you to follow the thread of a conversation that may lead in a fruitful direction as interview subjects add depth and breadth to the topic you are studying. You may also uncover unexpected insights that yield greater understanding. These emergent pieces of data often generate productive lines of inquiry for a current study and future direction.

Second, instead of random sampling techniques, interview studies typically employ a more purposive approach. *Purposive sampling* involves selecting respondents to participate based on the relevance of their knowledge and experiences to the objectives of the study. For example, if you are interested in understanding how a recent disaster impacted those with special needs in your community, a large-scale survey may not be necessary. Instead, you might conduct interviews at nursing homes, local shelters, or other appropriate places. In addition to beginning with a purposive approach, interview studies often proceed through the use of snowball sampling. *Snowball sampling* is an approach to recruiting additional participants to a study by getting recommendations from past respondents. For example, you might interview the director of public works about that department's role in responding to a recent disaster and he or she may recommend that you talk to specific people in the department to gain more detail. For disaster scientists, it may also be necessary to interview people in specific spatial zones such as the immediate impact area, outer areas, and non-affected areas. Imagine, for example, being able to track the flow of resources into an area from the outside to the inside as a way to study donations management.

Finally, while a major objective of survey research is to generalize findings from a sample of respondents to a much larger population, interview studies and qualitative approaches to research generally follow a different approach (Lincoln and Guba 1985). Qualitative research assumes that social reality rather than being patterned and predictable is fluid and dynamic, and while different social settings may be similar, they will always exhibit important differences. Instead of generalizability, which assumes that patterns identified among a relatively small sample of people can be inferred to exist in a much larger population, qualitative researchers focus instead upon transferability. *Transferability* is the degree to which insights gained from studying one social setting or group of people are applicable to others. In EM, transferability is a very useful concept. While disasters may create unique challenges for communities impacted by them, they also produce many of the same problems. Thus, by studying how one community dealt with those problems, we can learn valuable lessons that may not be directly generalizable to another community but are certainly transferable.

4.6.3 Observations

Observational research involves the systematic identification of patterns and trends in a social setting. It is an invaluable tool for disaster scientists because it offers a holistic view of activities in a post-disaster environment. While researchers often use observations in conjunction with interviews to gain a more comprehensive understanding of disasters, in some cases they must rely heavily on observations because respondents may not be readily available for interviews or a language barrier may exist. There are several important issues to consider when conducting observational research. First, of course, is deciding what to observe. Every social setting involves a tremendous amount of activity, even when it appears that nothing meaningful is happening. After a disaster, when researchers may feel overwhelmed and bombarded with information, they must make critical decisions about focusing their observations (Spradley 1980).

Second, you must devise an effective strategy for recording observations. With so much activity over a relatively wide area, it is not realistic to think after a disaster that you will be able to carry your laptop everywhere and enter observations directly. More often, researchers make notes of their observations throughout the day and enter them into a computer in more elaborate form later. *Visual methods* such as photographs and video recordings can supplement observations or serve as stand-alone techniques. In one unique study, researchers gave cameras to shelter residents to record their personal experiences, thus uncovering valuable lessons for shelter managers (Pike, Phillips, and Reeves 2006). This methodological approach, known as *photovoice*, utilizes participant-authored photographs and descriptions to convey local knowledge and can be useful for evaluating programs or advocating for unmet needs (Schumann, Binder, and Greer 2019).

Finally, researchers must make decisions about their degree of involvement in a social setting. *Participant observation* involves researchers becoming active members, at least to a degree, of the setting or group studied. Participatory action research involves researchers and people in the setting who work together to improve some aspect of social life. For example, in a classic disaster study, Taylor, Zurcher, and Key (1970) worked alongside others in a community struck by a tornado, all the while making observations about the group's activities, and later wrote a book about the experience. *Nonparticipant observation* involves maintaining a distance from the activities observed to minimize the researcher's role in and impact on a group or setting studied. In this approach, the researcher attempts to act as a "fly on the wall" by quietly observing the group or setting. In most cases, researchers find themselves playing a role between full-fledged participant and nonparticipant observer.

As with interviewing, observational research is a useful tool for capturing dynamic social processes as they unfold. Thus, observational methods are most often used for gathering data during the *response* and *recovery* periods. During those phases, things happen very quickly. If events are not thoroughly documented "on the spot," valuable information will perish. By conducting systematic observations and recording them in notes, photographs, or videos, we can more accurately reconstruct what happened during the response phase and chart the progress of recovery.

In the immediate aftermath of a disaster, with so much happening in a relatively short and condensed time frame, the challenge for those interested in gathering systematic information is often deciding what exactly to observe. It is impossible, of course, to observe everything, so you have to determine the focus of your observations on particular topics or issues. For example, if you are seeking to improve and strengthen communications among various city departments during emergencies and disasters, you might observe and document interactions of departmental representatives at the emergency operations center (EOC) when it is activated. In most cases, you will have multiple reasons for making observations, so a checklist of topics or issues upon which to focus may be helpful. In addition to the response and recovery phases, observation can also be a useful tool for gathering information about *preparedness*. Observations are often used, for example, in disaster drills and exercises to document what works and does not work and identify areas for improvement in the event of an actual disaster.

4.6.4 Archives

Archival information is another valuable source of data for those wanting to learn more about the impacts of disasters on communities (Wenger 1989). *Archives* are documents that attest to or provide an account of historical happenings. As society has grown in complexity and developed new technologies for producing, recording, and storing information, the amount of archival information available has vastly expanded. Indeed, the documents of life, as Plummer (2001) refers to archives, abound and are literally all around us.

Archival sources of data include newspapers, organizational memos, after-action reports, minutes of meetings, transcripts of congressional testimony, and other useful information. The major advantages of using these kinds of data are that they are plentiful, often easily accessible, and usually inexpensive to obtain. Additionally, archives are unobtrusive, which means they do not require the researcher to interact with people or risk disturbing a social setting (Webb et al. 1999). Disadvantages are that archival collections may be scattered or disorganized, data storage and retrieval systems become outdated, documents are sometimes illegible, and, in some cases, items may have been destroyed intentionally.

Many studies in the field of disaster science are based on archival data. For example, Kreps and his colleagues conducted extensive research on archives maintained by the DRC to study organizational dynamics in the aftermaths of disasters (Kreps 1989). Similarly, Mendonça and his colleagues (Mendonca, Webb, Butts, and Brooks 2014) used archival data from the 1995 bombing of the Murrah Federal Building in Oklahoma City and the 2001 attacks on the World Trade Center to study improvisation among first responders to disasters, a topic that will be discussed in-depth in Chapter 7.

Archives can provide useful information about the various phases of a disaster. Indeed, in launching a comprehensive study of a community and its experience with a disaster, the best place to start is often the local library. In terms of *preparedness*, published reports of special investigative commissions like those formed after September 11, 2001, and Hurricane Katrina can be valuable sources of information for understanding the degree to which various organizations were aware of potential threats and whether or not they took the threats seriously. A good example of the usefulness of these kinds of documents is a classic study by Barry Turner (1976), in which he argued that organizations often suffer from a "failure of foresight" by failing to think creatively and prepare for exigencies that in hindsight should have been foreseeable.

Although many *response* activities are unplanned, unscripted, and even undocumented, organizations nevertheless produce plenty of reports, memos, agendas, meeting minutes, and other documents that can be very useful. Archival data such as newspaper articles are well suited for studying recovery processes, particularly over the long term. Newspaper articles and other archives can also be helpful for gathering information about *mitigation*. Some researchers have examined challenges such as intergroup conflicts associated with community relocation – a strategy sometimes used in cases of severe environmental contamination (Shriver and Kennedy 2005). While these studies typically involve interviews and observations, they also tend to rely heavily on archival sources.

4.6.5 Spatial Tools

Recent advances in technology have dramatically expanded and enhanced our ability to gather massive amounts of data on all kinds of topics, including disaster and EM. Laptop computers and other portable devices, for example, make it much easier for researchers to process information, including observation notes and interview transcripts from the field. Digital voice recorders are much smaller and less obtrusive than old tape recorders and reel-to-reel machines that researchers carried into the field. Improved statistical software packages allow massive amounts of data such as those gathered from surveys to be analyzed rapidly and in increasingly sophisticated ways. All these advances have made the research enterprise much more efficient and far less daunting than it used to be.

In disaster science, perhaps the most important technological developments with the greatest potential for advancing the field are those designed to enhance spatial data collection and analysis. Geographical information systems (GIS) are probably the most common and widely used spatial applications in the hazards and disaster area (Dash 2002; Thomas, Ertugay, and Kemeç 2006; Siebeneck, Schumann III, and Kuenanz 2019). These programs allow researchers to attach spatial coordinates to various sources of data, all of which can then be visually depicted on maps. With appropriate GIS software, users can overlay all kinds of information on top of their geocoded data to show roads and bridges, waterways, and environmental hazards. In addition to GIS, researchers now have access to satellite imaging and remote sensing technologies that can be very useful after a disaster.

Spatial tools are becoming much more prevalent in the field of disaster science, and as technologies continue to improve, it is likely that these tools will become even more common in the future. For researchers and emergency managers, these tools have many possible applications during the four phases of a disaster. To ensure *preparedness*, for example, maps locating hospitals, schools, nursing homes, hazardous facilities, and other sites can be produced and distributed. Additionally, survey data on levels of household preparedness could be geocoded and mapped to provide emergency managers with snapshots of preparedness levels in their communities.

Researchers have also used GIS to identify and visually depict vulnerable populations in communities across the U.S. – those with high concentrations of poverty and high percentages of minority residents and those in close proximity to natural and technological hazards (Cutter 2001). GIS and remote sensing tools have also proven useful in the *response* phase, allowing researchers to rapidly, efficiently, and accurately conduct damage assessments based on visual displays of areas with high concentrations of damage. These tools can be valuable resources for emergency managers who need to prioritize response activities.

Spatial data collected during the response phase can serve as baseline data for assessing short- and long-term recovery in a community. As new maps and images are produced, they can be juxtaposed with earlier ones, allowing users to visually track recovery over time. Imagine, for example, the ability to spatially depict volunteer activities after a catastrophic event to allow better preparation for the next event (Greiner and Wikle 2008). As for *mitigation*, the maps used in the preparedness phase to identify hazardous places and vulnerable populations can and ideally would be used by city commissions, planning and zoning departments, and other public officials to make informed land use decisions that minimize future risks to their communities.

4.7 ETHICS

An important consideration in all fields of research is ethics. For disaster scientists, ethical concerns are perhaps more salient than in other fields because they deal with events and circumstances that entail enormous human suffering (Gaillard and Peek 2019). To some, Fritz's (1961) early characterization of disasters as "laboratories" for studying basic human social processes may seem callous and exploitative. Yet, if we want to enhance the safety of society, it is imperative that we study these tragic events to learn lessons from them that can be applied to the future. In other words, we hope that our research will produce tangible benefits to society in general and those who participate in our research in particular. While there are no definitive, universal standards of ethics against which to judge science and research, the U.S. government has provided helpful guidelines (Babbie 2017). The primary goal of these guidelines is to provide adequate protections to human subjects of research to minimize the risk of adverse effects – psychological, emotional, financial, or social – from their participation.

The first ethical guideline is *respect for persons*. To show appropriate respect for persons, researchers must demonstrate that subjects voluntarily consented to participate, that is, they were not tricked, misled, or coerced. Subjects must be informed of their right to withdraw their participation at any time without consequence, and researchers must take adequate measures to protect the confidentiality of information provided by subjects.

Benefits and risks constitute the second ethical guideline cited in federal policies governing research. Researchers must demonstrate that the benefits of the research to subjects, society, or the scientific community outweigh the potential risks to subjects.

While the risks to subjects from social science research are far less consequential than the risks from research on new medicines or experimental treatment regimes, we need to be mindful of and sensitive to the experiences of those who participate in our research.

The final ethical consideration is *justice*. This essentially means that both the risks and benefits of research should be distributed fairly in society. For example, it would be considered unjust if the only people who participated in test studies of new medicines were prison inmates or poor people in public hospitals. Similarly, it would be unjust if the new medicines that came from those studies were not made widely available, but instead were reserved for a select group of fortunate or prominent people.

It is important to note that not all research involves the participation of human subjects. For example, as described in the previous section, archival and spatial data can be gathered without interactions with people. In many cases, however, we are required to interact with people to gather the information we need. For researchers at universities, like many of those whose work is cited throughout this book, that means getting approval for a study before going into the field. That approval comes from an institutional review board (IRB). IRBs are committees that exist at all universities that receive federal support for research. The job of an IRB is to review research proposals submitted by faculty researchers to ensure that they have provided adequate protections to their subjects based on the ethical guidelines described previously.

4.8 RESEARCH CHALLENGES

In addition to providing adequate human subject protection, disaster scientists face other challenges in conducting studies (Kendra and Gregory 2019; Uekusa 2019). Of course, all research can be difficult, but the challenges of disaster research seem particularly pronounced. For example, disaster scientists face basic *logistical challenges* not present in other types of research. They must travel to disaster-stricken communities on very short notice, gain IRB approval for the research before they leave, find available and affordable lodging, and navigate debris-filled, barricaded communities upon arrival.

Researchers in all fields must find study participants and figure out ways to deal with those who decline participation. For disaster scientists, the problem of *respondent availability and accessibility* can be particularly pronounced. In studies aimed at understanding the impacts of disasters on ordinary citizens, researchers may have to travel to surrounding communities to track down survivors or visit with them in shelters or temporary "tent cities." Similarly, when researchers want to study public officials and their activities after a disaster (a common focus of research) they may find access very difficult for several reasons. First, it is possible or even likely that instead of working from their normal offices, the relevant public officials will work from an alternative temporary location such as an EOC or somewhere else in the community. Second, even when we locate such officials, it may be difficult for them to stop what they are doing and find time to talk with researchers. It is important, therefore, for researchers to be flexible and accommodating in the field.

In recent years, a new phenomenon has made it more difficult for researchers to access potential respondents. Indeed, the events of September 11, 2001, led to a noticeable change in post-disaster environments. Specifically, in the era of concern about homeland security, disaster sites are increasingly treated like crime scenes. As a result, law enforcement agencies have ramped up their efforts to restrict access to disaster-stricken communities and public officials appear less willing to talk to researchers, reporters, and the public at large about their activities. This is a disturbing trend because, as stated previously, a major goal of research is to learn lessons from past disasters to prevent mistakes in the future. If officials are unwilling to talk publicly about their activities, including their mistakes, the prospects for uncovering lessons learned are severely diminished.

Another prominent challenge in disaster research is dealing with *emotions and human suffering*. Disasters are tragic events. Although as researchers we approach them with a certain degree of scientific objectivity and emotional distance, the devastation caused by disasters cannot be totally ignored. Researchers in the field see the physical damage, social disruption, and human suffering caused by disasters. They also hear stories, both heroic and tragic, from respondents about what happened and can experience feelings of sadness, sympathy, and strong desire to help those suffering. One way of managing those feelings is to recognize the value of their own work. As stated previously, their studies may not produce immediate, tangible benefits to the community, but over time studies of disasters will contribute to a safer future.

***

SUMMARY

The term *emergency management* conjures up many images, but for most people scientific research is probably not what comes to mind when thinking about the profession. Yet, as we have seen in this chapter, the profession of EM and the field of disaster science have much in common, including a desire to improve society's ability to prepare for, respond to, recover from, and mitigate against future disasters. As a future emergency manager, you will benefit from understanding disaster science and by developing scientific literacy.

Whether you are interested in conducting a study of your own or finding out what others have already learned about a topic, this chapter provides a strong foundation to help you move forward. You are now familiar with the various methodological tools available for answering all kinds of disaster- and EM-related questions: how prepared are households and businesses in my community for a future disaster? What kinds of problems did agencies and departments in my community confront in responding to a past disaster? What is the status of my community's recovery from a past disaster as a whole, for businesses, and for certain groups in the population? And finally, how supportive are people in my community of a newly proposed mitigation measure?

Throughout your career, you will gain valuable knowledge through first-hand encounters with disasters. That kind of hands-on experience is essential to your professional development and will serve as a tremendous confidence builder. As we discussed in this chapter, however, disaster science is another important source of knowledge for you, and it is the best path for advancing the profession and building a safer and more resilient future.

Discussion Questions

1. Define and discuss disaster science. What academic disciplines have contributed to its growth? What are some examples of topics studied by disaster scientists from various disciplines (e.g., sociologists, geographers, psychologists, etc.)?

2. Why is disaster science important to the profession of EM? How can it contribute to the advancement of the profession?

3. What is scientific literacy? Why is it important for emergency managers of the future to possess this competency? What are some ways you can strengthen your own scientific literacy?

4. Locate and read a research article on a topic of interest to you published in one of the academic journals listed in Box 4.4. What was the primary research question? How did the researcher(s) gather data to answer the question? Do you agree with the findings? How could the research have been improved?

5. Imagine you work for a local EM office and your community was struck by a disaster, such as a tornado or a hurricane, two years ago. The City Council would like a report on the status of the community's recovery from the disaster. How would you go about preparing your report? What data would you need to assess the status of the recovery process? How would you gather those data? What kinds of charts and graphs might you need to visually illustrate recovery indicators?

Summary Questions

1. Distinguish between the kinds of research (e.g., basic and applied, qualitative and quantitative) and why each has value for disaster science.

2. Identify and describe ethical standards for taking care of people when they are research subjects. What specific actions should researchers take and what should they be concerned with?

3. Explain the value of each kind of data collection technique for both disaster science and the practice of EM (e.g., interviews, surveys, observations, archival research).

4. What challenges do disaster scientists face when they move into the field to conduct research?

REFERENCES

Babbie, Earl. 2017. *The Basics of Social Research*, 7th ed. Boston: Cengage.

Birkland, Thomas A. 1997. *After Disaster: Agenda Setting, Public Policy and Focusing Events*. Washington, DC: Georgetown University Press.

Birkland, Thomas A. 2007. *Lessons of Disaster: Policy Change after Catastrophic Disasters*. Washington, DC: Georgetown.

Bourque, Linda B., Kimberley I. Shoaf, and Loc H. Nguyen. 2002. "Survey Research." Pp. 157–193 in *Methods of Disaster Research*, ed. Robert A. Stallings. Philadelphia, PA: Xlibris/International Research Committee on Disasters.

Browne, Katherine E. 2015. *Standing in the Need: Culture, Comfort, and Coming Home after Katrina*. Austin: University of Texas Press.

Cutter, Susan L., ed. 2001. *American Hazardscapes: The Regionalization of Hazards and Disasters.* Washington, DC: Joseph Henry Press.

Dacy, Douglas C. and Howard Kunreuther. 1969. *The Economics of Natural Disasters.* New York: The Free Press.

Dash, Nicole. 2002. "The Use of Geographic Information Systems in Disaster Research." Pp. 320–333 in *Methods of Disaster Research*, ed. Robert A. Stallings. Philadelphia, PA: XLibris/International Research Committee on Disasters.

Donner, William and Walter Diaz. 2018. "Methodological Issues in Disaster Research." Pp. 289–309 in *Handbook of Disaster Research*, 2nd ed., eds. Havidan Rodriguez, William Donner, and Joseph Trainor. New York: Springer.

Drabek, Thomas E. and Gerard J. Hoetmer (Eds). 1991. *Emergency Management: Principles and Practice for Local Government.* Washington, D.C.: ICMA Press.

Dynes, Russell R. 1994. "Community emergency Planning: False Assumptions and Inappropriate Analogies." *International Journal of Mass Emergencies and Disasters* 12(2): 141–158.

Feldman-Jensen, Shirley, Steven Jensen, and Sandy Maxwell Smith. 2017. *The Next Generation Core Competencies for Emergency Management Professionals: Handbook of Behavioral Anchors and Key Actions for Measurement.* Emmittsburg, MD: FEMA Higher Education Program.

Fothergill, Alice and Lori Peek. 2015. *Children of Katrina.* Austin: University of Texas Press.

Fritz, Charles E. 1961. "Disaster." Pp. 651–694 in *Contemporary Social Problems*, eds. Robert K. Merton and Robert A. Nisbet. New York: Harcourt, Brace and World, Inc.

Gaillard, J. C. 2019. "Disaster Studies Inside Out." *Disasters* 43: 7–17.

Gaillard, J. C. and Lori Peek. 2019. "Disaster-zone Research Needs a Code of Conduct." *Nature* 575: 440–442.

Gershon, R. M., Marcie S. Rubin, Kristine A. Qureshi, Allison N. Canton, and Frederick J. Matzner. 2008. "Participatory Action Research Methodology in Disaster Research: Results from the World Trade Center Evacuation Study." *Disaster Medicine and Public Health Preparedness* 2: 142–149.

Greiner, Alyson L. and Thomas A. Wikle. 2008. "Episodic Volunteerism after Hurricane Katrina: Insights from Pass Christian, Mississippi." *International Journal of Volunteer Administration* 25(3): 14–25.

Gullion, JessicaSmartt. 2015. *Fracking the Neighborhood: Reluctant Activists and Natural Gas Drilling.* Cambridge, MA: MIT Press.

Hoffman, Susanna and Anthony Oliver-Smith, eds. 2002. *Catastrophe and Culture: The Anthropology of Disaster.* Santa Fe: School of American Research Press.

Jenkins, Sharon. 1998. "Emergency Workers' Mass Shooting Incident Stress and Psychological Reactions." *International Journal of Mass Emergencies and Disasters* 16(2): 181–195.

Kendra, James and Sarah Gregory. 2019. "Ethics in Disaster Research: A New Declaration." Pp. 311–333 in *Disaster Research and the Second Environmental Crisis: Assessing the Challenges Ahead*, eds. James Kendra, Scott G. Knowles, and Tricia Wachtendorf. Switzerland: Springer.

Killian, Lewis. 2002. "An Introduction to Methodological Problems of Field Studies in Disasters." Pp. 49–93 in *Methods of Disaster Research*, ed. Robert A. Stallings. Philadelphia, PA: Xlibris/International Research Committee on Disasters.

Kreps, Gary A., ed. 1989. *Social Structure and Disaster.* Newark: University of Delaware Press.

Kreps, Gary A. 1995. "Disaster as Systemic Event and Social Catalyst: A Clarification of the Subject Matter." *International Journal of Mass Emergencies and Disasters* 13(3): 255–284.

Lincoln, Yvonna S. and Egon G. Guba. 1985. *Naturalistic Inquiry.* Newbury Park, CA: Sage.

McNutt, Marcia. 2015. "A Community for Disaster Science." *Science* 348(630): 11.

Mendonca, David, G. Webb, C. Butts, and J. Brooks. 2014. "Cognitive Correlates of Improvised Behavior in Disaster Response: The Cases of the Murrah Building and the World Trade Center." *Journal of Contingencies and Crisis Management* 22(4): 185–195.

Michaels, Sarah. 2003. "Perishable Information, Enduring Insights? Understanding Quick Response Research." Pp. 15–48 in *Beyond September 11th: An Account of Post-Disaster Research*, ed. Jacquelyn L. Monday. Boulder, CO: Natural Hazards Research and Applications Information Center.

Norris, Fran H. 2006. "Disaster Research Methods: Past Progress and Future Directions." *Journal of Traumatic Stress* 19(2): 173–184.

Norris, Fran H., M. J. Friedman, and P. J. Watson. 2002a. "60,000 Disaster Victims Speak: Part II. Summary and Implications of the Disaster Mental Health Research." *Psychiatry* 65(3): 240–260.

Norris, Fran H., M. J. Friedman, P. J. Watson, C. M. Byrne, E. Diaz, and K. Kaniasty. 2002b. "60,000 Disaster Victims Speak: Part I. An Empirical Review of the Empirical Literature, 1981–2001." *Psychiatry* 65(3): 207–239.

North, Carol. S., L. Tivis, J. C. McMillen, B. Pfefferbaum, J. Cox, E. L. Spitznagel, K. Bunch, J. Schorr, and E. M. Smith. 2002. "Coping, Functioning, and Adjustment of Rescue Workers after the Oklahoma City Bombing." *Journal of Traumatic Stress* 15(3): 171–175.

Oliver-Smith, Anthony and Susanna Hoffman. 1999. *The Angry Earth: Disaster in Anthropological Perspective*. New York: Routledge.

Olson, Richard Stuart. 2000. "Toward a Politics of Disaster: Losses, Values, Agendas, and Blame." *International Journal of Mass Emergencies and Disasters* 18: 265–287.

Peek, Lori, Heather Champeau, Jessica Austin, Mason Matthews, and Haorui Wu. 2020a. "What Methods Do Social Scientists Use to Study Disasters? An Analysis of the Social Science Extreme Events Research Network." *American Behavioral Scientist* 64(8): 1066–1094.

Peek, Lori A. and Alice Fothergill. 2009. "Using Focus Groups: Lessons from Studying Daycare Centers, 9/11, and Hurricane Katrina." *Qualitative Research* 9(1): 31–59.

Peek, Lori, Jennifer Tobin, Rachel Adams, Haorui Wu, and Mason Mathews. 2020b. "A Framework for Convergence Research in the Hazards and Disaster Field: The Natural Hazards Engineering Research Infrastructure CONVERGE Facility." *Frontiers in Built Environment*. Available at https://www.frontiersin.org/articles/10.3389/fbuil.2020.00110/full.

Pfefferbaum, B., J. A. Call, and G. M. Sconzo. 1999. "Mental Health Services for Children in the First Two Years after the 1995 Oklahoma City Terrorist Bombing." *Psychiatric Services* 50(7): 956–958.

Phillips, Brenda D. 2002. "Qualitative Methods of Disaster Research." Pp. 194–211 in *Methods of Disaster Research*, ed. Robert A. Stallings. Philadelphia, PA: Xlibris/International Research Committee on Disasters.

Phillips, Brenda D. 2014a. *Qualitative Disaster Research*. Oxford: Oxford University Press.

Phillips, Brenda D. 2014b. "Qualitative Disaster Research Methods." Pp. 553–556 in *The Oxford Handbook of Qualitative Research Methods*, ed. Patricia Leavy. Oxford University Press, Inc.

Phillips, Brenda D. 2014c. *Mennonite Disaster Service: Building a Therapeutic Community after the Gulf Coast Storms*. Lanham, MD: Lexington Books.

Phillips, Brenda D., Deborah S. K. Thomas, Alice Fothergill and Lynn Pike, eds. 2010. *Social Vulnerability to Disaster*. Boca Raton, FL: CRC Press.

Pike, Lynn, Brenda D. Phillips and Patsilu Reeves. 2006. "Shelter Life after Katrina: A Visual Analysis of Evacuee Perspectives." *International Journal of Mass Emergencies and Disasters* 24(3): 303–330.

Platt, Rutherford H. 1999. *Disasters and Democracy: The Politics of Extreme Natural Events*. Washington, DC: Island Press.

Plummer, Kenneth. 2001. *Documents of Life 2*. Thousand Oaks, CA: Sage.

Quarantelli, E. L. 1994. "Disaster Studies: The Consequences of the Historical Use of a Sociological Approach in the Development of Research." *International Journal of Mass Emergencies and Disasters* 12: 25–49.

Quarantelli, E. L. 2002. "The Disaster Research Center (DRC) Field Studies of Organized Behavior in the Crisis Time Period of Disasters." Pp. 94–126 in *Methods of Disaster Research*, ed. Robert A. Stallings. Philadelphia, PA: Xlibris/International Research Committee on Disasters.

Ritchie, Liesel Ashley and Wayne MacDonald, eds. 2010. "Enhancing Disaster and Emergency Preparedness, Response and Recovery through Evaluation." *New Directions for Evaluation*, Number 126.

Rivera, Jason D. 2019. "Focus Group Administration in Disaster Research: Methodological Transparency when Dealing with Challenges." *International Journal of Mass Emergencies and Disasters* 37(3): 241–263.

Rivera, Jason D., ed. 2021. *Disaster and Emergency Management Methods*. Boca Raton, FL: Routledge.

Rubin, Herbert J. and Irene S. Rubin. 2005. *Qualitative Interviewing: The Art of Hearing Data*. Newbury Park, CA: Sage.

Schumann III, Ronald L., Sherri Brokopp Binder, and Alex Greer. 2019. "Unseen Potential: Photovoice Methods in Hazard and Disaster Science." *GeoJournal* 84: 273–289.

Shriver, Thomas E. and Dennis Kennedy. 2005. "Contested Environmental Hazards and Community Conflict over Relocation." *Rural Sociology* 70(4): 491–513.

Siebeneck, Laura, Ronald L. Schumann III, and Britt Kuenanz. 2019. "GIS Applications in emergency Management: Infusing Geographic Literacy in the Classroom." *Journal of Emergency Management* 17/2: 119–135.

Spradley, James P. 1980. *Participant Observation*. Fort Worth, TX: Harcourt, Brace, Jovanovich College Publishers.

Sylves, Richard. 2008. *Disaster Policy and Politics: Emergency Management and Homeland Security*. Washington, DC: CQ Press.

Taylor, James B., Louis A. Zurcher and William H. Key. 1970. *Tornado: A Community Responds to Disaster*. Seattle, WA: University of Washington Press.

Thomas, Deborah S. K., Kivanç Ertugay, and Serkan Kemeç. 2006. "The Role of Geographic Information Systems/Remote Sensing in Disaster Management. Pp. 83–96 in *Handbook of Disaster Research*, eds. Havidán Rogríguez, E. L. Quarantelli and Russell R. Dynes. New York: Springer.

Tierney, Kathleen J. 2020. "Pandemic and Disaster: Insights from Seventy Years of Social Science Disaster Research." Published May 21, 2020. Social Science Research Council: Items Insights from the Social Sciences. https://items.ssrc.org/covid-19-and-the-social-sciences/disaster-studies/pandemic-and-disaster-insights-from-seventy-years-of-social-science-disaster-research/

Turner, Barry A. 1976. "The Organizational and Inter-Organizational Development of Disasters." *Administrative Science Quarterly* 21: 378–397.

Uekusa, Shinya. 2019. "Methodological Challenges in Social Vulnerability and Resilience Research: Reflections on Studies in the Canterbury and Tohoku Disasters." *Social Science Quarterly* 100(4): 1404–1419.

Wachtendorf, Tricia. 2001. "Building Community Partnerships toward a National Mitigation Effort: Inter-Organizational Collaboration in the Project Impact Initiative." Invited paper presented at the annual workshop for the Comparative Study on Urban Earthquake Disaster Management, Kobe, Japan, January 18.

Wachtendorf, Tricia. 2019. "A Case for the Grand Challenge of Disaster Science." Pp. 335–343 in *Disaster Research and the Second Environmental Crisis: Assessing the Challenges Ahead*, eds. James Kendra, Scott G. Knowles, and Tricia Wachtendorf. Switzerland: Springer.

Wachtendorf, Tricia and Kristy Kompanik. 2000. "An Ongoing Assessment of the Project Impact Implementation Process: Recommendations and Lessons Learned." Poster presented at the Annual Project Impact Summit. Washington, DC, November 13.

Waugh, William. 2000. *Living with Hazards, Dealing with Disasters: Introduction to Emergency Management*. Armonk, NY: M. E. Sharpe.

Waugh, William. 2006. "Shelter from the Storm: Repairing the National Emergency Management System after Katrina." *The ANNALS of the American Academy of Political and Social Science* 604: 288–332.

Waugh, William L. Jr. and Kathleen Tierney (Eds.). 2007. *Emergency Management: Principles and Practice for Local Government*, 2nd ed. Washington, D.C.: ICMA Press.

Webb, Eugene, Donald T. Campbell, Richard D. Schwartz, and Lee Sechrest. 1999. *Unobtrusive Measures*, 2nd edition. Thousand Oaks, CA: Sage.

Wenger, Dennis E. 1989. "The Role of Archives for Comparative Studies of Social Structure and Disaster." Pp. 238–250 in *Social Structure and Disaster*, ed. Gary A. Kreps. Newark: University of Delaware Press.

Wright, James D., Peter H. Rossi, Sonia R. Wright, and Eleanor Weber-Burdin. 1979. *After the Clean-Up: Long-Range Effects of Natural Disasters*. Beverly Hills, CA: Sage.

RESOURCES

- The U.S. Census Bureau regularly collects and disseminates data on communities and households throughout the country and much of the data is relevant to emergency managers. To learn more, visit the official website at www.census.gov
- Both the DRC at the University of Delaware (drc.udel.edu) and the Natural Hazards Center at the University of Colorado (www.colorado.edu/hazards) house libraries vast amount of social science literature related to the social aspects of risks, hazards, and disasters.
- The UN Office of Disaster Risk Reduction maintains and shares extensive information about disasters worldwide through its International Strategy for Disaster Risk Reduction (www.unisdr.org).
- The Centre for Research on the Epidemiology of Disasters in Belgium maintains a database known as EM-DAT, the International Disaster Database, which provides information on the frequency, impacts, and consequences of disasters (www.emdat.be).

PART 2

Comprehensive Emergency Management

CHAPTER 5

Preparedness

CHAPTER OBJECTIVES

Upon completing this chapter, readers should be able to:

- Define preparedness, explain the importance of prioritizing preparedness, and discuss factors that affect preparedness levels.
- Describe how preparedness contributes to resilience.
- Explain how understanding social vulnerability can help emergency managers improve preparedness in their communities.
- Describe how preparedness is related to the other phases of disaster, including response, recovery, and mitigation, and discuss the value of the all-hazards approach.
- List specific preparedness activities and provide examples of preparedness initiatives at the state, national, and international levels.

KEY TERMS

- Cultural Competency
- Culture of Preparedness
- Disaster Subcultures
- Preparedness
- Resilience

- Risk Perception
- Social Vulnerability
- Sociocultural Literacy
- Whole Community

5.1 INTRODUCTION

In this chapter, we learn about preparedness, which serves as the most important phase prior to the onset of disasters and which can produce significant personal and social benefits (Stein et al. 2014). Despite its importance, however, preparedness levels have historically fallen short of where they need to be. Thus, this chapter begins by

DOI: 10.4324/9781003021919-7

explaining why we need to prioritize preparedness in order to ensure a safer and more resilient future. The remainder of the chapter defines preparedness; outlines different types of preparedness activities for households, organizations, and communities; identifies factors that influence preparedness levels; and provides examples of preparedness initiatives at the state, national, and international levels. It is our hope that the concepts and issues discussed in this chapter will help you both as an individual and as a future emergency manager to better prepare your own household, organization, and community for disasters.

5.2 PRIORITIZING PREPAREDNESS

Although disaster preparedness is vitally important to the well-being of our communities, the reality is that we are not doing enough to protect ourselves from future harm. As an emergency manager, prioritizing preparedness will be a major part of your job, and you will be much more effective at doing that by understanding the many reasons why preparedness levels are so low. In some cases, for example, people simply may not be aware of all of the hazards that exist in their communities, which may be particularly true of technological risks, such as those stemming from the storage, processing, or transportation of chemicals and other hazardous materials. In other instances, people may not fully understand risk probabilities, such as not knowing that a so-called 100-year flood has a 1% chance of occurring every single year, not just once every century. And then, there are those who may have full awareness and understanding of the risks they face but lack the sense of urgency that would prompt them to take appropriate protective actions, such as coastal residents who ignore evacuation orders and instead stay behind for hurricane parties.

Preparedness requires resources, and for many people, it is a luxury they simply cannot afford. For example, in households experiencing food insecurity or a lack of consistent access to adequate food and nutrition, storing three days of food and water is not possible. For them, engaging in additional preparedness actions, such as installing a storm shelter or purchasing a backup generator, would simply be cost prohibitive. As explained in Box 5.1, understanding *social vulnerability* is essential for emergency managers to improve preparedness in their communities.

Prioritizing preparedness requires emergency managers to involve the whole community (see Box 5.2), including individuals and households, businesses, volunteer groups, and others in building a *culture of preparedness*, which the Federal Emergency Management Agency (FEMA) has identified as its top strategic goal. To do this, "FEMA will focus on identifying ways to weave preparedness into people's everyday lives, connecting with individuals at the places they frequent, and incentivizing positive behavior..." (U.S. Department of Homeland Security 2018, p. 17). Recognizing the importance of culture is a critical step in prioritizing preparedness because it is a pervasive element of social life that envelops all of us. Culture provides us the language that we speak, and it embodies the norms and values that shape the way we view the world, our judgments about what is right and wrong, and ultimately how we behave. It is important, therefore, for emergency managers to understand culture and cultural diversity because it strongly influences the way in which people perceive risks and make decisions about preparing

BOX 5.1

LESSONS UNLEARNED: UNDERSTANDING SOCIAL VULNERABILITY TO IMPROVE PREPAREDNESS

As we have emphasized throughout this book, disasters are not equal opportunity events. Compared to others, some groups face greater exposure to environmental hazards, experience more severe impacts from disasters, and have greater difficulty recovering in the aftermath of those events. Researchers refer to these patterns as social vulnerability, and despite decades of research on this topic, many people in our communities remain at heightened risk (Thomas et al. 2013).

Recognizing social vulnerability and understanding its sources are crucial aspects of *cultural competency* and *sociocultural literacy*, which are essential attributes for emergency managers to possess if we are going to make meaningful progress toward better preparing the whole community for disasters.

Increasing their understanding of social vulnerability and their sensitivity toward those in greatest need should be a priority for all emergency managers. As stated in a recent book, "With each emergency and crisis, the lack of culturally respectable responses to diverse populations highlights the critical need for cultural competency education and training in higher education and practice" (Knox and Haupt 2020, p. 1). And as described in a report on *The Next Generation Emergency Management Core Competencies*, "emergency management professionals must understand the ways in which sociocultural factors contribute to population vulnerability" (Federal Emergency Management Agency [FEMA] Higher Education Program 2016, p. 4).

Over the years, researchers have identified numerous sources of social vulnerability, and by understanding what those are, emergency managers can significantly improve preparedness in their communities (Williams and Webb 2021). Poverty is a significant contributor to social vulnerability, and it explains why the vast majority of deaths occur in the poorest and least developed nations of the world (UNDRR 2016). Poverty also intersects with other factors, such as race and gender, to heighten people's vulnerability to disasters. For example, racial and ethnic minorities, particularly those with lower incomes, often face heightened risks from technological hazards such as hazardous materials sites (Bullard 1990). Minorities also suffer more severe impacts from all kinds of disasters, as reflected in the disproportionate deaths among African Americans in Hurricane Katrina in 2005 (Sharkey 2007). These alarming trends should tell us that increasing preparedness is vitally important to the safety and resilience of these communities.

Gender is also a source of social vulnerability, both before and after disasters (Llorente-Marrón et al. 2020). In the U.S., for example, an astounding 45.7% of single-parent, female-headed households with children under the age of six live below the poverty line (U.S. Census Bureau 2020, p. 14), making it virtually impossible for these households to afford taking preparedness actions. Age is another source of vulnerability, particularly for senior citizens who live alone, as was evidenced by their disproportionate deaths in the 1995 Chicago heat wave (Klinenberg 2002). Those living in nursing homes are also vulnerable, as revealed in the tragic deaths of 14 residents in a Florida nursing home in 2017 during Hurricane Irma, which underscores the critical importance of improving preparedness in these facilities (Gilmartin et al. 2019). At the other end of the age spectrum, children also face heightened vulnerability, as was vividly seen when a tornado destroyed an elementary school in Moore, Oklahoma, in 2013. But, at the same time, children can be important sources of resilience and should therefore be included in preparedness efforts (Fothergill and Peek 2015; Pfefferbaum, Pfefferbaum, and Van Horn 2018).

People with disabilities are also vulnerable to disasters, and it is imperative for emergency managers to consider their needs (Marceron and Rohrbeck 2019). Addressing the functional needs of those with disabilities requires emergency managers to consider such things as how they will communicate risk information to those with hearing, vision, or speech impairments, and how they can help ensure the safe evacuation and sheltering of those with mobility or sensory disabilities (ready.gov/disability).

Language can also be a source of social vulnerability, particularly for individuals with limited English proficiency (LEP) and in households where English is spoken as a second language (ESL; see Xiang, Gerber, and Zhang 2021). We know that disaster warnings and other risk communications are most effective when people are able to understand them and view them as coming from a credible source (see Chapter 7). Emergency managers must consider, then, how they will communicate with diverse audiences, which is challenging when you consider that in the Los Angeles area alone, more than 150 languages are spoken (U.S. Census Bureau 2009–2013 *American Community Survey*).

To best prepare our communities for disasters, we must also consider other vulnerabilities that may not immediately come to mind. Homeless people, for example, faced heightened exposure to the effects of disasters (Phillips 1996; Osborn, Every, and Richardson 2019). Emergency managers must therefore consider how they will communicate with the homeless in their communities to warn them of an impending disaster such as the severe ice storm that brought deadly low temperatures to Dallas, Texas, and other parts of the state in early 2021. Prison inmates are another vulnerable population that needs to be considered in disaster planning and preparedness (Gaillard and Navizet 2012; Purdum and Meyer 2020). In 2017, for example, thousands of inmates had to be evacuated from multiple Texas prisons during Hurricane Harvey.

Finally, we need to consider how we are going to prepare pets and livestock for disasters (Farmer and De Young 2019; De Young and Farmer 2021). Research has shown that, for example, people will sometimes choose not to go to a public shelter out of concern for their pets and not wanting to be separated from them. In more rural areas, including many of those in Texas impacted by Hurricane Harvey in 2017, livestock, such as cattle and horses, are especially vulnerable, particularly to widespread flooding, which can, of course, result in significant economic losses to ranchers.

Social vulnerability clearly impacts people's exposure to hazards, their experiences with disasters, and their capacity to prepare for future events. By developing a better understanding of the multiple sources of vulnerability, emergency managers can simultaneously enhance their own cultural competency and increase the level of disaster preparedness in their communities.

BOX 5.2

PREPAREDNESS AND THE WHOLE COMMUNITY

Recognizing that preparedness is a shared responsibility, it calls for the involvement everyone not just the government—in preparedness efforts. By working together, everyone can keep the nation safe from harm and resilient when struck by hazards, such as natural disasters, acts of terrorism, and pandemics.

Whole Community includes:

- Individuals and families, including those with access and functional needs
- Businesses
- Faith-based and community organizations
- Nonprofit groups
- Schools and academia
- Media outlets
- All levels of government, including state, local, tribal, territorial, and federal partners

The phrase "whole community" appears a lot in preparedness materials, as it is one of the guiding principles. It means two things:

1. Involving people in the development of the national preparedness documents.
2. Ensuring their roles and responsibilities are reflected in the content of the materials.

Source: https://www.fema.gov/glossary/whole-community, verbatim.

for disasters (Krüger et al. 2015; Webb 2018; Federal Emergency Management Agency 2019; Castañeda et al. 2020; Appleby-Arnold, Brockdorff, and Callus 2021).

Prioritizing preparedness and building a culture of preparedness is more important than ever before because the world is becoming a more hazardous place. Disasters are increasing in frequency and severity across the globe and new hazards are continually emerging. As recent events have shown us, communities must now prepare themselves for *compounding* disasters in which two or more events occur simultaneously or in rapid succession, such as hurricanes happening during the COVID-19 pandemic (U.S. Department of Homeland Security 2020a). We also must prepare ourselves for the *cascading* impacts of disasters in which the failure of one system causes ripple effects across other systems because of their interdependencies (U.S. Department of Homeland Security 2020b). In early 2021, for example, significant parts of Texas were severely impacted by an ice storm that crippled the state's power grid, and while residents may have been prepared for those outages, many were caught off guard by the loss of water that occurred when water treatment facilities could no longer operate due to the loss of electricity. In some places, communities must now prepare for hazards that were largely nonexistent in the past, as is the case in Oklahoma where induced seismicity (i.e., earthquakes), which is associated with hydraulic fracturing and wastewater reinjection, has become a prominent hazard (Wu, Greer, and Murphy 2020). As all these examples illustrate, the hazards we face are becoming more diverse and complex, and it is therefore important that we continue to embrace the all-hazards approach to emergency management (EM) and prepare ourselves for the widest range of possible threats.

Prioritizing preparedness is also important because it contributes significantly to *resilience*. As defined in Chapter 3, resilience refers to the ability of a social system (e.g., household, organization, or community) to anticipate, absorb, and bounce back from disruptions. In this context, disasters serve as the primary disruptions we are most concerned about, and getting ready for them is a critical first step toward achieving resilience. The next section of this chapter provides a definition of preparedness that emphasizes its role in enhancing response capacity, which is a defining characteristic of resilience; so, at its core, we can think of preparedness as being fundamentally concerned with promoting resilience.

5.3 DEFINING PREPAREDNESS

Preparedness is a central concept in disaster science and EM, and numerous definitions have been suggested over the years (Drabek 1986; Gillespie and Streeter 1987; Mileti 1999; Tierney, Lindell, and Perry 2001; Kirschenbaum 2002). *Preparedness* commonly refers to activities undertaken prior to the onset of a disaster to enhance the response capacities of individuals and households, organizations, communities, states, and nations. But what does it really mean to "enhance response capacities?"

At the most general level, *enhanced response capacity* refers to the ability of social units to accurately assess a hazard, realistically anticipate problems in the event of an actual disaster, and take precautionary measures to reduce impacts and ensure an efficient and effective response. We will discuss specific types of preparedness activities in the next section, but for now the general point is that we can dramatically improve our ability to respond to disasters by taking appropriate actions before they ever strike.

By defining preparedness in a way that emphasizes improving response capacities, we make an important assumption about disasters. Despite the best efforts of societies to mitigate natural and technological hazards, we are assuming in this chapter that *disasters will occur*. That is not to say that some disasters cannot be prevented or that mitigation efforts should be abandoned. Rather, by assuming that disasters will occur, we are simply acknowledging the reality of modern living and encouraging appropriate protective actions. Households, organizations, and communities must continue to devise effective means for protecting themselves against the threat of disaster.

It is important to remember that *preparedness is closely related to the other phases of emergency management*. It has already been noted that, for example, the primary goal of preparedness is to enhance response capacities so the relationship between preparedness and response is straightforward. Although less obvious, preparedness is also closely related to the mitigation and recovery phases. Drabek (1986, p. 21), for example, defines mitigation as "purposive acts designed toward the elimination of, reduction in probability of, or reduction of the effects of potential disasters," while preparedness activities "are predicated on the assumption that disasters of various forms will occur, but that their negative consequences may be…mitigated." Preparedness is also relevant to the recovery phase, in the sense that developing effective short- and long-term recovery plans prior to a disaster can facilitate a community's return to normalcy after an event has occurred.

5.4 TYPES AND LEVELS OF PREPAREDNESS ACTIVITIES

Preparedness can involve a range of activities, whether you are an individual, a member of a household unit, or responsible in some way for a larger organization or the broader community. As Figure 5.1 depicts, activities focus on securing life safety, protecting property and critical infrastructure systems, ensuring continuity of business operations, and educating the public about hazards and disasters. While each of us must accept some degree of responsibility for personal preparedness, as we will learn later, doing so may require support and assistance. Participating in neighborhood and community preparedness activities helps our neighbors and also allows them to help us if a disaster strikes. Furthermore, such efforts reduce the burdens of emergency responders, emergency managers, and community officials.

So, how prepared are we for disasters? The simple answer is: not very. But some individuals and households are more prepared than others; some organizations have more experience with disasters and are thus better equipped to respond; and some communities devote greater resources to EM and disaster preparedness than others. For states and nations, the picture is more complex and involves vast disparities in preparedness levels across countries and around the globe.

5.4.1 Individuals and Households

Individual and household preparedness activities are often measured by administering surveys that contain checklists of actions people may take prior to a disaster, such as (Tierney et al. 2001, p. 34):

* Obtaining disaster-related information.
* Attending meetings to learn about disaster preparedness.
* Purchasing food and water.
* Storing a flashlight, radio, batteries, and a first aid kit.
* Learning first aid.

FIGURE 5.1 Types of Preparedness Activities

- Developing and practicing a family emergency plan.
- Bracing furniture (in earthquake-prone areas), installing shutters (in hurricane-prone areas), or a safe room or storm cellar (in tornado-prone areas).
- Purchasing hazard-specific insurance.

As you can see from this list, individuals and households can take many steps to prepare for disasters. In light of all these possibilities, some people may become confused as to what exactly they should do to prepare. To simplify and clarify disaster preparation for the general public, the FEMA advises them to (1) get a disaster kit, (2) make a plan, and (3) be informed (www. ready.gov). As you can see in Box 5.3, FEMA recommends stocking disaster kits with three days' worth of basic provisions and other items, many of which appear on the above list.

Unfortunately, several decades of research on individual and household preparedness shows that overall preparedness levels remain alarmingly low even in disaster-prone regions. In a comprehensive review of preparedness studies conducted after the 1970s, Tierney et al. (2001) found that most respondents in survey after survey reported that they had not undertaken a single preparedness measure, and most of those studies were conducted in areas with high seismic activity. In another study, Kapucu (2008) found a similar pattern of underpreparedness among households in hurricane-prone Florida, with only 8% of respondents maintaining disaster supply kits stocked with enough basic provisions to shelter in place for three days (the FEMA recommendation).

Despite low, overall preparedness, variation does exist among households (Becker, Paton, and Johnston 2014; Martins et al. 2018). Preparedness levels tend to be higher among those with previous disaster experience and those who are more knowledgeable about hazards and perceive the risk of a disaster as relatively high in the short term. Additionally, higher socioeconomic status and levels of education, the presence of children, and home ownership all contribute to higher levels of readiness. Conversely, people with low incomes, racial and ethnic minorities, and renters tend to be less prepared (Mileti 1999; Tierney et al. 2001). Some preparedness activities are very costly, and even those that are relatively affordable to some may be cost-prohibitive to others. Thus, a major challenge for emergency managers is devising strategies to increase the preparedness levels of all the households in their communities.

5.4.2 Organizations

For organizations, including the public (government), private (business), and nonprofit sectors, typical preparedness checklists include many of the same activities that apply to households and some additional measures, such as (Webb, Tierney, and Dahlhamer 2000, p. 84):

- Talking to employees about disaster preparedness.
- Conducting drills and exercises.
- Receiving specialized training.
- Developing relocation plans.
- Obtaining an emergency generator.
- Purchasing business interruption insurance.

BOX 5.3

PREPAREDNESS RECOMMENDATIONS

When preparing for a possible emergency situation, think first about the basics of survival: fresh water, food, clean air, and warmth.

Recommended Items to Include in Basic Emergency Supply Kit

- Water (one gallon per person per day for at least three days) for drinking and sanitation
- Non-perishable food (at least three-day supply)
- Battery-powered or hand crank radio and a NOAA Weather Radio with tone alert and extra batteries for both
- Flashlight and extra batteries
- First aid kit
- Whistle to signal for help
- Dust mask to help filter contaminated air, plastic sheeting, and duct tape to shelter in place
- Moist towelettes, garbage bags, and plastic ties for personal sanitation
- Wrench or pliers to turn off utilities
- Can opener (if kit contains canned food)
- Local maps
- Cell phone with chargers

Additional Items to Consider Adding to Emergency Supply Kit

- Masks (for everyone ages two and above), soap, hand sanitizer, disinfecting wipes
- Prescription and nonprescription medications
- Prescription eyeglasses and contact lens solution
- Infant formula and diapers
- Pet food and extra water for pet
- Important family documents such as copies of insurance policies, identification, and bank account records in a waterproof, portable container
- Cash or traveler's checks and change
- Sleeping bag or warm blanket for each person
- Complete change of clothing appropriate for your climate and sturdy shoes
- Fire extinguisher
- Matches in waterproof container
- Feminine supplies and personal hygiene items
- Mess kits, paper cups, plates and plastic utensils, paper towels
- Paper and pencil
- Books, games, puzzles, and other activities for children

Source: www.ready.gov/kit.

As with households, organizations also vary in the degree to which they are prepared for disasters. Among public sector (i.e., governmental) organizations, for example, preparedness efforts of local EM agencies have improved significantly over the years (Wenger, Quarantelli, and Dynes 1986). As Mileti (1999) notes, these agencies are most effective when preparedness activities become integrated into daily operations of local government, are coordinated with other community organizations, and offer realistic disaster planning (see Chapter 6) based on how organizations and people actually respond to disasters (see Chapter 7). Police and fire departments and emergency medical service (EMS) units also devote significant efforts to preparing for disasters, but researchers have identified a number of problems in the approaches these organizations take around preparedness (Quarantelli 1983; Wenger, Quarantelli, and Dynes 1989; Mileti 1999; Tierney et al. 2001). Most notably, they tend to plan and prepare for disasters internally and in isolation from other community organizations, and they often fail to appreciate the significant difference between everyday emergencies and disasters. As a result, they often assume that disasters can be handled by simply expanding normal emergency procedures and fail to prepare at an appropriate scale.

Organizations in the private sector (i.e., businesses) are far less prepared than their public sector counterparts. Based on large-scale mail surveys of business owners in Tennessee, Iowa, California, and Florida, Webb et al. (2000) reported that when faced with a variety of hazards, such as floods, hurricanes, and earthquakes, business owners do very little preparation. In response to a checklist of 15 possible preparedness activities, business owners on average reported engaging in only four and the most common was obtaining first aid supplies. While such safety steps are certainly important, they do little to ensure operational continuity, continued profitability, and long-term recovery and survival. As we will see in Chapters 8 (Recovery) and 10 (Public and Private Sectors), businesses can play a vital role in a community's response to and recovery from a disaster.

5.4.3 Communities

Finally, at the community level of analysis, typical preparedness actions include many of the same organizational-level activities and some additional ones, including (Tierney et al. 2001, p. 27):

- Testing sirens, emergency alert, and other warning systems.
- Conducting educational programs and distributing disaster-related information.
- Conducting multi-organizational drills and exercises.
- Establishing mutual aid agreements with surrounding communities.
- Maintaining an emergency operations center.
- Conducting a hazard identification and risk analysis.

As you can see from the lists of activities for organizations and communities, drills and exercises are fairly common. However, as with developing disaster plans (discussed in detail in Chapter 6), simply participating in a drill or exercise does not guarantee success when a disaster strikes. Disaster drills and exercises are most effective as preparedness tools when they are based on:

- Realistic scenarios, including accurate assumptions about disaster-induced demands, resource shortages, and communication difficulties.
- Accurate assumptions about how people and organizations respond to disasters rather than myths of disaster (see Chapter 7).
- Meaningful involvement rather than ritualistic, symbolic, or mandated participation.
- Integration of multiple organizations and levels of government with citizen participants.
- Recognition that disasters do not always follow plans and often require participants to think creatively and improvise to solve unanticipated problems.

5.5 FACTORS INFLUENCING LEVELS OF PREPAREDNESS

In this section, we will find that preparedness is more than an issue of personal responsibility. We will uncover factors that influence how much and how effectively people prepare for disasters. Before reading this section, you might refer to Box 5.3 to see how well you have prepared for a disaster. How would you grade yourself in terms of personal preparedness? Next, consider each factor explained vis-à-vis your own level of preparedness. Do they ring true?

5.5.1 Previous Disaster Experience

Survivors of a previous disaster are far more likely to prepare for another even if the first one affected them only indirectly. Watching the tragedy of Hurricane Katrina unfold prompted a massive evacuation when Hurricane Rita threatened Texas a few weeks later. For individuals and households, the positive effect of a recent experience with disaster on future preparedness is firmly established in the research literature (Tierney et al. 2001). Past disaster experiences also stimulate organizational preparedness, including the private sector (Dahlhamer and D'Souza 1997). At the community level, repeated threats generate "local wisdom" that enhances the capacity to respond when disasters strike (Drabek 2010, p. 66).

Previous disaster experience tends to increase preparedness levels for several reasons. First, by witnessing a disaster, people and organizations develop *heightened hazard awareness and risk perception* that is positively associated with preparedness. Second, on the basis of past experience, people and organizations develop a more realistic understanding of what happens in a disaster and are thus more likely to take proactive measures to prevent or minimize potential problems from future disasters. Finally, at the community level, previous disaster experiences can contribute to the formation of what is called a *disaster subculture* of people and organizations that are extremely familiar with a threat and know what to do in a disaster (Drabek 2010). Think, for example, about "tornado alley," earthquake threats in California, and hurricane season in Florida.

While disaster subcultures often exhibit resilience in the aftermath of a disaster, they can also lead to *complacency and inaction*. As Drabek (2010, p. 67) suggests, certain "elements of the subculture … neutralize adaptive responses." He mentions hurricane parties at which people gather to "ride out" a storm despite evacuation warnings of public officials. Why do people who know better choose to stay? One reason may be that their experiences with a previous disaster were less traumatic and difficult than expected or possibly even positive. They may develop a *false sense of confidence* toward future disasters. Additionally, with the threat of a disaster always lingering in the background but usually not materializing, people tend to *normalize risk* and assume a disaster will not occur. As we will see in the next section, risk perception is an important influence on preparedness levels.

5.5.2 Risk Perception

Anyone who has watched driver education films and then ignored speed limits or traffic signs understands immediately that risk is not always respected. "It won't happen here … or to me" is a common response of people questioned about their own risks. With so many risks associated with modern living, we constantly judge what is safe and what is not. In making those judgments, we almost never calculate the statistical probabilities of illness, injury, or death. Instead, we draw on past experiences, pay vague attention to the warnings of experts, and sometimes consciously decide to take our chances. Think about the number of people who still smoke cigarettes despite their proven deleterious health effects and drivers who refuse to buckle up even when confronted with the prospects of traffic tickets, property damage, injury, or death in an accident.

Smoking and driving without a seat belt are examples of risky behaviors that present reasonably high chances of causing negative impacts. How do we act toward risks that have much lower chances of happening? Consider disasters, commonly called *low-probability/high-consequence events*. They are not nearly as common as other types of threats but have the potential to produce devastating effects. Thus, a major challenge for emergency managers is convincing a skeptical public, budget-strapped leaders, and overextended division heads and directors in local government to spend time and money to prepare for something that may not ever happen. People and organizations are much more likely to prepare when they perceive a risk as highly likely in the short term (Tierney et al. 2001).

Fortunately, research suggests that emergency managers can influence risk perceptions and promote greater levels of preparedness in their communities via effective risk communication (Faupel, Kelley, and Petee 1992; Mileti 1999; Tierney et al. 2001). Risk communication is intended to educate people and organizations about the hazards they face, inform them about risks and likelihoods that the hazards will produce disasters, and persuade them to take appropriate measures to protect themselves and better meet the challenges resulting from disasters. Risk communication, including educational campaigns to raise hazard awareness, is most effective when it is delivered through multiple channels, consistent across the channels, details the nature of threats and their possible impacts, specific about what people and organizations can do to protect themselves, and perceived as coming from credible sources (Mileti and Fitzpatrick 1993). As we will see in Chapter 7, issuing disaster warnings is a specific risk communication used when a disaster is imminent or has already begun. In this chapter, we are referring to ongoing risk communication utilized during normal times.

5.6 PREPAREDNESS INITIATIVES AT STATE, NATIONAL, AND INTERNATIONAL LEVELS

Earlier in this chapter, we discussed levels of preparedness at the household, organizational, and community levels, and we pointed out that preparedness levels tend to be low but with variations. We also identified various factors, including risk perception, previous disaster experience, and others, that influence preparedness levels. In this section we take a higher-level view and provide examples of preparedness initiatives at the state, national, and international levels. Our goal is not to measure how much various states and nations are doing, but instead to gain a sense of what can be and is being done to prepare for disasters beyond the household and community levels.

5.6.1 Examples of State-Level Preparedness Initiatives

Preparedness initiatives at the state and national levels typically involve educational campaigns, large-scale drills and exercises, and the development of disaster warning systems. A good example of a state-level educational campaign is the *Ready Oklahoma* campaign administered by the Oklahoma Office of Homeland Security (https://www.ok.gov/homeland/Ready_Oklahoma/index.html). This program urges individuals and households, organizations, neighborhoods, and businesses to prepare for all kinds of disasters. The activities it recommends are similar to those described in the checklists earlier in this chapter and consistent with the recommendations of FEMA's *Ready.gov* campaign mentioned earlier and described below in more detail. Importantly, specific information is provided for the elderly, those with disabilities, pet owners, and businesses. In other words, this campaign addresses the issues raised in this chapter about social vulnerability.

Another example of a state-level preparedness initiative is the *Great ShakeOut* earthquake drill campaign that started in California but has since widened its reach (http://www. shakeout.org). This is an earthquake drill that aims to educate the public about earthquakes and how to prepare for them. As part of the drill, people are instructed to "drop, cover, and hold on," and practice how they would protect themselves in a real earthquake. In 2008, a shakeout drill was conducted in Southern California and the program was expanded in 2009 to include all 58 counties in California. That year, 6.9 million people participated in the drill, and in 2010, there were 7.9 million participants. The drill has been extended even further to include other countries, and in 2020 more than 29 million people worldwide registered to participate.

5.6.2 Examples of National-Level Preparedness Initiatives

Preparedness initiatives at the national level include FEMA's *Ready.gov* and its *National Exercise Program* (NEP). *Ready.gov* is an educational campaign for encouraging individuals, households, organizations, and communities to prepare for disasters. The campaign provides vast amounts of information on its website, including specific information for children, the elderly, the disabled, military families, pet owners, and businesses. Importantly, the campaign recognizes the need to address the special needs of populations at risk.

Since 2000, FEMA has conducted annual exercises to assess response capabilities and identify problems of intergovernmental coordination in catastrophic scenarios. In 2007, these Tier I national-level exercises (NLEs), formerly known as TOPOFF due to the involvement of top officials from various federal agencies, became part of the NEP. The primary purpose of the NEP is to coordinate federal, state, and regional exercise activities. In the past, NLEs have been based on simulated large-scale terrorist attacks. The NLE 2020 was intended to be a two-year effort focused on cybersecurity, and while some preliminary workshops and other activities had already been held, the remainder of the exercise was suspended due to FEMA's need to prioritize its response to the COVID-19 pandemic. You can find more information at https://www.fema.gov/emergency-managers/national-preparedness/exercises/national-level-exercise.

The most significant attempt to improve disaster preparedness at the national level in the U.S. was the establishment of the National Preparedness Goal. On March 30, 2011, President Barack Obama issued Presidential Policy Directive/PPD-8: National Preparedness, which directed the Secretary of Homeland Security to establish a National Preparedness Goal and identify core capabilities needed to achieve that goal. The purpose of the Goal is to achieve "A secure and resilient Nation with the capabilities across the whole community to prevent, protect against, mitigate, respond to, and recover from the threats and hazards that pose the greatest risk" (U.S. Department of Homeland Security 2011, p. 1). In addition to directing Department of Homeland Security (DHS) to establish a goal and identify core capabilities needed to achieve the goal, PPD-8 also requires DHS to monitor the nation's progress toward achieving the goal and to publish the results in an annual report. According to the 2020 *National Preparedness Report*, the nation continues to make progress in the area of disaster preparedness; but there are areas where improvement is needed, particularly in terms of dealing with catastrophic, systemic, and emerging risks, such as global pandemics, cyberthreats, and other potential threats that are capable of producing widespread damage and resulting in cascading failures across multiple critical infrastructure systems (U.S. Department of Homeland Security 2020b).

5.6.3 Examples of International Preparedness Initiatives

Although we tend to think primarily about disasters that impact our own local communities, catastrophic events around the world, including the 2010 earthquake in Haiti, the 2011 tsunami in Japan, and many others in more recent years, have dramatically underscored the need to think about disasters on a global scale. As discussed in this text, the most impoverished and least developed nations in the world suffer the harshest impacts of disasters, including exorbitant financial costs, widespread physical damage, and massive death tolls. Given their extreme poverty under ordinary circumstances, these same nations face the greatest challenges in responding to disasters when they occur and desperately need help from the international community.

As Wachtendorf (2000) suggests, we also need to think about disasters in international terms because they sometimes defy national boundaries. For example, the 2004 tsunami impacted several countries in the region, and there have been many occasions on which floods have simultaneously impacted multiple countries in Western Europe. Cities in both the U.S. and Canada have also dealt with simultaneous flooding, and in

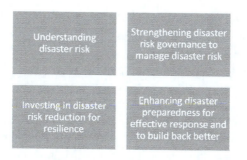

FIGURE 5.2 Priorities for Action in the Sendai Framework for Disaster Risk Reduction, 2015–2030

these events, cooperation and coordination between governments is critical and may be facilitated through pre-disaster preparedness efforts. Several studies have examined international preparedness levels in numerous countries, including Sweden, Turkey, New Zealand, and Japan (Karanci, Askit, and Dirik 2005; Paton et al. 2010; Guldåker, Eriksson, and Kristofersson 2015).

Recognizing the uneven impacts of disasters across the globe and the possibility of transnational events, the UN launched the *International Strategy for Disaster Reduction* in 2000, and it now maintains the UN Office of Disaster Risk Reduction. The primary aim of disaster risk reduction is to reduce disaster losses and build resilient nations by getting key stakeholders and decision makers to shift their focus from cleaning up after disasters to working to prevent them from occurring in the first place. Its activities include coordinating international disaster relief efforts, advocating for greater investment in disaster reduction activities, conducting educational campaigns about disasters and risk reduction measures, organizing global conferences, publishing reports on disasters across the globe, and encouraging nations to implement the Sendai Framework for Disaster Risk Reduction 2015–2030 (UNDRR 2019). As shown in Figure 5.2, this international framework consists of four major priorities for action, one of which is to enhance disaster preparedness for effective response and building back better in recovery.

5.7 WORKING AND VOLUNTEERING IN PREPAREDNESS

In reality, we all need to work and volunteer to achieve preparedness. It is not sufficient to be the local emergency manager who focuses on preparedness. That individual needs to be a leader who motivates others to work in the area. The emergency manager, for example, must reach out to and involve the media in crafting and disseminating preparedness messages and utilize social media to reach the widest possible audience (Wukich 2019). Other agencies also bear responsibilities for preparedness.

If a blizzard threatens an area, transportation agencies must inform the public of routes likely to close so that lives can be saved. Physicians and health care providers should ask their patients how prepared they are and distribute information to them. They can even use preparedness checklists as part of annual physical examinations. Teachers need to prepare their students for untoward events so that they respond as directed when situations warrant. Elected officials must inform themselves so that they can reach out to their constituents and encourage proper advance preparation; they bear a special responsibility for the most vulnerable among us who need protection.

Health care centers also employ preparedness experts. For example, hospitals sometimes advertise positions of emergency preparedness coordinators who will work in collaboration across the hospital and the community, design exercises and events, conduct training, and ensure continuity of operations for the hospital and its patients. These positions typically accept applications from individuals with degrees in nursing, biology, public health, environmental health, or EM, and require some experience in emergency preparedness and planning.

Students often ask us how to get that experience. Several routes open that door. One is internship experience in an agency that works on emergency preparedness. Another route is working at an entry-level job to gain experience and earn "boots on the ground" experience with preparedness, planning, training, and exercising. A final route emerges through volunteer efforts. In the U.S., FEMA has partnered with the AmeriCorps National Civilian Community Corps (NCCC) program and created FEMA Corps, which is a team-based service program that gives 18–24 years old participants the opportunity to serve communities impacted by disasters. You can learn more about this program at https://www.fema.gov/careers/position-types/peace-corps-americorps.

You do not have to join a group to become more involved in preparedness. Start with your own family and neighborhood (Andrews 2001). Host a neighborhood meeting or picnic and invite the fire department and EM agency to visit and distribute preparedness materials. Since the most trusted information comes from social networks, use yours to prepare those around you. Canvass your community and assess what is needed. Invite professionals to create safety programs for your neighborhood. Use your school club to launch a preparedness effort directed at elderly residents with disabilities or purchase resources for local schools. Gaining experience in preparedness can be as easy as knocking on your neighbor's door with a checklist from this textbook. Preparedness starts at home.

***

SUMMARY

In this chapter, we discussed both the good news and the bad news about disaster preparedness. The bad news, of course, is that disaster preparedness levels are alarmingly low for individuals and households, organizations, communities, states, and nations. Moreover, preparedness levels vary in large part because some people, households, and even nations simply do not have the resources to adequately prepare. As a result, when disasters occur they impact some groups much more harshly than others, which means we need to do more to address the preparedness needs of those most vulnerable.

The good news about preparedness is that steps can be taken to enhance readiness for disasters. Many of the activities described in this chapter are simple and relatively inexpensive. We can greatly increase the number of people taking those actions through effective educational campaigns like the ones described in this chapter, by understanding sources of social vulnerability, and by providing assistance when necessary. While disaster preparedness is in some sense a personal responsibility, it is also a shared, collective responsibility. By increasing readiness at all levels, from individuals and households to entire nations, we can greatly improve public safety and dramatically enhance the resilience of our communities to disasters.

Discussion Questions

1. What is the relationship between preparedness and resilience? How does preparedness contribute to resilience? What can we do as individuals and as emergency managers to promote greater resilience?
2. What is a culture of preparedness? Why is culture important in the context of disasters? How can we begin to build a culture of preparedness?
3. Why is all-hazards EM important for preparedness? What are some examples of new and emerging hazards that we will need to better prepare ourselves for in the future?
4. How does social vulnerability affect preparedness? What are some examples of socially vulnerable groups? What can you do as an emergency manager to assist them in preparing?

Summary Questions

1. What is the primary purpose of preparedness?
2. What are the different types of preparedness?
3. When was the National Preparedness Goal established and what is its major purpose?
4. What is the Sendai Framework and what are its major priorities for action?

REFERENCES

Andrews, Jill H. 2001. "Safe in the 'Hood: Earthquake Preparedness in Midcity Los Angeles." *Natural Hazards Review* 2(1): 2–11.

Appleby-Arnold, Sandra, Noellie Brockdorff, and Celia Callus. 2021. "Developing a "Culture of Disaster Preparedness": The Citizens' View." *International Journal of Disaster Risk Reduction* 56: 102133 ISSN 2212-4209 https://doi.org/10.1016/j.ijdrr.2021.102133.

Becker, Julia, Douglas Paton, and David Johnston. 2014. "Societal Influences on Earthquake Information Meaning-Making and Household Preparedness." *International Journal of Mass Emergencies and Disasters* 32(2): 317–352.

Bullard, Robert D. 1990. *Dumping in Dixie: Race, Class, and Environmental Quality.* Boulder, CO: Westview Press.

Castañeda, Javiera V., Nicolas C. Bronfman, Pamela C. Cisernas, and Paula B. Repetto. 2020. "Understanding the Culture of Natural Disaster Preparedness: Exploring the Effect of Experience and Sociodemographic Predictors." *Natural Hazards* 103: 1881–1904.

Dahlhamer, James M. and Melvin J. D'Souza. 1997. "Determinants of Business Disaster Preparedness in Two U. S. Metropolitan Areas." *International Journal of Mass Emergencies and Disasters* 15: 265–281.

De Young, Sarah E. and Ashley K. Farmer. 2021. *All Creatures Safe and Sound: The Social Landscape of Pets in Disasters*. Philadelphia, PA: Temple University Press.

Drabek, Thomas E. 1986. *Human System Responses to Disaster: An Inventory of Sociological Findings*. New York: Springer-Verlag.

Drabek, Thomas E. 2010. *The Human Side of Disaster*. Boca Raton, FL: CRC Press.

Farmer, Ashley and Sarah De Young. 2019. "The Pets of Hurricane Matthew: Evacuation and Sheltering with Companion Animals." *Anthrozoös* 32: 419–433.

Faupel, Charles E., Susan P. Kelley, and Thomas Petee. 1992. "The Impact of Disaster Education on Household Preparedness for Hurricane Hugo." *International Journal of Mass Emergencies and Disasters* 10(1): 5–24.

Federal Emergency Management Agency. 2019. *Building Cultures of Preparedness: A Report for the Emergency Management Higher Education Community*. Washington, DC: FEMA.

FEMA Higher Education Program. 2016. *The Next Generation Emergency Management Core Competencies*. Emmittsburg, MD: FEMA Higher Education Program.

Fothergill, Alice and Lori Peek. 2015. *Children of Katrina*. Austin: University of Texas Press.

Gaillard, J. C. and Fanny Navizet. 2012. "Prisons, Prisoners and Disaster." *International Journal of Disaster Risk Reduction* 1: 33–43.

Gilmartin, Mattia J., Wanda Raby Spurlock, Nicoda Foster, and Samir K. Sinha. 2019. "Improving Disaster Preparedness, Response and Recovery for Older Adults." *Geriatric Nursing* 40(4): 445–447.

Gillespie, David F. and Calvin L. Streeter. 1987. "Conceptualizing and Measuring Disaster Preparedness." *International Journal of Mass Emergencies and Disasters* 5: 155–176.

Guldåker, Nicklas, Kerstin Eriksson, and Tuija Nieminen Kristofersson. 2015. "Preventing and Preparing for Disasters—The Role of a Swedish Local Emergent Citizen Group." *International Journal of Mass Emergencies and Disasters* 33(3): 360–387.

Kapucu, Naim. 2008. "Culture of Preparedness: Household Disaster Preparedness." *Disaster Prevention and Management* 17(4): 526–535.

Karanci, Ayse Nuray, Bahattin Askit, and Gulay Dirik. 2005. "Impact of a Community Disaster Awareness Training Program in Turkey: Does It Influence Hazard-Related Cognitions and Preparedness Behaviors." *Social Behavior and Personality* 33: 243–258.

Kirschenbaum, Alan. 2002. "Disaster Preparedness: A Conceptual and Empirical Reevaluation." *International Journal of Mass Emergencies and Disasters* 20(1): 5–28.

Klinenberg, Eric. 2002. *Heat Wave: A Social Autopsy of Disaster in Chicago*. Chicago: University of Chicago Press.

Knox, Claire Connolly and Brittany "Brie" Haupt, eds. 2020. *Cultural Competency for Emergency and Crisis Management*. New York: Routledge.

Krüger, F., Bankoff, G., Cannon, T., Orlowski, B., and Schipper, L. F. (2015). *Cultures and Disasters: Understanding Cultural Framings in Disaster Risk Reduction*. London: Routledge.

Llorente-Marrón, Mar, Montserrat Díaz-Fernández, Paz Méndez-Rodríguez, and Rosario González Arias. 2020. "Social Vulnerability, Gender and Disasters: The Case of Haiti in 2010." *Sustainability* 12(9): 3574. http://dx.doi.org/10.3390/su12093574.

Marceron, Jennifer E. and Cynthia A. Rohrbeck. 2019. "Disability and Disasters: The Role of Self-Efficacy in Emergency Preparedness." *Psychology, Health & Medicine* 24(1): 83–93.

Martins, V. Nuno, Hans M. Louis-Charles, Joanne Nigg, James Kendra, and Sarah Sisco. 2018. "Household Disaster Preparedness in New York City before Superstorm Sandy: Findings and Recommendations." *Journal of Homeland Security and Emergency Management* 15(4). https://doi.org/10.1515/jhsem-2017-0002.

Mileti, Dennis. 1999. *Disasters by Design*. Washington, DC: Joseph Henry Press.

Mileti, Dennis and Colleen Fitzpatrick. 1993. *The Great Earthquake Experiment: Risk Communication and Public Action*. Boulder, CO: Westview Press.

Osborn, Elizabeth, Danielle Every, and John Richardson. 2019. "Disaster Preparedness: Services for People Experiencing Homelessness and the Pressure-Cooker Response." *Australian Journal of Emergency Management* 34(1): 58–64.

Paton, Douglas, Robert Bajek, Norio Okada, and David McIvor. 2010. "Predicting Community Earthquake Preparedness: A Cross-Cultural Comparison of Japan and New Zealand." *Natural Hazards* 54(3): 765–781.

Pfefferbaum, Betty, Rose L. Pfefferbaum, and Richard L. Van Horn. 2018. "Involving Children in Disaster Risk Reduction: The Importance of Participation." *European Journal of Psychotraumatology* 9(sup2), doi: 10.1080/20008198.2018.1425577.

Phillips, Brenda D. 1996. "Homelessness and the Social Construction of Places: The Loma Prieta Earthquake." *Humanity and Society* 19(4): 94–101.

Purdum, J. Carlee and Michelle A. Meyer. 2020. "Prisoner Labor throughout the Life Cycle of Disasters." *Risks. Hazards & Crisis in Public Policy* 11: 296–319.

Quarantelli, E. L. 1983. *Delivery of Emergency Medical Services in Disasters: Assumptions and Realities*. New York: Irvington Publishers.

Sharkey, Patrick. 2007. "Survival and Death in New Orleans." *Journal of Black Studies* 37(4): 482–501.

Stein, Robert, Birnur Buzcu-Guven, Leonardo Dueñas-Osorio, and Devika Subramanian. 2014. "The Private and Social Benefits of Preparing for Natural Disasters." *International Journal of Mass Emergencies and Disasters* 32(3): 459–483.

Thomas, Deborah S. K., Brenda D. Phillips, William E. Lovekamp, and Alice Fothergill, eds. 2013. *Social Vulnerability to Disasters*, 2nd ed. Boca Raton, FL: CRC Press.

Tierney, Kathleen J., Michael K. Lindell, and Ronald W. Perry. 2001. *Facing the Unexpected*. Washington, DC: Joseph Henry Press.

UNDRR. 2016. *Poverty and Death: Disaster Mortality, 1996–2015*. Geneva, Switzerland: United Nations Office for Disaster Risk Reduction.

UNDRR. 2019. *Global Assessment Report on Disaster Risk Reduction*. Geneva, Switzerland: United Nations Office for Disaster Risk Reduction.

U.S. Census Bureau. *2009–2013 American Community Survey*. Washington, DC: U.S. Census Bureau.

U.S. Census Bureau. 2020. *Income and Poverty in the United States: 2019*. Washington, DC: U.S. Government Publishing Office.

U.S. Department of Homeland Security. 2011. *National Preparedness Goal*, 1st ed. Washington, DC: U.S. Department of Homeland Security.

U.S. Department of Homeland Security. 2018. *2018–2022 Strategic Plan, Federal Emergency Management Agency*. Washington, DC: U.S. Department of Homeland Security.

U.S. Department of Homeland Security. 2020a. *COVID-19 Pandemic Operational Guidance for the 2020 Hurricane Season*. Washington, DC: U.S. Department of Homeland Security.

U.S. Department of Homeland Security. 2020b. *2020 National Preparedness Report*. Washington, DC: U.S. Department of Homeland Security.

Wachtendorf, Tricia. 2000. "When Disasters Defy Borders: What We Can Learn from the Red River Flood about Transnational Disasters." *Australian Journal of Emergency Management* 15(3): 36–41.

Webb, Gary R. 2018. "The Cultural Turn in Disaster Research: Understanding Resilience and Vulnerability through the Lens of Culture." Pp. 109–121 in *Handbook of Disaster Research*, 2nd ed., eds. Havidan Rodriguez, William Donner, and Joseph E. Trainor. Switzerland: Springer.

Webb, Gary R., Kathleen J. Tierney, and James M. Dahlhamer. 2000. "Businesses and Disasters: Empirical Patterns and Unanswered Questions." *Natural Hazards Review* 1(2): 83–90.

Wenger, Dennis E., E. L. Quarantelli, and Russell R. Dynes. 1986. *Disaster Analysis: Local Emergency Management Offices and Arrangements*. Newark: University of Delaware, Disaster Research Center. Final Project Report No. 34.

Wenger, Dennis E., E. L. Quarantelli, and Russell R. Dynes 1989. *Disaster Analysis: Police and Fire Departments*. Newark: University of Delaware, Disaster Research Center. Final Project Report No. 37.

Williams, Brian D. and Gary R. Webb. 2021. "Social Vulnerability and Disaster: Understanding the Perspectives of Practitioners." *Disasters* 45: 278–295.

Wu, Hao-Che, Alex Greer, and Haley Murphy. 2020. "Perceived Stakeholder Information Credibility and Hazard Adjustments: A Case of Induced Seismic Activities in Oklahoma." *Natural Hazards Review* 21(3): 04020017.

Wukich, Clayton. 2019. "Preparing for Disaster: Social Media Use for Household, Organizational, and Community Preparedness." *Risk, Hazards & Crisis in Public Policy* 10: 233–260.

Xiang, Tianyi, Brian J. Gerber, and Fengxiu Zhang. 2021. "Language Access in Emergency and Disaster Preparedness: An Assessment of Local Government "Whole Community" Efforts in the United States." *International Journal of Disaster Risk Reduction* 55: 102072, ISSN 2212-4209, https://doi.org/10.1016/j.ijdrr.2021.102072.

RESOURCES

- The best place to start learning more about disaster preparedness for individuals, households, and businesses in the U.S. is www.ready.gov.
- To learn more about disasters internationally, both in terms of their impacts and efforts to better prepare for them, visit the UN Office for Disaster Risk Reduction at www.undrr.org.
- More information on the role of nonprofit, voluntary organizations in preparing for disasters can be found on the National Voluntary Associations Active in Disaster website at www.nvoad.org.

CHAPTER 6

Planning

CHAPTER OBJECTIVES

Upon completing this chapter, students should be able to:

- Recognize that planning is a process.
- Discover that the planning process creates important social networks.
- Understand why long paper documents or boilerplate documents fail.
- Explain why evidence-based planning works.
- Describe the planning process for:
  - Households
  - Private and Voluntary Organizations
  - Governments
  - Cross-National Events
- Understand the role of Federal guidance in disaster planning.

KEY TERMS

- Business Continuity Planning
- Community-Based Planning
- Household Planning
- National Incident Management System
- National Response Framework
- Planning Process
- Social Networks/Social Capital
- Whole Community Planning

6.1 INTRODUCTION

In Chapter 5, we discussed what preparedness means, why preparedness is important, who prepares and does not prepare, and how preparedness works. This chapter explains how individuals, groups, and organizations should plan for disasters. A few

DOI: 10.4324/9781003021919-8

main themes run throughout this chapter. First, rather than considering a paper plan as an end product, planning should be a dynamic, continually evolving and improving, and participatory process among stakeholders and representatives at all relevant levels. Second, many planning tools can be found through publicly available sources to assist with developing various kinds of plans, including response, recovery, mitigation, and business continuity plans. Content also exists to help emergency managers plan for specific issues (e.g., socially vulnerable populations, pets, livestock, and families). For example, U.S. Federal planning documents include Comprehensive Preparedness Guide (CPG) 101, which will be discussed in this chapter. This chapter also provides an overview of how plans develop through stakeholder participation, including the importance of integrating research findings.

Planning must be undertaken by professional emergency managers using evidence-based best practices in order to serve their constituents well. However, consider the problems revealed following the 2010 Deep Horizon oil disaster in the Gulf of Mexico (CBSNEWS 2010; National Commission on the BP Deepwater Horizon Oil Spill and Offshore Drilling 2011). As the disaster unfolded, a BP representative stated that a plan was in place and that the proper authority had approved the plan (Fitzgerald 2010). In contrast, the Presidential Commission studying the aftermath of the event described the disaster planning process in the following manner (National Commission on the BP Deepwater Horizon Oil Spill and Offshore Drilling 2011, p.133):

> If BP's response capacity was underwhelming, some aspects of its response plan were embarrassing. In the plan, BP had named......a wildlife expert on whom it would rely; he had died several years before BP submitted its plan. BP listed seals and walruses as two species of concern in case of an oil spill in the Gulf; these species never see Gulf waters. And a link in the plan that purported to go to the Marine Spill Response Corporation website actually led to a Japanese entertainment site.

In short, best practices emphasize that planning is a process involving an array of stakeholders. The plan must reflect a carefully considered set of potential hazards that can impact a workplace, business, school, or agency. Plans must be worked through carefully by stakeholders involved and invested in outcomes beneficial to the community.

In the next sections, this chapter describes recommended steps in the planning process based upon research showing what works best. Examples will be given illustrating a range of planning that an emergency manager might become engaged in for their workplaces and communities. The chapter begins by understanding basic principles of planning.

6.2 PRINCIPLES OF PLANNING

Drawing upon extensive research, Quarantelli (1988, 1994, 1997) summarized these planning guidelines:

- *Disasters differ from day-to-day accidents and emergencies.* The magnitude, scope, and impact of a disaster require that a fuller set of partners join in the response and recovery efforts. Accidents and emergencies use only local first responders and medical professionals that are part of planned, everyday emergency response activities. By comparison, disasters (see Chapter 3) require many additional partners from both within and outside the community. Examples may include additional police, fire, paramedics, and emergency medical technicians (EMTs), public works employees, psychologists, faith-based community and volunteer organizations, engineering assessment teams, environmental protection specialists, animal rescue teams, shelter providers, housing reconstruction teams, and more. Representatives from state and federal government may also arrive to provide assistance and guidance. A disaster plan of any kind must consider all the people and organizations possibly needed, depending upon the hazard and its impact. In short, responding to a day-to-day emergency is much different than responding to a disaster. Disasters require a considerably larger scope and magnitude of planning with a wide array of partners.

- *A plan is not the final outcome of disaster planning – because planning never stops.* Plans must be living, actively revised documents that people know well (see Box 6.1).

New disasters unfold over time. For example, during the last 20 years, new kinds of terrorism attacks, pandemics, and cybercriminal incidents have happened. Other dynamic circumstances occur as well, which can change plans. Employees leave their positions, new technologies emerge, and office locations change. Plans need to be continually updated to reflect personnel changes and alterations of the built environment. The dynamic nature of our professional and personal lives thus compels us to revisit planning documents for currency and accuracy while also (re)connecting with existing and new representatives from other organizations to confirm or obtain new information. As one example, call down lists that are used to alert emergency response, partners change frequently and require continual updating. A community's demographics may also change. Plans must reflect new groups, such as evacuees, immigrants, or even newly disabled veterans that arrive in a community. Finding and working with representatives of these groups can enhance the plan and bring new people into the process. The result? A more comprehensive and stakeholder-driven plan that serves a broader population.

- *Creating a plan means assuming an agent generic approach toward planning – not creating a plan for each specific type of hazard.* Any given community typically faces a range of threats. Planning for each type of event requires time that most agencies cannot devote to a widespread effort. Many agencies also lack the personnel and expertise to do so. Further, certain needs occur commonly across disasters such as communication, coordination, and decision-making authority. By focusing on the common areas, a planner can achieve broadly based planning for a range of hazards. For example, creating the general components of an effective warning system is the same for a tornado or blizzard. Regardless of the event, the same organizations will be engaged with the response. In addition, the National Response Framework (NRF) in the U.S. uses the all-hazards approach. Within the NRF, emergency support functions (ESFs) address specific areas that

---

BOX 6.1

LESSONS UNLEARNED: DUSTING OFF THE PLAN

During one of the authors' field work training at the Disaster Research Center (DRC), the center's director Henry Quarantelli directed us to obtain a copy of the local disaster plan when possible. As part of our analysis, we would compare the written plan to the actual response. Quarantelli warned us, however, not to be surprised if the local emergency coordinator could not find the plan or would brush the dust off the top of the plan. Either way, these actions showed that the disaster managers and/or others did not use the plan during the disaster. Our team seemed a bit skeptical of his observations until we would travel to a disaster site and made a request to see the plan. And yes, either the coordinator could not find the plan or would take a second or two to wipe the dust off the top of the plan.

A few years later, one of us studied warning systems during flash floods in West Virginia for the U.S. Army Corps of Engineers. The Corps wanted to know why the warning system was so successful (i.e., no deaths). A small field team consisting of a geographer, hydrologist, and sociologist, along with a consultant, met at Dulles Airport and rented a car to drive to the flood-stricken city. Along the way, the consultant confidently stated, "I'll bet the second they heard the flood was coming, city officials pulled out the plan and followed it exactly....... That's why nobody was killed." The rest of us were skeptical, being well versed in the pattern of disaster plan use during response. Despite citing our experiences, the consultant felt so right, he bet us a steak dinner. We agreed.

Upon arriving at the city offices (officials were expecting us), we started to introduce ourselves to the local emergency manager and police chief. But even before we completed our introductions (and breaking our protocol for interviewing city officials), the consultant blurted out, "I'll bet you pulled those plans right off the shelf and used them for your warning – and that's why your warning was so successful." The local emergency coordinator looked at him rather oddly and replied, "You know, things happened so fast, we didn't even have time to use them. In fact, (she then pointed up, looking at a shelf on the wall), there they are ...... the same place they were before the flood." Lesson learned – the nature of a disaster often means that local disaster managers do not pull the plans off the shelf and use them. Events unfold too fast, and good coordinators know what is in the plan. And that night, the steak tasted pretty good, too.

---

guide a national response. ESF #6, for example, centers on mass care (sheltering, housing, and feeding), which is a common need regardless of the type of event. For most local plans, additional annexes address concerns such as terrorism or pandemics.

- *Plans must assume that unpredictable events will occur and that improvisation and group emergence will develop to respond to new situations.* Disasters involve problem-solving. Disaster plans provide a framework or starting place for response – they do not provide all the answers. As a result, unpredictable or overwhelming events may occur. For example, how does a community quickly mobilize volunteers and sandbags to save a neighborhood? To solve these problems, emergent groups of volunteers will often form. Or, various civic organizations may work together to obtain sand, bags, and a means to put sand in the bags, transport the sandbags to where they are needed, and recruit volunteers to place sandbags. New or strengthened personal or organizational relationships during the planning process often assist with emergence, which, in turn, may provide a more rapid and effective disaster response.

- *Plans must focus on coordination and flexibility, not on maintaining a rigid command and control bureaucracy.* Generally, rigid bureaucracies do not perform well under disaster circumstances. Disasters have a tendency to disrupt established routines and present new challenges. Keeping the day-to-day management structure for most organizations may lead to failure during a disaster. As events change, so must organizational structure. Consider, for example, when a Fujita scale (F3) tornado tore through Fort Worth, Texas, in 2000. A Federal Bureau of Investigation (FBI) building lost its windows along with some critical case files. The same happened in New Orleans after Hurricane Katrina to police offices. Retrieving and replacing evidence presented a new challenge, one that is typically not addressed in a plan. As another example, the attack on the World Trade Center resulted in the destruction of state-of-the-art emergency management (EM) facilities. To respond, surviving employees had to reconstruct a makeshift emergency operations center a few blocks away (Kendra and Wachtendorf 2003). Addressing such emerging challenges requires an ability to be flexible, innovative, and resourceful.

- *The planning process should create a set of general guidelines or principles for a disaster response.* Certainly, disaster managers and responders will draw upon some standard operating procedures such as initiating the steps for opening an emergency operations center, delineating the safety steps when responding to a hazardous materials event, or tuning on the sirens for a specific warning message. Disasters, however, generate a high degree of uncertainty. Rather, creating general guidelines and principles for planning and response are much more effective since they can be applied to a broad set of disaster threats. For example, consider the 2001 Super Bowl. Planners had worked diligently to protect the public from any potential terrorist attack at the big game. A blizzard, icy conditions, unusually low wind chill, and rolling blackouts caused unexpected disruption instead. The general set of communication guidelines established for the Super Bowl provided a foundation for managing the blizzard, which led to a more effective adaptation.

- *Disaster plans must avoid integrating the myths of such events as mass hysteria, panic, looting, and other incorrect assumptions of anti-social behavior by the victims.* Though you will learn more about disaster behavior in Chapter 7, you should know now that such behaviors like looting or panic are largely myths. Accordingly, if a planner anticipates that the first responders will be neighbors and friends, they can train neighborhood teams how to conduct basic search and rescue safely and render first aid until help arrives. Or, if a planner assumes that looting is actually less likely than pro-social behavior, they can deploy critical assets like National Guard troops to locations for search and rescue rather than waste their time on unnecessary "security." When disaster threatens, knowing that people usually do not panic should prompt early warnings to inspire evacuation. Disaster planners who rely upon disaster myths may create less effective plans.

- *The planning process must involve people working together on the plan within and across organizations.* Planning should never be conducted within one's own "silo." Organizations that will function together in a crisis event must plan together during noncrisis times. Doing so involves a range of partners within as well as across organizations. Janitors, typically at the bottom of an organizational hierarchy, will know a great deal about building layouts and resource locations, making them critical in an emergency. Similarly, the chief executive officer (CEO) must be involved because he or she will likely make decisions that determine the fate of a business or agency. Because agencies work across their silos in a disaster, they must sit at the planning table together. As an example, consider how a university might plan for a terrorist attack on a football stadium. Doing so requires involvement of university leaders as well as the temporary day labor used to route people into and out of the location. Police, paramedics, firefighters, and traffic control people are part of the operational team as are the university's communications personnel and public relations officer and high-level administrators. In short, disaster planners must network with central players when devising a disaster plan. Furthermore, planners must encourage others to work together formally and informally during the planning process. The development of predisaster networks and building social capital during this process will enhance the disaster response.

- *The planning process and plans must be guided by the science of disaster behavior.* Just as surgery requires expertise, with knowledge of what works and does not work for a given procedure, disaster planning and operations should follow the same route. To illustrate, consider that people impacted by Hurricane Katrina could not evacuate without assistance and hundreds had to be rescued after the levees broke in New Orleans. When evacuees landed in distant cities during the evacuation, people with disabilities had lost assistive devices and local shelters receiving them were hard-pressed to provide appropriate levels of support. Nonetheless, disaster scientists had been calling for planners to address vulnerable populations for some time prior to Katrina. Similarly, the COVID-19 pandemic resulted in inequitable outcomes for socially vulnerable populations, including during vaccine distribution. Despite decades of research on how to communicate risk information and a fair amount of pandemic planning, racial and ethnic minority vaccine rates fell quickly behind.

- *Although disaster planning is often considered part of the "preparedness" phase of disasters, planning should also plan for mitigation, response, and recovery.* As noted earlier, a range of planning exists in which a community may engage. Planners are increasingly recognizing the linkages between these kinds of plans and moving forward accordingly. For example, preparedness planning for households reduces the overall burden when response plans operationalize. Similarly, designing a recovery plan with mitigation initiatives improves disaster resilience for future events and reduces the burden placed on EM (see Chapters 8 and 9 for more).

After going over these points, several cross-cutting themes emphasize the main elements of community or organizational disaster planning:

- *Planning is a process, not a piece of paper.*
- *Network, network, and network.*
- *Plans are living documents.*

In short, the planning process helps in the following ways. First, those involved with the planning process will learn the plan. Learning occurs not by studying it, but by becoming active participants in creating and writing the plan. People learn by doing and, as a result, they do not have to search for the plan, find the correct page number, and follow a script while a disaster unfolds. Rather, they learn where and how to step into their roles through the planning process. Other activities such as training, drills, and exercises reinforce information related to the plan. In fact, when disasters strike, emergency managers need to know the plan, not have to look it up.

Second, the planning process helps create and enhance connections or networks among decision makers and key actors in the response, recovery, or mitigation phases. Planning together, followed by training and exercising on the plan, means the mayor gets to know the fire chief better, the head of public works learns how to work with the police chief, the city manager increases trust in the emergency manager, the director of the Red Cross works more closely with the CEO of the local hospital, and a committee representing faith-based groups establishes ties with similar community organizations. Related social capital accrues as trust builds, working relationships strengthen, and the community becomes safer as a result. Furthermore, creating plans collectively enhances interjurisdictional coordination. County government representatives may have to coordinate their plans with local or municipal governments. County sheriffs may have to synchronize with local police departments. Businesses and agencies will need to work with various levels of government. So, not only are individuals within an organization getting to know the disaster plan through the planning process, they are getting to know even better the people they will work with during a disaster.

Finally, plans need to be living documents that change and adapt. Change may come from people living a household or a workplace, which means that the plan must change to cover that loss or to integrate a new person. New hazards continually arise, such as a spate of cyberattacks that undermined businesses in 2021. The COVID-19 outbreak required massive adaptation, given the magnitude and scope of the pandemic. Preexisting plans for hospital surge were challenged by the volume of patients vis-à-vis available medical staff and medical devices like ventilators. As the vaccine became available, plans for points of distribution (PODs) to provide immunizations had to be created or modified in many locations worldwide to meet demand, followed by new strategies to reach herd immunity when vaccine demand waned. Plans must be adaptable and those tasked with implementing the plan must be adaptive. These principles hold true no matter which kind of plan has been written.

6.3 TYPES OF PLANNING

Planning occurs across all disaster phases. The majority of planning occurs before disaster strikes, particularly in the preparedness and mitigation phases. But, it is also true that despite recommendations from researchers and experts in the field, some mitigation and recovery planning occurs only after a disaster has struck. In this section, we review the kinds of planning typically conducted by emergency managers. Additional planning content can be found in the chapters on recovery, mitigation, and private/public sector partnerships.

6.3.1 Planning Across the Life Cycle of Emergency Management

A range of planning awaits those involved in managing disasters, including preparedness (see Chapter 5), response, recovery, mitigation, and business continuity planning.

Response plans are usually referred to as Emergency Operations Plans (EOPs). They can vary in their focus, length, and format but most center on how to coordinate activities, including warning the public, search and rescue, restoring utilities, opening shelters, and providing food and water. It is probably true that the most time spent on planning occurs around the response phase because here is where life-saving activities take place. As members of a human society, our shared value for human life compels us to concentrate on this critical planning phase.

In the U.S. and worldwide, response plans vary considerably, especially given available resources and expertise. In the U.S. since 1992, the NRF (and its precursors beginning with the Federal Response Plan [FRP]) and its ESFs drove response planning. With additions of the National Incident Management System (NIMS) and CPG 101, planning has become more standardized with certain expectations for structure and content.

Recovery, the phase that follows and overlaps with response, lacks much planning worldwide. Few jurisdictions expend time or resources to think through how they will plan out a recovery effort. Failure to do so, however, wastes valuable time in the aftermath of an event. The recovery time period, when sleep is sorely needed to drive efforts, visioning, and projects, demands an organized plan. Two types of recovery planning are typical. *Pre-event recovery planning* rarely occurs, but for those jurisdictions that do so, such as Los Angeles, efforts to restore normalcy can be expedited. *Post-event recovery planning* is more typical and unfortunately takes longer to conduct and implement. Sitting amidst the debris is not the time to plan, but most communities conduct recovery planning in the aftermath of a disaster. Common elements of any recovery plan address housing, roads and bridges, environmental resources, historic and cultural preservation, businesses, utilities, and more (see Chapter 8). Communities with the energy, time, and funding will benefit from careful planning. Doing so allows stakeholders to reconsider changes to enhance traffic flow, increase green space, reinvigorate a business sector, and mitigate future risks. Quality of life can be increased through recovery planning.

Emergency coordinators and planners conduct mitigation planning based upon identifying local threats and hazards, assessing the probabilities of where and how hazards could harm people and places, and selecting feasible ways to reduce their potential impact (see more in Chapter 9). Mitigation planning involves stakeholders such as the business, education, utility, and health care sectors with the public in identifying and prioritizing areas for risk reduction. Mitigation measures can include structural measures, such as the construction of levees along rivers that flood or installing rebar inside homes to resist earthquake shaking. Nonstructural efforts include those that do not involve built measures. Insurance is one example, because purchasing a policy affords the means to recover. Building codes serve as another example, when cities design rules for construction. In hurricane areas, for example, the city may require that builders install hurricane clamps on roofs to help them stay on during high winds. Locations that face wildfire threats may disallow wood shingles on roofs. Both kinds of mitigation measures can be considered as a way to reduce disaster impacts. In some organizations, resilience managers work alongside mitigation planners to enhance the ability to bounce back. Some cities have integrated similar efforts with sustainability. The City of Baltimore Office of Sustainability, for example, has hired planners for coastal resilience, climate change, environmental concerns, landscapes, and more (see https://www.baltimoresustainability.org/about/staff/, last accessed June 2, 2021).

6.3.2 Business Continuity Planning

In Chapter 10, which addresses public-private partnerships, you will learn more about business continuity planning. As a brief introduction, this type of planning addresses continuity of operations for workplaces and is also used for schools, health care settings, nonprofit agencies, and similar enterprises (Phillips and Landahl 2021). Unfortunately, most businesses lack much level of such planning, although research shows it can reduce damage (Webb, Tierney, and Dahlhamer 2000, 2002; Xiao and Peacock 2014). The scale of planning can move from smaller, home-based businesses to multinational corporations. Business continuity planning has, at its heart, addressing the critical functions that an enterprise must undertake to stay in operation. For a pizza restaurant, that might be producing and delivering food while for a hospital it would certainly mean being able to continue providing emergency and critical care. Business continuity planning tasks internal stakeholders with discerning critical functions, responsibility for maintaining them, how to sustain or restart functions, needed resources, and a timeline for resuming interrupted operations. The goal is to reduce downtime, when businesses are not in operation, and to anticipate disruptions. Revenue, products, and paychecks will be at stake, so business continuity planning helps to minimize losses.

Many businesses and schools faced the challenges of such disruptions during the COVID-19 pandemic. Schools worldwide closed for a time before moving to remote learning. Restaurants, fitness centers, conference facilities, and entertainment venues suffered significant losses economically. Business continuity planning helps to identify and work through hazard scenarios like pandemics, natural disasters, or terrorism and how everyone will respond.

6.4 LEVELS OF PLANNING

This section walks readers through the levels at which planning should occur and in which emergency managers should be involved. The first topic, personal- and household-level planning, addresses what emergency managers seek to inspire for individuals and families. Readers may benefit from trying some of the recommended planning advice as well. Next, community-level planning is discussed so that the full set of stakeholders can be considered and incorporated into planning. Finally, state and national planning guidance is considered specific to the U.S.

6.4.1 Individual- and Household-Level Planning

Many organizations and experts will tell you to be ready for disaster and to "make a plan" (Kohn et al. 2012). But what does it mean to make a plan at the individual and household levels? At this point you should have some good ideas about general preparedness and understand that you bear individual responsibility for your personal safety. To the greatest extent possible, you need to learn more, because exposing yourself and others to preparedness information makes people more likely to prepare (Thomas et al. 2015). Have you walked your family or roommates through planning for various scenarios from fire to severe weather to an extended period of isolation from a blizzard or pandemic?

And it is not enough to be familiar with just where you live but also in other environments, including school, work, restaurant, and tourist locations. Imagine, for example, going on vacation in another state and realizing that a tornado outbreak is occurring. You look at the weather map but have no idea where you are in relation to the threat. If you go outside and realize that it is hailing and need to seek immediate shelter, where do you go? Or, you are in the hotel when the fire alarm goes off. Did you read the emergency information the hotel provides before that occurred? Did you count the number of doors to the closest exit so that you can crawl under the smoke to safety?

Planning at the personal level starts with familiarizing yourself with area hazards and the risks they pose to you. Many Internet sites offer content that can help you understand the disaster history of the area as does your local library. A local EM agency probably offers information on their websites and may even have a preparedness and planning campaign with downloadable materials. At the national level, many government agencies like the Federal Emergency Management Agency (FEMA) or the New Zealand Ministry of Civil Defence and Emergency Management provide planning tools and templates (e.g., see FEMA 2021a). A National Seasonal Preparedness messaging calendar and social media toolkit for the U.S. can alert you to hazards at various times of the year (FEMA 2021b). FEMA (2021c) also provides personal information templates to use in the case of disasters. Why not put the book down for 15 minutes and start that process?

Several first steps should launch your plan (see Box 6.2). The first is what to do in case a disaster bears down as an immediate threat. You will need to plan out how to shelter in place or evacuate. To shelter in place requires that you know the safest place for the hazard you are facing. Should a disaster destroy your home when you are separated from family and friends, you should have a place to meet near the neighborhood. If that is possible, you will need a place within walking distance and it is good to designate a further reunification location too. Deciding how, when, and where to evacuate beyond your home requires considerably more planning effort. You will need to determine where you can go and how you will get there. Personal transportation may or may not be an option, so knowing people who can assist you to travel or how to use public transportation options is critical.

Not everyone can shelter in place or evacuate easily. Such factors as income, age, or a disability may make such an effort challenging. Although some communities have registries for people with transportation or sheltering needs, keeping it current and viable remains challenging (Metz et al. 2002; Hewett 2013). Other kinds of transportation planning can also help people at risk. Planners can work with organizations that support people at risk (e.g., local aging agencies, home health care agencies) to help individuals and their households plan or to assist them in a disaster. The use of Geographic Information System, coupled with demographic data and a hazard analysis, can help planners target specific areas for finding residents with accessibility needs such as a congregate care facility. Regardless of where such planning originates, people with accessibility needs and their advocates should participate actively in the planning process. Individuals who may be blind, deaf, or use mobility devices know best what works for them and can inform planners of their particular needs. At a minimum, planning should include ways to secure and evacuate (as needed) with medications, medical records, assistive devices and other technologies, and service animals. Caregivers must be active in the planning process so that they remain with an individual at risk during a disaster.

Members with particular needs also include pets and livestock (De Young and Farmer 2021). Ensure that you have planned for your pet, including transportable medical information, food, water, leashes, kennels, and comfort items, should an evacuation warrant. As part of your plan, be sure that someone remains alert to changing weather conditions so that pets can be brought indoors to safety, given heat, cold, and weather threats. Livestock can receive varying degrees of protection from the elements from farm buildings and shelters to evacuation to livestock shelters in areas outside of the immediate threat (DHS 2021a).

Finally, develop a communications plan. Assume that you will lose your cell phone or the charger or that callers will overwhelm cellular capacities after a disaster. What is your next strategy to let people know where you are and what you need? Planning an alternative means to communicate is critical. Land lines, e-mail, text messaging, and social media all serve as possible alternatives if the power stays on (Sutton and Tierney 2006). Currently, Twitter has developed a key means of communication by officials to the public, among family members and friends (e.g., Sutton et al. 2014). You should also designate certain people to serve as central communication points so that you can contact them and they can pass on information about what you may need, where you are, and your personal safety status. Most planning can take place over a couple of family or household dinners, which certainly seems a worthwhile investment of time given the alternative (Sutton and Tierney 2006).

6.4.2 Community-Based Planning

Community-based planning involves the whole community with understanding risk, discerning solutions, and sorting through strategies to implement. Why involve the community? A number of benefits accrue when planners and emergency managers

---

BOX 6.2

MAKE A HOUSEHOLD DISASTER PREPAREDNESS PLAN

Both FEMA/Department of Homeland Security (DHS) and the American National Red Cross provide similar suggestions for starting and maintaining a household disaster plan. Highlights of their recommendations include:

- Discuss among household members about making a plan.
- Analyze the possible types of hazards that present risks.
- Review how household members might be alerted for each of these hazards and the actions household members would take when a warning is received.
- Determine a location to meet if household members become separated during an event.
- Establish an appropriate shelter in place procedure and practice it before an event.
- Lay out steps to evacuate, including people with disabilities, seniors, pets, and service animals.
- Insure that each household member has contact information for other members such as:
  - Email
  - Phone
  - School or work
- Identify a contact person outside of your hazard area(s).
- Consider what important documents and medications each member may need.
- Put together kits to both shelter in place and to evacuate (see Chapter 5).
- Think about your pets, sheltering or evacuating with them, and their food, water, and medication needs.
- Practice your plan once or twice a year.

Sources: Red Cross (2021), FEMA (2021e).

---

invite the public to invest in their efforts (Chandra et al. 2013; Plough et al. 2013; Wells et al. 2013):

- People learn more about area hazards and the risks they present to themselves, their families, their neighbors, businesses and the local economy, pets, livestock, high risk populations, and government continuity. Acquiring information and education results in people being more willing to take preparedness measures, support local initiatives, and approve spending money to make their community safer.
- New ideas and insights surface. People from different cultures, languages, workplaces, residential areas, and ability levels bring new perspectives to community understanding of hazards and risks and produce social capital through their interactions. Elderly people and people with disabilities will be able to alert planners to their specific needs. People who have borne homelessness and their advocates will reveal new vulnerabilities that need to be addressed. New parents will have

questions about protecting extremely vulnerable infants. The knowledge that the community brings, which arises out of personal experience, enriches and deepens the planning process. By surfacing their knowledge and experiences, planners can anticipate their needs in a disaster better and craft a stronger plan.

- Knowledge accumulates too. When people learn about hazards and the plan to address risk, they leave the planning process more ready to help themselves and those around them. Planning may happen at a community forum, but it can then spread into households, neighborhood associations, congregate care centers, and workplaces. Raising awareness increases public safety.
- Resilience increases. When people become more aware and do something about their risks, they become more able to rebound sooner and better. Community participants may be surprised to learn that planners and emergency managers expect them to be able to care for themselves for up to 48 hours before emergency aid can arrive – and then do something to be ready. Planning serves to alert people to what they need to do.

How can planners involve community members? By creating multiple means for people to participate from going to their neighborhood community centers to offering public forums, online ways to join the conversation, surveys, and in-person planning charrettes. Planners should not expect people to come to them, because families juggle a lot with work, caregiving, school, and household duties. We need to go to them.

A common strategy is to identify scenarios of area hazards, like a flood. Then, planners can present a range of solutions with posters, news stories, door-to-door and online surveys, and other creative ways to invite feedback. Public events, like neighborhood or public fairs or sporting events, can be used as sites to invite people to respond and give opinions. Because emergency managers and planners will need public support, the time spent is well invested, especially when it comes time to ask the public for additional taxes or financial support to reduce flood risks through strengthening levees, managing dams, elevating historic structures or homes, or launching a relocation/buyout.

A more recent strategy being used in community-based planning is participatory action research (PAR) (Meyer et al. 2018). PAR involves citizens as scientists in identifying a problem, collecting data, and analyzing the information to produce actionable priorities. By working together, local residents can share their knowledge of the environment such as concerns about wildfire threats. They can also help to identify socially vulnerable populations and any local needs specific to their communities. Experts support local residents in learning more while simultaneously learning from residents about what they know, see, and experience by living in the risky environment. Insights can be gained to produce useful information for a range of plans, including response and recovery (Montesanti et al. 2021; Nolan et al. 2021). Together, they find solutions that make sense and that people will accept more readily and be willing to implement.

6.4.3 State and National Planning Guidance in the U.S.

In the U.S., the state's role generally is threefold. First, the states take federal guidance and create training opportunities for state and local government. For example, following the September 11 terrorist attacks, the U.S. required that all federal, state, and local officials involved in EM become trained in knowing how to use the NIMS (Federal Emergency Management Agency 2017). Second, states model their planning processes upon federal recommendations (McEntire and Dawson 2007). For example, CPG 101 suggests different ways states can approach planning to fit their own unique needs. The NIMS functions as the operational backbone of such planning. In addition, the NRF describes the role of the federal government for planning and response and serves as a structure for organizing at the national, state, and local levels.

CPG 101 provides federal planning guidance for local governments. The designers of CPG 101 integrated social science research, along with perspectives from emergency managers, to ground the overall approach to the plan in reality.

A primary evidence-based assertion of CPG 101 is that planning is a process that requires interaction and continual updating. Planning together means that response can ensue more effectively as the planning process built trusted partnerships based in what works and through strengthened relationships (FEMA 2020a).

CPG 101 also reinforces a number of ideas that enhance and improve planning (and with it, response). Many of these ideas you have already read about in this text. They include (FEMA 2020a):

- Focus on community-based planning.
- Include people with disabilities.
- Draw upon all stakeholders.
- Use an All-Hazards approach to identifying and managing risks.
- Incorporate existing resources to start your planning, including Mutual Aid Agreements or working with those you have in the past.
- Remember, planning is a process.

As illustrated in Figure 6.1, CPG 101 breaks the planning process into a series of steps. The first step, forming a planning team, seems simple and straightforward, but if it is not done properly, the entire process can be derailed. It is essential that the planning team reflects the diversity of the broader organization or community and that the team engages the whole community throughout the process. Once the team is assembled, the next step is to conduct a threat and hazard identification and risk assessment (THIRA; see more in Chapter 9). During this step, it is particularly important to adopt an all-hazards approach rather than focusing specifically on a single type of hazard.

Next, the team establishes goals and objectives. Here it is important to remember that plans are not intended to provide detailed scripts or recipes, but should instead provide general guidance and maximum flexibility. According to CPG 101, "plans are not scripts followed to the letter, but are flexible and adaptable to the actual situation" (FEMA 2010, p. i). Once the team identifies information and resource needs, it is time to write, review, approve, and disseminate the plan. It is absolutely essential at this stage to engage the whole community to maximize the plan's effectiveness and prevent it from being placed on a shelf and fading into obscurity.

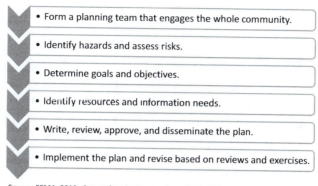

- Form a planning team that engages the whole community.
- Identify hazards and assess risks.
- Determine goals and objectives.
- Identify resources and information needs.
- Write, review, approve, and disseminate the plan.
- Implement the plan and revise based on reviews and exercises.

Source: FEMA. 2010. *Comprehensive Preparedness Guide 101*, p. 4-1. Washington, D.C.: U.S. Department of Homeland Security.

FIGURE 6.1 Steps in the Planning Process

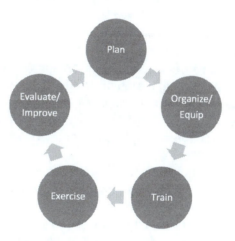

FIGURE 6.2 The Planning and Preparedness Cycle
Source: FEMA (2010), p. 1-4.

Once implemented, it is imperative that plans are continually maintained through regular reviews and revisions. It is also important to practice the plan by conducting drills and exercises, both tabletop and full scale, to identify shortcomings, inconsistencies, and sources of confusion. As depicted in Figure 6.2 and as described in this chapter, planning is best viewed as an ongoing process and it is an essential component of disaster preparedness.

The *NRF* emerged after the dual disasters of 1989 (see Chapter 1), when U.S. officials became concerned about dealing with overlapping and catastrophic disasters. Coordinated by FEMA, a large number of federal agencies and the American National Red Cross started to create a document to fix this problem. Initially called the FRP, it focused on coordinating federal agencies for specific tasks during a large-scale event. The development of ESFs specifically laid out which federal agency would coordinate or lead a task and which agencies would assist. While the FRP was being printed, Hurricane Andrew struck both the Atlantic (including Miami) and Gulf coasts. The government issued copies to those managing the disaster, but without adequate time to

BOX 6.3

HAZARD-SPECIFIC PLANNING: PANDEMICS

Although an all-hazards approach occurs routinely in EM planning, some hazards require specific plans, usually incorporated as Support Annex to a more general plan. Pandemics require a hazard-specific approach as a Support Annex. Specific units, like health care centers, will likely have a full-scale tested and exercised pandemic plan.

The need for pandemic planning was made abundantly clear during COVID-19. But preceding events launched significant levels of worldwide effort to produce actionable plans. In 2003, the severe acute respiratory syndrome (SARS) epidemic spread to over 20 countries and claimed approximately 800 lives (Cava et al. 2005; McDonald et al. 2004). Followed by an outbreak of H5N1 that same year, global concern led to pandemic planning. A significant amount of effort then developed, led in part by the World Health Organization (WHO) and respective national-level units like Public Health Canada.

Actions taken after 2003 mattered in subsequent pandemics. The Ebolavirus, led to over 28,000 deaths, particularly between 2013 and 2016 and primarily in African countries. This horrific disease, which causes internal hemorrhaging and fever in those affected, leads to rapid decline and high rates of death. The virus spreads easily, but various experimental medications do seem to be proving efficacious. Personal protective equipment (PPE) proved life-saving for medical professionals tasked with care of those who became ill with Ebola, which turned out to be a good rehearsal for COVID-19 (see Briand et al. 2014; Jacob et al. 2020).

Planning mattered again in late 2019 when a new virus that came to be known as COVID-19 spread rapidly worldwide. The first confirmed case (as of this writing) happened in December 2019. By late January 2020, the WHO declared a global health emergency as the virus spread rapidly through international travel and exposure. European nations closed rapidly, as patients overwhelmed health care systems in places like Italy, which went into a nationwide lockdown by February. Universities and schools worldwide shifted to remote learning by March and quarantines, masking, and other mitigation strategies went into place worldwide. As of this writing (June 2021), a total of 3,530,837 known deaths have occurred from the virus according to the WHO. It is the world's worst pandemic since the 1918 influenza pandemic, when approximately 50 million people died worldwide. As terrible as the COVID-19 pandemic has been, it could have been even worse without planning. Even with planning, COVID-10 overwhelmed health care centers and governments struggled to contain the spread of the virus, which was especially deadly to socially vulnerable populations (e.g., see Bodkin et al. 2020).

WHO recommends a three-phase approach to pandemic planning (visit https://www.who.int/influenza/preparedness/pandemic/essential_steps_influenza/en/ for more details):

Phase One: Preparation and Situation Analysis
   Prepare a Situation Analysis (similar to a THIRA, see Chapter 9)
   Increase awareness among planning participants and stakeholders

Review the Situation Analysis

Develop a work plan with budget, team members, and planners

Phase Two: Develop the Plan

Discuss and achieve consensus among planners and stakeholders

Consolidate Plan

Consult with stakeholders again

Phase Three: Evaluating, Finalizing, and Disseminating the Plan

Conduct a simulation exercise to test the plan (for details, see https://www.who.int/influenza/preparedness/en/)

Review and evaluate the exercise, then revise the plan

Finalize the plan

Seek relevant approvals

Disseminate the plan widely among agencies, stakeholders, the public

Core elements within a pandemic plan may seem more familiar after COVID-19:

- Patient Surge
- Rationing of health care
- Quarantine protocols
- Surveillance
- Infection control
- Quarantine protocols
- PPE
- Community education
- Mitigation testing
- Contact tracing
- Mass fatality management
- PODs for vaccine and medication distribution
- Planning for specific at risk populations (minorities, homeless, elderly)

Some locations, like Taiwan, have embraced pandemic planning at a high level since SARS. By training school children to wear a mask during influenza season, to engage in handwashing, and to receive vaccines – basic mitigation strategies – Taiwan kept its COVID-19 rates low (date June 2, 2021; see also Meyer et al. 2018). New Zealand, whose Ministry of Civil Defence and Emergency Management was led by a Director with a nursing and public health background, implemented a national lockdown with quarantine protocols. New Zealand limited COVID-19 deaths to 26 in comparison to the U.S. at 588,292 as of June 1, 2021 (per WHO Situation Report #42).

How will COVID-19 change planning as a worldwide and massively impactful event? Experts indicate that pandemics will continue to emerge in the future and that pandemic planning must continue to improve and expand.

Resources and References

- For more on SARS, see https://www.cdc.gov/sars/about/fs-sars.html and https://www.ncbi.nlm.nih.gov/pmc/articles/PMC3713824/, last accessed June 3, 2021.
- The WHO maintains Situation Reports (a routine EM reporting protocol) on its website for COVID-19. You can read more here: https://www.who.int/emergencies/diseases/novel-coronavirus-2019/situation-reports, last accessed June 3, 2021.
- Extensive pandemic planning lists can be found at WHO, https://www.who.int/influenza/preparedness/pandemic/en/, last accessed June 3, 2021.

Bodkin, Claire, Vaibhav Mokashi, Kerry Beal, Jill Wiwcharuk, Robin Lennox, Dale Guenter, Marek Smieja, and Timothy O'Shea. 2020. "Pandemic Planning in Homeless Shelters: A Pilot Study of a COVID-19 Testing and Support Program to Mitigate the Risk of COVID-19 Outbreaks in Congregate Settings." *Clinical Infectious Diseases* 72(9): 1639–1641.

Briand, Sylvie, Eric Bertherat, Paul Cox, Pierre Formenty, Marie-Paule Kieny, Joel K. Myhre, Cathy Roth, Nahoko Shindo, and Christopher Dye. 2014. "The International Ebola Emergency." *New England Journal of Medicine* 371(13): 1180–1183.

Cava, Maureen A., Krissa E. Fay, Heather J. Beanlands, Elizabeth A. McCay, and Rouleen Wignall. 2005. "The Experience of Quarantine for Individuals Affected by SARS in Toronto." *Public Health Nursing* 22(5): 398–406.

Jacob, Shevin T., Ian Crozier, William A. Fischer, Angela Hewlett, Colleen S. Kraft, MarcAntoine de La Vega, Moses J. Soka et al. 2020. "Ebola Virus Disease." *Nature Reviews Disease Primers* 6(1): 1–31.

McDonald, L. Clifford, Andrew E. Simor, Ih-Jen Su, Susan Maloney, Marianna Ofner, Kow-Tong Chen, James F. Lando, Allison McGeer, Min-Ling Lee, and Daniel B. Jernigan. 2004. "SARS in Healthcare Facilities, Toronto and Taiwan." *Emerging Infectious Diseases* 10(5): 777.

Meyer, Diane, Matthew P. Shearer, Yi-Chien Chih, Yu-Chen Hsu, Yung-Ching Lin, and Jennifer B. Nuzzo. 2018. "Taiwan's Annual Seasonal Influenza Mass Vaccination Program—Lessons for Pandemic Planning." *American Journal of Public Health* 108(S3): S188–S193.

develop, train, and exercise on the plan, the effort remained challenging (Neal 1993, 1995).

The NRP evolved into current guidance called the NRF, which is now in its fourth edition, and it retains but updates the ESFs discussed in Chapter 1 (Federal Emergency Management Agency 2019).

NRF support annexes now include the business and private sector, faith-based entities, and nongovernmental organizations (NGOs) and address financial management, international coordination, public affairs, tribal relations, volunteer and donations management, and worker safety and health (FEMA 2021c). This comprehensive document has served as the structure for many state and local response plans, particularly the use of the ESF and Support Annex sections (see Box 6.3). Doing so has enabled greater partnerships, communication, and coordination between governmental levels. After a major disaster, for example, FEMA will establish a Joint Field Office (JFO) where each ESF will be established along with support and resources. Key intergovernmental and voluntary agencies and partners will use those sites to coordinate a response effort.

The *NIMS*, based upon the ICS used by the fire services, drives how most response organizations interact and coordinate in the U.S. NIMS is required training for many, and readers would be well advised to secure NIMS certification as it is often mentioned in employment openings. Readers can start that journey at https://training.fema.gov/nims/, last accessed June 2, 2021. Please note also the "all-hazards" position specific training found on this page.

Why did NIMS become so important? Following the 9/11 terror attacks in the U.S., expert analysis suggested that numerous management, including coordination and communication, issues plagued the response, especially in New York City (*The 9/11 Commission Report* 2004). Homeland Security Presidential Directive 5 then required all levels of government to use NIMS during all disaster events (including terror attacks) with training to assist the private sector and other NGOs.

NIMS is based on the Incident Command System (ICS). Originating as a tactic to fight wildfire in the Western U.S., firefighters have used and enhanced ICS since the early 1970s. As shown in Figure 6.3, ICS is based on an organizational structure that includes a command staff, including the incident commander (IC), a public information officer (PIO), a safety officer, and a liaison officer, in addition to four section chiefs who oversee finance and administration, logistics, operations, and planning. The IC oversees and coordinates activities during an event. The PIO is the primary point of contact for the media and the public, while the liaison officer is the primary point of contact for representatives from various organizations, including governmental agencies, jurisdictions, NGOs, and others not included in the command staff. The safety officer monitors the health and safety of all response personnel involved in the incident. Individuals in charge of Finance, Logistics, Operation, and Planning report to the IC to share their

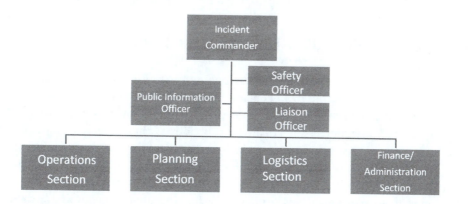

Source: FEMA. 2017. National Incident Management System, 3rd ed, p. 84. Washington, D.C.: U.S. Department of Homeland Security.

FIGURE 6.3 The Incident Command System

information so the IC can make well-informed decisions. The finance function keeps track of the budget. Logistics secures and delivers resources to the disaster site. Planning gathers information to determine what resources (e.g., people, equipment) are needed to perform needed tasks (e.g., debris removal). In theory, ICS has a simple organizational structure that can expand or contract as driven by the situation. Firefighters can use this basic structure to fight fires, or local, state, and federal governments can use this same type of structure, but with thousands of people, to respond to a larger event (PHE 2012).

NIMS reflects the ICS structure, but also includes the idea of "unified command." In theory, each jurisdiction and major task should be operating under the ICS structure. Yet, this means that the disaster response could have multiple ICs which could cause confusion about decision-making and who is in charge. Thus, through the unified command process, ICs collectively agree upon a decision and let their managers and responders know the decision (FEMA 2021d, pp. 2–3). In summary, a Unified Command should promote shared understanding, focused incident objectives, collaboration, information flow internally and externally, better use of resources, and a more streamlined effort.

NIMS and ICS are the standard and often required management structures used for events ranging from day-to-day emergency response (e.g., house fires) to large-scale catastrophes, such as a COVID-19-type event. As disaster planners and managers have attempted to implement and utilize NIMS and ICS, disaster scientists have studied these systems extensively (Buck, Trainor, and Aguirre 2006; Jenkins et al. 2009; Jensen and Waugh 2014; Jensen and Youngs 2015; Chang 2017; Chang and Trainor 2018, 2020). Among the concerns raised by researchers are that NIMS and ICS may stifle rather than promote flexibility; that volunteer and emergent groups may not be as well versed in NIMS and ICS terminology and therefore not be fully integrated into planning and response efforts; that catastrophic events may overwhelm and exceed the capacities of these systems; and that disparate and uneven patterns of NIMS implementation, in particular across different jurisdictions and different types of organizations, weaken the system's overall effectiveness (Neal and Webb 2006; Jensen and Thompson 2016).

6.5 WORKING AND VOLUNTEERING IN PLANNING

Jobs in disaster planning may be stand-alone opportunities or embedded within a more general position. Large EM agencies may be able to employ a planner or team or planners dedicated to the full array of needed plans. Or, the task may fall to a single key person. For example, someone who functions as the sole emergency manager for an agency, business, or university may find that planning rests on their shoulders along with the other tasks spanning the life cycle of disasters. Planners may also be found in a city's planning unit, where they work on emergency planning along with other kinds of city planning needs. Students who gravitate toward planning as a career would be well advised to take courses in urban planning, community development, and public speaking.

Volunteering opportunities exist also in the area of planning. This is particularly so in the areas of mitigation and post-disaster recovery planning. Because mitigation planning rolls out more slowly and in a stepwise fashion, it is easier to volunteer as part of a community-based group working to lessen area hazards. After a disaster occurs, communities also convene planning committees and usually offer the public various means to participate such as open forums, housing fairs, and planning charettes. To become more involved in other phases, volunteer for organizations designing preparedness campaigns and help distribute and explain information to people. Encourage personal and household planning in both your own home and across your neighborhood. Form efforts with EM officials to support seniors and others with household planning. Response planning typically occurs within the EM and first responder community. Depending on the size of the community and their commitment to public involvement, you may be able to participate in the planning process as part of a formal response group dedicated to serving during emergencies. Even if you are not part of the actual planning, your participation may be useful during exercises and drills to test the plan. Remain alert for opportunities to observe these events as well as they can provide insights and instruction to you for a future career path.

***

SUMMARY

Planning is best approached as a process that invites all stakeholders into the process of making communities more resilient. Several kinds of planning need to be conducted, which will be explored further in upcoming chapters on response, recovery, and mitigation. Planning also needs to consider the levels at which it should be focused for households, businesses, local through national and international plans. Planning should be conducted with people at risk deeply involved in the process. Community-based planning generates numerous benefits, from social capital to surface ideas to increased household preparedness. State and national guidance also exists. In the U.S., this guidance relies heavily on CPG 101, NIMS, and ICS structures. Most U.S.-based plans rely on the standardized ESF structure with Support Annexes for specific concerns such as terrorism and pandemics.

Discussion Questions

1. What are the types of activities that a local disaster manager can take to engage those in the public, private, and volunteer sector to enhance the planning process? During these activities, what goals are local emergency managers trying to meet?
2. When disaster strikes, why do good emergency managers and other officials and others still manage the disaster effectively without consulting the plan?
3. Consider how the use of disaster myths in plans and the belief of disaster myths by decision makers could create a poor response?
4. Have you ever been involved in any type of household disaster planning? If so, what type of event did you discuss (e.g., tornado, hurricane, flood)? What types of activities did you do to plan and prepare? How successful do you think these efforts were?

5. Effective disaster planning can only occur when all stakeholders are involved. Identify different publics (e.g., those with disabilities, tribal nations) that may reside in your community. Next, how might you reach out to these stakeholders? Consider what organizations may also help you reach out since they often represent these different groups.

6. Imagine you are a local disaster coordinator and are giving a 15-minute talk to a local club during lunch. Your talk will focus on effective disaster planning. What two or three themes would you stress during your short luncheon talk?

7. If you were a disaster planner, to enhance your planning efforts, what might you explicitly draw upon:
   a) CPG 101?
   b) The NRF?
   c) NIMS?

Summary Questions

1. Why is the planning process more important than creating a paper plan?
2. What can families begin to do to start their planning process?
3. What governmental entity (i.e., federal, state, local, tribal) coordinates the NRF and why?
4. CPG 101 provides guidance for many different organizations. But, what level of government does it see as a starting point and why?
5. What governmental entities and other organizations are supposed to use NIMS during a disaster response? What is the purpose of some/many organizing/adapting the NIMS and ICS management structure.

REFERENCES

Buck, Dick A., Joseph E. Trainor, and Benigno E. Aguirre. 2006. "A Critical Evaluation of the Incident Command System and NIMS." *Journal of Homeland Security and Emergency Management* 3(3). doi: 10.2202/1547-7355.1252.

CBSNEWS. 2010. "BP Didn't Plan for Major Oil Spill." Available at http://www.cbsnews.com/news/bp-didnt-plan-for-major-oil-spill/, last accessed June 2, 2021.

Chandra, Anita, Malcolm Williams, Alonzo Plough, Alix Stayton, Kenneth B. Wells, Mariana Horta, and Jennifer Tang. 2013. "Getting Actionable about Community Resilience: The Los Angeles County Community Disaster Resilience Project." *American Journal of Public Health* 103(7): 1181–1189.

Chang, Hsien-Ho. 2017. "A Literature Review and Analysis of the Incident Command System." *International Journal of Emergency Management* 13(1): 50–67.

Chang, Hsien-Ho and Joseph Trainor. 2020. "Balancing Mechanistic and Organic Design Elements: The Design and Implementation of the Incident Command System (ICS)." *International Journal of Mass Emergencies and Disasters* 38(3): 241–267.

Chang, Ray and Joseph Trainor. 2018. "Pre-Disaster Established Trust and Relationships: Two Major Factors Influencing the Effectiveness of Implementing the ICS." *Journal of Homeland Security and Emergency Management* 15(4): e20170050. doi: 10.1515/jhsem-2017-0050.

Department of Homeland Security (DHS). 2021a. "Prepare Your Pets for Disaster." Available at https://www.ready.gov/animals, last accessed June 2, 2021.

Department of Homeland Security (DHS). 2021b. "Presidential Policy Directive / PPD-8: National Preparedness." Available at https://www.dhs.gov/presidential-policy-directive-8-national-preparedness, last accessed June 2, 2021.

De Young, Sarah E. and Ashley K. Farmer. 2021. *All Creatures Safe and Sound: The Social Landscape of Pets in Disasters*. Philadelphia, PA: Temple University Press.

Federal Emergency Management Agency (FEMA). 2010. *Comprehensive Preparedness Guide 101, Version 2.0*. Washington, DC: U.S. Department of Homeland Security.

Federal Emergency Management Agency (FEMA). 2017. *National Incident Management System*, 3rd ed. Washington, DC: U.S. Department of Homeland Security.

Federal Emergency Management Agency (FEMA). 2019. *National Response Framework*, 4th ed. Washington, DC: U.S. Department of Homeland Security.

Federal Emergency Management Agency (FEMA). 2020a. "Developing and Maintaining Emergency Operating Plans: Comprehensive Preparedness Guide (CPG) 101 (Draft 2.0)." Available at https://www.fema.gov/sites/default/files/2020-05/CPG_101_V2_30NOV2010_FINAL_508.pdf, last accessed June 2, 2021.

Federal Emergency Management Agency (FEMA). 2020b. "National Response Framework." Available at https://www.fema.gov/emergency-managers/national-preparedness/frameworks/response, last accessed June 2, 2021.

Federal Emergency Management Agency (FEMA). 2021a. "Create Your Family Emergency Communications Plan." Available at https://www.ready.gov/collection/family-emergency-communication-plan, last accessed June 2, 2021.

Federal Emergency Management Agency (FEMA). 2021b. "Calendar." Available at https://www.ready.gov/calendar, last accessed June 2, 2021.

Federal Emergency Management Agency (FEMA). 2021c. "Create Your Family Emergency Communications Plan." Available at https://www.ready.gov/sites/default/files/2021-04/family-emergency-communication-plan.pdf, last Accessed June 2, 2021.

Federal Emergency Management Agency (FEMA). 2021d. "NIMS Implementation Objectives for Federal Departments and Agencies." Available at https://www.fema.gov/sites/default/files/documents/fema_nims-implementation-objectives-federal-departments-agencies_04-2021.pdf, last accessed May 31, 2021.

Federal Emergency Management Agency (FEMA). 2021e. "Make a Plan." Available at https://www.ready.gov/plan, last accessed June 2, 2021.

Fitzgerald, Alison. 2010. "BP Ready for Spill 10 Times the Gulf Disaster." Available at http://www.bloomberg.com/news/articles/2010-05-31/bp-told-u-s-it-could-handle-oil-spill-10-times-larger-than-gulf-disaster, June 2, 2021.

Hewett, Paul L., Jr. 2013. *Organizational Networks and Preparedness during Disaster Preparedness: The Case of an Emergency Preparedness Registry*. Doctoral Dissertation, Fire and Emergency Management Program (Department of Political Science). Stillwater, OK: Oklahoma State University.

Jenkins, J. Lee, Gabor D. Kelen, Lauren M. Sauer, Kimberly A. Fredericksen, and Melissa L. McCarthy. 2009. "Review of Hospital Preparedness Instruments for National Incident Management System Compliance." *Disaster Medicine and Public Health Preparedness* 3(S1): S83–S89.

Jensen, Jessica and Steven Thompson. 2016. "The Incident Command System: A Literature Review." *Disasters* 40(1): 158–182.

Jensen, Jessica and William L. Waugh, Jr. 2014. "United States' Experience with ICS." *Journal of Contingencies and Crisis Management* 22: 5–17.

Jensen, Jessica and George Youngs. 2015. "Explaining Implementation Behaviour of the National Incident Management System (NIMS)." *Disasters* 39(2): 362–388.

Kendra, James M. and Tricia Wachtendorf. 2003. "Elements of Resilience After the World Trade Center Disaster: Reconstituting New York City's Emergency Operations Centre." *Disasters* 27(1): 37–53.

Kohn, Sivan, Jennifer Lipkowitz Eaton, Saad Feroz, Andrea A. Bainbridge, Jordan Hoolachan, and Daniel J. Barnett. 2012. "Personal Disaster Preparedness: An Integrative Review of the Literature." *Disaster Medicine and Public Health Preparedness* 6(3): 217–231.

McEntire, David A. and Gregg Dawson. 2007. "The Intergovernmental Context." Pp. 57–70 in *Emergency Management: Principles and Practice for Local Government*, 2nd ed, eds. William L. Waugh, Jr. and Kathleen Tierney. Washington, DC: ICMA Press.

Metz, William, Paul Hewett, Edward Tanzman, and Julie Muzzarelli. 2002. "Identifying Special-Needs Households that Need Assistance for Emergency Planning." *International Journal of Mass Emergencies and Disasters* 20(2): 255–281.

Meyer, Michelle Annette, Marccus Hendricks, Galen D. Newman, Jaimie Hicks Masterson, John T. Cooper, Garett Sansom, Nasir Gharaibeh, et al. 2018. "Participatory Action Research: Tools for Disaster Resilience Education." *International Journal of Disaster Resilience in the Built Environment* 9(4–5): 402–419.

Montesanti, Stephanie, Kayla Fitzpatrick, Tara Azimi, Bryan Fayant, and Lorraine Albert. 2021. "Exploring Indigenous Ways of Coping after a Wildfire Disaster in Northern Alberta, Canada." *Qualitative Health Research* 31(8): 1472–1485.

National Commission on the BP Deepwater Horizon Oil Spill and Offshore Drilling. 2011. "Deep Water: The Gulf Oil Disaster and the Future of Offshore Drilling." Available at http://www.gpo.gov/fdsys/pkg/GPO-OILCOMMISSION, last accessed June 2, 2021.

Neal, David M. 1993. "Emergency Response Philosophy of the Federal Response Plan: Implications in the Case of a Catastrophic Disaster," *Proceedings of the 1993 National Earthquake Conference*: 511–518. Memphis, TN: May 2–5.

Neal, David M. 1995. "Hurricane Andrew and Federal Disaster Policy," *Forum for Applied Research and Public Policy* 10(1): 26–29.

Neal, David M. and Gary R. Webb. 2006. "Structural Barriers to Implementing the National Incident Management System." Pp. 263–282 in *Learning from Catastrophe: Quick Response Research in the Wake of Hurricane Katrina*, ed. Christine Bvec. Boulder: Natural Hazards Center – University of Colorado.

Nolan, James E. S., Eric S. Coker, Bailey R. Ward, Yahna A. Williamson, and Kim G. Harley. "Freedom to Breathe": Youth Participatory Action Research (YPAR) to Investigate Air Pollution Inequities in Richmond, CA. 2021. *International Journal of Environmental Research and Public Health* 18(2): 554.

Phillips, Brenda D. and Mark Landahl. 2021. *Business Continuity Planning: Increasing Workplace Resilience to Disasters*. Oxford: Elsevier.

Plough, Alonzo, Jonathan E. Fielding, Anita Chandra, Malcolm Williams, David Eisenman, Kenneth B. Wells, Grace Y. Law, Stella Fogleman, and Aizita Magaña. 2013. "Building Community Disaster Resilience: Perspectives from a Large Urban County Department of Public Health." *American Journal of Public Health* 103(7): 1190–1197.

Public Health Emergency (PHE). 2012. "Emergency Management and the Incident Command System." Available at https://www.phe.gov/Preparedness/planning/mscc/handbook/chapter1/Pages/emergencymanagement.aspx, last accessed June 2, 2021.

Quarantelli, E. L. 1988. "Assessing Disaster Preparedness Planning." *Regional Development Dialogue* 9: 48–69.

Quarantelli, E. L. 1994. "Research-based Criteria for Evaluating Disaster Planning and Managing." Available at https://udspace.udel.edu/bitstream/handle/19716/136/PP247-Research%20Based%20Criteria.pdf?sequence=1, last accessed June 2, 2021.

Quarantelli, E. L. 1997. "Ten Criteria for Evaluating the Management of Community Disasters." *Disasters* 21: 39–56.

Red Cross. 2021. "Make a Plan." Available at https://www.redcross.org/get-help/how-to-prepare-for-emergencies/make-a-plan.html, last accessed June 2, 2021.

Sutton, Jeanette, Emma S. Spiro, Britta Johnson, Sean Fitzhugh, Ben Gibson, and Carter T. Butts. 2014. "Warning Tweets: Serial Transmission of Messages during the Warning Phase of a Disaster Event." *Information Communication & Society* 17(6): 765–787.

Sutton, Jeanette and Kathleen Tierney. 2006. *Disaster Preparedness: Concepts, Guidance, and Research*. Boulder, CO: Natural Hazards Center, Institute of Behavioral Sciences.

Thomas, Tracy N., Michelle Leander-Griffith, Victoria Harp, and Joan P. Cioffi. 2015. "Influences of Preparedness Knowledge and Beliefs on Household Disaster Preparedness." *Morbidity and Mortality Weekly Report* 64(35): 965–971.

The 9/11 Commission Report. 2004. *Final Report of the National Commission on Terrorist Attacks upon the United States.* New York: W. W. Norton and Company.

Wells, Kenneth B., Jennifer Tang, Elizabeth Lizaola, Felica Jones, Arleen Brown, Alix Stayton, Malcolm Williams et al. 2013. "Applying Community Engagement to Disaster Planning: Developing the Vision and Design for the Los Angeles County Community Disaster Resilience Initiative." *American Journal of Public Health* 103(7): 1172–1180.

Webb, Gary R., Kathleen J. Tierney, and James M. Dahlhamer. 2000. "Businesses and Disasters: Empirical Patterns and Unanswered Questions." *Natural Hazards Review* 1(2): 83–90.

Webb, Gary R., Kathleen J. Tierney, and James M. Dahlhamer. 2002. "Predicting Long-Term Business Recovery from Disaster: A Comparison of the Loma Prieta Earthquake and Hurricane Andrew." *Global Environmental Change Part B: Environmental Hazards* 4(2): 45–58.

Xiao, Yu and Walter Gillis Peacock. 2014. "Do Hazard Mitigation and Preparedness Reduce Physical Damage to Businesses in Disasters? Critical Role of Business Disaster Planning." *Natural Hazards Review* 15(3): 04014007.

RESOURCES

- Personal planning and Preparedness: www.ready.gov serves as a portal to a comprehensive set of information on planning and preparedness.
- Planning guides can also be found at https://www.fema.gov/emergency-managers/national-preparedness/plan for various kinds of agencies and workplaces.
- The American Red Cross http://www.redcross.org/support/emergency-preparedness gives a good overall perspective on disaster planning.
- To learn more about CPG 101, visit https://www.fema.gov/sites/default/files/2020-05/CPG_101_V2_30NOV2010_FINAL_508.pdf
- The NIMS can be reviewed at https://www.fema.gov/national-incident-management-system.
- The NRF can be reviewed at http://www.fema.gov/national-response-framework. A version of the FRP can be found at https://www.hsdl.org/?abstract&did=781058.
- An extensive list of planning guides can be found at http://emergency.cdc.gov/planning/, a web site published by the Center for Disease Control and Prevention. This site provides informative links for planning for specific types of agents, personal and household locations, businesses, health care facilities, government, and lists documents related to legal issues.
- Basic checklists for pandemic planning can be seen at http://apps.who.int/iris/bitstream/10665/68980/1/WHO_CDS_CSR_GIP_2005.4.pdf.
- The American Planning Association (APA) provides advice and examples on recovery, https://www.planning.org/research/postdisaster/, https://www.planning.org/research/postdisaster/, and https://www.planning.org/divisions/hazardmitigation/.

7

Response

CHAPTER OBJECTIVES

Upon completing this chapter, readers should be able to:

- Define the response phase of disasters, identify problems and challenges that commonly arise when responding to disasters, and discuss the principles of effective emergency management (EM) best suited for addressing them.
- Describe the process of issuing disaster warnings and identify the characteristics of effective disaster warnings that lead people to take appropriate protective actions.
- Compare and contrast the myth- and research-based views of the response phase of disasters.
- Discuss response challenges in the context of international disasters.
- Discuss the future of response, including the characteristics of future disasters and the challenges they will pose for the profession of EM.

KEY TERMS

- Cascading Impacts
- Compounding Disasters
- Convergence
- Disaster Myths
- Disaster Research Center Typology

- Flexibility
- Improvisation
- Organizational Adaptation
- Resilience
- Warning Process

7.1 INTRODUCTION

It is very likely that when you hear or think about *emergency management*, you immediately think about the response phase of disaster. You might envision yourself

DOI: 10.4324/9781003021919-9

working in an ultramodern, high-tech emergency operations center (EOC), simultaneously monitoring network news coverage on multiple flat-panel televisions, keeping a close eye on your computer screen as response activities are logged and updated at near real-time speed into an advanced decision support software program, and handling nonstop telephone calls from colleagues out in the field and media seeking a good quote. Indeed, the image of a strong leader asserting command and control over a chaotic situation is one that many people have of the emergency manager. We will refer to this as the "command post" image of the emergency manager.

Despite the pervasiveness, and the appeal even, of this imagery, it is not entirely accurate. In fact, if your idea of an emergency manager is a person whose days are action-packed and spent in the EOC making split-second, life and death decisions, then you will likely be disappointed by the profession. There will be some of that, to be sure, but most of your time will not be spent in the trenches. Rather, you will spend time working to make the trench time effective, efficient, and smooth.

As a point of reference, consider the law enforcement profession. When we think of the police, we tend to imagine trained professionals who spend their days chasing criminal suspects, collecting highly sensitive evidence at crime scenes, and solving cold cases. Yet, if you talk to a recently hired police officer about his or her work, you will likely sense at least some disillusionment over how much idle time they have and, even more likely, how much time they spend writing reports.

This is not to say that you will spend all your time as an emergency manager at a desk, writing and reviewing disaster plans. Indeed, like a police officer called to the scene of a major crime, you will sometimes spring into action due to a disaster. It is important, however, to realize that responding to actual disasters is only one, albeit a very important, component of an emergency manager's job. Our purpose here is not to shatter your hopes and dreams of saving lives during a disaster, but instead to give you a more realistic view of the profession. The command post view of EM is inaccurate because it largely ignores the other phases of disaster and their relationship to the response period, it envisions widespread chaos, and it assumes that an effective response is characterized by strong command and control over a situation.

7.1.1 Ignoring Other Phases of Disaster

As we have discussed throughout this book, the life cycle of disasters includes preparedness, response, recovery, and mitigation. Because you will spread your time across all four phases, because actual disaster events are relatively rare, and because emergency managers have numerous job responsibilities, it is simply inaccurate to assume that most of your time will be spent managing response efforts. However, it is accurate to assume that you will spend a great deal of time *thinking* about response activities. The time you spend on preparedness-related activities, for example, including educating the public about the hazards and risks in your community, talking with organizations such as schools and businesses, and conducting drills and exercises, will pay tremendous dividends when it comes to responding to an actual disaster.

Similarly, if your community takes effective, proactive steps to mitigate possible threats, it is likely that disaster impacts will be less severe and enable more manageable responses. While response is the most prevalent phase in the common view of the emergency manager's work, the concept of comprehensive EM assumes that the other phases are equally important.

7.1.2 Envisioning Chaos

Another reason the command post view of the emergency manager comes to mind so readily is the common notion that disasters create chaos and social disorganization. In all that confusion, it is assumed by many that we need a calm, level-headed leader to make the right decisions and keep everyone else in line. The concept that disasters create chaos and massive social breakdown, however, is a myth. Instead, as we will see, individuals, organizations, and communities typically show remarkable resilience in the face of disasters.

As Dynes (2003) points out, we continually find "order in disorder" in the immediate aftermaths of large-scale disasters like the terrorist attacks of September 11, 2001. Similarly, Drabek (2013) characterizes the post-disaster environment as "organized-disorganization." However, for reasons we will discuss in this chapter, many people, including some EM professionals, continue to believe that chaos prevails in disasters. As a result, the command post image of the emergency manager persists in the minds of many.

7.1.3 Assuming Need for Command and Control

Because it envisions a chaotic scene after a disaster, the command post image also assumes that the best way to effectively manage a disaster is to assert strong command and control over the situation. According to Dynes (1994), this command-and-control model of EM is based on numerous false assumptions and inappropriate analogies. Generally, it assumes that civil society is fragile, and the post-disaster environment is like a wartime scenario. In the absence of a strong and assertive leadership, the expectation is that lawlessness and anarchy will spread. From this perspective, based largely on a military model of leadership, the emergency manager is essentially a commander, establishing firm control over a situation and unilaterally issuing orders to others. As we will see in this chapter, however, emergency managers are much more effective when they emphasize coordination and communication instead of command and control.

The post-disaster environment is fluid, dynamic, and constantly changing. Decisions must be made quickly, often based on very limited information. In those circumstances, a rigid, hierarchical, and centralized approach is likely to fail. Instead, a decentralized, flexible, problem-solving approach is much better suited to the complexities of the response phase of a disaster (Dynes 1994; Neal and Phillips 1995). Therefore, in sharp contrast to the command post image, it is much more accurate to view EM professionals as managers and coordinators, not as commanders.

7.2 GETTING STARTED: DEFINITIONS AND ACTIVITIES

Now that you understand that response is only one aspect of an emergency manager's job duties and have been cautioned against embracing a command post view of the profession, the remainder of this chapter will provide an in-depth look at the response period. In this section, we will consider various definitions of response and identify disaster-related activities typically performed during the response phase. In subsequent sections, we will discuss the process of issuing disaster warnings and identify factors that enhance their effectiveness; describe various myths about how people, organizations, and communities respond to disasters; debunk the disaster myths and describe actual responses, including typical patterns and common problems; and discuss the most effective principles of EM during the response phase, including the all-hazards model, coordination, and flexibility. Despite decades of research on the response phase, misunderstandings about reactions to disasters are still widespread. After reading this chapter, you will have a much better sense of what really happens during disasters and obtain clear guidance on managing responses effectively.

7.2.1 Defining Response

The response phase is defined as activities "... designed to provide emergency assistance for casualties ... seek to reduce the probability of secondary damage ... and to speed recovery operations" (National Governors' Association 1979, p. 13). More recently, Tierney, Lindell, and Perry (2001, p. 81) defined disaster response activities as "... actions taken at the time a disaster strikes that are intended to reduce threats to life safety, to care for victims, and to contain secondary hazards and community losses." They further explained that during the response phase, emergency managers must address two sets of demands: those generated from the disaster and those arising from the response effort.

Disaster-induced demands arise from the needs to care for victims and deal with physical damage and social disruption caused by the event. *Response-induced demands* are far less obvious but equally important and challenging for emergency managers. They include the need to coordinate the activities of the multitude of individuals and organizations involved in the response. As we will see later in this chapter, response-induced demands are plentiful in the wake of a disaster because so many different types of actors and organizations – some without clearly delineated disaster responsibilities – become involved in response efforts.

7.2.2 Typical Response Activities

Given the involvement of so many different individuals, groups, and agencies and the pressing needs brought on by disasters, the response period is typically packed with activity. Common components of the response effort include activating the EOC, warning the public, notifying appropriate authorities, mobilizing personnel and resources, initiating evacuation, opening shelters, providing medical services, search-and-rescue operations, and many others. To more accurately describe response activities, Drabek (1986) separates them into pre-impact mobilization and postimpact emergency action subphases. *Pre-impact mobilization* involves warning the public, initiating evacuation, and establishing shelters. *Postimpact emergency actions* include searching for survivors and providing medical care to the injured. Tierney et al. (2001, p. 75) categorize response activities in even greater detail, identifying four related areas of activity:

- Emergency assessment.
- Expedient hazard mitigation.
- Protective response.
- Incident management.

Emergency assessment includes monitoring hazards (natural, technological, and human-induced) in your community and assessing damages and other impacts when a disaster occurs. One of the main tasks of an emergency manager after a disaster is to conduct an emergency assessment, which in the U.S. initiates the process of applying for a presidential disaster declaration that releases federal disaster funding. To conduct a preliminary damage assessment (PDA), capable investigators enter the field to determine how bad things are after a tornado, flood, or earthquake has struck. The initial PDA, which will be followed by a more thorough investigation once the area is accessible, typically involves a "windshield survey" in which the EM team drives through the area and identifies quickly the number of houses, businesses, and infrastructure components compromised. To do so, they generally designate three levels: destroyed, major damage, and minor damage and tally a straightforward account of the apparent damage. Aerial reconnaissance and satellite imagery can also be used to assess damage, but, as with the windshield survey, the visual images just cannot reach inside a building. Therefore, the PDA is followed by more careful assessments made by qualified engineers to determine if buildings are safe to reenter or need to be torn down. The PDA thus serves to safeguard the public, determine the amount of damage to qualify for outside aid, and set up parameters by which voluntary organizations will determine the extent of their assistance. The PDA is, in short, the key step that bridges response into recovery (see more in Chapter 8).

Expedient hazard mitigation refers to activities undertaken just prior to or shortly after the onset of a disaster – sandbagging in a flood and boarding windows in a hurricane – aimed at protecting lives and containing damage. *Protective response* involves all the activities we typically think about in relation to disasters, including search and rescue, emergency medical services, sheltering, and others. *Incident management* requires establishing an EOC, interagency and intergovernmental coordination, media communications and public information activities, documentation, and administrative and logistic support.

As an emergency manager, it is highly unlikely that you would ever be directly involved in all these response activities. However, it is important that you understand what happens and will happen in your community after a disaster. It is even more important that you understand how best to facilitate *coordination* of all those activities, foster *communication* among all the responding entities, and recognize the value of *flexibility* in maximizing the effectiveness of your community's response to a disaster. These core principles of effective EM are particularly important in the response phase, as will be evident throughout this chapter.

7.3 DISASTER WARNINGS

Warning the public of an impending threat is a critical first step in responding to disasters. Of course, disasters vary significantly in predictability and length of forewarning. At one extreme, for example, hurricanes can be spotted and tracked well in advance, giving emergency managers and other public officials hours or possibly even days to establish an EOC, mobilize necessary resources, and urge the public to take appropriate protective actions. At the other extreme, an earthquake or chemical plant explosion offers virtually no advance warning. Between these extremes, tornadoes can be located and tracked fairly accurately, giving local officials some time, even if only minutes, to alert the public. Because of the great variability in forewarnings of disasters, it is critical in the preparedness phase for emergency managers to educate the public about the hazards in their communities, test their disaster warning systems, and provide clear guidelines for people and organizations to follow in the event of a disaster when every second counts.

In some sense, therefore, warnings can be considered both a preparedness and response activity. In the interests of simplicity and clarity of presentation, we will focus in this chapter only on actual disaster warnings and treat them accordingly as response activities. You should recognize however that while disaster warnings fall under response activities, other types of risk communication cut across the phases of disaster and focus on preparedness, recovery, and mitigation. Public education campaigns that seek to inform the public about common causes of wildfires and house fires or about the value of flood insurance are intended to prevent disasters from occurring in the first place or persuading people to take preventive measures that will assist them to respond to or recover from a disaster. In weather forecasting, a distinction is made between watches and warnings. Watches indicate that conditions are favorable for the emergence of a tornado, blizzard, hurricane, or ice storm. A warning indicates that a storm has been spotted. If these efforts are effective, people will pay attention to emergency warnings and respond appropriately, lessening the burdens on EM agencies and first responders.

In this section, our primary objective is to gain a better understanding of the disaster warning process and the factors that enhance the effectiveness of warnings. An effective disaster warning persuades people and organizations to take appropriate protective actions. Disaster warnings have been studied extensively for more than 40 years and we have learned a great deal (Sorensen 2000; Sorensen and Vogt-Sorensen 2006). Nevertheless, public officials continue to stumble, as evidenced in Hawaii in 2018 when authorities mistakenly issued a false warning to the public about an impending ballistic missile attack (DeYoung et al. 2019).

7.3.1 Warning Process

In the wake of Hurricane Katrina, some observers were surprised that so many people did not evacuate New Orleans at the urging of the city's mayor. Many observers attributed much of the suffering and human tragedy that ensued to the failures of some individuals to make the right decisions and leave the area. Inherent in that view,

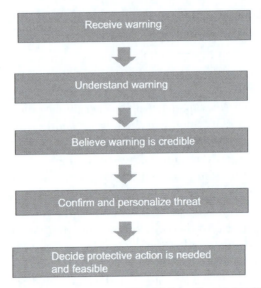

(*Sources*: Mileti 1999, p. 191; Sorensen and Vogt-Sorensen 2006, p. 191; National Research Council 2010, p. 8).

FIGURE 7.1 Warning Process

however, are the assumptions that everyone in the impacted area received warning messages; that the messages were clear and interpreted in the same way by all who received them; and that the residents had a level playing field in terms of ability to evacuate.

In reality, people do not always receive and interpret warning messages in the same manner; messages are not always effectively worded and delivered; and social factors such as socioeconomic status, disability, and others impact the ability of people to heed warnings and take protective actions. At first glance, the warning process seems simple and straightforward: public officials issue a warning and people comply with the instructions in the warning. Research, however, suggests that warnings are far more complex. As depicted in Figure 7.1, warning is a social process that involves several steps (Mileti 1999, p. 191; Sorensen and Vogt-Sorensen 2006, p. 191; National Research Council 2010, p. 8). As shown, there is a long way to go from public officials issuing a warning to the point where people and organizations take protective action. Every step presents uncertainties and intervening factors that can negatively impact the process.

7.3.2 Taking Protective Action

By issuing disaster warnings, emergency managers and other public officials hope to enhance life safety by urging citizens and organizations within their communities to take appropriate protective actions. Of course, the nature of a hazard determines what protective actions are appropriate. In the case of a tornado, for example, people are typically urged to get below ground or go to the center of their houses so that the walls protect against outside threats. However, in the days before a hurricane makes landfall, people may be asked to leave the area. At times, the primary purpose of a message is simply to urge people to stay tuned for more information and direct them to appropriate sources for additional information. During the winter months when inclement weather is expected, for example, public schools and universities often issue press releases and post announcements on their websites telling people to tune in to certain radio and television stations for important information about opening delays or cancellations.

For community-wide disasters, the primary protective actions are temporary sheltering and evacuation. Over the years, researchers have learned a tremendous amount about these measures and the insights they gained are extremely relevant to the practice of EM. If you are involved in setting up temporary shelters during a disaster, you may be surprised when very few people use them. Similarly, if you are involved in issuing an evacuation warning in your community, you may feel frustrated when many people stay put and ignore the warning. Researchers have consistently uncovered these patterns of behavior in their studies of numerous disasters, so we should not be surprised when people do not evacuate or utilize public shelters. In fact, by familiarizing themselves with research findings on sheltering and evacuation, public officials may dramatically improve their ability to persuade the public to take protective actions.

7.3.2.1 Evacuation and Temporary Sheltering

Sheltering and housing activities cut across the phases of disasters, beginning in the response phase and sometimes continuing through much of the recovery. In this section, we primarily consider temporary or emergency sheltering that falls into two broad types: public shelters and sheltering in place. *Sheltering in place* is a very common response to some hazards such as tornadoes. It involves urging people to stay where they are and giving them specific instructions on how best to protect themselves. For example, advice in a tornado is to seek shelter in a basement, storm cellar, or interior room of a house or building. A chemical or hazardous materials release may require that people remain indoors with windows closed and air conditioning systems turned off. *Public sheltering*, on the other hand, involves urging people to evacuate their homes and go to designated locations for safety. These locations often include school gymnasiums, common areas in churches, and large arenas, stadiums, or convention centers. In the U.S. we are starting to see communities, in areas of high risk, building congregate shelters to host hundreds of people at risk in a hardened facility.

In reviewing the major research findings on sheltering, we will limit discussion to public sheltering, which follows an official recommendation for people to evacuate a hazardous area. As mentioned previously, emergency managers may be puzzled when so few people actually show up at community shelters during and immediately after a disaster. Researchers have known about this pattern for a very long time. For example, in his comprehensive review of several decades of research on the topics of evacuation and sheltering, Drabek (1986) conclusively determined that most people in disaster-impacted communities do not go to public shelters.

Where do people go after a disaster, if not to public shelters? In every disaster, of course, a number of people will simply stay put. During the 1980 eruption of Mt. St. Helens in the state of Washington, a local resident named Harry Truman stubbornly refused to evacuate despite several warnings, and he is presumed to have died and been buried under several feet of ash from the volcano. According to Drabek (1986, 2010), most people who evacuate during a disaster will go to the homes of friends or relatives. While it is impossible for you to know ahead of time exactly how many people in your community will refuse to evacuate, how many will seek refuge with friends or family, and how many will use public shelters, you do not want, as many emergency managers do, to overestimate the amount of shelter use.

7.3.2.2 Factors Affecting Evacuation and Public Shelter Usage

In addition to relying largely on friends and family for safety, research has shown that several other factors affect the warning process and whether people take protective actions. These factors, described in this section, are summarized in various other publications (Drabek 1986; Mileti 1999; Tierney et al. 2001; Drabek 2010). While some of the social factors impacting people's ability and willingness to take protective actions may make perfect sense to you, others may be surprising. In both cases, you will benefit throughout your career by having a better understanding of these factors.

In their research on evacuation planning, Perry, Lindell, and Greene (1981, p. 160) identify various *community-level factors* that influence shelter usage among evacuees and suggest that "the use of public shelter increases when community preparedness is high, when the entire community must be evacuated, and when the evacuees anticipate that the necessary period of absence will be long." They go on to say that "even under these conditions, public shelters seem to attract only about one fourth of the evacuees at a given site." While Perry et al. recognize that shelter usage is typically low during disasters, they suggest that usage can be increased somewhat through enhanced community preparedness.

Researchers have also identified numerous *individual- and household-level factors* affecting warning responses and protective actions (Mileti 1999). These factors include gender, race, socioeconomic status, education level, knowledge and risk perception, and presence of children. While some of these factors positively impact the warning process, others decrease the likelihood that people will take protective action. Based on past research, it appears that protective actions are more likely to be engaged in by women, households with children, and those with higher socioeconomic status. Additionally, warning messages have more positive impacts on people with higher levels of education, greater knowledge about and heightened perception of risk, and those with more community involvement. On the other hand, racial and ethnic minorities, people of lower socioeconomic status, and those with less education are less positively impacted by official warnings and less likely to take protective actions. Social class significantly shapes exposure to hazards and the ability to escape them, as was dramatically revealed in Hurricane Katrina when many people simply did not have the necessary resources, including cars, to get out of the city.

Another factor stems from credibility of the person issuing the warning. A person issuing a warning should be as similar as possible to the population the warning should reach. Imagine, for example, someone with a New Jersey accent trying to convince someone in the Deep South to evacuate. A familiar voice will appear credible and thus motivate higher compliance.

Another impediment to public sheltering emerges when people believe that a shelter may not be ready for them. People with disabilities, for example, fear that shelters may not be able to accommodate their needs or perhaps a previous experience was unpleasant (van Willigen et al. 2002). We may also erroneously assume that everyone is warned. National Weather Service meteorologists noted a "hole" in the weather warning system: many systems bypass people with hearing disabilities (Wood and Weisman 2003). Senior citizens may prefer to remain in the comfort of their homes where they have medications, assistive devices, neighbors or family to help them, and pets to comfort them. Both groups experience lower incomes than the general public and have difficulties affording travel to, at, and from a shelter.

Other factors you may not have considered are far less intuitive. After Hurricane Katrina and other events, we learned that one major impediment to people seeking safety in public shelters was care of pets and service animals (Heath et al. 2001). Public shelters typically do not allow pets, even though owners, particularly the elderly, consider pets essential members of their families and are reluctant to leave them behind. Moreover, service animals provide necessary assistance to the vision impaired. Although public shelters are mandated to accept service animals (U.S. Department of Justice n.d.), not every shelter provider understands this (National Organization on Disability 2005).

Another less obvious impediment to evacuating and seeking refuge in public shelters is the fear of looting (Drabek 2010). As we will see later in this chapter, the idea that looting and stealing are rampant after a disaster is a major myth to which many people subscribe. Although these crimes are rare, people nevertheless make decisions about what protective actions they take on the basis of the looting myth. They fear that looters will target their property and steal their belongings if they leave their homes.

As all of this suggests, several impediments prevent people from taking protective action, in particular going to a public shelter after a warning is issued. Nevertheless, public officials and emergency managers often overestimate how much shelter space will be needed. Envisioning shelters overrun by thousands of frightened evacuees, they sometimes prepare for a massive onslaught that never occurs. As Fischer (2008) notes, it is important for emergency managers to recognize these factors and the actual behavioral patterns during disasters and open shelters accordingly. He suggests opening shelters "as needed," opening new shelters only after existing ones begin to fill.

Finally, we would be remiss if we did not also consider disaster warnings themselves as potential impediments to protective actions. Public officials sometimes wait too long to issue a warning; issue a warning that is too vague about who will be impacted by the impending threat and what actions should be taken; or convey contradictory messages to the public as events unfold. Because it is important for you to understand how to craft warning messages that are timely and accurate and effectively persuade as many people as possible to get out of harm's way, the next section discusses the research-based characteristics of effective warning systems.

7.3.3 Characteristics of Effective Disaster Warnings

Effective warning messages persuade those who receive them to take appropriate protective actions. Several established warning systems have been in operation for many years and new technologies promise to expand the reach and enhance the effectiveness of disaster warnings. Established warning systems include outdoor sirens used to warn of tornadoes and other weather events, the Emergency Alert System that scrolls messages across television screens, weather radio, and others. Newer technologies include cell phones, short message service (SMS) and text alerts, and social media websites including Facebook and Twitter (NRC 2010; Sutton et al. 2015; Canales, Pope, and Maestas 2019; Wehde, Pudlo, and Robinson 2019). In the wake of the tragic shootings at Virginia Tech University in 2007 many universities across the U.S. implemented text alert systems for informing students, faculty, and staff about emergencies on campus and providing brief instructions on what to do.

While researchers and EM professionals are hopeful that the new technologies can fill crucial gaps left by the older warning systems, we also must be mindful of the limitations of technology. Social media, for example, which has emerged as such an important tool for communicating risk and disaster information, can also be a major source of misinformation. To address that issue, the Federal Emergency Management Agency (FEMA) has launched a rumor control page to share trusted sources of information and discourage others from sharing information from unverified sources. As an example of this initiative, the webpage established for the COVID-19 pandemic can be viewed at https://www.fema.gov/disasters/coronavirus/rumor-control. Another limitation of new technologies is that they often improve the lives and safety of some but not all, creating a technological divide between those who have access to the technology and those who do not. Thus, in the realm of EM and disaster warnings, we would be wise to acknowledge that reality and recognize the limits of technology for keeping the public safe.

Past research suggests that several factors can enhance the effectiveness of disaster warnings (Aguirre 1988; Mileti 1999; National Science and Technology Council 2000; NRC 2010). All of these studies suggest that disaster warnings are most effective when they are:

- Broadcast frequently across multiple media.
- Consistent in content and tone over time and across media outlets.
- Crafted to reach diverse audiences.
- Specific and accurate about where the hazard is and to whom the message applies.
- Clear (no technical jargon), containing specific instructions on what actions to take, when, and why.
- Truthful and authoritative and delivered by an identifiable and credible source.

Drabek (2010, p. 105) offers additional advice for improving the effectiveness of disaster warnings. He suggests that community evacuation can be enhanced when emergency managers and other public officials:

- Encourage family planning for evacuation.
- Promote media consistency.
- Utilize forceful but not mandatory evacuation policies.
- Allay public fears of looting.
- Facilitate transportation.
- Establish family message centers.

Although research is fairly clear on what constitutes an effective disaster warning, warning systems that largely ignore the guidelines continue to be devised. For example, consider Department of Homeland Security's (DHS's) Homeland Security Advisory System (HSAS) put into place by Homeland Security Presidential Directive #3 and unveiled by the newly created DHS in the months following the attacks of September 11, 2001. Its purpose was to educate the public about the threat of terrorism, inform them about changes in risk levels, and encourage them to take precautionary measures.

To achieve those objectives, a color coded scheme was implemented in which green indicated a low risk of terrorist attacks, blue indicated a general risk, yellow indicated a significant risk, orange indicated a high risk, and red indicated a severe risk. However, based on the characteristics of effective disaster warnings described in this section, the HSAS had major shortcomings. As Aguirre (2004) aptly demonstrated, the terrorism alert system offered only a vague description of the hazard, was nonspecific in terms of to whom or even what region it applied, and failed to provide explicit instructions as to what people should do to protect themselves.

Additionally, the HSAS potentially suffered from what has been termed "warning fatigue," whereby the impact of a warning system on behavior is diminished when the public is continually warned about a hazard that does not materialize into a disaster (Sorensen and Vogt-Sorensen 2006). Because of these and other potential problems, the Secretary of Homeland Security, Janet Napolitano, ordered a review of the system. In September 2009, the Homeland Security Advisory Council submitted its written report, *Homeland Security Advisory System: Task Force Report and Recommendations*, concluding that "The system's ability to communicate useful information in a credible manner to the public is poor. Significant rethinking of how to communicate to this audience is warranted" (p. 1). As a result, in January 2011, Secretary Napolitano announced that the HSAS would be replaced by a new warning system, which is now called the National Terrorism Advisory System.

To better understand what constitutes an effective disaster warning system, consider news network coverage of severe weather in "tornado alley." If you live in or visit Texas, Oklahoma, or Kansas in the spring, you will undoubtedly experience severe weather and television coverage of it. During a typical broadcast, after a tornado has been spotted, meteorologists and weather forecasters inform viewers of its precise path, including its future trajectory and time estimates. Importantly, they tell viewers exactly what to do when the storm reaches their area. For example, viewers are typically told to go to a basement, storm cellar, or the center of the house away from windows. If you find yourself responsible for writing a disaster warning message in the future, think about the contrast between a detailed, highly specific tornado warning and the vague, ambiguous terrorism warning. To maximize the effectiveness of your warning message, model it more after the tornado warning than the terrorism alert.

7.4 DISASTER RESPONSE: MYTHS AND REALITIES

Despite what we have learned over the years about effective disaster warnings, some emergency managers and other public officials are still sometimes hesitant or reluctant to issue warnings to the public. Like the individual who refuses to go to a shelter out of fear of his or her home being looted, some officials fear that a premature warning will spark widespread panic in their communities. Indeed, fears about looting and panic in the aftermaths of disasters are fairly widespread among the public, and alarmingly, even among emergency managers. Looting and other antisocial behaviors are exceedingly rare in disasters and commonly called myths by researchers (Fischer 2008). In this section, we will explore these and other response myths in much greater detail, identify some of the sources of these myths, and contrast them with a more realistic, research-based view of the response phase.

At the most basic level, the myth- and the research-based views differ in terms of what they assume about social order in disasters. The *myth-based view* assumes that society is fragile and disasters cause a breakdown in social order, which leads to lawlessness, conflict, and chaos. However, the *research-based view* recognizes that society is resilient and disasters typically result in increased helping behavior, consensus, and enhanced social solidarity during the response phase. In fact, since the early 1950s, researchers have continually attempted to debunk the myths of disaster and instead document the recuperative and resilient capacities of societies (Quarantelli 1960; Fritz 1961; Quarantelli and Dynes 1977; Fischer 2008).

In this section, the myth- and research-based views are contrasted in terms of how they characterize disaster response at the individual, organizational, and community levels. The myth-based view assumes that individuals will suffer from reduced coping capacity, organizations will lack personnel, and communities will be torn apart. Conversely, the research-based view recognizes that individuals will actively contribute to the response effort, organizations will adapt and change to meet heightened demands, and communities will exhibit significant resilience. The primary purpose of our discussion is to introduce you to the research-based view and demonstrate its relevance to the effective practice of EM. Box 7.1 discusses these disaster myths in the context of the COVID-19 and explains how the scope, scale, and duration of disasters can affect the myths.

7.4.1 Myth-Based View of Disaster Response

When most people think of disasters, the myth-based view often comes immediately to mind. They envision massive piles of rubble, burning fires, blaring sirens, and traumatized victims milling around a devastated town. Under these tragic circumstances, it is difficult for many people to imagine anything but chaos and disorder. Associated with this imagery is the notion that the best way of dealing with the aftermath of a disaster is for authorities to swoop in and establish strong command and control over the highly disorganized scene.

At the *individual level*, the myth-based view assumes that panic and psychological breakdown will impede the ability of people to respond in an orderly, rational, and productive manner. In the simplest sense of the term, *panic* refers to highly individualistic or selfish, nonrational flight behavior accompanied by a complete disregard for social rules and attachments (Quarantelli 1954). Thus, the epitome of a panic-stricken person would be a person who abandons their own child to escape an impending threat or one who pushes, shoves, and tramples others to escape a burning building. The myth-based view assumes that because panic is a common response to disaster, emergency officials should postpone warning the public of a hazard until absolutely

BOX 7.1

DISASTER MYTHS AND THE COVID-19 PANDEMIC

Henry W. Fischer, PhD

Classic Experience. Social media, broadcast, and print media combine to help form our view of how people tend to respond to disasters. We learn to expect bad behavior. Why? Regardless of profession, most of us believe the way people behave in disasters is the same as what occurs in riots or civil disturbances. We have learned to believe people are likely to panic, loot, price gouge, prematurely evacuate, fill shelters quickly, become incapacitated by disaster shock, become psychologically dependent upon others, and require martial law to control the situation. We also often hear initial injury, death, and destruction estimates that are exaggerated. What is described here is the **classic disaster mythology**. These behaviors are normally *not* characteristic of natural disasters.

If **authorities** mount an **effective response** in support of the victims and survivors, reality diverges from the mythology. Survivors normally do not panic, they rationally respond to what they believe is needed to sustain their safety. Looting is extremely rare; crime actually declines in a disaster. The community usually rallies to help those in need giving free food, equipment, clothing, shelter. Price gouging may occur from outsiders, not locals. As fellow survivors bonded to the community, local businesses tend to give supplies away or sell at cost. Shelters tend to be the last choice of evacuees who seek the comfort of family, friends, or hotels. While survivors may be distraught, they are actually also the first responders. They initiate search and rescue as well as clean up. Martial law has never, yet, been declared in the U.S. Actual reports of death, injury, and destruction are often less than what are initially estimated.

On the other hand, if **authorities ineffectively respond**, myth can quickly become reality. For example, when forced to stay in the New Orleans Superdome post-Hurricane Katrina, the shelter lacked sufficient access to life supporting supplies. Many entered nearby stores to obtain what they needed. This was characterized as looting. Theft. Is this not rational behavior? Food is spoiling with the electricity out. Survivors need food... and take it to survive. Norms changed to meet the new needs. Similarly, response to these survivors was found to be slow, partially due to racist attitudes and fears by some of those sent to help.

Classic Disaster Myth versus Reality	
Myth	**Reality**
Panic Flight	Rational Decision-Making and Behavior
Looting	Crime Declines
Price Gouging	Giving Away Needed Items
Martial Law	Normal Law
Psychological Dependency	Ability to Respond to Needs
Disaster Shock	Sad, Yet Coping

Classic Disaster Myth versus Reality	
Myth	**Reality**
Evacuation – Don't Start Too Soon	Evacuation – People Hesitate, Start Early
Shelter Use – Fill Up Quickly	Shelter Use – Used as Last Resort
Exaggerated death/injury/damage estimates	Accurate death/injury/damage estimates

Contemporary Caveats. During the COVID-19 pandemic, U.S. authorities failed to speak with a consistent voice in recommending how to safely respond to the outbreak. Requiring mask wearing and social distancing varied greatly over the course of the disease spread. As a result, the number of cases and deaths increased dramatically more than was likely to have otherwise occurred.

Behavior differed from the classic findings during the pandemic. Price gouging occurred rather broadly. Rather than drawing together, there were great divisions among U.S. citizens. Political ideology, social class, and race seemed to exacerbate in conjunction with the authorities lacking consistency and clarity in their messaging. While many Americans still exhibited an altruistic response, there were quite a few deviations from the norm. Why? This is a very important question, as worldwide climate change will likely parallel and exceed the COVID-19 pandemic experience.

Scope, scale, and time. The scope or degree of disruption of normal life, coupled with the scale or breadth (how widespread) of the disruption and the length of time the event lasts, all combined to increase the suffering of the victims. And, responders faced an ever greater challenge. Can we expect to encounter behavior and response needs that are different (from those of a single community) when a disaster impacts an entire society (more catastrophic)? Most likely.

The next generation of disaster scientists and emergency managers is tasked, then, with discerning when the classic myths apply and when they do not. Best Practices will then need to vary to meet the different circumstances. To help with this process, we can utilize a *disaster scale* that differentiates between everyday emergencies, which are fairly limited in scope and cause only minor disruption; disasters, which are much wider in scope and cause more severe damage and disruption to a larger geographic area; and catastrophes, which can overwhelm entire regions or societies, such as COVID-19. Across this continuum, we can expect both citizen and EM needs and challenges to vary.

Reference:

For a more detailed discussion of the disaster mythology and the disaster scale, see: Fischer, III, Henry W. 2008. *Response to Disaster: Fact versus Fiction and Its Perpetuation*, 3rd ed. Lanham, MD: University Press of America.

necessary. It also assumes that a major part of the official response will involve controlling and containing all the panicked people in the community.

Another core assumption of the myth-based view about individuals is that disasters will cause severe psychological *shock and dependency*. Because of their psychological impairments, it is assumed that individuals will become immobilized and dependent on response agencies for basic needs. As with the panic myth, the assumption here is that individuals will not be available to participate actively in or contribute to the response. Rather, it is assumed that much of the official response effort must be devoted to addressing the pervasive and widespread psychological trauma brought on by the disaster. As Quarantelli (1960, p. 72) states, "the picture is one of docile and impotent individuals, waiting childlike for someone to take care of them."

At the *organizational level*, the myth-based view assumes that organizations will suffer personnel shortages and be largely ineffective. This assumption has two major components. First, it is often assumed that the only organizations that will respond will be those with clearly delineated disaster responsibilities such as police and fire departments and hospitals. Second, in light of the centrality of these organizations to the response effort, there is concern about the problem of role abandonment. *Role abandonment* is the failure of emergency workers to report to work and instead tend to their own personal or family needs. Because the myth-based view assumes that emergency-relevant organizations will not receive much help from other agencies and individuals in the community, the fear is that the effects of a disaster will be exacerbated if emergency workers do not report to work. Disaster myths also assume that organizations must assert strong command and control to counter the panicked and selfish responses of individuals, and that it is best to conform to rigid bureaucratic policies and procedures.

Finally, at the *community level*, the myth-based view assumes there will be intense community conflict, increased crime, and widespread social disorder. If you have watched any network news coverage of a recent disaster, the first thing you will notice is a focus on looting. Indeed, after Hurricane Katrina, the media devoted considerable attention to looting, playing a continuous loop of video footage of people removing merchandise from department stores and conveying reports of organized gangs terrorizing people in public shelters at the Superdome and New Orleans Convention Center. In addition to looting, the myth-based view emphasizes the breakdown of social order more broadly, for example, price gouging by greedy vendors who capitalize on the suffering of others and the emergence and spread of conflict and strife throughout a community.

If panic, looting, and social breakdown are myths, why do so many people, including the public, government officials, and even some emergency managers, believe them? As discussed in the next section, these myths persist despite several decades of debunking research. We can identify at least three primary reasons for the persistence of disaster myths. First, the *mass media* certainly plays a role in perpetuating disaster myths (Fischer 2008). In an effort to capture the attention of readers, listeners, and viewers (and thus satisfy advertisers), media outlets typically sensationalize disasters, focusing primarily on rare and isolated cases of antisocial behavior and presenting them as the norms rather than the exceptions. Second, as Tierney (2003) points out, various *institutional interests* benefit from depicting disasters as chaotic and lawless, including private security firms, advanced technology companies, and those seeking to establish an increased role for the military in civilian disaster response operations. Finally, Quarantelli (2002) suggests that the myth of panic and social breakdown may serve a useful function for *society at large*. Drawing insights from a classical sociologist named Emile Durkheim who argued that images of crime and criminals are functional for society because they reaffirm the importance of social rules, Quarantelli similarly suggests that perhaps images of panic, chaos, and social breakdown remind us all of the need to conform to cultural norms, maintain social relationships, and preserve social order, even during disasters.

7.4.2 Research-Based View of Disaster Response

The research-based view of disaster response contrasts sharply with the myth-based view. Its central premise is that individuals, organizations, and communities exhibit resilience in the face of disaster. In this context, *resilience* refers to the ability of individuals and social units to absorb and rebound from the impacts of a disaster. As will be discussed in more detail later in this section, certain vulnerable populations are at greater risk and some individuals, organizations, and communities rebound more easily and quickly than others, but the overall pattern of resilience is well established in the research literature (Dynes 2003).

At the *individual level*, the research-based view recognizes that disaster survivors will participate actively in the response effort (Yang 2021). Indeed, individuals possess important coping skills, and in times of disaster they typically exhibit remarkable self-efficacy and respond in an altruistic and caring manner. In virtually every disaster, survivors are typically the first responders on a scene, initiating search-and-rescue activities and providing preliminary care to the injured. This pattern was on vivid display during Hurricane Harvey in Houston in 2017 when dozens of citizen responders used their personal watercraft to conduct successful water rescues throughout the flooded city.

Rather than having to control panic-stricken people as they flee en masse, emergency managers instead find themselves struggling to manage and coordinate all the people and donations that quickly arrive at disaster scenes and in some instances, remain or return for long periods of time (Nelan, Penta, and Wachtendorf 2019; Nelan, Zavar, and Ray 2020; Penta, Wachtendorf, and Nelan 2020). This mass influx of people and supplies at the scene of a disaster is known as *convergence behavior*. In the first systematic study of the issue, Fritz and Mathewson (1957) identified several types of people who converge on a disaster site: returning survivors, curious spectators, volunteers, and those who seek to exploit the situation for economic gain. In addition to this kind of *personal convergence*, these researchers also discussed *informational convergence*, which in today's world would certainly include the mass media and its round-the-clock coverage of disasters, and *material convergence* – heavy equipment, other relief supplies, and donated items. In a much later study of convergence behavior, Neal (1994, 1995) documented the problems emergency managers faced in South Florida following Hurricane Andrew in 1992 when they were bombarded with unrequested donations, including winter coats and mismatched shoes. A similar pattern of excessive donations followed the explosion of a fertilizer plant in West Texas in 2013 and a tragic mass shooting at an elementary school in Newtown, Connecticut, in 2012. As Box 7.2 illustrates, the continuing problem of convergence and unrequested donations remains one of the most prominent unlearned lessons related to disaster response.

BOX 7.2

LESSONS UNLEARNED: DEALING WITH DISASTER DONATIONS

Disaster scientists have studied the mass influx of volunteers, supplies, equipment, and donations into disaster-stricken communities since the 1950s. They refer to this phenomenon as *convergence*, and for nearly eight decades, one of the most consistent findings of their research is that it can create significant problems for the very communities it is supposed to help. In particular, the onslaught of unrequested donations, including clothing, toys, and miscellaneous household items, can result in what has been termed a mass assault or even a second disaster. By understanding the long history of research on this topic, you will be in a batter position, both as an individual and as a professional emergency manager, to help alleviate these problems in the future.

You might be surprised to learn that, for example, most of the time, most things that people want to donate after a disaster are not needed. In disaster after disaster, people empty their closets and cupboards and send their used clothing and canned goods, often to places and people who do not need or cannot use what has been sent. Such unsolicited donations can cause significant problems when they require staff or volunteer time to sort and manage (Neal 1994). Though it is through a spirit of generosity that such donations arrive, the impact can be massive and cause significant problems for disaster-stricken communities.

Even more importantly, people who have lost everything need the right things at the right time in the right place, and your help in serving them *effectively* is needed. People who wear uniforms to work will need them replaced. If you do not have such uniforms in your closet (firefighter, police, medical, maid, delivery worker), then the most effective thing you can donate is money to purchase replacement uniforms – ones that are clean and in the right size. People may also need specialized, assistive devices like hearing aids, wheelchairs, scooters, walkers, canes, eyeglasses – and ones that work specifically for their specific needs. By donating money, an aid organization can move your money quickly through electronic means to that person with a specific need. Or, imagine the teenager who just desperately wants to fit in again – by wearing clothes that fit, and that are current, and that help them to express their own sense of individuality. Clothing symbolizes who we are, and when we donate money, aid organizations can issue vouchers so that teenagers can make their own selections. Regaining control in this manner also produces psychological benefits. Using the money locally stimulates the economy as well, and since most items can be purchased fairly close to a disaster area most of the time, your money can help restart local businesses.

Instead of holding a clothing or food drive, think about how to raise money for a reputable aid organization. Hold a garage sale, pass a bucket, or donate online. Sell used clothing at a yard sale. Set up a bake sale. Ask for donations from area businesses and hold a silent auction. Talk to companies in your area about donating a percentage of sales. Host a pancake breakfast. Put on a car wash. Donate your labor to mow yards in exchange for a donation. The money will be the most useful thing that you will send because it is the most flexible.

What happens when unsolicited donations do arrive? In big disasters, outside organizations help inventory, organize, and distribute goods or funds donated. In most disasters, the Seventh Day Adventists (a faith-based organization) set up a warehouse. They may get help from Americorps, the military, and other volunteers. From an online inventory, voluntary organizations can then log in to see what is available and then distribute items to people in need. Leftover items may be stored or offered to distribution sites set up by Goodwill or the Salvation Army stores. Used clothing is often sold to businesses that convert them into rags or other recyclable items and the voluntary organization then receives funds from the sale. The time that this can take might go on for months.

According to FEMA, cash is best because:

Financial contributions to recognized disaster relief organizations are the fastest, most flexible and most effective method of donating. Organizations on the ground know what items and quantities are needed, often buy in bulk with discounts and, if possible, purchase through businesses local to the disaster, which supports economic recovery.

To find a list of trusted organizations, visit National Voluntary Organizations Active in Disaster (nvoad.org).

Do not be part of the problem. Be part of the solution and do the right thing.

As far as the panic myth is concerned, extensive research suggests that it is rare or nonexistent (Quarantelli 1954, 1957; Johnson 1987, 1988; Clarke and Chess 2008). Norris Johnson (1987), a leading authority, studied victim behavior in a major nightclub fire in which 160 people perished and a crowd surge at a rock concert where 11 people died. On the basis of extensive research, he concluded that in both instances social norms and attachments continued to regulate behavior. For example, in the crowd surge, he found that people upheld norms of civility as evidenced by the fact that helping behavior became widespread. Moreover, helping behavior appeared to have been guided by prevailing gender role expectations. Specifically, he found that most women reported receiving help, while men were twice as likely to report giving than receiving help. In terms of social attachments, he found in the nightclub fire that the overwhelming tendency was for patrons to attempt to evacuate in the same social groupings – friends and family members – with whom they arrived, a very common phenomenon in building fires.

Many observers point to the attacks on the World Trade Center and remember the images of people leaping to their demise from the upper floors of the burning towers. Even in those desperate circumstances, we heard numerous reports of people first attempting to place phone calls and connect with loved ones before they perished. Indeed, the persistence of social norms and relationships in even the most extreme environments has led scholars in EM to question whether the concept of panic serves any useful purposes (Quarantelli 2002). Perhaps Johnson (1987, pp. 181–182) has addressed the matter most succinctly:

throughout the analysis I was struck not by the breakdown of social order but by its strength and persistence; not by the irrational, individual behavior of popular myth, but by the socially structured, socially responsible, and adaptive actions of those affected.

He goes on to conclude that "ruthless competition did not occur, and it did not occur because a functioning social order prevented it."

The issue of psychological stress and impairment has also been the subject of extensive research (for an excellent summary, see Edwards 1998). The basic conclusion is that disasters are capable of producing *both* negative and positive mental health effects. While the myth-based view focuses only on the negative effects and the debilitating impacts on individuals, the research-based view also calls attention to the possible positive effects. As Fritz (1961, p. 657) states, "The traditional emphasis on pathological 'problems' has focused only on the destructive and disintegrative effects of disaster; it has wholly neglected the observable reconstructive and regenerative human responses." Thus, although we should certainly be sensitive to the mental health needs of disaster survivors, we also need to recognize that survivors often experience heightened feelings of solidarity with others around them and a sense of empowerment as they contribute actively to a response effort. This is not to say that there is no need for psychological services after disasters, but just as they do with public sheltering decisions, emergency managers and other public officials sometimes dramatically overestimate demands for mental health services.

At the *organizational level*, the research-based view suggests that organizations are adaptive and resilient in the face of disasters. Rather than having to deal with personnel shortages from role abandonment, as assumed by the myth-based view, research suggests that organizations, especially those with disaster-related responsibilities, will instead be confronted with a massive onslaught of workers and volunteers. Consider the search-and-rescue and clean-up efforts at Ground Zero following the attacks on the World Trade Center. Firefighters, police officers, construction workers, and volunteers from all parts of the country toiled in the rubble for months, working exceedingly long hours and stopping only periodically to recuperate or attend funerals. Far from abandoning their roles, these workers overextended themselves, even placing their own health and safety at risk. Many of the first responders later suffered serious health problems as a result of the toxic exposures they faced at the site of the disaster, and as a result, the U.S. government passed legislation to address their medical needs.

The research-based view recognizes that numerous and diverse organizations are typically involved in responding to disasters. While police and fire departments and hospitals may be the operations that come to mind first, many other organizations step up after disasters. Thus, rather than focusing on command control within a single organization, the greatest need after a disaster is for improved communication between and coordination of multiple organizations. In an effort to more accurately describe the range of organizations involved in responding to disasters, the Disaster Research Center (DRC) developed what is now commonly known as the *DRC Typology* (Dynes 1970).

As you can see in Figure 7.2, organizations are classified in terms of their structures and the tasks they perform. Type I, or *established organizations*, such as police and fire departments, perform their regular tasks in a disaster, and in so doing rely on existing

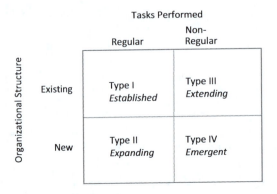

FIGURE 7.2 Types of Organized Responses to Disasters
Source: Adapted from Dynes (1970), p. 138.

structures. Type II, or *expanding organizations*, such as the Red Cross or Salvation Army, also perform regular tasks, but they rely on new structures – that is, they grow or expand from a small cadre of full-time professionals to large-scale operations of tens or hundreds of volunteers. Type III, or *extending organizations*, have established structures, but take on new tasks in the aftermath of a disaster – for example, a construction crew working on a project in town may lend its personnel and equipment to the clean-up effort. Finally, Type IV, or *emergent organizations*, such as informal search-and-rescue groups, do not exist prior to a disaster, form only after impact, and thus rely on new structures and perform non-regular tasks. The involvement of so many different organizations, as we will see later in this chapter, can create problems in terms of coordination and communication, and that is why rather than adhering to rigid bureaucracy, organizations must be flexible after disasters strike.

At the *community level*, the research-based view emphasizes resilience and social order rather than lawlessness and social breakdown. Instead of stealing from and fighting with each other, disaster survivors are much more likely to assist family members, friends, and neighbors. This increase in helping behavior after disasters led early researchers in the field to characterize the post-disaster environment as therapeutic in some respects for disaster-stricken communities. For example, Fritz (1961, p. 694) argued, "Contrary to the traditional pictures of man and society in the process of disintegration, disaster studies show that human societies have enormous resilience and recuperative power."

7.4.3 Sources and Limitations of Community Resilience

Researchers have identified various sources of community resilience in the face of disasters. First, although they are certainly tragic when they occur and disruptive to those they impact, many disasters are relatively low-impact events in relation to remaining community and societal resources, which allows societies to largely absorb the effects (Wright et al. 1979). Second, disasters are collectively shared experiences that often produce a unifying effect, whereby people feel heightened attachment to and responsibility for others and social distinctions and inequalities are temporarily suspended (Fritz 1961). Third, during a disaster, an emergency consensus typically arises, whereby community priorities that ordinarily are subject to competition and debate are simplified and oriented toward life safety activities (Dynes 1970). Finally, social capital, including cultural values, social norms and obligations, social relationships, and cultural traditions, ensures community survival and provides guidance and resources for responding to disasters (Dynes 2003).

Researchers also recognize however that disasters can and do produce negative effects and that societies can do much more to prevent them (Tierney 2014). Indeed, Tierney (2007) cautions researchers against overstating or exaggerating what she refers to as the "good news" paradigm in disaster research. Researchers have begun to identify various limitations of community resilience. First, for example, catastrophic events may severely limit the ability of a community or society to effectively rebound. The scope and magnitude of impact of a catastrophe, such as Hurricane Maria that caused massive damage in Puerto Rico in 2017, are so wide and devastating that even the capacity of surrounding communities to offer assistance is diminished. It is important to note however that even in catastrophes, people remain capable of and typically do exhibit pro-social, helping behavior, as demonstrated in Hurricane Katrina (Rodriguez, Trainor, and Quarantelli 2006).

Second, as discussed throughout the text, vulnerable populations, including the elderly, racial and ethnic minorities, the poor, and others, often suffer much greater impacts from disasters and steeper challenges responding to and recovering from them. Third, problematic pre-disaster conditions such as high crime rates and widespread political corruption may also limit the ability of a community to respond in a productive, pro-social manner, as these same dynamics will likely play out during the disaster (Fischer 2008). Fourth, a growing body of research in the field of environmental sociology suggests that technological disasters such as oil spills, rather than producing the therapeutic effects commonly observed in natural disasters, may instead create corrosive communities characterized by heightened psychological stress, intensified conflict over whom is to blame, and in some cases prolonged litigation (Picou, Marshall, and Gill 2004).

Finally, some types of disasters, such as riots, can involve intense conflict between first responders and community members, and in some cases, the response effort is actually thwarted by crowd members throwing rocks, bottles, and other objects at responders and otherwise attempting to undermine the response effort. These kinds of confrontations have occurred in several U.S. cities in recent years, including Baltimore, Maryland (2014), Ferguson, Missouri (2015), and Minneapolis, Minnesota (2020), where controversial police killings of civilians sparked widespread protests. In light of the conflict that accompanies these kinds of events, researchers have historically made a distinction between natural disasters, which typically evoke consensus and solidarity and conflict-type events, such as riots, which involve intentional acts of property damage and disruption (Peek and Sutton 2003).

7.5 DISASTER RESPONSE IN AN INTERNATIONAL CONTEXT

The myths and realities of human response to disaster discussed in this chapter are based largely on research conducted on events in the U.S. In light of that fact, it is reasonable to question whether the same kinds of response patterns would be present in another country. Do people in other countries respond to natural disasters in the same pro-social manner described above? Do they rely as heavily on informal social networks, including family and friends? Does the outpouring of support occur in response to international disasters? The simplest answer to these questions is that there are some basic similarities in disaster responses across countries but there are also important differences.

At the most basic level, international research suggests that societies across the globe exhibit varying degrees of resilience in responding to disasters. In the wealthiest, most developed countries of the world such as the U.S., Canada, Australia, Japan, E.U. nations, and others, disaster impacts are typically absorbed relatively effectively, and the general response pattern resembles the research-based view of response described in this chapter. While the financial impacts of disasters in those nations can be very high, loss of human life is typically relatively low. Indeed, on virtually any indicator, including financial loss, damage to the built environment, and death toll, the ratio of disaster impacts to remaining societal resources is usually relatively low in the most developed nations.

However, disaster impacts on all these dimensions are typically very high in developing nations and in the least developed countries of the world (Kulstad-González 2019; Rayamajhee and Bohara 2019; Kroll et al. 2021). But the initial social response to disaster in those countries is often very similar to the pattern observed in developed nations, including survivors actively engaging in search and rescue and other activities; friends, family members, and neighbors helping each other; and volunteers, supplies, and resources converging on the scene. In other words, *social capital* such as interpersonal relationships, community ties, cultural traditions, and other factors serves as a source of survival and resilience in all societies, from the most impoverished and least powerful to the wealthiest and most powerful (Ritchie 2012).

Disasters in the developing world, however, typically produce much greater devastation and much more complex and difficult response challenges than those in developed nations. Developing nations include Brazil, Guatemala, Honduras, Mexico, Haiti, Honduras, the Dominican Republic, India, Indonesia, Pakistan, Turkey, Thailand, Sri Lanka, and many others. There are many reasons for the *heightened disaster vulnerability* of these countries.

First, substantial portions of their populations live in *extreme poverty*. As a result, in daily life and certainly when disaster strikes, people have far fewer resources to draw upon than those living in wealthier nations. Second, these societies typically have *vulnerable physical infrastructures*. Because of that vulnerability, the physical impacts of disasters on their built environments are often far more extensive than what we see in the U.S. and other developed countries. Third, stemming from the vulnerable built environment, disasters in developing countries often produce *sizable death tolls*. The January 2010 earthquake in Haiti and the 2004 Asian tsunami, for example, each resulted in approximately 300,000 deaths, and a devastating earthquake in Nepal in 2015 killed thousands more. With such widespread loss of human life, disasters in the developing world cause much greater losses in social capital – a primary source of resilience – than they typically do in developed countries.

Fourth, developing countries often have *weak or ineffective political institutions*. Countries like Turkey, for example, are known to have reasonable building codes governing development but lack enforcement mechanisms, leading to questionable building practices and massive damage and loss of life when earthquakes occur. In 1999, for example, approximately 20,000 people died in an earthquake in Turkey, largely from building collapses. Fifth, in many cases developing countries are more vulnerable to disasters due to a *lack of effective warning systems*. The death toll in the Asian tsunami in 2004, for example, was so high in large part because the Indian Ocean, unlike the Pacific, was not protected by an advanced tsunami warning system. Finally, developing nations face increased technological hazards. As the wealthiest and most developed countries shift their manufacturing operations to the developing world in search of cheaper labor power and weaker environmental regulations, they are exposing people in those nations to new technological risks. In 1984, for example, thousands of residents of Bhopal, India, died from a toxic release at a chemical plant owned by Union Carbide, a U.S. company.

7.6 DISASTER RESPONSE AND PRINCIPLES OF EFFECTIVE EMERGENCY MANAGEMENT

Based on the topics covered in this chapter, it should be clear that disasters, even in an international context, generally do not produce the kind of chaos and social breakdown envisioned by the myth-based view. Problems arise, to be sure, particularly in developing nations, but they typically do not center on the need to control hordes of unruly people. Instead, the greatest challenge in effectively responding to disasters is organizing and focusing the activities of the numerous individuals, informal groups, voluntary organizations, and public agencies that invariably arrive at the scene of a disaster.

Indeed, probably the two most common problems identified in after-action reports about disasters are the lack of coordination among responding organizations and breakdowns in communication. Throughout your career, you can do your part in overcoming those challenges by remembering the principles of effective EM introduced in this book. In particular, the most effective strategies to embrace during the response phase are comprehensive EM, integrated EM, and flexibility.

7.6.1 Comprehensive Emergency Management

As discussed throughout this book, many hazards and disasters confront modern society. These threats vary, of course, in terms of the length of forewarning they afford and the scope, magnitude, and duration of their potential impacts. Each disaster agent is unique. Responding to a chemical, biological, or nuclear attack, for example, would certainly require the involvement of highly trained specialists and the use of specialized equipment not typically needed for natural disasters. *Comprehensive emergency management*, however, recognizes that various types of hazards share a great deal in common. For example, they are all capable of producing extensive physical damage, causing major injuries and deaths, and, importantly, creating major social disruption. Indeed, an event is only recognized as a disaster when it impacts human societies.

As social events, then, disasters of all types create some common social responses that have been described in this chapter and produce common management problems. Convergence behavior or rushing to the scene of a disaster is very likely to occur, regardless of the hazardous agent. Additionally, as predicted by the DRC Typology, numerous organizations, both formal and informal and official and unofficial, will invariably become involved in responding to disasters of all types. As a result, regardless of the type of disaster involved, emergency managers will always have to organize and focus the activities of multiple response organizations. By embracing the *all-hazards view*, emergency managers maximize their ability to respond effectively to the broadest range of threats (Buck 2020).

7.6.2 Integrated Emergency Management

Integrated EM recognizes that all kinds of organizations are involved in responding to disasters. From this perspective, a major challenge for the emergency manager is coordinating, organizing, and focusing the activities of so many different response agencies. Coordination is a vital and far-reaching task. Emergency managers must facilitate coordination of multiple levels of government, coordination of government and nongovernmental organizations (NGOs), coordination within single organizations and across multiple organizations, and interactions among official and unofficial response groups and organizations. They must also manage the flow of information throughout the community and through the media and direct the movement of equipment, supplies, and donations.

Based on such a tall order and complex and important tasks, it may be helpful to consider some strategies for improving coordination. Keep in mind that none of these strategies is guaranteed and each has limitations. First, for example, emergency managers can improve coordination through *enhanced EOC design*, setting a center up in a way that maximizes communication among responding organizations (Neal 2003, 2005). An EOC is best viewed as a communication hub, not as a command post, where EM professionals and representatives from all the responding organizations can come together to identify and address emergency response needs. Whether the EOC is set up as a stand-alone facility in a city-owned building or as a mobile operation in a motor home or trailer, its purpose is to monitor, manage, and share information so that officials can make proper decisions. To facilitate communication and assist in the decision-making process, EOCs today are equipped with numerous advanced technologies, including web-based software programs, such as WebEOC, which allow stakeholders to communicate and share information remotely. Unfortunately, many modern EOCs are so oriented toward advanced technology that they actually impede communication because representatives from agencies sit staring at computer screens rather than interacting with others. Thus, EOCs should always be set up and designed in a manner that maximizes communication and facilitates collaboration and coordination among the multitude of responding organizations.

Second, *incident management frameworks*, such as the National Incident Management System (NIMS), predicated largely on the Incident Command System (ICS) developed by the fire services, can be useful for improving coordination. These systems are aimed at providing common terminology and organizing response activities into standard, recognizable areas (finance, logistics, operations, and planning). In the U.S. it is expected that all levels of government will use NIMS in a consistent manner, but as with all federal policies, actual implementation varies significantly. In their study of the use of NIMS in responding to Hurricane Katrina, for example, Neal and Webb (2006) visited the EOC in New Orleans and the Joint Field Office in Baton Rouge and found wide variation in organizational training in and use of NIMS.

Finally, numerous *advanced technologies* can assist emergency managers in coordinating response activities. Geographic information systems (GISs) and global positioning systems (GPSs) can be used to locate and track response teams or map areas of heavy damage. Remote sensing technologies can produce aerial images for damage assessment, and decision support software can be used to log, track, and prioritize response activities. Advanced technologies, however, should be approached with some caution. One reason for caution is that not all jurisdictions have access to the most advanced technologies, creating somewhat of a technological divide in community readiness for disasters. Further, satellites cannot see inside a building to assess damage and may require ground truthing (Eguchi et al. 2003). Another reason is that technological glitches invariably arise, including data compatibility problems and lack of system interoperability. Finally, technology should be viewed with caution to the extent that it may foster overdependence and constrain the flexibility and creativity of users.

7.6.3 Flexibility in Emergency Management

In addition to embracing comprehensive and integrated EM, emergency managers can enhance their ability to overcome response challenges by recognizing the value of flexibility. As discussed in Chapters 5 and 6, preparedness and planning are critical aspects of EM. If done successfully, these activities can greatly reduce the amount of damage and disruption caused by a disaster, lessen the number of physical injuries and deaths, and dramatically improve a community's ability to respond. During the response phase, however, emergency managers and other public officials will invariably encounter new problems and unforeseen challenges for which they may not have been trained or to which they may not have been given much consideration. When that happens, responders need to think creatively and be flexible about possible solutions.

There are two broad categories of flexibility in responding to disasters. *Individual-level* flexibility refers to improvisations enacted by individual responders and can take various forms (Mendonca et al. 2014). For example, a responder may have to perform a task without his or her usual equipment and rely instead on makeshift provisions. In the aftermath of the bombing of the Murrah Federal Building in Oklahoma City in 1995, for example, first responders used blown-out doors in the fallen debris as stretchers for carrying victims of the blast. As one contributor to the final report on the bombing observed:

> Probably the greatest tool of all was the rescue workers' ingenuity. In the early stages of the incident, I saw many circumstances in which rescue workers adapted standard tools to complete tasks for which the tools were not originally designed.

The report concludes, "This expedited the rescues of dozens of people in the early stages of the incident" (*Final Report: Alfred P. Murrah Federal Building Bombing, April 19, 1995*, 1996, p. 154).

Organizational-level flexibility involves adaptations on the part of the organizations. Similar to individual improvising, organizational adaptations can take several forms and usually result from resource shortages, unforeseen contingencies, or unmet needs and demands. For example, in the aftermath of the September 11, 2001, attacks, New York City's EOC had to be relocated when the building housing it was destroyed (Kendra and Wachtendorf 2003). Also in that event, thousands of people were evacuated from lower Manhattan in an unplanned water rescue operation (Kendra, Wachtendorf, and Quarantelli 2003; Kendra and Wachtendorf 2016). At both the individual and organizational levels, flexibility is often necessary to fill gaps left by the planning process and meet heightened demands of a disaster (Schakel and Wolbers 2021).

Certainly there will be times in your career when you will need to think creatively and exhibit this kind of flexibility. In fact, in all professions, not just EM, a premium should be placed on creativity and flexibility because it typically produces positive results. Of course, improvisations occasionally fail or backfire and create undesirable outcomes. In other words, at times doing things "by the book" is the best way to go and at other times it is necessary to "think outside the box." Like the football quarterback who must decide in a split second whether to run a play as called by the coaches or make a quick change at the line of scrimmage, the most effective leaders in any context decide, based on past experience or intuition, which path to follow. As you gain experience in the field of EM, your skills in this area will sharpen over time.

Some organizations, however, develop *important limitations on flexibility*. As Webb and Chevreau (2006) suggest, several *internal organizational characteristics* limit flexibility. For example, many organizations actually stifle flexibility and creativity due to their strict adherence to written rules and procedures, extensive specialization of tasks with accompanying diffusion of responsibility, and overreliance on technology to solve basic problems. Rather than producing innovators and problem solvers, these organizations instead create conformists and ritualists who define their jobs in very narrow terms and rely exclusively on protocol and standard operating procedures to perform tasks. There are also important *external constraints* on organizational and individual flexibility. Drabek (2010) calls attention to the climate of litigation so prevalent in modern society and the possibility that individuals and organizations may be legally liable for damages possibly resulting from failures to follow proper protocol. Additionally, we could consider the broader bureaucratic context under which EM falls as a possible external constraint on flexibility. With the creation of DHS, for example, many observers feared that FEMA would lose its autonomy and flexibility to respond to natural disasters when it was placed under the umbrella of homeland security. Those concerns were validated by the federal government's initially slow and ineffective response to Hurricane Katrina (Waugh 2005).

7.7 THE FUTURE OF RESPONSE

We have said throughout this book that disasters continue to increase in both frequency and severity, and this trend will likely accelerate and intensify in the future. In fact, given our global experience with the ongoing COVID-19 pandemic, we can say in a very real way that the future is now. As shown in Figure 7.3, we can expect future disasters to be creeping, compounding, cascading, complex, and catastrophic.

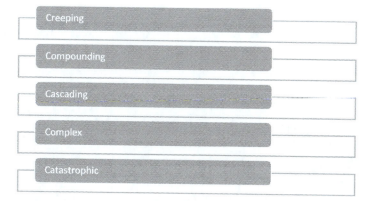

FIGURE 7.3 Characteristics of Future Disasters

Unlike conventional disasters, which are generally rapid onset events with a relatively short duration, *creeping* crises, such as climate change and the COVID-19 pandemic, develop slowly over time and are capable of producing disruptive impacts for months or even years (Boin, Ekengren, and Rhinard 2020). *Compounding* disasters occur when two or more events happen simultaneously or in rapid succession of each other. During COVID-19, for example, FEMA provided guidance to local communities on how to respond to hurricanes during the pandemic (U.S. Department of Homeland Security 2020a). Future disasters will also be capable of producing *cascading impacts* in which failures in one system cause ripple effects across multiple systems. In early 2021, for example, significant parts of Texas were impacted by a severe ice storm that resulted in widespread power outages. While residents may have been somewhat prepared to deal with the consequences of not having electricity, many were caught off guard when they lost water because the power outages shut down many water treatment facilities. To make matters worse, this all occurred in the midst of the COVID-19 crisis. With multiple disasters occurring at once and failures spreading across multiple systems, future disasters are clearly going to be more *complex* and difficult to manage. In short, because of their creeping, compounding, cascading, and complex characteristics, future disasters are likely to be far more *catastrophic*, defying geographic and political boundaries, impacting massive regions, and causing severe societal disruption.

As a result, future disasters will pose numerous challenges and place enormous strain on the EM profession. Obviously, given their increased frequency, scope, and complexity, future disasters will be *financially costly*. Responding to such large-scale events or to multiple events simultaneously will also *strain resources*. In addition to supplies and equipment, human resources, including first responders, health care professionals, emergency managers, and others, will be taxed, leading to possible *personnel shortages*, as occurred in 2017 when FEMA lacked sufficient personnel to deploy to Puerto Rico following Hurricane Maria because so many had already been deployed to Texas following Hurricane Harvey. Finally, with multiple disasters occurring simultaneously or in rapid succession, and with some events, such as the COVID-19 pandemic, lasting for months and years, we may find ourselves in a perpetual state of response and run the risk of experiencing *response fatigue*.

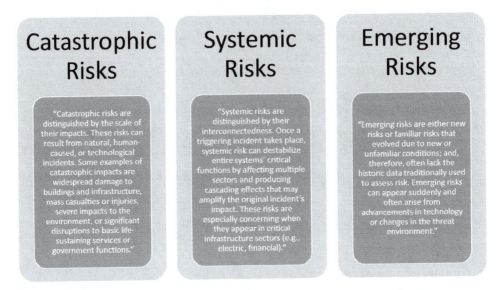

Source: Verbatim from U.S. Department of Homeland Security. 2020 *National Preparedness Report* Washington, D.C.: U.S. Department of Homeland Security. Pp. 16, 18, and 24.

FIGURE 7.4 Understanding Future Risks

To deal with these challenges, the EM profession is going to need to change in significant ways. As a first step, FEMA, in its *2018–2022 Strategic Plan*, established readying the nation for catastrophic disasters as one of its top strategic goals in recognition of the fact that disasters are growing in scope, severity, and complexity (U.S. Department of Homeland Security 2018). More recently, in its *2020 National Preparedness Report*, FEMA recognized that in order to enhance our ability to respond to future disasters, emergency managers will need to develop a better understanding of catastrophic risks, systemic risks, and emerging risks, which are defined in Figure 7.4 (U.S. Department of Homeland Security 2020b). Finally, to better equip future emergency managers to deal with challenging disasters in the future, the FEMA Higher Education Program emphasized both systems literacy and scientific literacy, in its report on *The Next Generation Core Competencies for Emergency Management Professionals* (Feldman-Jensen, Jensen, and Smith 2017). Scientific literacy, which was discussed at length in Chapter 4, is particularly important because it serves as the foundation for promoting evidence-based practice and advancing the profession of EM through science, which are major goals of this book.

7.8 WORKING AND VOLUNTEERING IN RESPONSE

As described in this chapter, considerable differences exist between first responders and emergency managers. Working in the response phase is only one of the activities of the emergency manager and is a role that involves coordination, communication, and collaboration across multiple agencies. In a small town, the emergency manager will likely play the role of EOC facilitator. In larger areas, EM professionals play more specific roles during the response period such as specializing in mass care (food and shelter), coordinating debris removal, handling massive unsolicited donations, assessing infrastructure damage and repair needs, reestablishing communications, and working with the media.

To be effective, an emergency manager must pursue education, training, and experience. Anyone who works in an EOC during a response period must be a highly trained professional capable of managing significant amounts of stress, working across agencies, and moving the community through crisis stage by stage. Although you are at the first stages in moving toward working in the response period, you can start by acquiring some knowledge beyond this chapter through the FEMA independent study courses. These free online courses offer insights into incident command, the NIMS, voluntary organizations, and more.

Volunteering during the response period also requires training. You can start with basic first aid and cardiopulmonary resuscitation (CPR) courses. Many disaster organizations like the Red Cross also offer shelter manager training and integrate volunteers well in advance into disaster action teams. After September 11, 2001, the U.S. also established the Citizen Corps (www.ready.gov/citizen-corps). Within your state, community, or possibly your university, you may be able to train for a community emergency response team (CERT) and be activated for crisis events or help with crowd management at a major sporting event.

Perhaps you have other kinds of interests. The Medical Reserve Corps integrates medical professionals into volunteer service. When coastal hurricanes threaten nursing home populations, for example, many residents are evacuated inland or to other host states. The Medical Reserve Corps receives, assesses, and cares for arriving evacuees. A fairly new program, called Map Your Neighborhood in the state of Washington, involves neighbors in identifying people who may need assistance and where neighborhood resources can be located for rescue purposes. If you volunteer for response, do not just show up and hope to help. Known as spontaneous unaffiliated volunteers (SUVs), such convergences of people create more problems than help. Enter a damaged area through an established organization for your own safety as well as that of those you seek to help.

***

SUMMARY

This chapter has addressed several important aspects of the response phase of disaster. Having read this chapter, you should now have a much better understanding what actually happens during the response phase and how to maximize the effectiveness of response efforts. For example, we identified the major characteristics of effective disaster warnings: consistency, specificity, and credibility. Additionally, we discussed the myth-based view of disaster that envisions chaos and pervades the popular imagination and contrasted it with the research-based view emphasizing resilience and adaptability.

While the public response to disasters is often productive, adaptive, and pro-social, we have also identified the most common response problems, including communication and coordination. We also discussed strategies for overcoming these challenges, including enhanced EOC design, appropriate incident management frameworks, and reasonable use of advanced technologies. For international disasters, we identified specific vulnerabilities of developing countries such as extreme poverty, vulnerable infrastructure, weak and ineffective political institutions, and other factors. We suggested that the key to effectively managing the response phase of disasters is to embrace core principles discussed throughout this book, including comprehensive EM, integrated EM, and flexibility. Finally, we discussed the future of response and suggested some important changes to help strengthen and improve the profession of EM for many years to come.

Discussion Questions

1. What can you do, both as an individual and as a professional emergency manager, to reduce the problems that occur when disaster-stricken communities are inundated with massive amounts of unrequested donations?
2. What role should social media play in disaster response? Is it an effective tool for issuing disaster warnings? What are some of its downsides and limitations?
3. What are the disaster myths? Where do they come from and why do they persist? Why is it important for emergency managers to understand them?
4. What would a worst-case scenario disaster look like? What challenges would it pose to emergency managers and are we currently equipped to deal with them? If not, what changes do you believe are necessary to strengthen the profession of EM and improve its ability to respond to future disasters?

Summary Questions

1. What are some activities that typically occur during the response phase?
2. What are the characteristics of effective disaster warnings?
3. What is a PDA and why is it important?
4. What should be the primary function of an EOC?

REFERENCES

Aguirre, Benigno E. 1988. "The Lack of Warnings before the Saragosa Tornado." *The International Journal of Mass Emergencies and Disasters* 6(1): 65–74.

Aguirre, Benigno E. 2004. "Homeland Security Warnings: Lessons Learned and Unlearned." *International Journal of Mass Emergencies and Disasters* 22(2): 103–115.

Boin, Arjen, Nagnus Ekengren, and Mark Rhinard. 2020. "Hiding in Plain Sight: Conceptualizing the Creeping Crisis." *Risks, Hazards, and Crisis in Public Policy* 11(2): 116–138.

Buck, Richard A. 2020. "A Better Approach to Managing COVID-19 and Its Effects." *Journal of Emergency Management* 18(7): 151–156.

Canales, Kristine L., JoEllen V. Pope, and Cherie D. Maestas. 2019. "Tweeting Blame in a Federalist System: Attributions for Disaster Response in Social Media Following Hurricane Sandy." *Social Science Quarterly* 100: 2594–2606.

Clarke, Lee and Caron Chess. 2008. "Elites and Panic: More to Fear than Fear Itself." *Social Forces* 87(2): 993–1014.

DeYoung, Sarah, Jeannette Sutton, Ashley Farmer, David Neal, and Katherine Nichols. 2019. "Death Was Not in the Agenda for the Day: Emotions, Behavioral Reactions, and Perceptions in Response to the 2018 Hawaii Wireless Emergency Alert." *International Journal of Disaster Risk Reduction* 36. doi: 101078.10.1016/j.ijdrr.2019.101078.

Drabek, Thomas. 1986. *Human System Responses to Disaster: An Inventory of Sociological Findings*. New York: Springer-Verlag.

Drabek, Thomas E. 2010. *The Human Side of Disaster*. Boca Raton, FL: CRC Press.

Drabek, Thomas E. 2013. *The Human Side of Disaster*, 2nd ed. Boca Raton, FL: CRC Press.

Dynes, Russell R. 1970. *Organized Behavior in Disaster*. Lexington, MA: Health Lexington Books.

Dynes, Russell R. 1994. "Community Emergency Planning: False Assumptions and Inappropriate Analogies." *International Journal of Mass Emergencies and Disasters* 12(2): 141–158.

Dynes, Russell R. 2003. "Finding Order in Disorder: Continuities in the 9–11 Response." *International Journal of Mass Emergencies and Disasters* 21(3): 9–23.

Edwards, Margie L. Kiter. 1998. "An Interdisciplinary Perspective on Disasters and Stress: The Promise of an Ecological Framework." *Sociological Forum* 13(1): 115–132.

Eguchi, R., C. Huyck, B. Adams, B. Mansouri, B. Houshmand, and M. Shinozuka. 2003. *Resilient Disaster Response: Using Remote Sensing Technologies for Post-Earthquake Damage Detection*. Buffalo, NY: Multidisciplinary Earthquake Engineering Research Center.

Feldman-Jensen, Shirley, Steven Jensen, and Sandy Maxwell Smith. 2017. *The Next Generation Core Competencies for Emergency Management Professionals: Handbook of Behavioral Anchors and Key Actions for Measurement*. Emmittsburg, MD: FEMA Higher Education Program.

Fischer, Henry W. 2008. *Response to Disaster*, 3rd ed. Lanham, MD: University Presses of America.

Fritz, Charles E. 1961. "Disasters." Pp. 651–694 in *Contemporary Social Problems*, eds. Robert K. Merton and Robert A. Nisbet. Riverside: University of California Press.

Fritz, Charles E. and J. H. Mathewson. 1957. *Convergence Behavior in Disasters: A Problem in Social Control*. Washington, DC: National Academy of Sciences, National Research Council.

Heath, Sebastian, Philip Kass, Alan Beck, and Larry Glickman. 2001. "Human and Pet-related Risk Factors for Household Evacuation Failure during a Natural Disaster." *American Journal of Epidemiology* 153(7): 659–665.

Homeland Security Advisory Council. 2009. *Homeland Security Advisory System, Task Force Report and Recommendations*. Washington, DC: Department of Homeland Security. Available at http://www.dhs.gov/xlibrary/assets/hsac_final_report_09_15_09.pdf, last accessed May 26, 2011.

Johnson, Norris. 1987. "Panic and the Breakdown of Social Order: Popular Myth, Social Theory, and Empirical Evidence." *Sociological Focus* 20(3): 171–183.

Johnson, Norris. 1988. "Fire in a Crowded Theater: A Descriptive Investigation of the Emergence of Panic." *International Journal of Mass Emergencies and Disasters* 6(1): 7–26.

Kendra, James M. and Tricia Wachtendorf. 2003. "Creativity in Emergency Response after the World Trade Center Attack." Pp. 121–146 in *In Beyond September 11th: An Account of Post-Disaster Research*, ed. Jacquelyn L. Monday. Special Publication #39 Natural Hazards Research and Applications Information Center, University of Colorado: Boulder, CO.

Kendra, James M. and Tricia Wachtendorf. 2016. *American Dunkirk: The Waterborne Evacuation of Manhattan on 9/11*. Philadelphia, PA: Temple University Press.

Kendra, James M., Tricia Wachtendorf, and E. L. Quarantelli. 2003. "The Evacuation of Lower Manhattan by Water Transport on September 11: An Unplanned Success." *Joint Commission Journal on Quality and Safety* 29(6): 316–318.

Kroll, Alexander, Christa L. Remington, Pallavi Awasthi, and N. Emel Ganapati. 2021. "Mitigating the Negative Effects of Emotional Labor: A Study of Disaster Response and Recovery Workers after the 2010 Haiti Earthquake." *Governance* 34: 87– 106.

Kulstad-González, Tess. 2019. "Transborder Disasters and Vulnerability: The Case of the 2010 Earthquake in Haiti." *Human Organization* 78(4): 278–287.

Mendonca, David M., Gary R. Webb, Carter T. Butts, and James Brooks. 2014. "Cognitive Correlates of Improvised Behaviour in Disaster Response: The Cases of the Murrah Building and the World Trade Center." *Journal of Contingencies and Crisis Management* 22(4): 185–195.

Mileti, Dennis. 1999. *Disasters by Design*. Washington, DC: Joseph Henry Press.

National Governors Association. 1979. *Comprehensive Emergency Management*. Washington, DC: National Governors Association.

National Organization on Disability. 2005. *Special Needs Assessment of Katrina Evacuees*. Washington, DC: National Organization on Disability.

National Research Council, Committee on Public Responses to Alerts and Warnings on Mobile Devices: Current Knowledge and Research Gaps. 2010. *Public Response to Alerts and Warnings on Mobile Devices: Summary of a Workshop on Current Knowledge and Research Gaps*. Washington, DC: The National Academies Press.

National Science and Technology Council, Committee on Environment and Natural Resources. 2000. *Effective Disaster Warnings: Report by the Working Group on Natural Disaster Information Systems, Subcommittee on Natural Disaster Reduction*. Washington, DC: National Science and Technology Council.

Neal, David M. 1994. "Consequences of Excessive Donations in Disaster: The Case of Hurricane Andrew." *Disaster Management* 6(1): 23–28.

Neal, David M. 1995. "Crowds, Convergence, and Disasters." *Crowd Management* 2(1): 13–16.

Neal, David M. 2003. "Design Characteristics of Emergency Operating Centers." *Journal of Emergency Management* 1(2): 35–38.

Neal, David M. 2005. "Case Studies of Four Emergency Operating Centers." *Journal of Emergency Management* 3(1): 29–32.

Neal, David M. and Brenda D. Phillips. 1995. "Effective Emergency Management: Reconsidering the Bureaucratic Approach." *Disasters* 19: 327–337.

Neal, David M. and Gary R. Webb. 2006. "Structural Barriers to Implementing the National Incident Management System." Pp. 263–282 in *Learning from Catastrophe: Quick Response Research in the Wake of Hurricane Katrina*, ed. Christine Bvec. Boulder: Natural Hazards Center–University of Colorado.

Nelan, Mary M., Samantha Penta, and Tricia Wachtendorf. 2019. "Paved with Good Intentions: A Social Construction Approach to Alignment in Disaster Donations." *International Journal of Mass Emergencies and Disasters* 37(2): 174–196.

Nelan, Mary M., Elyse Zavar, and Stephanie J. Ray. 2020. "Chasing Utopia: Disaster Memorial Volunteers at the Joplin Memorial Race." *International Journal of Disaster Risk Reduction* 44. doi: 10.1016/j.ijdrr.2019.101413

Peek, Lori A. and Jeannette N. Sutton. 2003. "An Exploratory Comparison of Disasters, Riots, and Terrorist Acts." *Disasters* 27(4): 319–335.

Penta, Samantha, Tricia Wachtendorf, and Mary M. Nelan. 2020, "Disaster Relief as Social Action: A Weberian Look at Postdisaster Donation Behavior." *Sociological Forum* 35: 145–166.

Perry, Ronald W. Michael K. Lindell, and Marjorie R. Greene. 1981. *Evacuation Planning in Emergency Management*. Lexington, MA: Lexington Books.

Picou, J. S., B. K. Marshall, and Duane Gill. 2004 "Disaster, Litigation, and the Corrosive Community." *Social Forces* 82: 1497–1526.

Quarantelli, E. L. 1954. "The Nature and Conditions of Panic." *American Journal of Sociology* 60: 267–275.

Quarantelli, E. L. 1957. "The Behavior of Panic Participants." *Sociology and Social Research* 41: 187–194.

Quarantelli, E. L. 1960. "Images of Withdrawal Behavior in Disasters: Some Basic Misconceptions." *Social Problems* 8: 68–79.

Quarantelli, E. L. 2002. "The Sociology of Panic." Pp. 11020–11023 in *International Encyclopedia of the Social and Behavioral Sciences*, eds. Paul B. Baltes and Neil Smelser. New York: Elsevier.

Quarantelli, E. L. and Russell R. Dynes. 1977. "Response to Social Crisis and Disaster." *Annual Review of Sociology* 3: 23–49.

Rayamajhee, Veeshan, and Alok K. Bohara. 2019. "Natural Disaster Damages and Their Link to Coping Strategy Choices: Field Survey Findings from Post-Earthquake Nepal." *Journal of International Development* 31(4): 336–343.

Ritchie, Liesel A. 2012. "Individual Stress, Collective Trauma, and Social Capital in the Wake of the Exxon Valdez Oil Spill." *Sociological Inquiry* 82: 187–211.

Rodriguez, Havidán, Joseph Trainor, and E. L. Quarantelli. 2006. "Rising to the Challenges of a Catastrophe: The Emergent and Prosocial Behavior following Hurricane Katrina." *The ANNALS of the American Academy of Political and Social Science* 604: 82–101.

Schakel, Jan Kees and Jeroen Wolbers. 2021. "To the Edge and Beyond: How Fast-Response Organizations Adapt in Rapidly Changing Crisis Situations. *Human Relations* 74(3):405–436.

Sorensen, John. 2000. "Hazard Warning Systems: A Review of 20 Years of Progress." *Natural Hazards Review* 1: 119–125.

Sorensen, John H. and Barbara Vogt-Sorensen. 2006. "Community Processes: Warning and Evacuation." Pp. 183–199 in *Handbook of Disaster Research*, eds. Havidan Rodriguez, Enrico L. Quarantelli, and Russell R. Dynes. New York: Springer.

Sutton, Jeannette, C. B. Gibson, E. S. Spiro, C. League, S. M. Fitzhugh, C. T. Butts. 2015. "What It Takes to Get Passed On: Message Content, Style, and Structure as Predictors of Retransmission in the Boston Marathon Bombing Response." *PLoS ONE* 10(8): e0134452. doi: 10.1371/journal.pone.0134452.

The City of Oklahoma City. 1996. *Final Report: Alfred P. Murrah Federal Building Bpmbing, April 19, 1995*. Stillwater, OK: Fire Protection Publications.

Tierney, Kathleen J. 2003. "Disaster Beliefs and Institutional Interests: Recycling Disaster Myths in the Aftermath of 9-11." Pp. 33–51 in *Terrorism and Disaster*, ed. Lee Clarke. New York: Elsevier.

Tierney, Kathleen J. 2007. "From the Margins to the Mainstream? Disaster Research at the Crossroads." *Annual Review of Sociology* 33: 503–525.

Tierney, Kathleen J. 2014. *The Social Roots of Risk: Producing Disasters, Promoting Resilience*. Stanford, CA: Stanford University Press.

Tierney, Kathleen J., Michael K. Lindell and Ronald W. Perry. 2001. *Facing the Unexpected*. Washington, DC: Joseph Henry Press.

United States Department of Justice. n.d. *The ADA and Emergency Shelters*. Available at http://www.ada.gov/pcatoolkit/chap7shelterprog.pdf, last accessed January 25, 2011.

U.S. Department of Homeland Security. 2018. *2018–2022 Strategic Plan, Federal Emergency Management Agency*. Washington, DC: U.S. Department of Homeland Security.

U.S. Department of Homeland Security. 2020a. *COVID-19 Pandemic Operational Guidance for the 2020 Hurricane Season*. Washington, DC: U.S. Department of Homeland Security.

U.S. Department of Homeland Security. 2020b. *2020 National Preparedness Report*. Washington, DC: U.S. Department of Homeland Security.

van Willigen, Marieke, Bob Edwards, Terri Edwards, and Shaun Hessee. 2002. "Riding out the Storm: The Experiences of the Physically Disabled during Hurricanes Bonnie, Dennis, and Floyd." *Natural Hazards Review* 3(3): 98–106.

Waugh, William. 2005. "The Disaster that Was Katrina." *Natural Hazards Observer*. Available at http://www.colorado.edu/hazards/o/archives/2005/nov05/nov05d1.html, last accessed January 25, 2011.

Webb, Gary R. and Francois-Regis Chevreau. 2006. "Planning to Improvise: The Importance of Creativity and Flexibility in Crisis Response." *International Journal of Emergency Management* 3: 66–72.

Wehde, Wesley, Jason M. Pudlo, and Scott E. Robinson. 2019. "Is There Anybody Out There?: Communication of Natural Hazard Warnings at Home and Away." *Social Science Quarterly* 100: 2607–2624.

Wood, V. T. and Weisman, R. A. 2003. "A Hole in the Weather Warning System." *Bulletin of the American Meteorological Society* 84(2): 187–194.

Wright, James, Peter Rossi, S. R. Wright and E. Weber-Burdin. 1979. *After the Clean-Up: Long-Range Effects of Natural Disasters*. Beverly Hills, CA: Sage.

Yang, Xheng. 2021. "Understanding Spontaneous Volunteering in Crisis: Towards a Needs-based Approach of Explanation." *Social Science Journal*. doi: 10.1080/03623319.2021.1884778

RESOURCES

- To learn more about training and educational opportunities available to first responders and emergency managers, visit the FEMA Emergency Management Institute (EMI) at training.fema.gov/emi.aspx.
- To learn about Citizen Corps and various educational and volunteer opportunities that may be available to you, visit www.ready.gov/citizen-corps.
- To learn more about the National Incident Management System, visit https://www.fema.gov/emergency-managers/nims.
- To learn more about the National Response Framework, visit https://www.fema.gov/emergency-managers/national-preparedness/frameworks/response.

CHAPTER 8

Recovery

CHAPTER OBJECTIVES

Upon completing this chapter, readers should be able to:

- Define, describe, and understand recovery as a process that occurs in both short- and long-term periods.
- Discern and explain how social justice and equity issues influence the speed of recovery for historically disadvantaged populations.
- Base recovery processes on principles that promote a holistic and sustainable outcome to promote resilience in future events.
- Situate recovery planning as a community-based process that produces a consensus-based vision.
- Describe how to involve the whole community in recovery planning to promote a more equitable outcome for all concerned.
- Reveal the full array of recovery functions needed so that everyone in a community can rebound equitably.
- Encourage mitigation as a central element of recovery planning.
- Offer insights into green recovery processes that provide valuable returns for damaged communities.
- Identify opportunities for both professional work and volunteer service in the area of disaster recovery.

KEY TERMS

- Cultural Resources
- Emergency Shelter
- Functional Needs
- Historic Properties
- Needs Assessment
- People-Centered Recovery
- Permanent Housing
- Preliminary Damage Assessment
- Reconstruction
- Recovery

DOI: 10.4324/9781003021919-10

- Rehabilitation
- Restitution
- Restoration

- Social Capital
- Temporary Housing
- Temporary Shelter

8.1 INTRODUCTION

As you learned in Chapter 3, a disaster means that numerous community functions have been disrupted, well beyond a personal emergency. Schools and businesses close. People lose their homes. The disaster compromises access to health care, food sources, and work opportunities. Streets, bridges, or ports become impossible to pass through. Utility companies must restore services. Sports and recreational events cease. People experience varying degrees of trauma, including personal injuries, family separation, and psychological harm. Debris and disaster effects can damage the natural environment, historical sites, and cultural heritage. Nothing feels normal or routine. The goal of recovery efforts, from planning to implementation, is to restore functioning to societies. Recovery also presents an opportunity to build back better in ways that restore equity, increase resilience, and reduce future risks. This chapter embeds this triple focus by defining recovery, explaining how to assess damage, laying out various recovery challenges, and walking through community-based recovery planning. A traditional section then concludes this chapter by looking at opportunities to work and volunteer during the recovery period.

8.1.1 Defining Recovery

After a disaster, politicians often go on camera and say, "we will build back." What disaster scientists and experienced emergency managers prefer they say is "we will build back *better*." Politicians refer to the process of *reconstruction* or the time period when communities repair and rebuild homes, businesses, and damaged infrastructure (Quarantelli 1998). By having a pre-disaster plan in place (which is rare) or by launching a focused post-disaster recovery plan, reconstruction might enable communities to repel future disasters and to address situations that foster inequitable outcomes. Integrating mitigation measures is a critical step (see Chapter 9), such as incorporating storm-resistant hurricane shutters and roof clamps, safe rooms, and elevations and by making these features accessible. By funding and implementing such mitigation measures in low-income areas and in homes for people with disabilities, recovery managers can reduce injuries, deaths, and property loss in future disasters. Reconstruction can also introduce more energy-efficient homes and businesses that reduce costs for homeowners and companies. The reconstruction period could also promote green space to absorb runoff, improve storm water systems, and relocate utilities resistant to the next disaster. In a wildfire area, increased use of native plants and reduced invasive plants can decrease fire risks.

A resilient reconstruction period should also move beyond *rehabilitation*, where recovery might improve a property but not address related issues. For example, public outcry arose when the U.S. Housing and Urban Development in conjunction with the Housing Authority of New Orleans tore down public housing and reintroduced mixed-income housing after Hurricane Katrina. The decision resulted in fewer homes for those at lower-income levels. *Restoration*, another term used in recovery, may be appropriate in some cases, albeit with added features. An historic structure, for example, can reuse elements saved during debris removal to retain meaningful historic character. Recovery managers can also integrate mitigation features like elevations, storm doors, and evacuation procedures for places like museums, libraries, or art galleries to safeguard the cultural and historic heritage sites that foster a sense of identity and place. Emergency managers can now raise floodwalls in Venice, Italy, to prevent repetitive flooding from inundating its historic business sector, cathedrals, and galleries.

Finally, the term *restitution* suggests that some kind of legal action or compensation is due after a hazardous materials spill, a levee failure, or a terrorist attack (Quarantelli 1998). After multiple California wildfires, for example, utility companies faced legal action by homeowners and communities that lost a massive number of structures. Recovery managers can also rethink restitution as a means to restore equity caused by historic injustices produced by segregation, prejudice, and discrimination. The Lower Ninth Ward in New Orleans, a historic community with a predominant African American population, faced catastrophic losses after Katrina. A strengthened levee system now protects the community better, but local residents still live in a sector of the city with food deserts and lack of access to affordable health care. Building back *better*: this means not just addressing the structures but also the people who live and work within them.

8.1.2 Recovery Is a Process

Clearly, mindful approaches to recovery need to take place, which requires collaboration and collective decision-making with those affected. Simultaneously, recovery managers will feel pressed to return a community to normal as quickly as possible. By focusing on two phases, both necessary steps and longer-term planning can be undertaken. First, *short-term recovery* involves assessing damages, restoring utilities and infrastructure, and placing people into temporary housing. Communities and people can then begin to restore daily routines while working through the more time-consuming reconstruction period. Second, the *long-term recovery* phase involves a community in tackling how, when, and where to build back better, often by launching a recovery planning effort. The process typically starts with damage assessments that form short-term period priorities and lay a foundation for long-term recovery planning. What is important to keep in mind is that emergency managers will need to walk people through the recovery process, which various populations and locations will experience at different rates. Rebuilding housing lost by people who are elderly, poor, or both may take a much longer than hoped. The process begins by determining what kinds of destruction occur and what the community needs.

8.2 DAMAGE ASSESSMENT

To launch recovery, emergency managers often participate in two kinds of assessments. First, preliminary damage assessment (PDA) totals the kinds of damage sustained by buildings, infrastructure, utilities, natural and cultural resources, environmentally sensitive areas, parks and recreational facilities, and businesses. Emergency managers then share the PDA with insurance companies, relief organizations and nongovernmental organizations, and government agencies. Second, needs assessments identify what people need to move forward, from social services and health care to psychological support and recreational opportunities.

8.2.1 Preliminary Damage Assessment

The PDA provides an overview so that others can know what kind of resources to send. In any disaster site, you will need to assess at a minimum the following:

- The number and type of houses damaged as well as the extent of damage, from minor to completely destroyed. A geographic information system (GIS) overlay of socioeconomic characteristics can identify low-income areas where people will need help the most. Relief agencies and voluntary organizations will be very interested in this information so that they can begin to explore places to set up long-term rebuilding efforts.
- High-risk locations. Within the damaged area can be found congregate or group living sites. A PDA should identify damage to nursing homes, assisted living facilities, rehabilitation centers, state schools, and group homes. Owners, agencies, and responders will then prioritize these areas for restoration of utilities, repairs to damaged roads, and rebuilding.
- People and businesses rely on infrastructure. Impacts to local utilities, including power, telephone, cell towers, gas, water, and Internet, may already be underway by the companies or agencies that own these sites but should be assessed. Damage to critical infrastructure such as bridges, underpasses, railroads, subways, airports, waterways, and roads may require a combination of emergency manager-driven assessments and those by appropriate offices, like public works. Emergency managers will need to gather and map that information. Mapping these kinds of infrastructural damages with an overlay of population demographics (including pre-disaster homelessness) can pinpoint areas of high need. Utility companies, for example, may need to focus on hospitals and health care sites for immediate restoration. A damaged community sector may need roads repaired so that small businesses can reopen or people can return to work. Communities that historically face health care, food, or transportation deserts will certainly need to be a priority as their situations will have worsened.
- A PDA should not overlook impacts to local cultural, historical, and environmental resources that represent a shared identity and heritage. Damage to such sites may also impact tourism and the local economy. Environmentally sensitive areas may be damaged with debris, overflow, projectiles, and contaminants and require specialized treatment. Often overlooked, such sites have recently been incorporated into the newest version of the U.S.-based National Recovery Framework (see Box 8.1).

BOX 8.1

FEMA NATIONAL RECOVERY FRAMEWORK

In the U.S., the Federal Emergency Management Agency (FEMA) has organized six Recovery Support Functions (RSFs) in its National Recovery Framework, with an emphasis on mitigation of future disasters by promoting resilience and sustainability.

- *Economic Recovery.* The Department of Commerce leads efforts to restore the health of the economy by involving the private sector, nonprofits, and local, state, and tribal governments. The goals are to share information, communicate, and collaborate.
- *Community Planning and Capacity Building.* Here, the Department of Homeland Security (DHS) and FEMA facilitate efforts to conduct community-based recovery planning and management with help from other federal agencies and private partners. The goal is to help communities make post-disaster recovery decisions that may impact a local area for years to come.
- *Housing Recovery.* The U.S. Housing and Urban Development Agency leads housing recovery and aims to deliver housing solutions that promote a sustainable and resilient recovery with adequate, affordable options that feature accessibility.
- *Health and Social Services.* The U.S. Health and Social Services Agency coordinates this RSFs. The objectives include assessing affected health and social service needs, restoring health care and social services, and attending to the well-being of those affected by the disaster.
- *Infrastructure Systems.* The U.S. Army Corps of Engineers coordinates infrastructure recovery, including planning, technical assistance, and support with navigating relevant processes and policies. A prime objective is to mitigate future disasters when rebuilding and to use green technologies.
- *Natural and Cultural Resources.* The U.S. Department of the Interior, with support from a wide array of other agencies, focuses on historic properties, cultural resources, and natural resources. Museums, green space, heritage sites, and more are supported with planning, technical assistance, and funding to preserve, conserve, rehabilitate, and restore natural and cultural resources at risk.

Source: For more information, visit https://www.fema.gov/emergency-managers/
national-preparedness/frameworks/recovery, last accessed February 5, 2021.

- The hit taken by the full array of local businesses, including home-based, locally owned, franchise, corporate, and major industrial sectors, should also be assessed. People will need their paychecks to rebuild their lives and area governments will need to restore the tax base. Government agencies and chambers of commerce will need the PDA information to know where to assist. Given that small businesses, often owned at higher rates by women and minorities, experience higher failure rates after a disaster, this PDA will prove crucial to making equitable investments in business recovery funding.

In short, emergency managers should be deeply involved in damage assessment as a starting point to launch community recovery. The various damage assessments can rely on windshield drive-by views or drone flyovers followed by detailed engineering inspections and mapping. The PDA starts the recovery process by understanding the impact on the built environment. A needs assessment can then help recovery managers discern the impacts on the people who live, work, and learn inside those structures.

8.2.2 Needs Assessment

A second type of evaluation is a needs assessment, which emergency managers, social service agencies, and voluntary organizations will need to launch relief efforts. Emergency managers should be aware of, support, and coordinate needs assessments, because knowing how the disaster has affected people will prove key to organizing a full and holistic recovery. Needs assessments will range from critical needs to quality of life issues, including:

- Food and nutrition availability, with particular attention to food deserts where people cannot easily obtain nutritional groceries.
- Clothing, particularly that suitable to work and school. Typically, clothing donations overwhelm locally impacted areas with inappropriate items. For people to return to work, they may need specialized uniforms or footwear. Children will need clothing that fits and enables them to blend in, as a way to help them recover psychologically and socially.
- Health care, including medical, dental, and psychological services, may have been disrupted. Assessing for these services, including accessibility and affordability, will help to surface specific needs to secure help from social service agencies and voluntary organizations. Professional medical services have mobile units they can deploy to health care deserts, and funding from civic organizations may help to meet this need.
- Job loss may have occurred and emergency managers may need to work with local offices to offer job fairs, retraining, and grants to provide for temporary disaster-related work. In the COVID-19 pandemic, local chambers of commerce offered business continuity seminars, personal protective equipment, and resources followed by job fairs.
- Childcare will certainly be a need. An assessment can reveal when and where childcare services will be needed. Specific voluntary organizations provide such care using trained and credentialed volunteers. Some also provide children's camps to help them process their disaster experience. Emergency managers can make that connection happen.
- Recreational areas and services matter. Having a place to go to relax, to gather with friends and family, and to get away from the stress of disaster can help. After Katrina, the City Park was devastated. After cleanup, it became an important place to walk, talk, and greet returning evacuees. Returning to sports venues,

concert settings, and club sites mattered a great deal as COVID-19 became increasingly under control.

- Schools will need to reopen, so that parents can manage rebuilding and/or return to work and children can experience normal routines. Temporary buildings may need to open or educators may need to launch online courses to reduce educational disruption.
- Animals also suffer in disasters, including pets, livestock, and zoo or aquarium animals. Restoring veterinarian care may be needed, as may efforts to establish rescue, shelter, reunification, and adoption services. Voluntary organizations may also arrive to help with injured or wandering livestock or to provide food, water, and first aid.

Recovery managers may undertake a needs assessment in several ways, from door-to-door surveys to online apps that collect needed information. Information collectors must take care to avoid missing people who are homeless, immigrants, minorities, or tourists. During the COVID-19 pandemic, for example, many states launched vaccine appointments using websites or apps. Elderly residents, who made up the group most likely to die from the virus, lacked technology or digital skills to access the sites. Language and literacy levels also matter, and providers needed to offer vaccine information in multiple languages and at appropriate levels. Trust levels will influence people's willingness to come forward to report needs (Phillips, Garza, and Neal 1994). A mass evacuation can also compromise abilities to secure information, when people scatter across a nation like after Hurricane Katrina (Bell 2008; Weber and Peek 2012). A variety of tools and approaches will be needed to identify needs, from traditional surveys to open forums to online apps.

Recovery managers can overcome obstacles to collecting information by partnering with trusted community organizations. Homeless advocates, shelters, and food banks can help with gathering information. Home health care agencies can reach out to elderly people living alone. Spanish-speaking health care personnel can reach undocumented workers. What community partners and advocates have is credibility, because they have provided for needs prior to the disaster. Working with these community-based and community-trusted partners increases an emergency manager's ability to collect useful information that is actionable toward recovery.

8.3 RECOVERY FUNCTIONS

Disasters disrupt community functioning, which recovery efforts seek to address. This section looks at the areas recovery managers typically address, with an emphasis on facilitating a more equitable recovery so that all can build back better, safer, and with resilience to thwart future events.

8.3.1 Shelter and Housing

Displaced persons generally move through four phases to secure shelter and housing (Quarantelli 1982). In the first phase, *emergency shelter*, survivors use cars, tents, overpasses, or other short-term means to protect themselves. Cyclone Nargis, which struck Myanmar/Burma in 2008, resulted in a massive number of fatalities when the military government refused access to external aid organizations. Thousands perished in emergency shelters. After Katrina, both formal and informal aid groups rescued survivors from overpasses and rooftops in New Orleans, where well over 1,300 people died. Isolation and long-term disruptions to the power grid from Hurricane Maria meant that people lacked access to suitable protective sites for some time in Puerto Rico.

The second phase, *temporary shelter*, happens when organizations supply food, water, and cover in more secure sites like tent cities, gyms, worship centers, or public buildings. Equity differences often affect such locations, as we saw in the 2010 Haiti earthquake when deeply entrenched global inequalities lengthened life in tent cities from the weeks to years. In the U.S., several types of temporary shelters may develop. General population shelters open to the public on an as-needed basis, and about 20% of the evacuating public will use them. The American Red Cross opens most shelters in the U.S.; though given a large enough disaster, communities may open a range of shelters (Phillips et al. 2011). General population shelters are required to admit people with disabilities and service animals, and many open colocated pet shelters, which spurs evacuation (Heath et al. 2001; DeYoung et al. 2021). Another type of shelter is currently named a *functional needs shelter* that opens for people with medical needs (Mace and Doyle 2017). Highly trained medical staff usually operate these types of shelters and often with the support of the federal and state governments. Such shelters decrease the potential for loss of life, particularly among seniors and people in fragile health situations.

Ideally, survivors will move quickly into the third phase, *temporary housing*, and reestablish a household routine. Such sites may continue to be tent cities in historically impoverished areas, or communities may use rental units, trailers, and mobile homes. Equity issues can again resurface, with survivors needing temporary housing close to work. However, disasters undermine affordable housing, which can result in permanent job loss or increased transportation costs. Moving people into trailer parks can also lose valuable social networks that provide child and elder care as well as access to food sources and health care. As another example, disability organizations sued the U.S. federal government over a lack of post-Katrina accessible trailers, which lengthened temporary shelter stays for people with disabilities. Finding or providing temporary housing can be challenging based on the magnitude and scope of the disaster, the income levels of those affected, and lingering patterns of inequity. In many developed nations, people assume they will find temporary housing locations (the third phase in moving from displacement to relocation) like a rental unit or another house while crews repair or rebuild their insured home. Some countries, such as the U.S., may provide eligible applicants with funding to rent units or in some instances, a travel trailer or mobile home. FEMA may use trailers when massive damage depletes temporary housing stock or in areas that lack rental units and/or affordable housing.

The fourth phase, *permanent housing*, occurs when people do not have to move again. Again, equity issues surface to prevent people from securing permanent housing. After Hurricane Andrew, income issues prevented families from securing permanent housing for up to ten years (Dash et al. 2007). Strategies to return people to permanent housing typically fall into four strategies (Comerio 1998). The *redevelopment model* involves national agencies in designing a recovery under a master plan. A second model, *capital infusion*, occurs when nongovernmental organizations (NGOs) render aid due to a lack of sufficient resources within the affected nation. A third model for permanent housing recovery, which is more typical in developed nations, is the *limited intervention model*. Here, people use personal insurance to recover from their losses. In many nations, government assistance will be available as material resources, grants, expertise, loans, or personnel. Again, equity reappears as those with insurance and personal income are most likely to regain permanent housing sooner. Without government assistance and help from NGOs, low-income households may experience delays (Tierney and Oliver-Smith 2012). The last approach, the *market model*, lets survivors try to secure permanent housing with limited outside support. To think through the impact of this model, consider how much insurance and money you or your family have available at this moment. Consider also the circumstances of elderly people living on a fixed income or people trying to survive in developing nations. Clearly, this model results in "winners and losers" based on income, often affected by systemic inequalities (Comerio 1998, p. 127).

What recovery managers can do includes (see also Box 8.2):

- Recognizing that equity issues will cause suffering and that emergency managers will need to address these matters to help survivors regain housing.
- Working with local government to prioritize mitigation measures for historically marginalized and/or low-income groups.
- Involving stakeholders and survivors in pre-disaster recovery planning to become fully aware of the issues they will face.
- Seeking out funding specifically for population groups likely to face a longer return to temporary and permanent housing.
- Inviting a range of NGOs into recovery planning, with an emphasis on people-centered housing approaches (discussed in an upcoming section).

8.3.2 Businesses

Preparedness is key to surviving disaster, but most businesses do little to prepare (Webb, Tierney, and Dahlhamer 2000; Phillips and Landahl 2020). Take a minute and think about the place where you or family member works. What would happen should that business have to close due to a disaster? *Downtime* occurs when disasters close businesses. As many businesses experienced in the COVID-19 pandemic, even short closures to save lives caused significant economic harm. Alternatively, consider how a power outage affects utilities that businesses rely on. Restaurants, dry cleaners and, coffee shops cannot operate without water. Employees cannot ring up sales and banks cannot offer any services without power. Without being open for business, employees lose their paychecks and cannot commence their own repairs. *Displacement* can also occur in a disaster. Even a few feet of water inside a business can cause relocation for close to a year with new costs for moving, rental, and reopening.

BOX 8.2

LESSONS UNLEARNED, EQUITY ISSUES IN SHELTER AND HOUSING

What works better to return people into permanent housing is an approach named people-centered housing recovery (Maly 2018). This approach involves survivors in decision-making to determine what works for them.

Internationally, the Sphere Project (2018) provides guidelines for establishing temporary shelter, and key standards address issues that undermine success in shelter and housing for historically marginalized people. For shelter and settlement (housing) planning, Sphere standards include:

- *Planning.* Stakeholders should be involved and their preferences honored. Planners should work to ensure safety and well-being of those in a shelter or settlement and think about recovery. Documented reports of assaults and abductions of women and youth have occurred in some post-disaster shelters, and planners should work to reduce such risks. Needs assessments should be integrated into planning so that shelters and settlements prove useful for and respond to the affected population.
- *Location.* Reconstruction should rely on local practices to create shelters, situating shelter and housing in its environmental context, using local workers, and timeworn building practices. Sites should also link people to their social networks and close to their work to fuel psychological and economic recovery. Homes built after the 2004 Indian tsunami became sweltering domiciles when rebuilding organizations failed to consider preferred layout and utility situations (Jordan, Javernick-Will, and Amadei 2015). Similarly, homes rebuilt in Sri Lanka failed to include traditional kitchens and lacked space for fishing gear (De Silva and Yamao 2007). Well-meaning rebuilding efforts can actually worsen people's situation when local practices are not considered.
- *Living Space.* People have the right to privacy and dignity within a living space, with consideration of age, gender, and cultural matters. To encourage a holistic and healthy home-based return to normal, space should allow for sleeping, washing, cooking, socializing, dressing, and playing.
- *Household Items.* Culture often dictates what we need inside our homes, from cooking practices to clothing. Clothing appropriate for the climate and for work will be needed rather than the often inappropriate donations that arrive. Equipment should be suitable to local needs, from cooking appliances and utensils to work vehicles. Donors should give careful thought to donations, with consideration around usage or replacement costs. Donating a gas stove when locals have always used a wood-burning unit means an extra expense when the gas runs out.
- *Technical Assistance.* Experts should provide support and assistance in a timely manner. As with previous recommendations, officials and especially outsiders should always consult and involve local residents and use local professionals. Local, sustainable, and familiar resources should be used during reconstruction and repairs, with an eye on how to increase resilience given the disaster that has

happened. Technical assistance can help locals interpret or revise building codes to increase resilience, but in a way that makes sense locally.

- *Security of Tenure.* Displaced persons should not lose their historic rights to housing or face eviction after resecuring housing. In many low-income areas, residents may pass on housing from generation to generation, with official paperwork lost over time. Proving tenancy can be challenging, and disputes can displace people again.

In short, whether working internationally or locally, listen to what people tell you they need. Anticipate those needs by involving them in planning before disaster strikes. Do not be surprised that people cannot use what others assume disaster victims need. An emergency manager's inability to anticipate and plan for everyone's needs in a disaster elongates suffering and reflects an insensitive, thoughtless lack of professionalism.

The structural losses could also be significant enough to cause permanent relocation. Disasters can also cause content losses, from computerized operations to inventory needed to make products.

Consider also the range of businesses that may need assistance. Small businesses face the highest risk of disaster impact usually because they have less cash flow and fewer resources to use after a disaster. Women and minority groups are more likely to operate small businesses, which have higher failure rates in disasters. Small businesses that are home-based are particularly at-risk, including home repairs, carpentry and cabinetmaking, consulting, childcare, and sewing, because the loss of a home is also the loss of a business (Enarson 2001). Larger businesses have more employees to help with the recovery and may have alternative locations to provide an infusion of goods, services, and funds (Webb et al. 2000).

Business recovery can be challenging, but recovery managers, local governments, and chambers of commerce can help. During the COVID-19 pandemic, for example, small businesses like restaurants pivoted to curbside and takeout. Museums gave virtual tours and theaters offered video plays. Educators, health care providers, and accountants worked from home using virtual tools. Yet, those deemed "essential workers" faced a frightening work environment, including health care workers, grocery clerks, postal carriers, and employees in food and agricultural production. Death rates appear to have been higher in some industries that did not accommodate public health precautions, including the meat packing industry (Dyal et al. 2020).

External assistance may not be readily available for businesses. In the U.S., the Small Business Administration offers loans of up to $1.5 million for up to 30 years of repayment for those who qualify. Economic Injury Disaster Loans may also be available. In other locations, businesses may need external aid. After the tsunami destroyed the commercial sector in Vailankanni, India, Oxfam and other partners rebuilt small businesses enabling them to open within a few months.

What recovery managers can do includes:

- Encouraging pre-disaster business continuity planning to scope out the full range of disasters that could cause disruption and plan accordingly.

- Working with the local business community to plan before and after a disaster so that the full economy can rebound efficiently. Include chambers of commerce, unions and employee groups, and professional associations that link to women and underrepresented minorities.
- Identifying small businesses at risk and prioritizing them for displacement relocation, employee assistance programs, and inventory restoration.

8.3.3 Infrastructure and Lifelines

Communities need a functioning infrastructure, including roads, ports, bridges, utilities, cellular, and Internet connectivity. The Haiti earthquake damaged the air and water ports significantly, causing considerable delays for arriving search and rescue teams. Outside military teams had to rebuild the airport to enable planes to arrive with life-saving supplies and teams. A derecho in 2020 left Iowa communities without power or cell service for a month. Ice storms can shut down travel and the delivery of goods and services for days to weeks. A cyberattack on a U.S. pipeline in 2021 meant that people had to pivot back to working from home. A structural problem with a bridge on Interstate 40 in the U.S. the same year meant that up to 40,000 vehicles a day had to be rerouted.

Two kinds of disruptions can occur: direct and indirect losses. A direct impact happened in Joplin, Missouri, when an Enhanced Fujita (EF) scale EF5 tornado badly damaged the local hospital and surrounding community. The tornado disrupted all utilities, damaged roads, and delayed outside help. Employees transported patients to alternate sites even as seriously injured and dying tornado victims arrived at the damaged emergency department. Indirect damage can result from power losses, like when a dry cleaner cannot operate without power or a domestic violence shelter loses its security systems. After the 1994 Northridge earthquake, businesses sustained an average of $150,000 in losses even without a direct hit (Tierney 1996). Social impacts occur too, from caring for family members to getting ready for work. Family members may need power for wheelchairs or oxygen systems. Employees may experience disrupted travel to work, resulting in lost wages and productivity. Students will not be able to go to work or study, resulting in increased stress around childcare.

Inequities also clearly exist with access to infrastructure, as we saw in the COVID-19 pandemic. Children in lower-income neighborhoods lacked devices or Internet connections to access remote learning. South Bend, Indiana, addressed that problem by putting Internet-enabled school buses into lower-income neighborhoods. Similar problems occurred in rural areas and people in developing nations were especially hard-hit. The spring 2021 COVID-19 surge devastated India when the virus overran available hospitals. Problems in delivering sufficient oxygen supplies caused unnecessary deaths. Frantic family members turned to social media, imploring friends to help them find life-saving resources for loved ones.

Infrastructure systems also interconnect, so that damage causes rolling effects. For example, a power outage results in nonworking traffic signals, street congestion, and communication disruptions (Zimmerman 2003). Banks and ATMs cannot function without power and people cannot use their bankcards to pay for food or fuel – if those locations can even open. You may remember the opening day of fall semester

2020, when online learning platforms and video delivery systems failed to cope with pandemic-related demand. We rely on infrastructure for so much, and recovery managers must address disruptions to help communities return to normal functioning.

The ultimate goal of an infrastructure-focused recovery is to build a more robust system able to resist future disasters. Bridges can become more structurally flexible for earthquakes. Blast-resistant windows and doors can deter wind-borne debris and external attacks. Stronger levees can resist flooding and storm surges. Companies can place utilities underground in many areas subject to strong winds and trim tree limbs to reduce outages. Communications systems can build in redundancies and rerouting options.

What recovery managers can do includes:

- Being present at meetings and public hearings when infrastructure is discussed and identify opportunities to mitigate disaster risks to roads, ports, airports, bridges, cellular transmission, and Internet connectivity.
- Encouraging infrastructure managers to integrate resilience, robustness, and adaptability as infrastructure is built or rebuilt (Zimmerman 2003). The American Society of Civil Engineers in 2021 awarded the grade of C– to the U.S.-built infrastructure (see https://infrastructurereportcard.org, last accessed April 23, 2021). Upgrades will be needed to sustain the nation into the future.
- Recognizing that infrastructure also contains inequities, including access to public transportation, sufficient Internet connections, and safe water.
- Addressing inequity in public infrastructure by insuring that rebuilt infrastructure does not sustain or exacerbate access to Internet, safe utilities, or public transportation.

8.3.4 Psychological Impacts

Many misconceptions exist about the impact of disasters on the human spirit. Media messages often lead us to assume that everyone impacted is immediately subject to Post Traumatic Stress Disorder (PTSD). However, PTSD rates remain low after most disasters. What is more common are stress reactions and higher levels of anxiety than normally found in the general public along with socioeconomic distress (Norris, Friedman, and Watson 2002; Norris et al. 2002; Makwana 2019). While most of the time people respond fairly well to such stress, in conditions of significant magnitude it is important to recognize when it is necessary to intervene and offer psychological recovery programs.

First, exposure to the disaster influences how we respond. Massive disasters that undermine response capabilities, leave survivors open to the elements, and cause deaths and injuries of loved ones, often increase stress. In areas where disasters force people to flee or lose valued social networks, our coping abilities may be undermined. The magnitude of a disaster may also influence our stress levels, as many of us experienced during quarantine, with job loss or while serving as essential workers throughout the COVID-19 pandemic.

Second, age appears to matter. One study after September 11 discovered that about 18% of children exposed to the trauma experienced a stress reaction (Fairbrother et al.

2004). People who are middle aged serve as key caregivers for both young and old which can increase stress (Norris, Friedman, and Watson 2002; Norris et al. 2002). However, older survivors may actually react better than we expect, in part because they have a lifetime of coping skills to draw upon (Prince-Embury and Rooney 1988).

Third, disasters are not equal opportunity events. Psychological impacts may be more likely for women and racial and ethnic minorities. Experts believe this is so because of prior and historic traumas they have experienced, which the present disaster complicates. It is also clear that the age-related caregiving, mentioned earlier, tends to fall heavier on the shoulders of women. Finally, historic patterns of segregation have placed racial and ethnic minorities in harm's way, including floodplains or closer to environmentally dangerous areas (Cutter 2006; Bolin and Kurtz 2018). Thus, exposure and magnitude due to systemic racism and sexism may actually be the cause rather than gender, race, or ethnicity.

Because many readers are considering a career in the field, good mental health is something that we should all work toward so that we can not only handle stress but assist survivors. Training and education for what to expect in a disaster helps as does experience. It is also good to process any disaster experience with a trained professional (Jenkins 1998; Phillips et al. 2008). And never forget the importance of social networks. After the 1995 Oklahoma City (U.S.) bombing, firefighters turned to their family and relatives as their most common strategy for addressing stress (North et al. 2002).

What recovery managers can do includes:

- Being a role model for others by building strong personal and work relationships before a disaster.
- Encouraging people to build strong personal and work relationships before a disaster.
- Supporting local efforts that bring people and families together.
- Inviting people to access and use employee assistance programs.
- Recognizing that disasters are not equal. Remember to include caregivers in disaster recovery planning because of the added burden they shoulder. Involve social service and advocacy organizations for historically marginalized people and their communities in recovery planning efforts, including psychological recovery.
- Broadcasting resource information widely and in multiple languages using people from the affected communities as spokespersons.
- Bringing people together to support each other, such as through reuniting families, developing support groups, forming neighborhood work teams, and convening community-based recovery committees, can be helpful. The goal is to enable people to reconnect socially to help them psychologically.
- Organizing events from anniversary remembrances to recovery celebrations. Community memorials are common after disaster, often at the one-month and one-year anniversaries (Eyre 2006).
- Supporting parks and recreation personnel in crafting events that bring people together from all over the community.
- Encouraging people to take time off, to pursue personal fitness, to eat nutritionally, and to minimize the use of alcohol and drugs.

- Accessing resources for your community. The Red Cross offers trained and credentialed mental health support. Church World Services outlines a code of conduct for disaster spiritual care and Lutheran Disaster Response trains and certifies chaplains.

- Partnering with schools to offer programs, an especially important step when a school is directly impacted.

- Involving mental health professionals in working with children and restoring normal elements of children's worlds. Encourage disaster planning for future events, because people will be motivated now more than ever.

8.3.5 Environmental Concerns

Disasters carry the potential to harm our environment, such as through the release of a hazardous material or through poor decisions regarding how we manage debris, rebuild homes, and treat nature's resources. When considering the environment around us, it is important to think through how we rebuild communities. Community recovery planning considers how to build and strengthen resilience for animals, plant life, water quality, and the air (to name a few).

Emergency managers now have options available to rebuild in a "green" manner that draws from renewable resources, promotes energy efficiency, and not only sustains but enhances environmental quality (Mileti et al. 1995; Mileti 1999). Consider, for example, what you can do with disaster debris. It might surprise you to discover that you can reuse mud, sand, and dirt that accumulates from floods and landslides. Properly managed, it can be used as topsoil or for landfill cover. Shingles torn off by hurricanes can be reused for resurfacing asphalt roads. Metals torn from vehicles, billboards, and homes can be sorted and sold, producing a profit for the affected community. Flooded buildings can be stripped and salvaged and windows, cupboards, and other items can be resold or reused. Communities can also mulch tree limbs and green matter to use in parks, schools, and other public locations. Creative thinking can minimize the debris sent to overburdened landfills and reduce rebuilding costs (Brickner 1994; EPA 1995; FEMA 2007; Habib and Sarkar 2017).

Public education about the environment is also important. Recovery leaders should inform the public of their responsibility to sort home debris properly and safely into recyclable, reusable, and hazardous piles. Officials need to follow careful guidelines for removal, disposal, and incineration of debris (FEMA 2007). Debris management must be carefully monitored so that the environment is not damaged further by hazardous materials that could leak into the ground and groundwater.

Some events represent environmental disasters by themselves. In 2010, BP Petroleum had an accident with its Deepwater Horizon Well. The explosion and resulting damage leaked extensive amounts of oil into the U.S. Gulf. As a result, commercial and recreational fishing had to be shut down and beaches closed for cleanup. Happening right at the start of shrimping season as well as the onset of summer tourism, the economic damage became significant. Agencies and organizations worked diligently to save wildlife, endangered wetlands, and fragile estuaries. Studies by Environmental Protection Agency (EPA) and other researchers found impacts to water quality and air quality from spilled and burned oil as well as infiltrations into the food chain (e.g., see Beland and Oloomi 2019).

What recovery managers can do includes:

- Building partnerships with environmental advocates and agencies prior to disaster and involve them in disaster recovery planning.
- Implementing pre-disaster mitigation efforts to safeguard protected species and sites from disaster impacts.
- Monitoring environmental impacts and environmentally sensitive areas after a disaster occurs and implement recovery plans or design ones that allow you to make sustainable decisions.
- Relying on experts in environmental protection and sustainability to guide recovery decisions after an event.
- Encouraging residents to integrate environmentally friendly features into rebuilt homes, such as permeable surfaces, native plantings, and solar energy.

8.3.6 Historic and Cultural Resources

All communities have rich origins and histories. Artifacts representing that legacy connect people with each other, build a sense of personal and collective identity, and give people a strong desire to return home. By working to identify historical and cultural resources and protect them before and after a disaster, an emergency management (EM) professional can help people retain their sense of ancestry and social connections and encourage people to rebuild their communities. Historic properties are defined as "any prehistoric or historic district, site, building, structure, or object included in, or eligible for inclusion in, the National Register of Historic Places" (FEMA 2005). Cultural resources include the built environment, monuments, and the art and sculpture found inside museums and around our communities and the ways of life that represent a shared cultural heritage.

Think about this for yourself. Where do you live? What is important to you where you are located? If you are a student in a college or university program, are you wearing your school colors today? Perhaps a t-shirt or cap with the name or mascot? If you "bleed" scarlet and gray, then you probably connect to The Ohio State University and know what "the Shoe" means to fellow buckeyes (like two of your authors). The "mean green" play football at the University of North Texas (your third author's university and alma mater).

Besides historical and cultural value, places also yield economic value. We travel to coastal areas to enjoy the beaches and ocean, to major cities to tour museums, and into areas that feature the culture and history of our ancestors. Such travel and tourism will generate significant amounts of dollars and taxes that support local economies. Restoration of those locations means that people will retain their livelihoods and the local tax base will benefit, yielding funds to restore the damaged community and maintain services.

The National Historic Preservation Act (NHPA) in the U.S. requires FEMA and other federal agencies to consider how any action they would take, such as demolition, relocation, or rebuilding, would affect the historic value of the property, including tribal areas. A Heritage Emergency National Task Force of 41 federal agencies and historic preservation organizations provides support (Quarantelli 2003). Each state or tribal area in the U.S. also has a State/Tribal Historic Preservation Officer who can serve as a key source for identifying historical and cultural heritage and offering strategies to maintain the integrity of the property or item. Indigenous communities will merit special attention and protection for their cultural and historical resources. Many communities have local historical associations that work to preserve locally meaningful places. Together, they can serve as important resources for a community recovery planning effort. In the U.S., the Digital Index of North American Archaeology (DINAA; http://ux.opencontext.org/archaeology-site-data/dinaa-overview/) identifies sites at risk from climate change. Readers can also visit U.S.-based National Historic Landmarks at the National Park Service website (https://www.nps.gov/subjects/nationalhistoriclandmarks/list-of-nhls-by-state.htm).

More globally, numerous World Heritage Sites have been identified for protection and preservation (for a list and pictures, visit https://whc.unesco.org/en/list/). Sites include ancient buildings, environmental areas, and sites that reflect specific cultures on every continent and in many nations. A number of such sites have been damaged by climate change, particularly flooding. Some have also been the target of terrorists because of the symbolic and emotional impact that intentional devastation can render.

What recovery managers can do includes:

- Integrating historic preservationists and experts into pre-disaster recovery planning.
- Conducting a pre-disaster inventory of historic properties and cultural sites that could be damaged by a disaster.
- Integrating mitigation measures into protecting those sites.
- Planning with local leaders how to protect sites during a disaster, such as evacuating art or artifacts.
- Engaging in post-disaster assessments of such sites and plan ways to restore appropriately historic properties and cultural sites.
- Involving a wide array of community members in the discussion so that locally meaningful sites are not lost, particularly those that represent the diversity of communities present.

8.4 PEOPLE-CENTERED RECOVERY

To ensure that the previous functions are covered in a disaster recovery plan, communities and their stakeholders must be involved in making decisions about recovery. Through participation, people bring fresh ideas and unique insights to the planning table that an emergency manager working alone might miss. We call what people bring in *social capital*. Think of social capital as akin to money, which people produce through social interaction, which can surface useful connections to build disaster resilience (Uphoff 2000; Woolcock 2000; Nakagawa and Shaw 2004; Ntontis et al. 2020). *Bonding* social capital occurs when people connect across similarities. After Hurricane Katrina, for example, the state of Mississippi held forums across affected areas so that people with similar interests could view and comment on rebuilding options. Similarities might result from long-held ancestral ties to an area, out of historic interests, or from shared economic livelihoods like restaurant owners. Coming together reveals those ties and yields useful and actionable information.

Bridging social capital accrues when people from different backgrounds problem-solve together. For example, university experts in sustainability can provide conceptual approaches to environmental preservation, and environmental advocates can specify where and how those approaches might work best. Or, parents needing post-disaster childcare might benefit from interacting with businesses that can provide locations and funds. People also produce *linking* social capital (Woolcock 2000) when new partners come to the table, such as city officials, NGOs, and the faith community. The linkages they produce and leverage might enable people with lower incomes or the elderly to return home faster.

Structural social capital reflects who we are in our communities. An architect brings knowledge of how to build structures, often with disaster-resistant designs that reflect local historical and cultural character. Trash collectors can visibly see the impact of debris on the environment and where storm water drains may be clogged. Mothers offer insights into what teenagers need, who may be at risk for domestic violence after disaster, and how to connect across a neighborhood. In short, no one should be excluded from participating because of their position in society. Rather, structural social capital results when we invite everyone to share their perspectives as knowledge embedded in our various family and community roles.

Finally, *cognitive* social capital includes perspectives brought from the rich array of cultures, faith traditions, and socioeconomic backgrounds that influence our worldviews (Woolcock 2000). Attitudes can spur or impede community planning. As one example, viewing recovery as an opportunity opens the door to possibilities: integrating mitigation measures, creating green spaces, prioritizing low-income families, harnessing solar and wind power, and more. Experts concur that planning is a process that should involve the entire community (Quarantelli 1997; Schwab et al. 1998; Norman 2004; FEMA 2005). In short, *people* serve as the heart of disaster recovery planning, both before and after an event. The job of a recovery manager is to facilitate their input to give their communities the best chance of making a robust and resilient recovery.

8.4.1 Kinds of Recovery Planning

Two kinds of recovery planning occur, either before or after an event. Ideally, pre-disaster recovery planning needs to be done well in advance to give a community sufficient time to produce a thoughtful and informed plan. Unfortunately, post-disaster planning occurs most commonly, often in the context of confusion, sadness, and very long workdays.

Whether before or after a disaster, a recovery task force should be convened with a local leader at the helm. Initial efforts should involve a wide array of stakeholders to generate social capital and produce useful insights and actionable results. A comprehensive plan should be developed that addresses key elements, identifies appropriate partners for the work, links the projects to funding, and generates a timeline. Recovery plans should include parts that address (at a minimum):

- *Housing.* Who should be involved? Too many times, rebuilding efforts fail to integrate people's real needs for their livelihoods, the local environment, the family structure, and regional cultures. People must be centrally involved in determining what works, because people-centered housing recovery works best (Maly 2018). On a related matter, how should homes be rebuilt after a disaster? Recovery plans should address new codes that can be applied to rebuilding efforts to safeguard residents from future events and create more resilient structures, which can be cost-prohibitive for low-income households and regions. Recovery planning also allows for the integration of green features that reduce reliance on utilities and protect the environment into the future. Homes need to reflect people's real needs so that they can sustain families, livelihoods, social networks, and both historic and cultural elements. Plans should address the rebuilding process, including involving outside organizations to focus on homes of single parents, low-income households, or the elderly. What is the process? Most locations require a permitting process. In the aftermath of a disaster, this process can be tedious and time-consuming, which often deters people now living even more complicated lives. Making the process user-friendly will be necessary while also ensuring that rebuilding is done correctly to avoid future disasters.
- *Businesses.* In many cities, tax revenue from businesses supports key social and governmental services. That revenue makes recovery possible. Addressing businesses also enhances the chances that people will be able to sustain their livelihoods, pay mortgages and rent, afford to eat, and go to school. Businesses of all kinds need to be at the planning table from the small or home-located businesses to major corporations. A wide range of considerations will need to be made, because planners may need to recommend strategies tore-route traffic, reestablish parking areas, and encourage that customers return. Employees may need paycheck support during downtime as many nations provided during the COVID-19 pandemic. Planning can identify temporary locations to address possible displacement. Bridging social capital might surface new conversations between utility providers and businesses that depend on them. During planning, the business sector can plan to rebuild green by using environmentally friendly building materials, paint, chemicals, lights, heating, cooling, and boiler systems (Smart Energy Design Assistance Center 2021).
- *Environmental Resources.* Planning around environmental concerns should address several elements. First, planners should identify environmentally sensitive areas and endangered or threatened wildlife. Planners should encourage viewpoints from environmentally knowledgeable experts and advocates and from local residents who know the area (Gibson, Hendricks, and Wells 2020). Second, appropriate strategies should link to regional initiatives focused on the environment, such as addressing runoff, best practices for green construction, increasing green space, or low-impact transportation options. Third, consider how to repair damage to the environment appropriately, such as tree plantings which also

absorb future storm water and promote energy efficiency when placed correctly around homes and businesses. Fourth, consider proactive strategies to thwart future disasters, such as reducing invasive eastern red cedars and eucalyptus trees that fuel wildfires. Fifth, plan to monitor the environment so that a disaster that involves environmental contaminants can be assessed over time. In the aftermath of September 11, long-term studies of airborne particulates have been crucial to understanding how first responders were affected (Moline, Herbert, and Nguyen 2006).

- *Historic Properties and Cultural Resources.* Shared places and their meanings will bring people to the planning table. Participants may come from museums, community organizations, genealogy clubs, cultural groups, or historic preservation enthusiasts. Recovery planning should address what to do beforehand, from protecting endangered sites, people, and resources in situ (where they are) to how to evacuate or rescue items during and after a disaster appropriately. The World Trade Centers, destroyed in the September 11, 2001, terror attacks, contained valuable art, some of which was retrieved, cleaned, and restored through careful, meticulous efforts. In 2019, fire severely damaged Notre Dame de Paris Cathedral, a medieval cathedral considered to be one of the most important symbolic sites in Paris, France. Fire destroyed the classic spire and vaulted ceiling, causing smoke damage to artwork and religious relics. A fundraising effort quickly secured resources to repair the building, scheduled to reopen in 2024.

- *Infrastructure.* The cost of infrastructure repairs can be so costly that in many countries, like the U.S., the infrastructure lags behind and requires considerable updating. Disasters afford an opportunity to do such work. Roads can be redesigned to improve traffic flow and to manage storm water runoff better. Bridges can be rebuilt with new earthquake-resistant standards. Ports can benefit from new docks and traffic routing technologies. Utilities can be placed underground or companies can introduce flexibility and redundancies to address future outages. Water treatment plants and sewage systems can be updated against regional hazards. The power grid can be made more robust. Newer types of technologies can be introduced, including wind and solar power options. Internet and cellular capacities can be strengthened or made publicly available. Public transportation options can be increased, including bicycle lanes. What can and should be done does not overlook people across and within the communities present in a region. Determining what is needed, where it is needed, and how people would use and benefit from such changes requires input. Funding will also be needed, which will require public investment through elected officials making critical, people-centered decisions.

- *Psychological Recovery.* Planners often fail to include social and psychological concerns in recovery plans. Yet even those most resilient to disasters, including emergency managers, face the enervating effects of daily struggles to rebuild. Moving past debris piles for months or years can be mentally draining. The COVID-19 pandemic left health care providers, public health officials, hospitality industries, and emergency managers exhausted, with some changing their profession as a result (Bufquin et al. 2021). Many of us remember how debilitating quarantine felt, especially by our elders in congregate care facilities. By addressing social and psychological concerns, community, household, and individual capacities can be supported and even restored. Nearly all communities have a cadre of social workers, faith leaders, and psychologists able to recommend and offer programs for the public. The diversity of that public should be considered. Because they must deal with a frustrated and exhausted public, attention should be given to our public employees through time off, debriefings, support, and recognition. Experts should be tapped to develop programs for children, seniors, historically disadvantaged groups, and others who may be at higher risk for disaster-related stress. Programs can represent a range of options as well, including public celebrations of reopened businesses and rebuilt homes, anniversaries of the event, and individual and group therapy. Public events might also include picnics, housing fairs, fitness initiatives, and sporting events.

8.5 WORKING AND VOLUNTEERING IN RECOVERY

There are always more than enough opportunities to work and volunteer during disaster recovery. One common route to disaster recovery work is to volunteer for a service organization or to hire on as a temporary employee.

Communities need volunteers more during recovery than in any other phase of disaster, including response. The best practice to follow is to volunteer for an experienced disaster organization (for a list in the U.S., visit www.nvoad.org), secure relevant training, including safety issues, and enter an area with the approval of local authorities. Once there, volunteers can pick up, clean up, muck out, sort debris, move furniture, install roofs, tape and mud sheetrock, paint, and help people move back in. Many volunteer organizations exist around the world, including:

- *Faith-based Organizations.* Most denominations provide volunteer opportunities through mission activities and experienced disaster-related organizations within their churches, synagogues, or mosques. Presbyterian Disaster Assistance, Buddhist Tzu Chi Foundation, Islamic Relief, NECHAMA Jewish Response to Disaster, and Mennonite Disaster Service work on rebuilding projects for years. Typically, the faith-based volunteer works on homes of the least fortunate with the most destruction. Without their assistance, many people could not go home again.
- *Community Organizations.* A number of community-focused organizations also dive into volunteer activity when disaster occurs. Habitat for Humanity is one that may have local or state chapters in existence or may set up one specific to the disaster site itself. Local community organizations may also recruit and commit volunteers to efforts in their home locations or they may facilitate the influx of external volunteers.
- *Civic Organizations.* Perhaps you or a family member belongs to a civic-minded organization such as the Lions Club, Rotary, or Kiwanis. These organizations exist to serve the public, usually through a specific capacity. By joining such an

organization, you can be ready to join in an effort they launch to assist those affected by disasters.

Once you have determined an appropriate organization, register with them and seek out any training they offer. Should a disaster occur where you live or where you would like to volunteer, go with an experienced organization that is working hand in hand with locals. Do not be the spontaneous unaffiliated volunteer ("SUV") who shows up – well intentioned – but ultimately not as useful as a full team arriving months to years later and fully equipped to meet needs that others have forgotten about.

A second option might be to volunteer as an intern for an affected EM agency. In the COVID-19 pandemic, such agencies needed help with messaging, serving a diverse community and in multiple languages, supportive office work, vaccine centers, computer and social media support, data gathering and analysis, and much more. You might also apply for paid work through a local, state, or federal agency. In large disasters, federal or provincial agencies will hire temporary workers to go to the site or to provide backfill support for employees deployed to the field. It is not unusual for a temporary position to turn into a more permanent career.

***

SUMMARY

Recovery takes time, particularly for communities and populations that lack resources. Recovery managers, including emergency managers, will be needed to think through short- and long-term recovery needs, including housing, psychological needs, businesses, infrastructure and lifelines, the environment, historic and environment resources, and more. Both preliminary damage and needs assessments should be conducted in order to build an understanding of what is needed, where, and for which neighborhoods, business sectors, and population groups. People-centered recovery is recommended as the best route forward, in order to accumulate and leverage the social capital that accrues when people work together. Community-involved recovery is likely to surface needs that various areas and populations require, enriching the range of perspectives made available for future-thinking recovery planning. Recovery and emergency managers need to lean in to the recovery process to offer needed insights and expertise and to facilitate communication between the various groups that require assistance.

Discussion Questions

1. Why is people-centered recovery valuable? How can involving people in planning for a recovery surface and enhance social capital?
2. Which recovery function interests you the most? What kinds of courses should you take in order to be able to help with housing, businesses, infrastructure, environmental, and historic resources?
3. Which kind of social capital sounds like it would be the most useful and why?

4. How would you launch a needs assessment in order to make sure that no one is left out? Who would be your key community partners?
5. What is the value of a PDA? Can you find examples on the Internet to discuss in class?

Summary Questions

1. What is the difference between short- and long-term recovery?
2. Why is recovery a process? Why is it an inequitable process?
3. What do recovery managers need to do during a preliminary damage and then a needs assessment?
4. How has recovery been defined and why do those definitions matter?
5. What are the areas of the National Recovery Framework (or a similar framework in another country) and why are those areas important?

REFERENCES

Beland, Louis-Philippe and Sara Oloomi. 2019. "Environmental Disaster, Pollution and Infant Health: Evidence from the Deepwater Horizon Oil Spill." *Journal of Environmental Economics and Management* 98: 102265.

Bell, Holly. 2008. "Case Management with Displaced Survivors of Hurricane Katrina: A Case Study of One Host Community." *Journal of Social Service Research* 34(3): 15–27.

Bolin, B. and Kurtz, L. C. 2018. "Race, Class, Ethnicity, and Disaster Vulnerability." Pp. 181–203. *Handbook of Disaster Research*, eds. Havidan Rodriguez et al. New York: Springer-Verlag.

Brickner, Robert. 1994. "How to Manage Disaster Debris." *C & D Debris Recycling* : 8–13.

Bufquin, Diego, Jeong-Yeol Park, Robin M. Back, Jessica Vieira de Souza Meira, and Stephen Kyle Hight. 2021. "Employee Work Status, Mental Health, Substance Use, and Career Turnover Intentions: An examination of restaurant employees during COVID-19." *International Journal of Hospitality Management* 93: 102764.

Comerio, Mary. 1998. *Disaster Hits Home: New Policy for Urban Housing Recovery*. Berkeley: University of California Press.

Cutter, Susan. 2006. "The Geography of Social Vulnerability: Race, Class, and Catastrophe." Available at https://items.ssrc.org/understanding-katrina/the-geography-of-social-vulnerability-race-class-and-catastrophe/, last accessed June 1, 2021.

Dash, Nicole, Betty Hearn Morrow, Juanita Mainster, and Lilia Cunningham. 2007. "Lasting Effects of Hurricane Andrew on a Working-Class Community." *Natural Hazards Review* 8(1): 13–21.

De Silva, D. A. M., and Masahiro Yamao. 2007. "Effects of the Tsunami on Fisheries and Coastal Livelihood: A Case Study of Tsunami-Ravaged Southern Sri Lanka." *Disasters* 31(-4): 386–404.

DeYoung, Sarah et al. 2021. *All Creatures Safe and Sound*. Philadelphia: Temple University Press.

Dyal, J. W., M. P. Grant, K. Broadwater, et al. 2020. Covid-19 Among Workers in Meat and Poultry Processing Facilities = 19 States, April 2020. *Morbidity and Mortality Weekly Report* 69: 557–561.

Enarson, Elaine. 2001. "What Women Do: Gendered Labor in the Red River Valley Flood." *Environmental Hazards* 3: 1–18.

Environmental Protection Agency (EPA).1995. *Planning for Disaster Debris*. Washington, DC: U.S. Environmental Protection Agency.

Eyre, Anne. 2006. "Remembering: Community Commemoration after Disaster." Pp. 441–455 in *Handbook of Disaster Research*, eds. Havidán Rodríguez, Enrico L. Quarantelli, and Russell R. Dynes. New York: Springer.

Fairbrother, G., J. Stuber, S. Galea, B. Pfefferbaum, and A. R. Fleischman. 2004. "Unmet Need for Counseling Services by Children in New York City After the September 11th Attacks on the World Trade Center: Implications for Pediatricians." *Pediatrics* 113(5):1367–1374.

FEMA. 2005. *Integrating Historic Property and Cultural Resource Considerations into Hazard Mitigation Planning*. Washington, DC: FEMA Publication 386-6.

FEMA. 2007. *FEMA 325*. Available at http://www.fema.gov/government/grant/pa/demagde. shtm. Accessed July 28, 2008.

Gibson, Jamesha, Marccus D. Hendricks, and Jeremy C. Wells. 2020. "Defining Partnership: Incorporating Equitable Participatory Methodologies in Heritage Disaster Recovery Planning for Socially Vulnerable Groups." Pp. 50–66 in *Learning from Arnstein's Ladder*, ed. Mickey Lauia. New York: Routledge.

Habib, Muhammad Salman and Biswajit Sarkar. 2017. "An Integrated Location-allocation Model for Temporary Disaster Debris Management under an Uncertain Environment." *Sustainability* 9(5): 716.

Heath, Sebastian E., Philip H. Kass, Alan M. Beck, and Larry T. Glickman. 2001. "Human and Pet-related Risk Factors for Household Evacuation Failure during a Natural Disaster." *American Journal of Epidemiology* 153(7): 659–665.

Jenkins, Sharon. 1998. "Emergency Workers' Mass Shooting Incident Stress and Psychological Reactions." *International Journal of Mass Emergencies and Disasters* 16(2): 181–195.

Jordan, Elizabeth, Amy Javernick-Will, and Bernard Amadei. 2015. "Post-disaster Reconstruction: Lessons from Nagapattinam District, India." *Development in Practice* 25(4): 518–534.

Mace, Sharon E. and Constance J. Doyle.2017. "Patients with Access and Functional Needs in a Disaster." *Southern Medical Journal* 110(8): 509–515.

Makwana, Nikunj. 2019. "Disaster and Its Impact on Mental Health: A Narrative Review." *Journal of Family Medicine and Primary Care* 8(10): 3090.

Maly, Elizabeth. 2018. "Building Back Better with People Centered Housing Recovery." *International Journal of Disaster Risk Reduction* 29: 84–93.

Mileti, Dennis. 1999. *Disasters by Design*. Washington, DC: Joseph Henry Press.

Mileti, Dennis S., JoAnne Darlington, Eve Passerini, Betsy Forrest, and Mary Fran Myers. 1995. "Toward an Integration of Natural Hazards and Sustainability." *The Environmental Professional* 17(2): 117–126.

Moline, Jacqueline, Robin Herbert, and Ngoctram Nguyen. 2006. "Health Consequences of the September 11 World Trade Center Attacks: A Review." *Cancer Investigation* 24(3): 294–301.

Nakagawa, Y., and R. Shaw. 2004. "Social Capital: A Missing Link to Disaster Recovery." *International Journal of Mass Emergencies and Disasters* 22(1): 5–34.

Norman, Sarah. 2004. "Focus on Recovery: A Holistic Framework for Recovery." Pp. 31–46 in New *Zealand Recovery Symposium*, ed. S. Norman. New Zealand: Ministry of Civil Defence & Emergency Management.

Norris, F. H., M. J. Friedman, and P. J. Watson. 2002. "60,000 Disaster Victims Speak: Part II. Summary and Implications of the Disaster Mental Health Research." *Psychiatry* 65(3): 240–260.

Norris, F. H., M. J. Friedman, P. J. Watson, C. M. Byrne, E. Diaz, and K. Kaniasty. 2002. "60,000 Disaster Victims Speak: Part I. An Empirical Review of the Empirical Literature, 1981–2001." *Psychiatry* 65(3): 207–239.

North, C. S., L. Tivis, J. C. McMillen, B. Pfefferbaum, J. Cox, E. L. Spitznagel, K. Bunch, J. Schorr, and E. M. Smith. 2002. "Coping, Functioning, and Adjustment of Rescue Workers after the Oklahoma City Bombing." *Journal of Traumatic Stress* 15(3): 171–175.

Ntontis, Evangelos, John Drury, Richard Amlôt, Gideon James Rubin, and Richard Williams. 2020. "What Lies beyond Social Capital? The Role of Social Psychology in Building Community Resilience to Climate Change." *Traumatology* 26(3): 253.

Phillips, Brenda D., Elizabeth Harris, Elizabeth A. Davis, Rebecca Hansen, Kelly Rouba, Jessica Love. 2011. "Delivery of Behavioral Health Services in General and Functional Needs Shelters." in *Behavioral Health Response to Disasters*, ed. Martin Teasley. Boca Raton, FL: CRC Press.

Phillips, Brenda D. and Mark Landahl. 2020. *Business Continuity Planning: Increasing Workplace Resilience to Disasters.* Cambridge, MA: Butterworth-Heinemann.

Phillips, Brenda, Dave Neal, Tom Wikle, Aswin Subanthore and Shireen Hyrapiet. 2008. "Mass Fatality Management after the Indian Ocean Tsunami." *Disaster Prevention and Management* 17(5): 681–697.

Phillips, Brenda., Lisa Garza, and David M. Neal. 1994. "Issues of Cultural Diversity in Times of Disaster: The case of Hurricane Andrew." *Journal of Intergroup Relations* 21(3): 18–27.

Prince-Embury, S., and J. F. Rooney. 1988. "Psychological Symptoms of Residents in the Aftermath of the Three Mile Island Accident and Restart." *Journal of Social Psychology* 128(6): 779–790.

Quarantelli, E. L. 1982. *Sheltering and Housing after Major Community Disasters: Case Studies and General Observations.* Newark: Disaster Research Center, University of Delaware.

Quarantelli, E. L. 1997. "Ten Criteria for Evaluating the Management of Community Disasters." *Disasters* 21(1): 39–56.

Quarantelli, E. L. 1998. "The Disaster Recovery Process: What We Do and Do Not Know from Research." Available at http://dspace.udel.edu:8080/dspace/handle/19716/309?mode=simple. Accessed January 28, 2011.

Quarantelli, E. L. 2003. *The Protection of Cultural Properties: The Neglected Social Science Perspective and Other Questions and Issues that Ought to Be Considered.* University of Delaware, Disaster Research Center, Preliminary Paper #325.

Schwab, James, Ken C. Topping, Charles C. Eadie, R. E. Deyle and R. A. Smith. 1998. *Planning for Post-disaster Recovery and Reconstruction.* Washington, DC: FEMA/American Planning Association.

Smart Energy Design Assistance Center. 2021. *Energy Efficiency Basics.* Available at https://smartenergy.illinois.edu/, last accessed June 1, 2021.

Sphere Project, The. 2018. *Humanitarian Charter and Minimum Standards in Humanitarian Response.* Retrieved February 10, 2021 from https://handbook.spherestandards.org/en/sphere/#ch001.

Tierney, Kathleen. 1996. *Business Impacts of the Northridge Earthquake.* Newark: University of Delaware Disaster Research Center.

Tierney, Kathleen and Anthony Oliver-Smith. 2012. "Social Dimensions of Disaster Recovery." *International Journal of Mass Emergencies & Disasters* 30(2): 123–146.

Uphoff, N. 2000. "Understanding Social Capital: Learning from the Analysis and Experience of Participation." Pp. 215–250 in *Social Capital: A Multifaceted Perspective*, ed. P. D. a. I. Serageldon. Washington, DC: The World Bank.

Webb, G., K. Tierney, and J. Dahlhamer. 2000. "Businesses and Disasters: Empirical Patterns and Unanswered Questions." *Natural Hazards Review* 1(3): 83–90.

Weber, Lynn and Lori Peek. 2012. *Displaced: Life in the Katrina Diaspora.* Austin: University of Texas Press.

Woolcock, M. 2002. *Social Capital in Theory and Practice* 2000 [cited 2002]. Available from http://poverty.worldbank.org/library/view/12045/.

Zimmerman, Rae. 2003. "Public Infrastructure Service Flexibility for Response and Recovery in the Attacks at the World Trade Center, September 11, 2001." Pp. 241–267 in *Beyond September 11th*, ed. J. Monday. Boulder, CO: Natural Hazards Center.

RESOURCES

- FEMA Recovery Management Toolkit; retrieved February 5, 2021, from https://www.fema.gov/emergency-managers/national-preparedness/frameworks/community-recovery-management-toolkit.
- National Organizations Active in Disaster; https://www.nvoad.org.
- New Zealand recovery framework; https://www.civildefence.govt.nz/cdem-sector/the-4rs/recovery/.
- Canada Public Safety recovery program; https://www.publicsafety.gc.ca/cnt/mrgnc-mngmnt/rcvr-dsstrs/index-en.aspx.

CHAPTER 9

Mitigation

CHAPTER OBJECTIVES

Upon completing this chapter, readers should be able to:

- Explain the steps involved in a threat and hazard identification, risk assessment, and community capability assessment process.
- Define mitigation and give examples of structural and nonstructural mitigation.
- Discuss the advantages and disadvantages of various kinds of mitigation measures.
- Explain how mitigation efforts can increase resilience.
- Describe strategies for involving people at risk in mitigation planning.
- Design a basic mitigation planning effort.
- Identify career and volunteer opportunities mitigation and resilience.

KEY TERMS

- Building Codes
- Buyout
- Capability Assessment
- Citizen Science
- Code Enforcement
- Community-Based Planning
- Community Engagement
- Crowdsourcing
- Dam
- Elevation
- Hazard Identification
- Insurance
- Land Use Planning
- Levee
- Mitigation
- Mitigation Planning
- Nonstructural Mitigation
- Relocation
- Resilience
- Retrofit
- Risk Assessment
- Social Vulnerability Assessment
- Structural Mitigation

DOI: 10.4324/9781003021919-11

9.1 INTRODUCTION

Resilient communities – those that can repel or rebound from disasters – embrace mitigation strategies that address and reduce known threats and hazards. Emergency management (EM) professionals lead their communities, businesses, neighborhoods, and individuals through a process to do so. This process involves a series of steps to identify threats and hazards, assess discovered risks, and outline strategies to reduce the impacts of disasters. This chapter explains and illustrates those steps, followed by a discussion of common mitigation strategies that can be pursued. The end goal is to empower communities at risk to become more resilient together. To do so, this chapter describes and explains how community-based mitigation planning can decrease disaster impacts and improve an area's ability to repel, resist, recover from, and be more resilient when threatened. That effort typically begins by understanding the risks that a community might face.

9.2 WHAT ARE THE RISKS?

Emergency managers lead efforts to determine what risks exist in their jurisdictions or workplaces. Whether situated in a state or provincial EM agency or functioning as an industry-placed emergency manager, that work requires a careful assessment of what could happen given the area's natural, technological, and human-induced threats. In the U.S., the Federal Emergency Management Agency's (FEMA's) process is called the National Threat and Hazard Identification and Risk Assessment (THIRA; see https://www.fema.gov/sites/default/files/2020-06/fema_national-thira-overview-methodology_2019_0.pdf, last accessed August 4, 2020). THIRA lays out a series of steps that an emergency manager undertakes to determine area threats and hazards, followed by a capability assessment and a risk assessment. Determining these three key items will influence what mitigation measures will need to be undertaken to promote resilience for people and places at risk.

9.2.1 Threat and Hazard Identification

Stop for a moment and think about the area where you currently live. What potential threats and hazards exist around you? Natural hazards, like an earthquake or tornado, might exist as could the possibility of floods or heat waves. You might also live in an area considered a likely target for a terror attack or near industrial sites that handle potentially dangerous chemicals. A threat and hazard identification starts by generating a list of such potential threats and hazards using an array of information sources (for ideas, see Box 9.1). Once an initial list has been developed, the next steps involve looking at the local history of that hazard and the probability that it might happen again. EM agencies typically lead such efforts.

Natural hazard histories can often be determined using existing sources. The U.S. Geological Survey (USGS), for example, offers detailed assessments of past earthquakes. The U.S. National Oceanic and Atmospheric Administration (NOAA) provides histories of past hurricanes and gives seasonal predictions. The U.S. Environmental

BOX 9.1

THREAT AND HAZARD INFORMATION SOURCES

The following sites currently contain information on an array of potential threats and hazards, last accessed August 4, 2020:

- Climate Change: https://data.worldbank.org/topic/climate-change and https://ec.europa.eu/eurostat/web/climate-change/data/database.
- Cyclones and Hurricanes: https://www.nhc.noaa.gov/climo/ and https://www.nhc.noaa.gov/outreach/history/.
- Earthquakes: https://www.usgs.gov/natural-hazards/earthquake-hazards/earthquakes.
- Floods, U.S.: https://www.weather.gov/marfc/HistoricalFloods.
- International Disaster Database: https://www.emdat.be/.
- Space Weather, https://www.swpc.noaa.gov/.
- Terrorism database: https://www.start.umd.edu/research-projects/global-terrorism-database-gtd.
- Tornado History: https://www.weather.gov/oun/history.
- Wildfire: https://www.usgs.gov/products/data-and-tools/real-time-data/wildfire and https://data.gov.au/data (search bushfire).

Protection Agency (EPA) maintains a list of hazardous waste sites that are undergoing remediation. Another source of information on hazards comes from the area's historical society, libraries, and historians. EM-DAT (https://www.emdat.be) provides a comprehensive, global database. You can find historical tsunami information as well (https://www.ngdc.noaa.gov/hazard/tsu_db.shtml). Such sources can be reviewed for their relevance to where you live or work to identify threats and hazards.

Many jurisdictions, especially at the state or provincial levels, have already generated a threat and hazard identification that planning teams can use (e.g., see https://drought.unl.edu/archive/plans/GeneralHazard/state/IN_2019.pdf, last accessed August 4, 2020). Professional agencies also participate in assessing criminal and terror threats, often through a fusion center where information is shared, assessed, and disseminated. Though typically not available to the general public, fusion center materials can be accessed by professional emergency managers (see https://www.in.gov/iifc/, last accessed August 4, 2020). In short, a threat and hazard identification effort will produce a list of possible risks, their historic occurrence and impacts, and the probabilities of that event happening again.

9.2.2 Capability Assessment

What capabilities would an EM agency need to address identified threats and risks? For example, if a hazard identification revealed a significant flood risk, what capabilities would be needed to address flooding? Three measures are used for capability assessment in the FEMA framework: impacts, critical tasks, and time frame metrics. As a starting point, what kind of impact might be expected? Most people remember

---

BOX 9.2

THREAT AND HAZARD IDENTIFICATION AND RISK ASSESSMENT

A THIRA can be produced in a table format to summarize information and walk through the process from initial hazard identification to mitigation implementation. A table can be as detailed and statistical as needed but can also provide a qualitative assessment (see below) that translates more effectively to a broad audience.

Threat/Hazard	History in Area	Probability of Reoccurrence	Loss Estimation	Risk Assessment	Mitigation Measure
Flood – due to river in area and increasing precipitation.	1913, 1953, 2005, 2018	One hundred-year event, reoccurrence increasing.	Significant impact to downtown, estimated $1.7 billion in structural and content losses.	High probability, high consequence.	Strengthen levee system, install flood pumps, increase insurance, design evacuation plans.
Cyberattack	2018, phishing scheme captures city payroll data, shuts down city operations.	Unknown, but attacks occur routinely and daily at some enterprises	Loss of personal identity information, captured personal data, infiltration of bank or credit card accounts	Medium probability, high consequence.	Educational campaign about phishing, ransomware, etc. Increase virus protection software. Update computers to provide higher resistance.
Pandemic	1918, 2020	Unknown, must always be ready	Significant loss of life and long-term health complications	Medium probability, high consequences	Wear a mask, wash hands, socially distance
Enter a local hazard here					

the impacts of COVID-19, which overwhelmed many health care systems as governments struggled to build the appropriate capabilities to respond. Hospitals ran out of personal protective equipment (PPE), which proved critical to protect health care workers, and had to ration care in some locations. The time frame metric was "now" to save the lives of those responding to critically ill and highly vulnerable patients.

Understanding risks that the hazard present will determine the depth of capabilities and the time frame needed to save people and places (see Box 9.2). For example, minor flash flooding (impact) would requires that a local jurisdiction alert the public and establish barricades (capabilities) to prevent people from driving into flash flood waters (rapid time frame). On a different scale, flooding could be so significant that capabilities would include dam and levee systems, sandbagging protocols, evacuation planning, and more. The time frame to build dams and levees could be decades and would require a significant amount of planning and funding. Capability assessment ultimately requires understanding the nature of the threat or hazard, inventorying appropriate and available resources, and laying out a timeline and circumstances under which to use those resources, acquire additional mitigation measures, or request outside assistance when resources prove insufficient.

9.2.3 Risk Assessment

A risk assessment gives an overview of how threats and hazards might impact the people, places, properties, and processes in a specific area. Risk assessments involve emergency managers in taking a step back to scientifically consider identified threats and hazards and what can be done to reduce related risks. Proximity plays an important role in such an assessment. Consider, for example, where people live in relation to a chemical plant, which may have a potential for leaks or explosions. If sufficient distance exists, area residents may not face any significant risk of exposure. However, the people who work at the plant may bear a disproportionate risk. Businesses, schools, and other places in close proximity will also experience a potentially higher risk. Historically, communities of color have borne a disproportionate impact due to practices of segregation (e.g., Cutter 2005; Sharkey 2007). Such impacts have become a well-understood issue of social and environmental justice, which emergency managers can address through mitigation and community-based planning.

The properties on which such types of places are located could face damage or annihilation such as the world saw in the 2020 explosion in Beirut or the 2013 fertilizer plant explosion in West Texas. Often hidden from consideration in a risk assessment are the processes that can be affected by a threat or hazard, such as the process of elections under a cyberattack, or the logistics processes that companies use to deliver goods and services in a major winter storm, or the process of providing health care access given historic racial inequalities. Such interruptions matter, because the damage can be significant, as we witnessed in the COVID-19 pandemic with severe economic impacts and disproportionate illness and death among racial and ethnic minorities, senior citizens, and people with high-risk health conditions.

Risk assessments are based on scientific data that reveal how people and places might be affected. Many experts like seismologists, meteorologists, and hydrologists calculate probabilities of an event happening quantitatively and assess the impact on people and places through social science research. Such calculations require careful analysis of historic occurrences and their intervals as well as the various magnitudes, levels, or speeds of an event and the demographics of people who would be impacted. Their work often results in statements that characterize a flood, for example, as 100- or 500-year events. If you live in an area with a 500-year flood, the odds sound good about whether it might or might not happen in your lifetime. However, such probabilities are actually more complex. A 500-year event could happen tomorrow and then not again for 1,000 years, but it could also happen again next month. The 500-year event is not an interval, it is a probability. Similarly, you could gamble at a casino and win the jackpot which might be a 1 in 5,000 likelihood. You might never win again, but you could win again tomorrow. Probabilities tell us about the odds of something happening rather than an interval between events. Probabilities increase in places with histories of racial discrimination and segregation (Phillips, Jenkins, and Stukes 2012; Kroll-Smith, Baxter, and Jenkins 2015).

As another challenge, consider that some hazards occur seasonally like tornadoes, but you will not know if the tornado will be a small Enhanced Fujita (EF)1 scale or the more devastating EF5. Where you live might help you to determine those odds better, such as living in tornado alley rather than the desert. To make it even more challenging, tornado spikes occur outside the traditional spring season (in the U.S.), including during November. Tornadoes can generate from a severe thunderstorm moving across the U.S. Midwest, but may also spawn from a hurricane along the Gulf Coast. Severe weather may appear extremely threatening but pass over without much rain, hail, or rotation. The time of day also matters. Late afternoon storms tend to produce stronger tornadoes because the sun heats up conditions that generate vortices. Overnight tornadoes, which could range from EF1 to EF5, are considered particularly dangerous because sleeping people miss warnings, resulting in more injuries and deaths. Living in a well-built home with a safe room decreases risk, while those who cannot afford sturdier shelter face higher risk of injuries, death, and property damage. Thus, statistical probabilities can provide insights, but so can the location and context of where people live and work.

Understanding probabilities is hard for the public to grasp. When hurricanes approach land, a "cone of uncertainty" is often used to depict where the hurricane might land. Linear graphics, sometimes called spaghetti models, depict where the storm might move. But hurricanes can take a sudden, unexpected turn. Risk assessment can thus be somewhat challenging to determine. Emergency managers play a role in explaining risk to the public, despite the complexity. One common way to help the public understand risk is to use the idea of low, medium, and high risks coupled with low, medium, and high consequences. A terror attack might be low risk in a given area, but if it happened, it would have high consequences. Therefore, people should be alert and if they see something concerning, say something. Similarly, a flood might happen on a frequent basis but with the right mitigation, carry low consequences. Helping the public understand why they are vulnerable and how to take the best risk reduction efforts saves lives and property.

9.2.3.1 Social Vulnerability Assessment

An additional, required level of assessment concerns the people in a community. Who lives in or near the areas of risk that have been identified and what threats and hazards do they face? For example, low-income households are more likely to face higher consequences with less means to mitigate threats and hazards. People who live in mobile homes, for example, have a higher risk of death, injury, and property loss with a small tornado compared to residents who have the means to own sturdier houses. But a group tornado shelter can save their lives.

Knowing where economically vulnerable households exist means that emergency managers can map out locations of households at risk against known threats and hazards. As described throughout this volume, disasters are not equal opportunity events. Emergency managers, as part of their ethical responsibilities, must understand how historic patterns of discrimination and economic marginalization have increased risk for some people more than others (Cutter 2005; Sharkey 2007; Phillips, Stukes, and Jenkins 2012; Kroll-Smith et al. 2015). COVID-19 also demonstrated differential vulnerability to the risks associated with pandemics, with rates 4.7 times higher for infection among African Americans than among non-Hispanic whites. Why? Experts linked the higher rates to lack of health care access which increased high-risk conditions. Coupled with higher exposure levels on the job, often as essential workers, African Americans became much more vulnerable (Marshall 2021).

Emergency managers need to understand the history of how people have become marginalized to understand social vulnerability. By learning about race and ethnic history, gender studies, disability studies, and poverty, emergency managers can acquire useful insights into why risks have been higher for some people than others. With disabilities, for example, people have been assumed to be dependent when, in fact, many people with disabilities lead independent lives as vital workforce members. But if people with disabilities have not been at the planning table to help emergency managers understand their specific concerns in a disaster, emergency managers will have overlooked an opportunity to reduce risk. Understanding vulnerability also means that we need to understand the complexity of a given group's risk. Someone who has been deaf for life, for example, will be more likely to know how to access warning messages than an elderly person with late-onset deafness.

Emergency managers also need to understand the complex intersectionality that exists within a particular group at risk. For example, women often live longer than men, yet older men often experience higher levels of social isolation that places them at higher risk. Poverty also increases with aging as people retire and aging introduces new disabilities associated with health and mobility. Emergency managers can change risks and reduce losses by understanding and involving the diverse set of people in their communities in mitigation efforts.

9.2.3.2 Loss Estimation

How much can a homeowner, business, or city bear to lose in a disaster? Loss estimation calculates the physical and economic impacts that could occur, which may motivate people to engage in mitigation measures that offset potential impacts. The kinds of losses that can occur may also point an individual or a community in directions that should be prioritized for mitigation. For example, if a significant flood exists that could threaten the downtown business sector, those alerted to losses might be more willing to fund a levee system to protect downtown businesses and tax revenues. Local foundations dedicated to social justice might be willing to pay for a congregate tornado shelter, support vaccine distribution efforts, or fund a community-based mitigation planning effort.

Loss estimation looks at several kinds of potential impacts such as *structural loss* when a tornado tears apart a home or business. A typical home in the Midwestern U.S. might cost $150,000 to rebuild (the same home in California would cost over $1 million). Thus, a mitigation measure to offset losses would be to purchase sufficient insurance to cover the amount of rebuilding. Structural loss estimation thus focuses on the built environment and what it would cost to replace it. Emergency managers can also consider the impact beyond a specific site such as a business. A primary production facility that is damaged in an explosion could cause ripple effects to related facilities and other enterprises dependent on that facility's manufactured goods. The 2011 tsunami in Japan did just that, when a damaged paint production facility caused slowdowns for vehicle manufacturers worldwide.

Loss estimation also considers *contents* inside a structure. For example, a homeowner might have items inside their home such as computers or valuable jewelry. Homeowners would want to do a careful inventory of those items to see if additional insurance coverage is needed for specific items. Students can undertake this kind of loss estimation as well. Stop and look around where you live and study. Inventory what you have and need to continue pursuing your degree: books, computers, a bed, clothes, food, and a phone. What is the cost of those items together? Next, determine the resources you have available to cover losses if a cyberattack damages a computer that must be repaired or replaced. If a tornado or flood destroyed your books, what means do you have to replace them? What would it cost to move to a new dorm room or apartment? Or do the same kind of assessment for your office or home. A flood of just a few feet inside a business can stop its operations, causing downtime and related loss of revenue until business functions can be restored. If the flood damages enough of the business, it might be displaced to another location or fail completely. Loss estimation can reveal what a homeowner, renter, or business owner needs to consider. How much loss can be tolerated from damage to the structure and contents? How much downtime can be endured before the business fails? What would displacement mean to a business? What can be introduced to offset risks? Upcoming sections will introduce mitigation measures to consider how to reduce risks from area hazards.

9.3 WHAT IS MITIGATION?

Nature has always had a plan for how heavy rains flow. From a systems theory perspective, though, people do not always respect what nature intended and build homes and businesses on beautiful coastlines, along recreational lakes and rivers, and in or near floodplains. But when we build a structure on the ground, water flows differently around it. The ground has less potential to absorb runoff which carries debris into streams and sewers not designed to handle branches and trash. Debris backs up and causes flooding, and then contaminates or damages waterways, bridges, and sewer systems. Given that flooding represents the top hazard in many nations, systems theory requires us to think carefully about how to interact with our natural environment.

Mitigation means taking intentional efforts to reduce the risks associated with such threats and hazards (Tables 9.1 and 9.2). Mitigation measures that can be considered for reducing threats and hazards typically fall into two kinds: *structural* and *nonstructural* measures. Structural measures include physical or tangible ways to reduce impacts like the Plexiglas barriers used in open reception areas during the pandemic as well as wearing masks that significantly reduced the spread of the disease. Nonstructural mitigation measures come from less tangible ways to reduce risks, such as socially distancing and washing hands as public health and EM experts advocated during COVID-19 and for other infectious diseases. Still, people refused to adopt mitigation measures like those recommended during the pandemic. The failure to adopt even such inexpensive or free mitigation measures led to the deaths of hundreds of thousands of people, many of them elderly, from historically disadvantaged populations and/or with preexisting health conditions. It takes a relentless champion for communities to put mitigation measures into place, which is the work of both disaster scientists and emergency managers (see Box 9.3). Let's turn to some opportunities to mitigate risk in your communities next. Two kinds cover most mitigation strategies: structural and nonstructural mitigation measures.

TABLE 9.1 Structural Mitigation

Defined: a built, physical, or tangible means to reduce the impact of a specific kind of disaster.
Goal: reduce loss of life, injuries, property damage, community disruptions, and economic and environmental impacts.

Types	Definition	Hazard Use	Advantages	Disadvantages	Example of where it is used
Dam	Structure designed to hold back water, typically on a lake, reservoir, or river.	Flooding, heavy precipitation, snowmelt.	Reduced water flow or flooding to protect downstream populations and places.	Expensive, usually requires governmental funding. Often engineered around rather than with nature. Often in poor condition.	Used extensively in many nations.
Levee	Structure, often earthen, built alongside a river to keep water inside riverine boundaries.	Flooding, heavy precipitation, snowmelt, storm surge.	Works in concert with existing river system.	Can be very expensive to reach the highest levels of protection, such as a category 5 storm surge. Maintenance, replacement, or strengthening costs can be quite high.	The City of New Orleans relies on levees as so many communities with rivers are subject to flooding.
Elevation	Structural means to raise a building above an inundation area.	Flooding, heavy precipitation, hurricane storm surge, snowmelt, sea level rises due to climate change.	Allows structure to remain in place and near livelihoods, including historic buildings.	Costly, requires significant effort.	Frequently used along coastal areas subject to frequent storm surge or future sea level rise; used inland for areas of repetitive flooding.
Retrofit	Structural reinforcement of the interior of a building.	Earthquakes.	Allows existing built environment to remain in place.	Challenging to structurally reinforce a building or bridge without significant cost and intrusion.	California earthquake-prone areas.

continued ...

Types	Definition	Hazard Use	Advantages	Disadvantages	Example of where it is used
Safe room	A room, often underground, reinforced to protect from high winds and projectiles. Can also be used to protect from an attack.	Tornadoes, hurricanes, active attackers.	Relatively inexpensive, often supported by government grants.	If accompanied by flooding, potential for loss of life.	Tornado alley in the U.S.
Pumping system	Flood gauges and pumps remove water from areas subject to inundation.	Floods.	Removes intrusive flooding.	May not be sufficient alone given inundation levels.	New Orleans.
Roof clamps	Used to reinforce roof rafters and keep roofs on during high wind events.	High winds in tornadoes, hurricanes, and derechos.	Relatively inexpensive.	May not withstand highest wind loads.	U.S. Gulf Coast.
PPE	Varies from hazmat suits to N95 masks and more, to protect from inhalation of respiratory threats or exposure threat from chemicals, radiation, and more.	Hazardous materials events, infectious disease outbreaks.	Can provide a high level of personal protection.	Can be expensive for larger industries, may not protect from all potential hazards, and requires replacement and related costs.	First responders, various industries, health care sectors, and places subject to infectious outbreaks and/or with chemicals on the worksite.
Generator	A portable or permanent unit that uses gas to generate power.	Blackouts, loss of power in a disaster.	Power for heating, cooling, food preservation, and medical devices. Can be used to power key sections of health care sites.	Improper use can lead to carbon monoxide poisoning. Requires availability of fuel to power generator.	Often at the homeowner and industry levels (homes, hospitals). Cost-prohibitive for many families (smallest units for minimal power cost about $600).

TABLE 9.2 Nonstructural Mitigation

Defined: nontangible means to reduce the impacts of disaster. Goal: reduce loss of life, injuries, property damage, community disruptions, and economic and environmental impacts.					
Types	Definition	Hazard Use	Advantages	Disadvantages	Examples of where used
Land use planning and zoning	Deliberate effort to design or limit a given area using government-based planning processes.	Hazardous materials, industrial sites, flood zones, wildfire urban interface.	Situates properties in safer locations to reduce losses.	Reduces options for where people want to live and work.	Most governmental jurisdictions.
Building codes and enforcement	Outlines how a structure must be built to resist area hazards.	Floods, hurricanes, tornadoes, wildfires, and more.	Increases built environment resilience.	May increase time spent to comply, may increase local contention.	Most governmental jurisdictions where possible (exceptions in impoverished nations).
Insurance	A purchased coverage typically with a deductible that pays out money to repair or replace damaged property or lost items.	Most hazards are covered but not all. Some areas may require government-assisted insurance plans.	Considerable savings when disaster strikes a home or business.	May be unavailable for some hazards or too expensive. Massive disasters can raise rates for everyone, including those not directly impacted.	Widely available, except in some specific areas (e.g., flood zones).
Relocations/ buyouts	Typically a government purchase of land and related structure so that residents can move to a safer location.	Floods, wildfire, earthquakes, all offer possibilities.	Allows people in an area of repetitive risk to relocate.	Can be expensive, even if government covers the cost. May involve loss of social networks, neighborhoods, and cultures.	Often found in areas of repetitive flood risk.

continued ...

Types	Definition	Hazard Use	Advantages	Disadvantages	Examples of where used
Evacuation planning	A process designed to identify those at risk and design a means to spur or assist evacuation to a safer location.	Wildfire, hurricane, flood.	Saves lives, especially for those lacking a means to evacuate.	Can be time-consuming and expensive, may not be possible in a rapid onset event.	U.S. Gulf Coast, global jurisdictions subject to tsunamis, floods, cyclones.
Mitigation planning	A stake-holder and government-driven effort to identify risks and prioritize mitigation measures appropriate to local hazards.	All local hazards.	Involves stakeholders, layouts options clearly, invites collective decision-making.	Can be time-consuming, may not generate public interest until after a disaster.	Most U.S. jurisdictions require some degree of mitigation planning.
Business continuity planning	A workplace-based plan to continue oper-ating despite a disaster.	All local hazards.	Focuses a team on critical functions to take to stay in business.	Lack of knowledge about how to plan or lack of resources, especially for small businesses.	Most large industries and school systems have some type of continuity planning.
Response planning, drills, and exercises	Can be done in any unit and occurs commonly among first responders and emergency managers.	All local hazards.	Can increase efficiency and effectiveness of a responding unit.	Lack of knowledge among those outside of emergency professions.	All police, fire, emergency medical service (EMS), EM agencies conduct response planning. Many industries do so as well as schools (e.g., fire and tornado drills).

Types	Definition	Hazard Use	Advantages	Disadvantages	Examples of where used
Educational campaigns for cybersecurity	Teaching the public and workers about intrusion measures like phishing, ransomware, viruses.	Cybersecurity.	Often inexpensive; virus protection can be more costly.	Human behavior, criminal action can all result in failures.	Higher education, corporate settings, home-based work.
Xeriscaping	Use of low water and native plants resilient in a warm climate.	Wildfire, drought, climate change.	Reduces need for water in a drought.	Not widely known or used in many areas.	U.S. Southwest and West.
Public hygiene campaign	Teaching proper protocol to reduce illness such as mask wearing, handwashing, social distancing, hand sanitizer.	Pandemic, seasonal influenza.	Relatively inexpensive.	Noncompliance.	COVID-19, SARS, H1N1, seasonal influenza.
First aid and cardio-pulmonary resuscitation/automated external defibrillator (CPR/AED) training	Basic skills designed to save lives and tend to people who are injured or ill.	Accidents, heart attacks, drownings, injuries from disasters.	Relatively inexpensive, quickly learned, even young children can learn the basics.	Failure to keep skills updated or to learn procedures correctly.	Workplaces, schools, and households all benefit from such training.

9.3.1 Structural Mitigation

Structural mitigation centers on the built environment. Examples include dams to hold back water, levees alongside waterways, blast-resistant windows for tornadoes, or concrete barriers to deter curbside attacks.

One example of a planned environment that strives to reduce risks comes from physical structures such as dams or levees. In the U.S., the U.S. Army Corps of Engineers typically takes responsibility for the creation of major flood risk reduction projects. Across the U.S., thousands of such structures – large, small, and even makeshift – exist. U.S. dams are in trouble, though. The American Society of Civil Engineers (ASCE 2021; https://infrastructurereportcard.org) has awarded the grade of "D" to U.S. dams, a grade that has not changed in some time. Thousands of high hazard dams (with an increased likelihood of failure) exist across the U.S. ASCE estimates that billions of dollars annually would be needed for repairs, a sum that would have to be shouldered mostly

BOX 9.3

LESSONS UNLEARNED, FROM CHAMPIONS OF DISASTER MITIGATION

Mitigation requires both solid, scientific knowledge of what works (like how to build a levee) as well as how practitioners can design and implement the best ways to become more resilient. Coming from both the scholarly and practitioner communities, three leaders in the U.S. have emerged as tireless champions for mitigation, working to convince policy makers, practitioners, and those at risk to heed disaster science or bear the consequences since the 1940s.

Gilbert White

Gilbert F. White, known worldwide as the "father of floodplain management" joined the University of Colorado Boulder (CU) faculty in 1970 as a professor of geography and director of the Institute of Behavioral Science where he remained active in academic work into his 90s. He founded CU's Natural Hazards Research and Applications Information Center, the nation's leading repository of knowledge on human behavior in disasters, in 1974. White's work in natural hazards changed the way people deal with nature and made the world safer for people to inhabit. "Floods are 'acts of God,' but flood losses are largely acts of man" he wrote in 1942 in his doctoral dissertation, which has since been called the most influential ever written by an American geographer.

White earned his degrees from the University of Chicago, then worked for the Federal government in the late 1930s where he studied the Mississippi River Basin. White served as the Gustavson Distinguished Professor Emeritus of Geography at CU where he founded and led the Natural Hazards Center. He was a member of the National Academy of Sciences, the American Academy of Arts and Sciences, and the Russian Academy of Sciences. His numerous awards include the nation's highest scientific honor, the National Medal of Science, presented in 2000. Among White's numerous other honors are the National Geographic Society's highest award, the Hubbard Medal; the UN' Sasakawa International Environmental Prize; and the Association of American Geographer's Lifetime Achievement Award. He received an honorary doctorate from CU in May 2006.

FEMA Director David Paulison recalls him as "a pioneer in a field which protects people and their homes." "At a time when the main stream thought was to build bigger and stronger flood control devices, Mr. White was investigating creative – and effective – methods that promoted safety, but not at the cost of damaging rivers and waterways. His legacy is a program that keeps people safe, protects the environment and makes smart investments in mitigation activities at all levels of government" (FEMA 2006, Release Number: HQ-06-145; see also Mabey 1986).

James Lee Witt

James Lee Witt served as the director of the Federal Emergency Management Agency under President Bill Clinton. His career began in Arkansas, where he owned a construction company, served as a county judge, and then became head of the Arkansas Office of

Emergency Services. While serving in FEMA, President Clinton made the FEMA director-ship a cabinet-level position. As the first politically appointed director with a background in EM, Witt made significant transformations in the agency (Goss 2015).

In his book, *Stronger in the Broken Places*, he said "Mitigation – which means to moderate in force or intensity – should be the goal of every crisis manager. Why prepare to clean up more efficiently after a disaster when you can prepare to lessen its effect in the first place" (Witt and Morgan 2002, p. 6).

One of FEMA's signature projects during his tenure was Project Impact. The effort partnered government with private and nonprofit communities to design mitigation ef-forts such as tornado safe rooms or flood reduction works (Holdeman and Patton 2008). Project Impact began as a grassroots program, which encouraged local stakeholders to determine what worked best for them – and to work together to design and implement solutions. Although Project Impact ended in 2001, the partnerships it inspired contin-ued in a number of communities. Tulsa, Oklahoma's Project Impact efforts, for example, dramatically reduced flooding following widespread flooding in the 1980s (Wachtendorf et al. 2002; Meo, Ziebro, and Patton 2004). As James Lee Witt said, "mitigation is the ulti-mate application of common sense to the challenges the world throws our way" (Witt and Morgan 2002, p. 7). After leaving FEMA, Witt formed his own consulting business and went on to manage reconstruction projects for the state of Louisiana after Hurricane Ka-trina and remains active in the field (Goss 2015).

Dennis Mileti

"Dr. Dennis Mileti was a luminary in the field of hazards and disaster research. During his tenure as director, he led the second assessment of natural hazards research, which cul-minated in the publication of *Disasters by Design*. The work leveraged the knowledge of more than 130 of the nation's disaster experts and established a framework for sustainable hazard mitigation in the United States. Mileti is also widely recognized as one of the world's leading risk communication scholars. He was an advocate of creating messages and warn-ings that encouraged people to prepare for and respond appropriately to disaster risks. He knew that moving this research into action could save lives.

Mileti earned his PhD in Sociology at the University of Colorado Boulder, where he studied under Natural Hazards Center founder Gilbert White. He graduated in 1975 after contributing to the first Assessment of Research on Natural Hazards. He returned to CU in 1994 to become the third director of the Natural Hazards Center and professor in the Department of Sociology. During his tenure, which ended in 2003, he worked to advance research on the societal aspects of hazards and disasters and to support the next gener-ation of researchers and practitioners." Dr. Mileti died from complications of COVID-19. In his memory, remember the lessons that he offered to make the world a safer place.

Source: Dennis Mileti, verbatim: https://hazards.colorado.edu/news/center-news/dennis-mileti-november-7-1945-to-january-30-2021.

References

Goss, Kay C. 2015. "James Lee Witt." *The Encyclopedia of Arkansas History and Culture*. Available at http://www.encyclopediaofarkansas.net/encyclopedia/entry-detail.aspx?entryID=3709, last accessed March 3, 2016.

Holdeman, Eric, and Ann Patton. 2008. "Project Impact Initiative to Create Disaster-Resistant Communities Demonstrates Worth in Kansas Years Later." *Emergency Management Magazine*, December 12, 2008. Available at http://www.emergencymgmt.com/disaster/Project-Impact-Initiative-to.html, last accessed March 4, 2016.

Mabey, Richard. 1986. *Gilbert White: A Biography of the Author of the Natural History of Selbourne*. Charlottesville: University of Virginia Press.

Meo, Mark, Becky Ziebro, and Ann Patton. 2004. "Tulsa Turnaround: From Disaster to Sustainability." *Natural Hazards Review* 5(1): 1–9.

Wachtendorf, Tricia, Rory Connell, and Kathleen Tierney, Kristy Kompanik. 2002. *Final Project Report #4 Disaster Resistant Communities Initiative: Assessment of the Pilot Phase-Year-3*. University of Delaware, Disaster Research Center.

Natural Hazards Center. Retrieved February 5, 2021 https://hazards.colorado.edu/news/center-news/dennis-mileti-november-7-1945-to-january-30-2021.

Witt, James Lee and James Morgan 2002. *Stronger in the Broken Places*. New York: Times Books.

Information on Gilbert White provided courtesy of University Communications, University of Colorado Boulder. With permission.

through taxpayer dollars, which is an economic burden that people may not want to share. Hard choices have to be made to put such structural mitigation measures into place. *Levees*, often earthen structures, are situated alongside rivers to prevent overtopping when floods occur. Levees in the U.S. include 100,000 miles of flood mitigation works that, in the ASCE estimation, earn a grade of D. The National Committee on Levee Safety estimates $100+ billion would be needed to improve existing levees. How many people do they protect? FEMA estimates that about 43% of the U.S. population benefits from levee protection, which includes about "14 million people who live or work behind the structures" (ASCE 2013). The 2005 levee failure in New Orleans after Hurricane Katrina represents a measure that failed to protect – in large part, because political and economic choices determined expenditures for the levee protection system, where to place homes and businesses, and allocations for maintenance costs. The pre-Katrina system provided protection from a Category 3 storm. Katrina pushed a Category 5 surge into the levee system which flooded the entire city. Close to 2,000 people died. The levee system has since been rebuilt or strengthened back to a Category 3 level.

Another way to deal with flood risks is to raise a home or business above expected flooding levels, which is called an *elevation*. A number of successful elevations took place after Hurricane Katrina and some in ways that addressed historic social vulnerability. The community of Pass Christian, Mississippi, created a long-term recovery committee and recommended clients to disaster voluntary organizations, such as Mennonite Disaster Service. Donations subsidized about 20 expensive elevations that averaged about $50,000–$70,000 in addition to the cost of rebuilding the home 5–20 feet above the ground. The combination of funds and volunteer labor were essential to enabling people to return home safely, including homes owned by single parents, elderly residents, African Americans, and Native Americans (Phillips 2014).

Another structural mitigation option is to bring an older building up to the current codes. In earthquake areas, *retrofitting* a building to make it stronger on the interior can reduce potential collapses. The cost can be significant, however. Far cheaper are strategies like securing cupboards, bookcases, and chimneys that fall and injure or kill people or teaching people to turn off the gas to avoid an earthquake-caused fire. *Safe rooms* can protect people from tornadoes and high winds. About 1,200 tornadoes occur annually in the U.S., although they have also been reported in South America, Europe, Africa, Asia, Australia, and New Zealand (National Weather Service, n.d.). One of the worst tornadoes to hit the U.S. occurred in Joplin, Missouri, in 2011. An EF5-level tornado, the twister stretched as far as a mile wide, and devastated homes, businesses, schools, and the local hospital. The human toll included 158 lives lost and over 1,000 people sustained injuries. Seventeen people died in a single assisted living facility, including residents and staff. Safe rooms, built to specific standards, can protect people from such storms. For example, the U.S. state of Kansas has funded safe buildings large enough to protect over 700 people. For individual homeowners, a safe room may cost $2,000–$3,000. Government programs in the U.S. have subsidized these costs in high-risk areas.

Blast performance is one element of making a building more structurally resilient in the face of a natural disaster or terrorist attack (see Box 9.4). Efforts might include placing barriers around buildings to reduce explosive-laden vehicles from penetrating the perimeter. Fencing, guards, and security procedures can also reduce the possibility that someone intent on harm can carry out their plans. Windows, doors, and storefronts can be strengthened by installing blast resistant products. Sometimes called "hardening," the process of assessing and incorporating materials and procedures – when coupled with emergency planning and public education – can save lives, reduce injuries, and minimize economic losses.

The benefits of implementing structural mitigation measures should be obvious. In short, lives are saved. The costs of rebuilding homes, infrastructure, and buildings lessen. People can return home faster, earn livelihoods, and continue to work. Insurance companies do not have to raise premiums to offset payments. The local economy and tax base rebound faster. The psychological impacts of being injured or grief-stricken, living in tents or temporary housing, or trying to return to work diminish because exposure lessens. Structural mitigation promotes resilience of the built environment, made possible through human choices, so that people and places can return to normal faster. Side benefits also exist. Recreational opportunities abound in areas served by dams and generate tourist income. Large-scale hydroelectric dams provide energy.

BOX 9.4

ASSESSING BUILDING VULNERABILITY TO TERRORISM

Are you safe where you work or go to school? How about places you visit such as a hospital or public mall? FEMA has published guidance on ways to assess vulnerability and mitigate terrorist attacks, and many of the items mentioned below also fit with other hazards (such as a flood entering a building and disrupting utilities). Their materials include assessments of many things you should start looking at when visiting public buildings (this is a selective list; for more, see the full document at the source given below):

- *The site.* Where is the facility and what kinds of other facilities are around it? Could they become targets and your building be affected? Can a vehicle (with an explosive) be parked close to your building? Are access procedures in place to prevent entry, such as key cards or barriers?
- *The architecture.* Does the building design allow for being able to see visitors and others coming into the location? Do the windows have blast resistance? Would the way the building was put together allow for places to hide from an intruder? Do places exist where explosive devices could be hidden? Are there ways to safely exit the building?
- *Structural systems.* Will the building withstand the impact of an explosion? Is it wood, steel, or concrete? What kinds of impacts would happen under certain circumstances? What can be done to strengthen or reinforce the building? Will parts of the building fail or pancake in an attack? Where are the weaknesses?
- *The building envelope.* Can the exterior withstand an assault or explosion? The building itself as well as the windows and doors?
- *Utility systems.* Where do water, gas, and electricity come from? What kinds of dependencies exist? Are any of these sources vulnerable to penetration or disruption? What about transformers in the area? Backup units? Generators? Is there a reliable source of utilities that can be depended on externally in a major attack?
- *Mechanical systems.* Are any parts of heating or air conditioning open to penetration or assault? What about air intake and air filtration? What would happen in a biological or chemical attack? Are there fire walls and fire doors?
- *Fire alarm systems.* Are the fire extinguishers, smoke detectors, and alarms working? Are there sprinklers? Are fire drills conducted? Are fire alarm panels protected from unauthorized personnel?
- *Communications and information technology (IT) systems.* How are telephones organized and operated? Is there a backup system? Is the emergency alert system secured and how many people have access to it? Is the wiring secured? Will the Internet be accessible in an emergency? Are records secured? What is the backup?
- *Security systems.* Is there a television system that monitors and records what happens? How long are these materials saved? Who can access them and what

procedures are in place when such information is needed in an emergency? Are they exterior, interior, or both?

Source: For an even more extensive set of ideas and suggestions, see FEMA 2005. FEMA 452, A How-To Guide to Mitigate Potential Terrorist Attacks against Buildings. Washington D.C.: FEMA. Available at http://www.fema.gov/media-library/assets/documents/4608, last accessed March 3, 2016.

Such dams do not come without controversy, however, as some have been charged with causing damage to the ecosystem, particularly riparian habitats with native flora and fauna. The advantages of structural mitigation must always be offset with the disadvantages – and hard choices will have to be made by those affected and those who serve the public. The most common critique concerns the high costs of structural mitigation. The costs to rebuild the New Orleans area levee system reached the $14 billion mark seven years after the storm. Other consequences may result as well. People may place their faith in structural mitigation measures and refuse to evacuate despite advice to do so. Still, mitigation measures pay off even if far down the road in terms of time. An investment now may pay off decades later.

9.3.2 Nonstructural Mitigation

Nonstructural mitigation includes disaster reduction efforts that are not tangible or built like decisions over land use, written building codes, insurance, or social distancing. Land use planning relies heavily on making informed choices about both location and design of the built environment, including not permitting building in a flood zone (Godschalk, Kaiser, and Berke 1998; Burby et al. 2000; Schuch et al. 2017). Land use planning requires stakeholder involvement, from elected and appointed officials to community members. Their collective work will require review of the hazard identification and risk assessment: are new locations being considered where hazards might generate losses and impacts? Or perhaps cause runoff that impacts other areas? Nonstructural land use planning can generate more sustainable and green places that naturally promote resilience and deter a hazard from becoming a disaster (Godschalk et al. 1998, p. 86; Schuch et al. 2017). Still, while land use planning makes sense in terms of disaster risks, emergency managers may find themselves caught between city planners, developers wanting to invest in the community, and constituents who may want to live in a desirable but hazardous location. Should you develop an area to help the community's economic well-being? Or, should the area be preserved or have limited growth to preserve environmental resources (Burby et al. 2000)?

Building codes require developers, builders, and homeowners to secure permits, go through inspections, and comply with a written code. For example, hurricane clamps that cost less than $200 can decrease roof damage. Or, a local code could require installing utility lines underground to reduce damage and power outages from high winds and ice. Code enforcement requires code inspectors and strict compliance. The degree to which code enforcement is kept has been questionable in some areas. After Hurricane Andrew tore off roofs across southern Florida in 1992, it was clear that codes did not match wind speeds (Ayscue 1996). To their chagrin, public officials watched as television crews filmed inside homes where nails had clearly failed to attach the roof to the rafters – something that inspectors should have caught during construction. Allegations of bribery and corruption erupted. Haiti's earthquake in 2010 serves as another example as well as providing evidence of the disproportionate impacts of lingering poverty and global inequality. The building code for the entire nation was a scant four pages with nearly nonexistent code enforcement, an outgrowth of deep poverty across the nation. Buildings pancaked, entombing many of the 200,000+ victims. In contrast, a similar magnitude earthquake in Chile – where building codes are more in place and monitored – led to significantly fewer deaths, injuries, and property damage.

When people and places face repetitive losses from disasters, a *relocation* or a "buyout" can enable people to move to a new location outside of a floodplain or an area contaminated with hazardous materials. Relocation is often fraught with difficulty because people do not want to leave homes, neighborhoods, and familiar locales that mean something to them. Conversely, staying in place may increase exposure, risk their lives, and damage their properties. But relocation might also be viewed as a threat to a way of life, a commitment to the land, and a social network that enables survival and provides rich, meaningful relationships. People hold strong ties to the land, such as Native American or First Nations communities. Princeville, North Carolina, for example, flooded multiple times since its inception as being the first town in the U.S. incorporated by African Americans. Flooded again in 1999, the community refused a buyout in a close vote. They did so out of allegiance to previous generations who survived race-based attacks, economic deprivation, and segregation as well as close kinship among trusted social networks (Phillips, Stukes, and Jenkins 2012). After the 2004 tsunami, efforts to move fisher families away from the Sri Lankan shoreline failed. People needed to stay closer to their livelihoods and moved back into what should have been a buffer zone (Karunasena and Rameezdeen 2014). A volcano that threatened families near Colima, Mexico, resulted in some relocation amid great suspicion that the effort was actually a land grab. Many stayed in place, so the government created an evacuation plan instead (Galivanes-Ruiz et al. 2009; Cuevas Muñiz and Luján 2005).

Carrying personal *insurance*, even if you are a renter, gives you the chance to replace a computer, clothing, or furniture. Renter's insurance can be surprisingly inexpensive, and although you may not want to pay even a small amount on a limited budget, contrasting your potential losses with a paid monthly premium may put things into perspective. Still, people may not have the financial means to purchase insurance, especially when specific coverage (wind, floods, earthquakes) increases the premium. Many insurance policies do not cover flooding and sometimes wind damage. To make up for this, the U.S. government offers the National Flood Insurance Program. Private insurance companies sell and service the policies which insure homes and contents up to certain amounts.

Because structural elements can be costly to install and maintain, nonstructural measures may represent a more affordable option. In the case of pandemic planning, for example, educating the public to engage in healthy behaviors as simple as the low cost of washing your hands can stem a potential outbreak. Targeting public education to those most likely to become ill from particular outbreaks, such as seniors or expectant mothers, can save lives. That was the focus of the 2016 Zika virus efforts that affected pregnant women. Though some degree of financial investment in a non-structural mitigation measure is usually needed, such as with insurance, the payoffs can be enormous. With sufficient coverage, you will be able to build back and to replace furniture, clothing, and computers. Or, land use planning can serve the public good and enhance quality of life by setting aside green space to absorb runoff and reduce flood risks. Building codes protect people inside, from employers to employees and the customers, clients, and patients who visit their facilities. Code enforcement insures that roofs stay on, safe rooms stop projectiles, and people emerge safely from the tornado that passed over.

People also see nonstructural mitigation measures as problematic, as we saw when people refused to wear a mask or socially distance during the COVID-19 outbreak. Some nonstructural mitigation options may be too costly for some families, like insurance coverage in earthquake or flood-prone areas. Relocations may threaten entire cultures and disrupt important social connections between people who live and work near kin. Regardless of the mitigation measure that should be considered, emergency managers will need to work diligently to educate, inform, involve, and support the public in taking on the best measures to reduce individual and collective risks.

9.4 MITIGATION PLANNING WITH STAKEHOLDERS

Mitigation efforts can return a monetary investment average of 4:1, which significantly reduces response and recovery costs (Rose et al. 2007). But making that investment requires dedicated time across a wide set of stakeholders. The best efforts come from community-based processes that involve those at risk in identifying and determining the best ways forward. Emergency managers play a vital role in working with their communities to create a successful mitigation plan.

9.4.1 Resilience

Given that disasters will continue to occur and that socially vulnerable people and places still require disaster risk reduction efforts, emergency managers must engage in mitigation planning that promotes resilience. Emergency managers also play a role in promoting a "culture of resilience" as recommended by the National Academy of Sciences (2012, see Chapter 3). Using the THIRA described earlier, emergency managers need to engage their stakeholders in mitigation planning to produce a series of actions that promote resilience. In this section, readers first explore general mitigation planning followed by engagement strategies that involve the whole community potentially at risk.

9.4.2 Mitigation Planning Basics

FEMA recommends that the planning process involve several basic steps: (1) organize resources, (2) assess risks, (3) develop a mitigation plan, and (4) implement the plan. It sounds straightforward, but it can take time to complete and secure financial resources for implementation. Step one involves a mitigation leader in assessing community support (see resources section for FEMA Mitigation Planning materials). It is likely that the mitigation leader, often an emergency manager, will spend considerable time explaining the process and value of mitigation planning to the public and to community officials. A public education effort might take the form of a series of media stories that take people back in time to area disasters, describe their impacts, and map out risk areas. Efforts to convince public officials often center on the long-term cost effectiveness of mitigation, with the idea that investment now pays dividends later (FEMA, see resources section).

The second step actively involves the mitigation planning team in creating or reviewing an existing or new THIRA, including loss estimation for structural and content losses. Once the data are accumulated and analyzed, the team should present the information to the public to raise concern and support – and be creative in doing so. Attend worship services, speak at service organizations, hand out flyers, involve scout troops in walking door-to-door, distribute information at parent-teacher meetings, go to senior centers, and invite civic and neighborhood associations to hear your concerns (FEMA, see resources). Get people concerned and excited, noting the considerable payoffs that could result.

Step three leads the community, in all its residential and workplace diversity, through mitigation planning that can rely on planning charettes, town halls, or virtual conversations (Fordham 1998; Krajeski and Peterson 2013). The planning process then moves toward identifying a set of mitigation measures and prioritizing what comes first – for implementation and for funding. Step three can take a significant amount of time as an emergency manager works to maintain interest and momentum on a topic that is often not a high priority unless a recent disaster has occurred. The ways in which a mitigation leader engages the community matter a great deal, which this chapter will turn to shortly.

In step four, the planning team develops an implementation strategy and timeline to mitigate future risks. Communities may opt for a range of mitigation measures depending on available funding and local preferences. Continual efforts will need to be made to secure funding as once the planning is complete, the process may fall from public view and interest. Though your work in mitigation may seem unending, and the payoff far in the future, this return will come someday. The lives and properties your efforts save may be your grandchildren, your neighbors, those with whom you worship, or people you don't even know. Mitigation is a payment toward the future and a more resilient community.

9.4.3 Inclusive Mitigation Planning

Mitigation planning must involve the whole community, in all its diversity of people and places, to become more resilient. Such a coalition becomes an "essential vehicle" to decrease disaster risks (National Academy of Sciences 2012, p. 119). To reduce vulnerability, planning must involve an array of stakeholders: educators, businesses, utilities, recreational and tourist facilities, government (including tribal) and nongovernmental organizations, renters, homeowners, health care industries, farmers, congregate care facilities, and more. Planning teams must also include socially vulnerable groups and their advocates: single parents, racial and ethnic minorities, seniors living alone or in assisted living facilities, low-income families, people with disabilities, caregivers, pets, and livestock. An intentional, inclusive effort will be needed to surface concerns and design best solutions. People who use assistive technologies should be enabled to join in (National Council on Disability 2009). Children should have input. Veterinarians can contribute as can medical providers. Business settings need to be represented too, from home-based enterprises through multinational factories. People who live in doorways, trailer parks, expensive downtown apartments, public housing, and single-family homes should be able to weigh in. No groups at risk should be excluded, and efforts must be made to make meetings accessible with appropriate languages, translations, technologies, and literacy levels (Peguero 2006; National Council on Disability 2009; Santos-Hernández and Morrow 2013).

Planning should also reflect local culture. Perhaps your community appoints formal committees to accomplish public tasks or relies on talking circles, which are more common to some Native American communities (Picou 2000; Krajeski and Peterson 2013). Honoring the local ways of meeting and connecting leverages the community's existing social networks and knowledge bases and makes people feel more welcome at the planning table. That planning table could be anywhere: in workplaces, community centers, neighborhood gathering spaces, or online. In California, three separate jurisdictions, including the Berkeley Unified School District, the City of Berkeley, and the University of California, Berkeley, worked together to reduce risks from earthquakes, wildfires, and other events (Chakos, Schulz, and Tobin 2002). Berkeley benefited from a community culture that believed deeply in "participatory democracy" where people join in actively over collective matters. With such broad stakeholder involvement, Berkeley residents voted to fund $30 million in mitigation projects.

Planning, especially step three, should also reflect the realities of people's lives as they juggle work and family. Strategies that can increase participation include:

- Paying people for their participation.
- Providing culturally appropriate meals.
- Using local venues that are convenient to encourage participation.
- Diversifying outreach communications through traditional and social media, social networks, trusted people and places, and through various languages.
- Providing transportation to the venue.
- Offering electronic alternatives and devices to join the conversation.
- Creating safe childcare services so that families can participate.
- Selecting accessible sites for people with disabilities, senior citizens, and families.
- Offering multilingual interpretation, including sign language.
- Enabling advocates to represent historically marginalized people.
- Encouraging credible and diverse local leaders to participate at high levels.
- Listening to everyone's voice and opinions and ensuring transparency around those conversations.

Why does an inclusive effort work? Because it surfaces what social scientists refer to as social capital. One particular form, called bridging social capital, arises out of people working across their differing points of view, workplaces, cultures, and locations. A classic example comes from involving both the janitor and the chief executive officer (CEO) of a company. While the CEO knows and understands how to manage a team and where to secure funding for a mitigation effort, the janitor is the person who knows where real risks lie in a building or operation. Their combined knowledge produces new insights and ideas to serve the business better and reduce risks (Phillips and Landahl 2020). Similarly, a community that has faced continual flooding risks because of historic segregation knows where the first breaches will occur, when, and who will be affected. They also know the community places and people who can contribute to the conversation and produce champions for focused mitigation efforts.

9.4.4 Strategies for Community Engagement

Emergency managers can consider several strategies to design community-based mitigation planning efforts. Those strategies range from traditional approaches that rely on formal committees and meeting structures to those that move into and rely on potentially affected communities with high levels of local participation. Traditional, formal, and standardized approaches often rely on an external consultant to guide the process through a templated process that results in a hazard mitigation plan. While efficient, such formal efforts have been critiqued as overemphasizing standardization at the expense of locally lived realities. Formal processes also tend to deter local participation and often miss critical perspectives from across the community's diverse population and business types (e.g., see Haverkamp 2017). Take a minute and think about your own preferred ways to become engaged. Would you prefer listening to someone present a PowerPoint for hours or would you prefer to talk through the issue with others from your community, tour high-risk locations, and learn about options to mitigate disasters?

Because local culture and ways of doing things matter, disaster scientists recommend that emergency managers should design a mitigation planning effort that relies on a local, *participatory* effort. Participatory means that people at risk – homeowners, business owners, renters, organizations, and government – are all involved in a meaningful way. Though traditional mitigation planning can produce a plan, it might not reflect what local people know about their communities and whether they will accept and invest in a plan. To illustrate, Alaskan Native villages have been facing melting permafrost, increased flooding, and loss of protective barriers that have impacted area species on which they rely (Ristroph 2018). These types of climate change will be experienced locally, as they impact the means on which people exist. Called subsistence living, protection of the environment has become a critical tool in conserving Alaskan Native cultures and food sources as well as reducing disaster impacts like flooding. One study found that consultants using templates in such areas ignored practical advice offered by the community. People who lived locally recommended creating an inexpensive evacuation "mound" that people could easily reach rather than a new, expensive, and extended road out of the area. After multiple mitigation plans, the community still did not have the mound or the road (Ristroph 2018).

One strategy to involve locals meaningfully is called participatory action research, where community members become engaged in identifying a problem, gathering information and data about the problem, analyzing the problem, and identifying solutions that work locally. By training *citizen scientists*, useful data can be reliably collected using people's local ecological knowledge (Meyer et al. 2018). Such an approach would have been beneficial in the study of Alaskan Native Villages, which remain waiting for viable solutions to climate change.

Participatory strategies have expanded in recent years to include digital technologies that engage stakeholders. One effort relied on an app where high school students collected data subsequently analyzed by community members with university faculty and student support (Meyer et al. 2018). Participatory geographic information systems (PGIS) also generate visual images of what is happening locally. In a Houston area effort, a diverse group of Hispanic and African American students collected data by using the Environmental Systems Research Institute's "Collector for ArcGIS" app (Meyer et al. 2018). Participants also collected survey data by going door-to-door in multilingual teams. Local stakeholders gave tours to the academic participants and then a series of meetings unfolded to analyze the data, surface solutions, and design a master plan. The result? The mitigation plan called for increasing green space by removing unused parking lots and abandoned buildings among other ideas (Meyer et al. 2018). Reasonable solutions surfaced that could be implemented to reduce flooding by involving people who knew the places and the people at risk.

Another digitized technique can come from crowdsourcing information, where emergency managers ask the public to share information through easily available technologies (Kankanamge et al. 2019). Given the widespread use of cellphones, mitigation planning can be informed by people even in remote locations. In one study, Taiwan officials crowdsourced and geotagged historical photographs to reveal debris flow hot spots (Chu and Chen 2018). To do so, a government agency provided a website for people to upload photos, which were then analyzed by scientists. As another example, CyberFlood, a cloud-based product, enabled citizen scientists to upload visual data via smart phones to facilitate flood risk management and increase flood awareness (Wan et al., 2014). In the U.S., anyone can participate in a crowdsourced app called "Did You Feel It?" that collects earthquake information (see it here: https://earthquake.usgs.gov/data/dyfi/; Harrison and Johnson 2016). Such information leverages groups effectively to produce data that can inform a THIRA and mitigation planning.

9.5 CAREERS AND VOLUNTEERING IN MITIGATION AND RESILIENCE

Many emergency managers work in mitigation on a regular basis (see Box 9.5). In quite a few locations, they may be the only emergency manager in their city or county, thus the work of all four phases falls on their shoulders. To accomplish mitigation work, they would likely collaborate with planners, public officials, community members, business leaders, school personnel, health care providers, and others. They will also work with state-, regional-, tribal-, or national-level governments to align their plans with those outside of their jurisdiction, because disasters do not recognize jurisdictional boundaries. They may interact with insurance companies, engineers, construction firms, and others to design and implement mitigation measures. Emergency

---

BOX 9.5

MITIGATION AND RESILIENCE CAREER EXAMPLES (VERBATIM FROM SOURCES)

"*Supervisory Emergency Management Specialist/Mitigation* (FEMA, posted November 2020, Oakland, California). The ideal leader for this position will possess the professional experience to address long-term risks caused by disasters through mitigation planning efforts, application of building codes and environmental standards to enhance the resiliency of states, tribes, territories, and communities. Oversight of $1 billion in grant programs. This position starts at a salary of $154,687 (GS-15).

In this position, you will serve as the Mitigation Division Director within FEMA Region 9, advancing disaster resilience through innovative partnerships and creative application of federal and other resources. The ideal candidate for this position will be well-versed in pre- and post-disaster mitigation efforts, urban planning, architecture or building sciences, and have experience in leading people within an organization. Typical assignments include:

- Managing all aspects of the regional Mitigation Division, overseeing programs related to: Risk Analysis, Hazard Mitigation Assistance, Floodplain Management and Insurance, and Environmental Planning and Historic Preservation.
- Serving as the resilience subject matter expert in the region, bringing a wealth of knowledge in the fields of urban planning and building sciences to ensure the region applies a resilience lens across all activities, identifying the region's resilience challenges and bringing together cross-sector stakeholders to develop solutions.
- Advocating for the implementation of resilience programs to engage all stakeholders in reducing the frequency, severity, and cost of disasters.
- Providing direct oversight on funding for eligible mitigation projects that reduce disaster losses to disaster-impacted State, local, tribal, territorial, nongovernmental organizations, and private sector partners.
- Ensuring regional mitigation operations are executed in accordance with agency guidance and that they follow emergency management-related directives, federal regulations, and environmental and historic preservation laws and executive orders."

"*Emergency Management Specialist, U.S. Department of Homeland Security/FEMA.* $121,316 to $157,709 per year. Posted January 2021.

The Department of Homeland Security (DHS) is calling on those who want to help protect American interests and secure our Nation. DHS Components work collectively to prevent terrorism; secure borders and our transportation systems; protect the President and other dignitaries; enforce and administer immigration laws; safeguard cyberspace; and ensure resilience to disasters. We achieve these vital missions through a diverse workforce spanning hundreds of occupations. Make an impact; join DHS. In this position, you will act as a senior expert in the Office of the Chief Administrator Officer, Installation and Infrastructure Division, coordinating and supporting the implementation of disaster services and programs. Typical assignments include:

- Analyzing resource requirements and capabilities to enable program delivery and performance.
- Providing expert advice, guidance, and policy interpretation on a significant number of issues.
- Developing and implementing emergency management standards, regulations, practices, training, and procedures to facilitate disaster operations.
- Preparing reports, information papers and briefings which identify emergency management operating practices.

The ideal candidate would have developed a program in the past; wrote SOP's and policies; worked in disasters; and understand FEMA's mission and how it correlates with the regions and states. The ideal candidate will be a data focused individual, one that knows how to take raw information and turn it into reports and operational decision tools."

managers will also connect with many people and places to educate them about risk reduction measures and to motivate them to join in.

Emergency managers may also work exclusively in mitigation and resilience activities. In larger cities or in state, regional, tribal, or national government, they may be the sole person tasked with developing a mitigation planning process and implementing the prioritized results. Grant writing will likely serve as one of their chief activities, as they work to secure funds for various projects. Perhaps they will focus exclusively on a mitigation project, like dam construction or a statewide safe room initiative. They could also work within an industry, conducting loss estimations and recommending strategies to remain economically strong. Perhaps insurance could serve as a place of employment, with the goal of risk reduction and overall savings to people, organizations, communities, and governments.

But mitigation work can and should involve the rest of us too. Everyone should be involved in being personally responsible to mitigate what risks they can for themselves as well as their families, friends, and coworkers. We can also volunteer to serve on a mitigation planning process. As citizens of a community at risk, we can help with fundraising and educational efforts to reduce dangers. We can volunteer on projects to increase public safety, from hosting insurance fairs to setting up public displays of safe rooms. Mitigation is everyone's responsibility.

***

SUMMARY

Mitigation reduces losses from hazards. Two main kinds of mitigation can be pursued: structural or nonstructural. Structural mitigation focuses on the built environment and involves creating or altering structures to be more resilient. An example might be an elevation, which raises a home or business out of an area of repetitive flooding.

Earthquakes can also threaten structures, so building them to be more seismically resistant also introduces a viable structural mitigation measure. Hurricane-centered structural mitigation might include metal shutters, hurricane clamps on roofs, or siting buildings away from areas of risk.

Nonstructural mitigation includes a range of less tangible measures. For example, communities will decide land use and how to site buildings in relation to area hazards. Public officials will also design and implement building codes about how homes or businesses should be constructed and enforce those codes through permits and inspections. Insurance can also serve as a nonstructural mitigation effort designed to reduce losses by providing post-disaster recovery funds. Mitigation planning represents a means to involve a wide range of stakeholders in identifying hazards, assessing risks, determining vulnerabilities, and prioritizing mitigation measures. Community-based mitigation, which requires a high level of attention to local culture and social vulnerability, requires an inclusive approach for all potentially affected stakeholders.

Discussion Questions

1. Define mitigation and then explain and give examples of the differences between structural and nonstructural mitigation.
2. Identify and give examples of standard practices for structural mitigation.
3. Identify and give examples of standard practices for nonstructural mitigation.
4. Explain why social vulnerability should be considered when designing a mitigation planning effort.
5. Describe best practices for walking stakeholders through a mitigation planning effort.

Summary Questions

1. Why can it be so difficult to convince people at risk to invest in mitigation measures?
2. How would you convince your community members to practice a mitigation measure such as insurance, hurricane roof clamps, or wearing a mask in a pandemic?
3. What would you say to convince a set of stakeholders (businesses, homeowners, government) to invest in mitigation measures?
4. Who would you invite to a mitigation planning effort where you live or work?
5. What do you see as the long-term benefits of mitigation measures?

REFERENCES

American Society of Civil Engineers. 2013. *Report Card for America's Infrastructure 2013*. Washington, DC: American Society of Civil Engineers. Available at http://www.infrastructurereportcard.org/grades/, last accessed February 23, 2016.
Ayscue, Jon. 1996. "Hurricane Damage to Residential Structures: Risk and Mitigation." Working Paper #4 at http://www.colorado.edu/hazards/publications/wp/wp4/wp4.html, last accessed January 31, 2011.

Burby, Raymond J., Robert E. Deyle, David R. Godschalk, and Robert B. Olshansky. 2000. "Creating Hazard Resilient Communities through Land-Use Planning." *Natural Hazards Review* 1(2): 99–106.

Chakos, Arrietta, Paula Schulz and L. Thomas Tobin. 2002. "Making it Work in Berkeley: Investing in Community Sustainability." *Natural Hazards Review* 3(2): 55–67.

Chu, Hone-Jay and Yi-Chin Chen. 2018. "Crowdsourcing Photograph Locations for Debris Flow Hot Spot Mapping." *Natural Hazards* 90: 1259–1276.

Cuevas Muñiz, Alicia and José Luis Seefoo Luján. 2005. "Reubicación y Desarticulación de La Yerbabuena: Entre el riesgo volcánico y la vulnerabilidad política." *Desacatos* 19: 41–70.

Cutter, Susan. 2005. "The Human Geography of Social Vulnerability: Race, Class, & Catastrophe." Available at https://items.ssrc.org/understanding-katrina/the-geography-of-social-vulnerability-race-class-and-catastrophe/, last accessed January 7, 2021.

Fordham, Maureen. 1998. "Participatory Planning for Flood Mitigation: Models and Approaches." *Australian Journal of Emergency Management* 13(4): 27–34.

Godschalk, David, Edward J. Kaiser, and Philip R. Berke. 1998. "Integrating Hazard Mitigation and Local Land Use Planning." Pp. 85–118 in *Cooperating with Nature*, ed. Raymond J. Burby. Washington, DC: Joseph Henry Press.

Harrison, Sara E. and Peter A. Johnson. 2016. "Crowdsourcing the Disaster Management Cycle." *International Journal of Information Systems for Crisis Response and Management* 8(4): 17–40.

Haverkamp, Jamie A. R. 2017. "Politics, Values, and Reflexivity: The Case of Adaptation to Climate Change in Hampton Roads, Virginia." *Environment and Planning* 49(1): 2673–2692.

Kankanamge, Nayomi, Tan Yigitcanlar, Ashantha Goonetilleke, and Md Kamruzzaman. 2019. "Can Volunteer Crowdsourcing Reduce Disaster Risk? A Systematic Review of the Literature." *International Journal of Disaster Risk Reduction* 35: 1–12.

Karunasena, Gayani and Raufdeen Rameezdeen. 2014. "Post-disaster Housing Reconstruction: Comparative Study of Donor vs. Owner-Driven Approaches." *International Journal of Disaster Resilience in the Built Environment* 1(2): 173–191.

Krajeski, Richard, and Kristina Peterson. 2013. "Involving the Community in Mitigation and Outreach." Pp. 151–194 in *Natural Hazard Mitigation*, eds. Alessandra Jerolleman and John J. Kiefer. Boca Raton, FL: CRC Press.

Kroll-Smith, Steve, Vern Baxter, and Pam Jenkins. 2015. *Left to Chance: Hurricane Katrina and the Story of Two New Orleans Neighborhoods*. Austin: University of Texas Press.

Marshall, William F. 2021. "Coronavirus Infection by Race: What's Behind the Health Disparities?" Available at https://www.mayoclinic.org/diseases-conditions/coronavirus/expert-answers/coronavirus-infection-by-race/faq-20488802, last accessed January 7, 2021.

Meyer, Michelle Annette, Marccus Hendricks, Galen D. Newman, Jaimie Hicks Masterson, John T. Cooper, Garett Sansom, Nasir Gharaibeh et al. 2018. "Participatory Action Research: Tools for Disaster Resilience Education." *International Journal of Disaster Resilience in the Built Environment* 9(45): 402–419.

National Academies of Science. 2012. *Disaster Resilience: A National Imperative*. Washington D.C.: National Academies of Science.

National Council on Disability. 2009. *Effective Emergency Management: Making Improvements for Communities and People with Disabilities*. Washington, DC: National Council on Disability.

National Weather Service. n.d. *Severe Weather 101: Tornado Basics*. Available at http://www.nssl.noaa.gov/education/svrwx101/tornadoes/, last accessed March 1, 2016.

Peguero, Anthony. 2006. "Latin Disaster Vulnerability: The Dissemination of Hurricane Mitigation Information among Florida's Homeowners." *Hispanic Journal of Behavioral Sciences* 28(1): 5–22.

Phillips, Brenda and Mark Landahl. 2020. *Business Continuity Planning*. Cambridge, MA: Elsevier Press.

Phillips, Brenda, Patricia Stukes, and Pam Jenkins. 2012. "Freedom Hill Is Not for Sale and Neither Is the Lower Ninth Ward." *Journal of Black Studies* 43(4): 405–426.

Phillips, Brenda. 2014. *Mennonite Disaster Service: Building a Therapeutic Community along the Gulf Coast.* Lanham, MD: Lexington Books.

Picou, J. S. 2000. "Talking Circles as Sociological Practice: Cultural Transformation of Chronic Disaster Impacts." *Sociological Practice* 2(2): 77–97.

Ristroph, Elizabeta Barrett. 2018. "Improving the Quality of Alaska Native Village Climate Change Planning." *Journal of Geography and Regional Planning* 11(10): 143–155.

Rose, Adam, et al. 2007. "Benefit-Cost Analysis of FEMA Hazard Mitigation Grants." *Natural Hazards Review* 8(4): 97–111.

Santos-Hernández, Jennifer and Betty Morrow. 2013. "Language and Literacy." Pp. 265–280 in *Social Vulnerability to Disasters*, ed. D. Thomas et al. Boca Raton, FL: CRC Press.

Schuch, Gemma, Silvia Serrao-Neumann, Edward Morgan, and Darryl Low Choy. 2017. "Water in the City: Green Open Spaces, Land Use Planning and Flood Management–An Australian Case Study." *Land Use Policy* 63: 539–550.

Sharkey, Patrick. 2007. "Survival and Death in New Orleans: An Empirical Look at the Human Impact of Katrina." *Journal of Black Studies* 37(4): 482–501.

Wan, Zhanming et al. 2014. "A Cloud-Based Global Flood Disaster Community Cyber-Infrastructure: Development and Demonstration." *Environmental Modelling & Software* 58: 86–94.

RESOURCES (LAST ACCESSED JANUARY 7, 2021)

- Extensive free guides can help you to assess your risks and design mitigation measures. Visit https://www.ready.gov/be-informed.
- FEMA Mitigation Planning tools and guides, https://www.fema.gov/emergency-managers/risk-management/hazard-mitigation-planning.
- FEMA on building resilient infrastructure and communities, https://www.fema.gov/grants/mitigation/building-resilient-infrastructure-communities.
- Mitigation benefit cost analysis tools, https://www.fema.gov/grants/guidance-tools/benefit-cost-analysis.
- Risk assessment tools and business impact analysis information, https://www.ready.gov/risk-assessment.
- THIRA tools, https://www.fema.gov/emergency-managers/risk-management/risk-capability-assessment.

PART 3

Working and Volunteering in Emergency Management

CHAPTER 10

Public and Private Sectors

CHAPTER OBJECTIVES

Upon completing this chapter, readers should be able to:

- Understand the role of the public sector in disaster at all levels of government.
- Discuss the ways in which the private sector is involved in preparedness, response, recovery, and mitigation.
- Describe the impacts disasters have on the private sector and patterns of preparedness among businesses.
- Understand the importance of business continuity planning and the steps involved in the process.
- Discuss the importance of establishing partnerships between the public and private sectors, particularly in terms of protecting critical infrastructure systems.

KEY TERMS

- Business Continuity Planning
- Community Lifelines
- Critical Infrastructure Systems
- National Critical Functions

- Private Sector
- Public and Private Partnerships
- Public Sector

10.1 INTRODUCTION

Preparing for, responding to, recovering from, and mitigating for disasters involves the whole community, including individuals and households, voluntary associations and nongovernmental organizations, and both the public and private sectors. Yet, when many people think about disasters, particularly responding to them, the first

DOI: 10.4324/9781003021919-13

and perhaps only thing that comes to their mind is government. This chapter emphasizes the importance of both the public and private sectors across the emergency management (EM) life cycle. First, we describe the role of the public sector in disaster at all levels of government, including local, state, and national. Next, we discuss the impacts of disasters on businesses and describe the numerous and varied roles of private sector companies in disaster preparedness, response, recovery, and mitigation. Finally, we discuss the importance and value of strengthening public and private partnerships to promote greater societal resilience to disasters.

10.2 THE PUBLIC SECTOR

As many have stated, all disasters are local. With this assumption, we will begin our discussion of the public sector by looking at the roles of local public officials. In addition to emergency managers, we include city managers, mayors, city council members, and elected county officials. A discussion of the public sector should also include other parts of local government such as public works, parks and recreation, planning departments, and emergency services (i.e., police, fire, medical). Next, we look at the role of state government, including the governor, the state office(s) of EM and/or homeland security, and other related state agencies. Finally, we review the role of the Federal government, focusing primarily on the duties and responsibilities of the Executive Branch (including Federal Emergency Management Agency [FEMA]) and Congress. We also outline the process of Presidential disaster declarations (PDDs), which involves all levels of government. Overall, we stress that the public sector's approach to disaster is "multi-organizational." By that, we mean that government representatives from local, state, and Federal sectors much work together, perhaps in different or new ways from every day operations, in order to succeed before, during, or after disaster (Drabek 2013).

10.2.1 Local Government

In this section, we will identify various local governmental actors and agencies and describe their roles and activities in EM. As you read this section, you will notice that in addition to departments that have clearly delineated disaster-related responsibilities, such as police and fire departments, many others contribute to EM activities.

10.2.1.1 Elected Officials and the Emergency Management Offices

In general, by law the highest elected local official carries the main decision-making responsibilities for EM. For county government in many states, this could be the county judge or the head county commissioner. For city governments, depending upon the exact type of local government structure, it could be the mayor or the president of the city council. These elected officials have many different tasks to manage on a day-to-day basis, so they do not have time to oversee an emergency management department on a full-time, daily basis. As a result, elected officials delegate these crucial EM tasks to the designated local emergency manager.

Furthermore, local governments may locate the office of EM differently. Generally, we see the office of EM embedded within fire or police departments. Such a pattern has developed historically because officials did not see EM as a separate profession. Instead, local officials saw the office as part of "emergency services" with a focus on response. Thus, local officials would fill the position with a person having experience in a "command and control" or emergency response background. Thus, when a police officer or firefighter was given the title and duties of the local emergency manager, he or she had a fire or police chief to report to, the chief reported to the city or county manager, who, in turn, reported to the elected official. As a result, the position of emergency manager often got buried under local government bureaucracy. Being buried under bureaucracy and many bosses, their job becomes more difficult before, during, and after disaster (Waugh and Streib 2006).

Today, we see some increasing evidence that an office of EM reports directly to the top official in local government. In many ways, this location is ideal to promote outreach, networking, and interacting across government, private, and volunteer sectors. But the problem is not unique to local government, as this same problem of organizational location plagues state government and FEMA. This problem can also be observed in the private sector, where business continuity planners are either part of the information technology (IT)/computer offices or fall under safety and security. Overall, emergency managers and business continuity planners may pass through many layers of a bureaucracy to get to the main decision maker. Rare is the case where the emergency manager has direct access – even during a disaster – to key decision makers (McEntire 2006; Edwards and Goodrich 2007). Since the creation of the Department of Homeland Security (DHS), the problem of access has further developed with an implicit "top-down" or command and control approach to EM (Waugh and Streib 2006). More recently, DHS has been moving to a command and "manage" approach, with an emphasis on collaboration and communication among DHS partner agencies.

10.2.1.2 Local Departments

Before disaster strikes, local government departments do their normal day-to-day tasks. When disaster strikes, some of these operations may continue or will focus on bringing capabilities back to normal. Sanitation departments work on debris removal and disposal. The utilities ensure that power and gas lines are safe to use. Water and sewage departments test the water and sewage systems for safety and that they work properly. As Dynes (1970) and Drabek (2013) stress, during and after disaster, many parts of local government (and others from government, business and volunteer organizations) may change their tasks or integrate themselves into a broader local response. For example, workers from parks and recreation may be moved to other departments to help, or their facilities may be used as staging sites for material resources or coordinating outside volunteers. Budget and finance offices will keep track of monies spent so that the Federal government can reimburse local government for disaster expenses. In broader situations, mutual aid agreements come into effect where police or fire departments may cross jurisdictions to help another community. In extreme cases, such as the City of Salt Lake during extreme flooding in 1983, a city may totally alter its organizational structure and tasks to focus strictly on preventing the whole city from flooding (Neal 1985).

Following disaster, local government must find ways to work with state and Federal governments and with local residents to enhance the recovery process (Smith and Wenger 2007; Phillips 2015). In short, local departments become central players before, during, and after a disaster, and must be willing to work together for the response and recovery to be effective. Preexisting relationships and effective communication built before the disaster can assist with effective event management.

10.2.2 State Government

State governments also play an important role in EM. Governors, for example, declare states of emergency after disasters strike, which is a crucial step in initiating subsequent response activities on the part of the Federal government. Some state agencies refer to themselves as offices of EM while others are known as offices of homeland security. In other locales, they may have both a DHS and Office of Emergency Management. Regardless of their names and bureaucratic locations, these agencies play vital roles in promoting preparedness at the local level, assisting in response activities, and facilitating recovery. For example, state offices play central roles in obtaining monies for local training, preparedness, and mitigation activities. They also assist in gathering information for the Governor to obtain additional funding for the presidentially declared disasters. Interorganizational coordination between local governments and state agencies during normal times must exist so that response and recovery will go more smoothly when disaster occurs.

10.2.2.1 Role of the Governor

Similar to the model of local government, the highest elected official of any state, the Governor, is the state's lead emergency manager. The state director of EM (see below) typically serves at the will of the Governor and promotes his or her policies. Although a state director of EM and/or homeland security can make recommendations, the ultimate decisions related to EM rest with the Governor (Sylves 2015, pp. 114–115).

A state's Governor has a number of important roles during a disaster response. First, only the Governor has the power to activate the state's National Guard to assist with response-related activities. Second, only through the Governor can a state make the formal request to the FEMA regional office to secure funding through a presidentially declared disaster. Third, the Governor can lobby both the President and Congress for additional funding or changes in policy in order to assist states with disaster issues. Governors' interactions with the FEMA regional offices before, during, and after disasters can also assist in obtaining a wide range of Federal resources. Overall, the office of the Governor becomes a central conduit between local and Federal governments to work together to meet their goals (Sylves 2015, pp. 114–115). Overall, Governors must set a leadership example by being willing to work with local government and the Federal government, including the FEMA regional office, Congress, and even the President. Importantly, the Governor sets the tone for developing intergovernmental relationships and partnerships.

10.2.2.2 Emergency Management and Homeland Security Offices

In general, the state office of EM and/or homeland security takes care of the day-to-day operations of EM. Similar to FEMA, these organizations are much more than a response agency such as providing training opportunities for local governments. It also helps to fund some initiatives for local EM offices. These state EM agencies also serve as an important conduit for Federal information and monies to local government. The state office also assists local governments in gathering data for disaster declaration applications and provides the information to the regional FEMA office. In general, state offices help to promote effective and responsive EM.

The development of the DHS as a cabinet-level post following the September 11, 2001 terror attacks further complicated matters for state officials. The creation of DHS placed FEMA within the DHS structure, and the Director of FEMA reported to the DHS director (DHS 2021a). Many States created their own Homeland Security office, adding further bureaucracy to their disaster management capabilities. Similar to the situation with local EM offices, one could find the state EM or homeland security office in many possible organizational locations. Possible options among states include (FEMA 2021):

- Governor.
- Adjutant General/Military.
- Homeland Security.
- Public Safety.
- State Police.
- Other.

Thus, except for those organizations reporting directly to the Governor, EM or homeland security directors may have bureaucratic roadblocks reaching the governor. For example, the State of Minnesota has the Division of Homeland Security and Emergency Management as one office. However, the division is located within the State Department of Public Safety, thus having no direct organizational access to the Governor (Minnesota Department of Public Safety 2021). Following the 9/11 terrorist attacks, California created its own DHS in addition to keeping its Governor's Office of Emergency Services. However, within a few years, the Governor and State Legislature merged the two offices and changed the name to the California Emergency Management Agency. In 2013, further organizational changes occurred and the name changed back to its historical roots – Office of Emergency Services. Although the office today covers a wide range of hazards and potential terror attacks, much of its budget and grants it receives focuses upon homeland security (AllGov 2021; California Office of Emergency Services 2021).

Oklahoma takes another approach. The Oklahoma Department of Emergency Management reports directly to the Governor, and the Governor appoints the state director. Tasks of this office include assisting with emergency and disaster declarations, helping victims and communities obtain financial assistance following a disaster, and providing training opportunities for a wide range of hazards across all four phases of disaster (Oklahoma Department of Emergency Management 2021). On the other hand, the Office of Homeland Security is located within the Oklahoma Department of Public Safety (Oklahoma Department of Public Safety 2021). Although appointed by the Governor, the Director of Homeland Security reports to the Director of Public Safety.

Homeland Security's main purpose is to protect the state from various types and forms of terrorist attacks. In addition, this office also manages most of the grants the State receives related to homeland security and EM (Oklahoma Office of Homeland Security 2021).

In sum, no one model exists where EM and homeland security are located within state organizational charts. EM in Texas, for example, was dramatically reorganized after Hurricane Harvey in 2017. For many years, the Texas Division of Emergency Management (TDEM), the state's lead EM agency, was housed under the Texas Department of Public Safety (DPS), the primary law enforcement agency in the state. That changed after Hurricane Harvey. Following the recommendations of the *Eye of the Storm* after-action report, which was published in 2018, TDEM was removed from DPS and placed under the auspices of the Texas A&M University (TAMU) System (Governor's Commission to Rebuild Texas 2018). As a result, the state's top EM official now holds the dual titles of Chief of TDEM and Vice Chancellor for Emergency and Disaster Services for the TAMU System.

10.2.3 Accrediting State and Local Governments

The Emergency Management Accrediting Program (EMAP) focuses upon improving state and local government (i.e., organizational) capabilities. During the National Emergency Management Association's (NEMA) annual meetings in 1997, the organization decided to create a set of EM standards for state and local governments. If state and local governments met these standards, they would become an "accredited" organization. Since NEMA's efforts are directed by the state directors of EM in the United States, this effort carried a lot of weight. The criteria that governmental organizations must follow are known as the Emergency Management Standard. These standards, developed by state and local emergency managers and EM organizations (e.g., NEMA, IAEMS, DHS), consist of (EMAP 2021a):

- Self-assessment and documentation.
- On-site assessment by a team of trained, independent assessors.
- A committee review and recommendation.
- Accreditation decision by an independent commission.
- Maintaining accreditation.

In all, EMAP uses 16 general standards that a state or local government must meet to become accredited. Although too many to list here, examples of some of the general criteria include (EMAP 2021b, verbatim):

- Program Management.
- Administration and Finance.
- Laws and Authorities.
- Hazard Identification, Risk Assessment and Consequence Analysis.
- Hazard Mitigation.
- Prevention.
- Operational Planning.

- Incident Management.
- Resource Management and Logistics.
- Mutual Aid.
- Communications and Warning.
- Operations and Procedures.
- Facilities.
- Training.
- Exercises, Evaluations and Corrective Action.
- Crisis Communications, Public Education and Information (end verbatim).

At this time, 35 states have EMAP accreditation as does the District of Columbia, and a number of major United States cities, disaster related federal agencies, and even three universities have achieved EMAP accreditation (EMAP 2021c).

10.2.4 Federal Government

The Federal government helps set disaster policy and guidance for state and local governments and other organizations. It also provides money for activities related to preparedness, response, recovery, mitigation, and prevention. Whereas all disasters may still be local, the Federal government drives and helps finance much of these activities. Here, we review the main activities by the Executive Branch (including the PDD process) and Congress.

10.2.4.1 The Executive Branch

Generally, the President obtains emergency powers through the Constitution. Article 2 Section 3 of the U.S. Constitution says that the President must ensure that laws of the nation are executed properly. Article 2 of the Constitution makes the President the Commander in Chief of the Military, giving the President the power to use military resources. In addition, the Constitution also allows the President under times of crisis to use the authority given to the two other branches of government: legislative and judicial. Only twice have Presidents used this power. Abraham Lincoln used it during the Civil War and Franklin Roosevelt used it during World War II. Although rarely used, the President could draw upon this authority in time of a catastrophic event (Sylves 2015, pp. 91–92).

The President also has various cabinet-level posts that generally make up a large percentage of what we refer to as the "Federal Bureaucracy." Over the last 50 years, cabinet-level posts have stayed generally the same. In 2021, the cabinet consists of the Vice President and the heads of the 15 executive departments, including (The White House 2021):

- Department of Agriculture.
- Department of Commerce.
- Department of Defense.
- Department of Education.
- Department of Energy.
- Department of Health and Human Services.

- Department of Homeland Security.
- Department of Housing and Urban Development.
- Department of the Interior.
- Department of Justice.
- Department of Labor.
- Department of State.
- Department of Transportation.
- Department of the Treasury.
- Department of Veteran Affairs.

FEMA currently resides under the DHS. Beginning with President Clinton's administration in 1993, FEMA had become a designated cabinet-level post. As a result, the FEMA director had direct access to the President and matters dealing with disasters often moved much more quickly and efficiently. However, with the formation of the DHS in 2003, FEMA moved under DHS. Many in EM expressed concern about the organizational location of FEMA, its perceived diminished importance due to the change, and potential problems with direct communication with the President. These fears became reality during and following Hurricane Katrina in 2005 (Waugh 2005, 2006). The added layer of bureaucracy proved to be a major hindrance to the response effort.

DHS, with FEMA now under its jurisdiction, serves as the central cabinet post for disaster and homeland security issues. Yet, resources and expertise within all layers of the cabinet enhance the Federal government's response capabilities during a disaster. As laid out in the National Response Framework and its Emergency Support Functions (ESFs), a representative from one cabinet-level post may coordinate the efforts to mobilize resources from other cabinet organizations. For example, to coordinate the activities related to public health during any disaster (ESF #8), Health and Human Services would serve as the primary agency and ESF coordinator. Thirteen Federal agencies from different cabinet posts would support or assist with ESF #8. To illustrate, some of these 13 agencies would include the Department of Justice, Department of Labor, Department of State, and the Environmental Protection Agency.

Coordinated activities by DHS and FEMA (i.e., executive branch) also lay the foundation for assisting state and local governments. For example, the Comprehensive Preparedness Guide (CPG)-101 disaster planning guide promotes communication and coordination among Federal, state, local agencies, and other entities. CPG-101 stresses that disaster planning should be local and it must include stakeholders from the whole community. Thus, partnerships among public, private, and volunteer organizations are crucial if planning and response are to be effective. The whole document stresses engaging all parts of a community.

The President makes the final decision on PDDs. Through these declarations, the executive branch passes monies through state governments that directly or indirectly reimburse or assist locally affected entities. For many, including politicians and victims, the Presidential declaration process may seem confusing, and it has changed through the years. To initiate the process, local government officials provide detailed damage assessments to the state's Governor. The Governor then sends these reports to the FEMA Regional office. Both their assessments then go to FEMA National Headquarters. Top officials at FEMA make their assessment and the Director of FEMA passes along a recommendation to the President. The President makes the final decision. The President does not accept all requests. In fact, from 1989 to 2013, Presidents rejected almost 20% of all disaster declaration requests (Sylves 2015, p. 119).

Some declarations may be controversial despite the President and others following guidelines. For example, a localized event (Enhanced Fujita [EF]-4 scale tornado) with extensive damage and deaths may not meet a threshold for a disaster declaration, but a widespread event lasting days (e.g., a slow rising flood) with no deaths and few injuries may quickly be declared a disaster. As a result, disaster declarations may appear to be political decisions rather than one based on need. Related research (Reeves 2009; also see Sylves and Buzas 2007) suggests that at times, small, subtle political factors may influence the declaration process. States with large populations that appear friendly to the President may have a slight advantage in obtaining a Presidential declaration over other states with large populations that may not always support the President. The annual percentages of requests accepted by a President since May 1953 generally vary from 75% to 80%. In sum, politics may enter the equation, but probably only slightly.

10.2.4.2 Congress

Congress has a much less hands-on role than the Executive Branch. Certainly, Congress passes the budgets that allow the Executive Branch to operate, and it provides funding (e.g., grants, matching funds) to state and local governments for specific disaster projects and initiatives. Congress also provides funding for the President's Disaster Relief Fund. Although the President authorizes monies for disaster relief, Congress must approve the funding – and, to date, Congress has always approved the majority of needed funding. Congress may also provide emergency supplements in bills related to disaster needs (Sylves 2015, pp. 111–114).

Finally, a constant tension often exists regarding how much the Federal government can explicitly dictate specific local disaster policy to local governments. This issue of Federalism runs constant through the U.S. history and is part of EM policy. On the one hand, Federal mandates can provide consistent standard approaches to disasters nationwide. On the other hand, each community and state has different cultures and ways of seeing the world, meaning how one state approaches a disaster issue may be different from another. Federalism can both improve and impede disaster management issues across the four phases of EM. Some claim that Federalism, in part, created the poor response to Hurricane Katrina (Burby 2006; Menzel 2006).

Throughout this chapter, we have discussed the roles and responsibilities in the U.S. of the local, state, and Federal government. We also need to consider transnational government. The EU, for example, consists of more than two dozen countries throughout Europe. While each country has local, regional, and national governments, they also participate in the EU. Because of major flooding and heat waves in EU countries in recent years, and because of large-scale disasters in other nations outside of Europe, the EU changed its EM infrastructure. In 2001, the EU created the Civil Protection Mechanism (CPM), which is depicted in Figure 10.1 (Wendling 2010). Central to the CPM is the Emergency Response Coordination Centre (ERCC), which monitors events and disasters within the EU and worldwide. When necessary, the ERCC coordinates

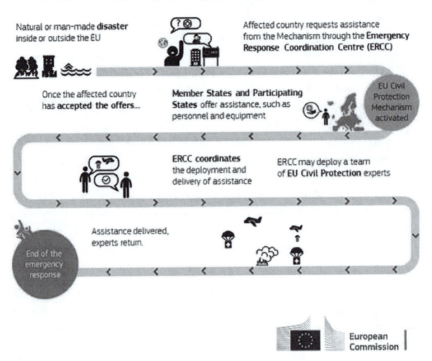

FIGURE 10.1 The EU Civil Protection Mechanism
Source: https://ec.europa.eu/echo/what/civil-protection/emergency-response-coordination-centre-ercc_en

resources and activities among EU nations to assist in providing aid within the EU or other nations. In addition to response capabilities, the ERCC also assists with preparedness activities, disaster exercises, and hazard awareness (EU 2021).

10.3 THE PRIVATE SECTOR

When we think about disasters and EM, we think of police and fire departments, local EM agencies, FEMA, and other public agencies rather than businesses and the private sector. For their part, researchers have also largely ignored the private sector. As we have seen throughout this book, much of what we know about disasters and EM is based on studies of households, broader communities, and organizations, primarily those in the public sector.

10.3.1 The Importance of the Private Sector

In recent years, however, the situation has begun to change with people paying more attention to the private sector. There are three primary reasons why it is important to consider the private sector in the context of disasters and EM. First, a major impetus for increased concern about the private sector is the growing awareness of the staggering *financial costs of disasters*. In 2020, during a single year, the U.S. experienced 22

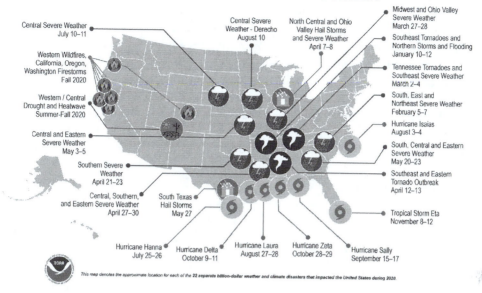

U.S. 2020 Billion-Dollar Weather and Climate Disasters

Central Severe Weather
July 10–11

Western Wildfires,
California, Oregon,
Washington Firestorms
Fall 2020

Western / Central
Drought and Heatwave
Summer-Fall 2020

Central and Eastern
Severe Weather
May 3–5

Southern Severe
Weather
April 21–23

Central, Southern,
and Eastern Severe Weather
April 27–30

Central Severe
Weather - Derecho
August 10

North Central and Ohio
Valley Hail Storms
and Severe Weather
April 7–8

South Texas
Hail Storms
May 27

Hurricane Hanna
July 25–26

Hurricane Delta
October 9–11

Hurricane Laura
August 27–28

Hurricane Zeta
October 28–29

Hurricane Sally
September 15–17

Midwest and Ohio Valley
Severe Weather
March 27–28

Southeast Tornadoes and
Northern Storms and Flooding
January 10–12

Tennessee Tornadoes and
Southeast Severe Weather
March 2–4

South, East and
Northeast Severe Weather
February 5–7

Hurricane Isaias
August 3–4

South, Central and Eastern
Severe Weather
May 20–23

Southeast and Eastern
Tornado Outbreak
April 12–13

Tropical Storm Eta
November 8–12

This map denotes the approximate location for each of the 22 separate billion-dollar weather and climate disasters that impacted the United States during 2020.

FIGURE 10.2 Billion-Dollar Weather Disasters in the U.S. in 2020
Source: https://www.ncdc.noaa.gov/billions/

separate billion-dollar weather and climate disasters, shattering the previous record of 16 such events in 2017 (see Figure 10.2). On a global scale, the picture is even more bleak. According to a recent report by the UN Office of Disaster Risk Reduction, between 2000 and 2019, disasters produced nearly $3 trillion in global economic losses (UNDRR 2020). Unfortunately, most projections are that these costs will continue to rise exponentially in the coming years as we continue to face more and worse disasters.

Second, the private sector now plays a larger role *responding to disasters*. In the U.S. and other countries, private companies own and operate much of the critical infrastructure, including electricity, telecommunications, and transportation. When those systems sustain damage or fail during a disaster, the effectiveness of the overall response effort largely hinges on the ability of company workers to restore services in a timely fashion. As we emphasize throughout this chapter, with so much involvement by the private sector, the challenge of coordinating response activities is even more pronounced for emergency managers. Thus, in order to aid communication and coordination during the response period, all levels of government must reach out to businesses and include them in broader community preparedness initiatives before a disaster strikes.

Finally, we need to pay more attention to the private sector because of its integral role in *stimulating overall community recovery from disaster*. Local governments rely heavily on sales tax revenues to support their basic operations, provide essential services, and launch new community initiatives. When disasters strike, those funds can be dramatically impacted if numerous businesses are damaged and forced to close. Not only do individual businesses suffer from disaster-induced interruptions and sales losses, but the broader community also suffers as a result of reduced sales tax income. The sooner local businesses are able to resume normal operations, the sooner the community as a whole can get on the long path to recovery (e.g., Hackerott 2016). Recovery is a process involving numerous stakeholders, including individuals and households, community groups, and governmental agencies. And, we must also add businesses to that list.

Clearly, the private sector is highly relevant to the study of disasters and the practice of EM. In the next section, we will describe the typical kinds of impacts that disasters have on the private sector, including physical damage to businesses, loss of electricity and other lifeline services, and many others. Then, we will discuss the private sector in relation to the life cycle of disasters and EM, highlighting the types of preparedness activities that best equip businesses to cope with disaster impacts, the typical kinds of things private sector companies do during the response phase, factors that affect business recovery outcomes, and the role of the private sector in mitigation. Given the centrality of the private sector to all four phases, we conclude the chapter by discussing and emphasizing the need for greater cooperation and coordination between the public and private sectors in preparing for, responding to, recovering from, and mitigating future disasters.

10.3.2 The Impacts of Disasters on the Private Sector

Disasters can produce enormous financial impacts. In measuring those impacts, we often think about losses over an extended period of time or at broad levels such as state, regional, or national economies (Webb, Tierney and Dahlhamer 2000). These measures give us useful information about the economic consequences of disasters, but they can overshadow and distort what happens to individual businesses. To understand what happens, in this section we look at the direct, indirect, and remote impacts on businesses.

10.3.2.1 Direct Impacts

In addition to their broader financial impacts, disasters can directly affect individual businesses in a number of ways. Indeed, when we think about businesses and disasters, the direct impacts are the ones that come immediately to mind. Direct disaster impacts on businesses include:

- *Physical damage* to the building in which a business is housed.
- *Forced closure* of a business as a direct result of damage.
- *Loss of utility lifelines* at the site, including electricity, water, sewage, and telecommunications.

In their study of disaster impacts on businesses and long-term recovery of businesses from disasters, Webb, Tierney, and Dahlhamer (2002) found that these kinds of impacts are widespread. In South Florida, for example, fewer than 10% of business owners reported experiencing no physical damage to their facility as a result of Hurricane Andrew in 1992. Among owners whose businesses were damaged, more than 75% indicated that the damage was disruptive or very disruptive to their operations. The vast majority of businesses were forced to close for at least some period of time, with 35% of those businesses closing for more than 22 days. Beyond physical damage to the property, loss of utility lifelines such as electricity, water and sewer, and telephone services can also force businesses to close after a disaster.

Research suggests that the immediate disaster impacts felt by businesses can have significant long-term consequences. In particular, what happens in the immediate aftermath of a disaster can profoundly shape recovery outcomes for individual businesses and the community as a whole. For individual businesses, those forced to close over longer periods of time are less likely to experience positive long-term recovery outcomes than those not forced to close or closed for shorter periods of time (Webb et al. 2002). When businesses suffer losses, sales tax revenues also decline, which negatively impact broader community recovery efforts. During the COVID-19 pandemic, many businesses of all types were forced to close their doors for prolonged periods of time because of stay at home orders, social distancing, and other protective measures that were taken to slow the spread of the virus. As shown in Box 10.1, FEMA provided guidance to assist organizations, including businesses, in their efforts to resume operations.

10.3.2.2 Indirect Impacts

In addition to physical damage, lifeline outages, and forced closure, businesses can also experience a range of indirect disaster impacts. These are things that occur off-site but that nevertheless negatively affect the ability of a business to operate. Typical indirect effects include (Webb et al. 2000):

- Employees unable to get to work.
- Suppliers unable to deliver necessary items.
- Customers declining.

In each of these instances, the effects on business operations can be significant, yet individual business owners can do little to prevent this from happening. For example, workers may be unavailable because they must deal with their own disaster-induced problems at home. Similarly, supply chain disruptions may be the result of direct physical damage to a supplier's facility, blocked transportation routes that impede deliveries, or even employees getting to work. Customers may need to manage damage to their own homes, navigate damaged routes to business districts, and shift spending priorities in the aftermath of a disaster leading to gains for some businesses and losses for others.

As with physical damage, utility outages, and forced closure, indirect impacts experienced immediately after a disaster can also have longer-term consequences. For example, the more operational problems a business faces, like the ones described here, the less likely they are to have positive recovery outcomes over the long term (Webb et al. 2002). Therefore, owners should develop realistic business continuity plans to help them deal with the full range of direct and indirect disaster impacts they may face. As we will see in our discussion of private sector preparedness, in developing those plans, business owners must consider employees, suppliers, nearby businesses, local government agencies, and others to maximize their effectiveness.

10.3.2.3 Remote Impacts

Disasters can produce remote impacts on businesses, which are similar to but larger in scope and more difficult to predict and control than the indirect impacts, described in the previous section. We have already illustrated that disasters are becoming increasingly complex in modern society. A driving force behind the growing complexity of crises and disasters is the increased interdependence of nations and the emergence and

BOX 10.1

RESUMING OPERATIONS DURING THE COVID-19 PANDEMIC

"In these uncertain times, organizations across the nation are grappling with when and how to resume operations while protecting the well-being and safety of their employees and communities. Many organizations will be returning to a new normal and are asking: When is it safe to bring people back? Do we need to modify how we operate? How do we keep our employees, customers, and community safe? How do we maintain a safe and sanitary environment?

An organization may need to adapt and adopt new processes, address physical and psychological impacts to personnel, recover records and files, reestablish communications and IT equipment, or acquire specialized equipment to regain full functionality. Planning for reconstitution requires expertise and coordination from the entire organization and coordination with partners and stakeholders throughout the community.

General Reconstitution Planning Considerations

- Begin now by developing a plan and procedures for how operations will be resumed. Organizations may need to consider a time-phased approach to prepare a facility to be reoccupied. Offices, functions, and returning personnel may need to be prioritized or work in staggered shifts.
- Communicate with employees and inform them of the process for returning to work. Consider providing online training and guidance for employees before returning.
- Coordinate with partners and stakeholders. Determine what methods will be used to inform employees, customers, vendors, and stakeholders that operations are being resumed.
- Identify and implement additional facility maintenance tasks necessary to safely reopen closed buildings.
- Address physical and psychological impacts to personnel through employee and family support plans and other human resource measures.
- Develop an after-action report/improvement plan to note lessons learned and improve plans."

Source: https://www.fema.gov/press-release/20210318/planning-considerations-organizations-reconstituting-operations-during-covid, verbatim.

growth of a global economy. When a disaster strikes in one part of the world, its impacts are often felt in many different places at once. In other words, disasters are now capable of producing remote effects, many of which directly impact businesses in the private sector. As Quarantelli, Lagadec, and Boin (2006) point out, the effects of modern disasters multiply rapidly and are increasingly felt across geographical boundaries.

To illustrate the remote effects of disasters on the private sector, consider instances in which an event in one place has produced cascading effects across an entire region or even the entire world. In 2010, for example, a volcanic eruption in Iceland affected air travel worldwide. To start, a massive cloud of volcanic ash stranded passengers going to or from major airports throughout Europe. For days, airlines cancelled, delayed, or rerouted flights all around the world. The airline industry suffered major disruptions and enormous financial losses. As another example, consider the Deepwater Horizon spill in the Gulf of Mexico in 2010. It certainly dealt a major blow to the local communities along the Gulf Coast, but it also adversely impacted the supply and prices of seafood and other commodities for the entire nation. These examples show how economic impacts transcend the local level and reverberate across large geographic regions. As a result, business owners and emergency managers promoting higher levels of preparedness must consider a wide range of hazards. Direct impacts, including physical damage, utility outages, and forced closure, are the most obvious ones. But, planners must not neglect considering indirect impacts and remote effects when preparing for disasters and developing effective business continuity plans.

10.3.3 The Private Sector and the Life Cycle of Emergency Management

As we have seen, disasters can have significant impacts on the private sector. The financial costs of catastrophic events continue to rise and the impacts of those events on businesses continue to increase in severity. The private sector is also actively involved in responding to disasters. As McEntire, Robinson, and Weber (2003, p. 453) explain:

> It is apparent that the private sector plays both vital and varied roles in emergency management. In fact, it is not an exaggeration to state that the contributions of businesses in mitigation, preparedness, response, and recovery activities have been woefully underestimated …The private sector interacts frequently with the public sector to fulfill necessary community disaster functions. Therefore, the lines between the public and private sectors appear to be blurring, disappearing, or perhaps even artificial.

In this section we learn about the important role of the private sector across all four phases of disasters, including preparedness, response, recovery, and mitigation.

10.3.3.1 Preparedness

Disasters are not a priority for most businesses and many do little to prepare. For example, on surveys containing checklists of 15–20 possible preparedness actions, such as storing a first aid kit, purchasing hazard-specific insurance, developing business continuity plans, or having their building assessed by a structural engineer, business owners on average report undertaking only about four of the items on the lists (Webb et al. 2000). However similar to trying to persuade individuals in households, businesses generally are not prepared for what they see as low probability events. Business owners, particularly those who own small, local establishments, have more pressing concerns. With bills to pay, payrolls to meet, and profits to protect, paying for engineering assessments, continuity plans, or higher insurance premiums becomes a low priority.

When they do prepare, businesses tend to prefer certain types of activities, namely those that are *simple, inexpensive, site-specific* and geared toward *life safety* (Webb et al.

2000; Tyler and Sadiq 2020). By site-specific preparedness measures, we are referring to activities that businesses can do independently, without having to coordinate with other businesses or governmental agencies. Thus, the most common types of preparedness measures undertaken by businesses include obtaining first aid supplies, storing water, and talking to employees about disasters. While important to ensure the life safety of business owners and employees, these kinds of activities do little to prepare businesses for the kinds of impacts described in the previous section, particularly those originating off-site, such as supply chain interruptions. As described in Box 10.2, there are several key principles to better prepare businesses for disasters and thus improve business continuity planning.

BOX 10.2

LESSONS UNLEARNED: IMPROVING BUSINESS DISASTER PREPAREDNESS

Although much of the research on disaster preparedness has focused on individuals and households, disaster scientists have also learned a significant amount about the preparedness patterns among businesses. Unfortunately, those patterns generally mirror what we see in households, namely alarmingly low levels of preparedness. For businesses, the problem is more pronounced because, even when they do make efforts to prepare, business owners typically focus on things that, while important, do little to ensure their ability to remain open and viable. Thus, to improve business continuity planning and maximize the effectiveness of preparedness efforts, business owners should consider the following *preparedness principles*, all of which are well established in the research literature:

Think Beyond Life Safety

When business owners prepare for disasters, the first thing they often consider, understandably, is the safety and well-being of their employees. This is an important first step, and while it is certainly necessary, it is not sufficient to ensure business continuity. Storing a first aid kit may provide us peace of mind and it may be used on some very rare occasions, but it will not help business owners navigate the multiple, complex problems they will face after a disaster, many of which originate from far away locations.

Think Beyond Direct Impacts

When thinking about disasters and their potential consequences, business owners tend to think almost exclusively about the impacts on their specific location. As a result, they may install storm shutters to try to minimize the physical damage to their building and inventory, they may purchase a backup generator for a short-term supply of electricity, or they may backup data and secure their computers. However, these measures will do little to address indirect disaster impacts that originate off-site, including supply chain disruptions or blocked transportation routes that may limit customer access and many others.

Think Beyond a Few Days

Although households are encouraged to prepare themselves for three days in the event of a disaster, businesses need to consider a much longer time frame. Even if they experience little or no damage themselves, businesses may not be able to reopen immediately because of off-site disruptions. If they do experience severe damage, they may need to find an alternate location to resume operations temporarily. During COVID-19, many businesses were forced to close for months, and while that is not typical in most disasters, it underscores the importance of preparedness and continuity planning for businesses.

Think Beyond Individual Businesses

Just as we hope individuals will think beyond their own households and assist their families, friends, and neighbors with preparedness, we also need to think beyond individual businesses to include the broader business community. Preparedness efforts are more effective when businesses coordinate their own activities with other businesses and with local governmental agencies. Fostering cooperation among businesses can be difficult because they are accustomed instead to competing with each other for customers, but existing institutions, such as a local Chamber of Commerce, can play a vital role in fostering cooperation and encouraging greater preparedness.

Unfortunately, however, few businesses engage in that kind of proactive planning (Webb et al. 2000). As Clarke (1999) points out, planning in the private sector often amounts to little more than the production of *fantasy documents*. These are symbolic plans businesses produce to give the public, governmental regulators, and themselves the sometimes false impression that they are ready for a disaster. Clarke focused his research on the oil industry and its lack of readiness for the *Exxon Valdez* oil spill in 1999, but the concept of fantasy documents applies much more broadly to all kinds of businesses.

A key to improving business preparedness for disasters is for them to engage in more realistic and more effective planning. *Business continuity planning* refers to the basic process of preparing and planning for a disaster (DHS 2021b; Phillips and Landahl 2021). As shown in Figure 10.3, the business continuity planning process involves several steps, including:

- Conducting a business impact analysis.
- Identifying, documenting, and implementing ways to recover business functions and processes.
- Organizing a team to write the business continuity plan.
- Undertaking training for the business continuity group.
- Testing and exercising the plan.

10.3.3.2 Response

The private sector has a diverse and varied role during response (McEntire et al. 2003). To illustrate, restaurant franchises, large-scale retailers, home improvement chains,

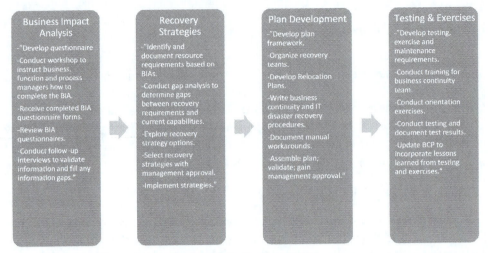

Source FEMA, https://www.ready.gov/business-continuity-plan, verbatim

FIGURE 10.3 Business Continuity Planning Process

heavy equipment rental stores, and many others often donate badly needed provisions, supplies, and services in the aftermath of major disasters. Telecommunications and computer hardware and software companies may provide necessary equipment and technical expertise. Other important response activities, such as debris removal, typically rely heavily on the services of paid subcontractors.

Examples abound of major disasters in which the private sector played pivotal roles during the response phase. For example, after the 1995 bombing of the Murrah Federal Building in Oklahoma City, much of the media coverage of the event focused on the heroic efforts of firefighters and emergency medical teams, but working alongside them at the scene were numerous representatives from the private sector. Workers from natural gas and electric companies in the state were there to shut down those services and ensure the safety of the site, telecommunications companies set up mobile equipment to facilitate the use of cellular telephones, and contractors from major construction firms operated heavy equipment to lift and clear debris for rescue workers (The City of Oklahoma City 1996). Similarly, the response to the September 11 attacks at the World Trade Center relied heavily on private utility and telecommunications companies, construction workers, and others to perform numerous critical tasks. These actions included debris removal, technical software support, mass fatality management, sanitation services, perimeter security and fencing, donations management, infrastructure repair, and others (McEntire et al. 2003).

During the response to Hurricane Katrina, Wal-Mart provided trucks and supplies to the devastated area, often times beating Federal and state aid efforts (ABC News 2005). The private sector played a central role with debris removal. Because of its wide scope of impact, the hurricane produced enormous amounts of wreckage and debris (Mendonça and Hu 2006), and numerous private entities, including waste management companies, landfill operators, and other contractors, were involved (U.S. Government Accountability Office 2008). More recently, during Hurricane Harvey in 2017, the owner of a large furniture business, Jim McIngvale, also known as "Mattress

Mack," opened several of his stores to provide temporary shelter to people displaced from their homes because of the severe flooding (Calfas 2017). In the early stages of the COVID-19 pandemic in 2020, several private sector companies temporarily suspended their normal operations to assist in producing personal protective equipment (PPE) for frontline responders and other essential safety products, as happened when some distilleries that normally produce bourbon and whiskey began instead using their facilities to make hand sanitizer (Browning 2020). Perhaps one of the most notable examples of private sector involvement in disasters is the Waffle House chain of restaurants. The company's commitment to remaining open whenever possible during several recent hurricanes led former FEMA Administrator Craig Fugate to coin the term "Waffle House Index" to gauge the severity of a disaster: the more Waffle Houses that are closed, the more severe the disaster (Touchberry 2018).

Our examples punctuate the private sector's active role in disaster response. Such widespread involvement magnifies the importance of coordination and communication during the preparedness and planning phase. While the private sector often provides necessary equipment, skills, and expertise that local governments may not have, we must also point out the potential for abuses with so much private sector involvement. For example, some companies may win contracts that others may see as unfair or biased. In other cases, some companies may exploit the situation and overcharge for services provided. Thus, appointed officials, including emergency managers, must recognize the importance of the private sector to the overall response effort, but also keep a close eye on potential abuses, always striving for integrity, fairness, transparency, and maximum effectiveness.

10.3.3.3 Recovery

The private sector also plays an important role in the community recovery process (Zavar, Lavy, and Hagelman 2020). When businesses quickly resume operations and return to profitability, the entire community benefits from sales tax revenues used to fund various services, including public safety, parks and recreation, public works, and many others. In this section, we will discuss what we know about business during the recovery period, including factors that promote or impede business survival.

There are two common ways to think about the economic impacts of disasters (Webb et al. 2000). On the one hand, disasters have devastating impacts, driving many firms out of business altogether. On the other hand, regional, state, and national economies absorb local disaster impacts (Wright et al. 1979). Disasters appear not to have negative long-term economic impacts. In reality, the answer lies somewhere between these two extremes.

Perhaps the best way to think about the issue is to recognize that disasters produce *winners and losers*. At a broad level, most businesses do recover from disasters, that is, they at least return to their pre-disaster level of functionality and profitability. However, some businesses have an easier time getting there and may even come out ahead. Factors associated with positive recovery outcomes over the long term include size, sector, financial condition, and market scope. Large businesses and those in good financial shape prior to a disaster typically fare better during the recovery phase than their smaller and financially struggling counterparts. Also, businesses in certain sectors, including the construction industry, often experience dramatic increases in profits as the rebuilding process begins. Conversely, small retail stores often suffer severe declines, primarily because that sector tends to be crowded and highly competitive under normal conditions, so even modest short-term declines in sales can have devastating effects. Finally, businesses whose primary markets extend beyond the local area, such as those with high internet sales, tend to rebound more quickly because they are less dependent on local customers (Scanlon 1988; Webb et al. 2000, 2002).

Two factors that we would expect to facilitate recovery among businesses, namely preparedness and the use of post-disaster financial aid, do not always produce the desired results. In other words, businesses with higher levels of preparedness and those who receive some form of financial aid are no more likely to report positive recovery outcomes than those who prepare less and do not make use of post-disaster aid. To explain the apparent ineffectiveness of business disaster preparedness, researchers have suggested that the efforts of business owners are misguided. As noted above, business owners are primarily interested in protecting themselves and their employees. Yet, they fail to prepare themselves for the indirect and remote impacts we discussed earlier. Many owners instead turn to personal savings and help from friends and family to get through a disaster (Webb et al. 2000; Haynes, Danes, and Stafford 2011).

In short, we need to pay more attention to businesses during the recovery process. Their survival and continued profitability is central to the recovery of the broader community. However, we should point out that close relationship between business recovery and community recovery can potentially be a source of conflict. Following a major disaster, as recovery money begins flowing into the community from various sources, community stakeholders may disagree on how best to use those funds. Some, for example, may promote the idea of economic development and want to use the money to help businesses. Others may be more interested in providing support to families and households. Therefore, local officials, including emergency managers, must be aware of these conflicts, and implement a recovery process that considers multiple perspectives and develops sensible, fair, and effective solutions.

10.3.3.4 Mitigation

As with the preparedness, response, and recovery, the private sector is also very important to the mitigation phase. Because of its innovation, entrepreneurship, and willingness to take chances, the private sector has enhanced the quality of life in our local communities and for society. Businesses create jobs, perform critical services, and provide us with limitless opportunities for leisure and recreation. However, business activity can also be risky, not just for the entrepreneur with money at stake, but for society as a whole when things go wrong.

Think, for example, about the 2010 Deepwater Horizon oil spill in the Gulf of Mexico. British Petroleum (BP) obviously saw the potential for huge profits by drilling for oil offshore in extraordinarily deep waters and decided that it was an acceptable risk. The company had to convince governmental regulators and a skeptical public these activities were safe. As a result, catastrophic damage was done to the environment and local communities, many of which depended heavily on tourism and fishing. Related impacts included mental health issues, standard of living declines, joblessness, and stress caused by prolonged litigation (Gill et al., 2014; Ritchie, Gill, and Long 2018). Also, consider the example of wastewater reinjection, associated with hydraulic fracturing and natural gas exploration, which has caused a dramatic increase in seismic activity in Oklahoma, requiring households and businesses in that state to increase their preparedness for earthquakes, which has not historically been the case (Greer, Wu, and Murphy 2020). In his influential book, *Disasters by Design*, Mileti (1999) proposes a model of *sustainable hazards mitigation* to reduce these kinds of risks and increase the safety and resilience of our communities. This approach simultaneously allows for continued economic success for businesses, maintains and protects safety and quality of life for residents, and preserves the surrounding natural environment. Some of the tools for achieving sustainable mitigation include:

- Land Use Planning and Management.
- Building Codes and Standards.
- Insurance.
- Prediction, Forecast, and Warning.
- Engineering.

While all of these elements currently exist, this approach provides substantial room for improvement. Some local city councils and planning commissions, for example, continue to allow builders to develop flood-prone and other hazardous areas. Yet, there are substantial opportunities to reenvision how these spaces can be used, including after disasters, to improve the quality of life, safety, and resilience of our communities (Zavar and Hagelman 2016; Zavar 2019; Binder, Greer, and Zavar 2020). Building codes provide another opportunity for mitigation, but we must recognize that as these codes evolve, newly constructed buildings continue to get safer but many older buildings badly need retrofitting. In places like Florida and California, people find it extremely difficult, if not impossible, to afford hazard insurance; so there is clearly a need for some kind of innovation or reform in the insurance industry.

Ultimately, the solutions to the problems we face in preparing for, responding to, recovering from, and mitigating disasters will require increased coordination and cooperation between the public and private sectors. In this section, we have discussed the relevance and importance of the private sector to all four phases of disasters and EM. The remainder of this chapter discusses strategies for enhancing the relationship between the public and private sectors.

10.4 PUBLIC AND PRIVATE PARTNERSHIPS

Building partnerships between the public and private sectors is essential to achieving greater societal resilience to disasters. As described in this chapter, the private sector is heavily involved in all four phases of disasters and therefore has a significant role to play in EM. The private sector possesses knowledge, skills, resources, and capacities that can complement those of the government. Because of that, FEMA has prioritized strengthening the relationship between the two sectors, as reflected in the CPG-101, which states, "The private sector plays a critical role in any disaster, and it is important to ensure that they are active participants in the process, including involvement in jurisdictional training and exercise programs" (FEMA 2010, p. 53). FEMA's emphasis on building these relationships is also evident in more recent publications, including the *2020 National Preparedness Report* (U.S. Department of Homeland Security 2020) and the *National Response Framework, Fourth Edition* (U.S. Department of Homeland Security 2019).

The U.S. Chamber of Commerce is also heeding the message that businesses need to work with government to prepare for disasters. For example, the Chamber stated:

> Improving our emergency response strategies would prevent the loss of billions of dollars in future damages and business interruptions, which is typical of major disasters... Now is the time to advance 'disaster 2.0' principles—focusing on readiness and resiliency, rebuilding communities to be more sustainable, and educating the different sectors on how to work together effectively.
>
> (U.S. Chamber of Commerce January 16, 2009).

Following up on this message, another emerging thrust has focused on cybersecurity. Business and government representatives worked together on making a series of recommendations to enhance cybersecurity within both sectors (U.S. Chamber of Commerce 2011); more recently, both sectors together advocating and creating more resilience buildings in the case of disaster or terror attacks (U.S. Chamber of Commerce 2014).

Perhaps the area in which public and private partnerships are most needed is in strengthening the resilience of *critical infrastructure systems*, including power, water, telecommunications, transportation, health care, and many other vital systems. As shown in Figure 10.4, FEMA refers to these systems as *community lifelines*, defined as, "...those services that enable the continuous operation of critical government and business functions and are essential to human health and safety or economic security"

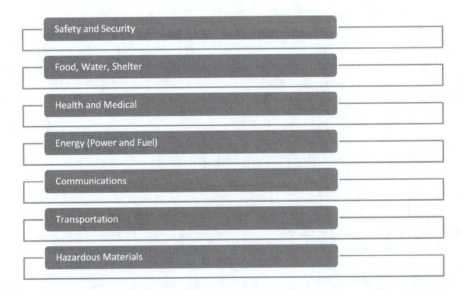

Safety and Security

Food, Water, Shelter

Health and Medical

Energy (Power and Fuel)

Communications

Transportation

Hazardous Materials

Source: U.S. Department of Homeland Security. 2019. *National Response Framework, Fourth Edition.* Washington, D.C.: U.S. Department of Homeland Security.

FIGURE 10.4 Community Lifelines

(U.S. Department of Homeland Security 2019, p. ii). In 2019, the U.S. DHS Cybersecurity and Infrastructure Agency (CISA) began referring to these systems as National Critical Functions (NCFs), defining them as, "The functions of government and the private sector so vital to the United States that their disruption, corruption, or dysfunction would have a debilitating effect on security, national economic security, national public health or safety, or any combination thereof" (CISA 2021).

We rely extensively on these systems, and when they fail, the results can be catastrophic. Since 2014, for example, a water crisis has been unfolding in Flint, Michigan. As a cost savings measure, city officials decided to draw water directly from the Flint River rather than through a pipeline from another city's water treatment facility, which caused severe corrosion and contamination throughout the water distribution system, leaving residents without safe water for months, even years, and exposing children to harmful levels of lead contamination.

Critical infrastructure systems are also highly interdependent, and failures in one can cause cascading impacts on others. In early 2021, for example, significant parts of Texas experienced a severe ice storm that crippled the power grid and shut down many water treatment facilities, leaving millions of residents without power and water for days and in some cases, weeks. Two other examples from 2021 further illustrate the vulnerability of our critical infrastructure systems. In one case, a major pipeline was temporarily shut down by computer hackers, causing fuel shortages and price spikes along the East Coast, and in the other, a major bridge along Interstate 40 in Memphis, Tennessee, was closed when inspectors discovered a massive crack with the potential of causing a catastrophic failure. The latter example reminded many of the tragic Interstate 35 bridge collapse in Minneapolis, Minnesota, in 2007 that resulted in more than a dozen deaths.

In addition to being essential to the smooth functioning of society and highly interdependent, critical infrastructure systems, particularly in the U.S., are also highly privatized (U.S. Department of Homeland Security 2020). For-profit companies own and are primarily responsible for operating and maintaining many of these systems, and consumers pay them to provide such essential services as electricity and natural gas, internet and television service, cellular telephones, and many others. Thus, when disasters strike, these same companies will play vital roles by restoring essential services to households, local governments, businesses, and communities. As a result, in the fourth edition of the National Response Framework, FEMA added a new ESF #14: Cross-Sector Business and Infrastructure (U.S. Department of Homeland Security 2019). According to FEMA, its purpose is to, "…coordinate multi-sector response operations between (or across) the government and private sector for natural or human-caused catastrophic incidents that jeopardize national public health and safety, the economy, and national security" (U.S. Department of Homeland Security 2020, p. 56).

10.5 WORKING AND VOLUNTEERING IN THE PRIVATE SECTOR

As we noted earlier in this text about the public sector, the private sector also has numerous opportunities to volunteer or work in. So, when you think about volunteering, seeking out an internship, or applying for jobs, you should look beyond the most obvious places and consider the private sector. For example, business continuity and/or disaster recovery specialists are needed for banks, chemical companies, hospitals, manufacturing firms, accounting firms, social services, and more. Looking for internships and jobs in the private sector may also suggest slightly different thinking about other majors or minors. Those looking for internships and jobs in the private sector must show a wide range of skills and capabilities. For example, some business offices for business continuity include health and safety or security. Those with additional background, training, or experience in occupational safety, fire, or law enforcement can enhance their internship and job opportunities. In many industries, such as chemical companies and manufacturing plants, they need safety compliance officers, risk managers, and emergency response personnel. Computer skills, especially with networks and communications backgrounds or training, can also complement those interested in disaster recovery. In some cases, if you have basic computer skills, the company will provide additional training while on the job.

As you may recall, the International Association of Emergency Managers awards the Certified Emergency Manager (CEM), which is generally oriented toward the public sector. For those seeking careers in the private sector, one can also obtain various levels of certification oriented toward the business community. With the growing interest and opportunities, we have identified at least three different organizations providing certification opportunities for those in the private sector. For example, the Disaster Recovery Institute International (DRII) offers seven different types of accreditation based upon different foci and areas of expertise. These include (DRII 2021a):

- Certified Functional Continuity Professional (CFCP).
- Certified Business Continuity Auditor (CBCA and CBCLA).
- Certified Business Continuity Professional (CBCP).
- Master Business Continuity Professional (MBCP).
- Certified Public Sector Continuity Professional (CPSCP).
- Certified Healthcare Provider Continuity Professional (CHPCP).

Obtaining and maintaining these various certifications include attending pre-exam seminars (not required but helpful), taking exams, attending continuing education-related training, and paying an annual membership fee (DRII 2021a, 2021b).

The Business Continuity Management Institute (BCMI) also offers a wide range of certification options. They include (BCMI 2021; verbatim):

- Business Continuity Certified Planner (BCCP).
- Business Continuity Certified Specialist (BCCS).
- Business Continuity Certified Expert (BCCE).
- Disaster Recovery Certified Specialist (DRCS).
- Disaster Recovery Certified Expert (DRCE).
- Business Continuity Certified Auditor (BCCA).
- Business Continuity Certified Lead Auditor (BCCLA).

- Crisis Management Certified Planner (CMCP).
- Crisis Management Certified Specialist (CMCS).
- Crisis Management Certified Expert (CMCE; end verbatim).

Obtaining each of these certificates requires obtaining specific levels of education/training and experience (BCMI 2021).

The Business Resilience International Consortium (BRCI 2021) provides certificates in business continuity, IT, and business continuity/disaster resilience auditing. Training classes provide much of the foundation for obtaining these certificates.

These are just some of the examples of certification opportunities that could enhance one's job entrée and advancement in the private sector. We do not endorse any of these programs. Rather, this information may serve as a starting point for exploring options. We recommend that you talk with experienced employees in the private sector to see which type of certification may be best for you. You may also obtain an understanding of which certification is recognized by your profession in your geographical area.

Although we commonly think of EM as a responsibility of the public sector, the private sector has an equally valuable role. This role also increases opportunities for internships, volunteer work, and jobs. As disasters continue to threaten our communities and their financial impacts continue to climb, we believe that positions in business continuity and disaster recovery will continue to expand.

***

SUMMARY

Both the public and private sectors play vital roles before, during, and after disasters. Government, especially at the local level, is the starting place for effective EM across all disaster phases. Local government must work with its state and Federal government to enhance its disaster capabilities. An important component for local government after a disaster strikes is understanding and using properly the process to obtain a PDD. Otherwise, local government (and its residents) may not get proper funding and reimbursement, and in a timely manner, to provide assistant for response and recovery.

The private sector has a number of priorities, and managing disasters is not typically one of them. Yet, many businesses suffer greatly and may even go out of business from a disaster. Business managers and executives must recognize that surviving disturbances and disasters are a central component to having, in the long run, a successful and profitable business. Making disaster awareness and resiliency as part of the organizational culture creates an important step for a successful business to survive a disaster.

A key to strengthening the resilience of our communities is forging more effective public and private partnerships. Both sectors possess valuable resources and expertise, and when disasters strike, both sectors are impacted by them and both play prominent roles in their aftermath. By working together, the public and private sectors can harness their capacities to better prepare for, respond to, recover from, and mitigate future disasters.

Discussion Questions

1. Research your own state's organizational structure of EM. Are the offices of Homeland Security and Emergency Management two distinct offices or are they combined? Do these offices report directly to the governor or another office (e.g., Adjunct General), who then reports to the governor? What implications might these arrangements have for dealing with disasters or terrorism before, during, or after any event?

2. What can businesses do to become more resilient? As a starting point, you might want to consider from whom they buy products from, various types of transportation routes (e.g., roads, rail, ports, airports), location of their offices and/or manufacturing areas, where they locate their offices and other facilities, and how those facilities are constructed.

3. Thinking of your own hometown, consider some of the following questions. What might be some important business representatives (e.g., both businesses and organizations that represent businesses) that could team with local government to develop public/private partnerships? What do you think might be some good forums or opportunities that would provide officials from the public and private sector to meet?

4. Thinking again of your own hometown, what are the most critical infrastructure systems or community lifelines that would need to be protected during a disaster? What are some of the vulnerabilities of those systems? Who is responsible for operating and maintaining them? What would happen if one or more of those systems failed during a disaster?

Summary Questions

1. What is the executive branch of government and how is it relevant to EM?
2. Identify three types of impacts disasters have on businesses?
3. What are community lifelines?
4. What are NCFs?

REFERENCES

ABC News. 2005. "What Can Wal-Mart Teach FEMA about Disaster Response?" Available at http://abcnews.go.com/WNT/HurricaneRita/story?id=1171087, last accessed June 2, 2021.

AllGov. 2021. "California Office of Emergency Services." Available at http://www.allgov.com/usa/ca/departments/office-of-the-governor/california_emergency_management_agency?agencyid=217, last accessed June 2, 2021.

BCMI. 2021. "Certification." Available at http://www.bcm-institute.org/certification, last accessed June 2, 2021.

Binder, Sherri Brokopp, Alex Greer, and Elyse Zavar. 2020. "Home Buyouts: A Tool for Mitigation or Recovery?" *Disaster Prevention and Management* 29(4): 497–510.

BRCI. 2021. "Certification Program." Available at http://www.brcci.org/index.php/certification/business-continuity-certification-overview, last accessed June 2, 2021.

Browning, Kellen. 2020. "Distilleries Raced to Make Hand Sanitizer for the Pandemic. No Longer." *New York Times.* August 4, 2020. https://www.nytimes.com/2020/08/04/business/-distilleries-hand-sanitizer-pandemic.html, last accessed June 2, 2021.

Burby, R. J. 2006. "Hurricane Katrina and the Paradoxes of Government Disaster Policy: Bringing about Wise Governmental Decisions for Hazardous Areas." *The ANNALS of the American Academy of Political and Social Science* 604: 171–191.

Calfas, Jennifer. 2017. "Meet the Man Who Turned His Furniture Stores into Shelters for Harvey Victims." *Time* August 30, 2017. https://time.com/4922108/hurricane-harvey-mattress-mack-houston/, last accessed June 2, 2021.

California Office of Emergency Services. 2021. "About Cal EOS." Available at http://www.caloes.ca.gov/Cal-OES-Divisions/About-Cal-OES, last accessed June 2, 2021.

CISA. 2021. *National Critical Functions.* Washington, DC: U.S. Department of Homeland Security, Cybersecurity and Infrastructure Agency. Available at https://www.cisa.gov/national-critical-functions, last accessed June 2, 2021.

Clarke, L. 1999. *Mission Improbable: Using Fantasy Documents to Tame Disaster.* Chicago: University of Chicago Press.

DHS. 2021a. "Creation of the Department of Homeland Security." Available at https://www.dhs.gov/creation-department-homeland-security, last accessed June 2, 2021.

DHS. 2021b. "Business Continuity Plan." Available at https://www.ready.gov/business/implementation/continuity, last accessed June 2, 2021.

Drabek, Thomas E. 2013. *The Human Side of Disaster,* 2nd ed. Boca Raton, FL: CRC Press.

DRII. 2021a. "Certification – Maintaining Certification Overview." Available at https://www.drii.org/certification/maintaincert.php, last assessed June 2, 2021.

DRII. 2021b. "Certification." Available at https://www.drii.org/certification/maintaincert.php, last accessed June 2, 2021.

Dynes, Russell R. 1970. *Organized Behavior in Disaster.* Lexington, MA: Heath.

Edwards, Frances L. and Daniel C. Goodrich. 2007. "Organizing for Emergency Management." Pp. 39–56 in *Emergency Management: Principles and Practice for Local Government,* 2nd edition, eds. William L. Waugh and Kathleen J. Tierney. Washington, DC: ICMA Press.

Emergency Management Accreditation Program (EMAP). 2021a. "EMAP History." Available at https://www.emap.org/index.php/program-resources/steps-to-accreditation, last accessed June 2, 2021.

Emergency Management Accreditation Program (EMAP) 2021b. "Emergency Management Standard." Available at https://www.emap.org/index.php/what-is-emap/the-emergency-management-standard, last accessed June 2, 2021.

Emergency Management Accreditation Program (EMAP) 2021c. "EMAP Accredited Programs." Available at https://www.emap.org/index.php/what-is-emap/who-is-accredited, last accessed June 2, 2021.

EU. 2021. "Emergency Response Coordination Centre." Available at http://ec.europa.eu/echo/what/civil-protection/emergency-response-coordination-centre-ercc_en, last accessed June 2, 2021.

FEMA. 2010. *Comprehensive Planning Guide 101.* Available at http://www.fema.gov/pdf/about/divisions/npd/CPG_101_V2.pdf, last accessed June 2, 2021.

FEMA. 2021. "Emergency Management Agencies." Available at https://www.fema.gov/-emergency-management-agencies, last accessed June 2, 2021.

Gill, Duane A., Liesel A. Ritchie, J. Steven Picou, Jennifer Langhinrichen-Rohling, Micha. Long, and Jessica W. Shenesey. 2014. "The Exxon and BP Oil Spills: A Comparison of Psychosocial Impacts." *Natural Hazards* 74: 1911–1932.

Governor's Commission to Rebuild Texas. 2018. *Eye of the Storm: Report of the Governor's Commission to Rebuild Texas.* Austin, TX: Office of the Governor.

Greer, Alex, Hao-Che Wu, and Haley Murphy. 2020. "Household Adjustment to Seismicity in Oklahoma." *Earthquake Spectra* 36(4): 2019–2032.

Hackerott, Caroline. 2016. *A Jolt to the System: Measuring Disaster-Induced Social Disruption through Water Consumption, Sales Tax Revenue and Crime Data.* Ph.D. Dissertation. Stillwater, OK: Fire and Emergency Management Program, Oklahoma State University.

Haynes, George W., Sharon M. Danes, and Kathryn Stafford. 2011. "Influence of Federal Disaster Assistance No Family Business Survival and Success." *Journal of Contingencies and Crisis Management* 19(2): 86–98.

McEntire, David A. 2006. "Local Emergency Management Organizations." Pp. 168–182 in *Handbook of Disaster Research*, eds. Havidán Rogríguez, Enrico L. Quarantelli, and Russell R. Dynes. New York: Springer.

McEntire, David A., Robie J. Robinson, and Richard T. Weber. 2003. "Business Responses to the World Trade Center Disaster: A Study of Corporate Roles, Functions, and Interaction with the Public Sector." Pp. 431–457, in *Beyond September 11th: An Account of Post-Disaster Research.* Special Publication #39. Boulder: Natural Hazards Research and Applications Information Center – University of Colorado.

Mendonça, David and Yao Hu. 2006. "Hurricane Katrina Debris Removal Operations: The Role of Communication and Computing Technologies." Pp. 283–304 in *Learning from Catastrophe: Quick Response Research in the Wake of Hurricane Katrina*, ed. Christine Bvec. Boulder: Natural Hazards Center – University of Colorado.

Menzel, D. C. 2006. "The Katrina Aftermath: A Failure of Federalism or Leadership?" *Public Administration Review* 66(6): 808–812.

Mileti, Dennis. 1999. *Disasters by Design.* Washington, DC: Joseph Henry Press.

Minnesota Department of Public Safety. 2021. "Homeland Security and Emergency Management." Available at https://dps.mn.gov/divisions/hsem/about/Pages/default.aspx, last accessed June 2, 2021.

Neal, David M. 1985. *A Comparative analysis of Emergent Group Behavior in Disaster: A Look at the United States and Sweden.* Ph.D. Dissertation. Columbus, OH: Department of Sociology, The Ohio State University.

Oklahoma Department of Emergency Management 2021. "About Us." Available athttps://oklahoma.gov/oem/about-odemhs.html, last accessed March 26, 2016.

Oklahoma Department of Public Safety. 2021. "Home." Available at https://oklahoma.gov/dps.html, last accessed June 2, 2021.

Oklahoma Office of Homeland Security 2021. "About OKOHS." Available at https://www.ok.gov/homeland/About_OKOHS/index.html, last accessed June 2, 2021.

Phillips, Brenda D. 2015. *Disaster Recovery*, 2nd ed. Boca Raton, FL: CRC Press.

Phillips, Brenda D. and Mark Landahl. 2021. *Business Continuity Planning: Increasing Workplace Resilience to Disasters.* Oxford: Butterworth-Heinemann.

Quarantelli, E. L., Patrick Lagadec, and Arjen Boin. 2006. "A Heuristic Approach to Future Disasters and Crises: New, Old, and In-Between Types." Pp. 16–41 *Handbook of Disaster Research*, eds. Havidan Rodriguez, E. L. Quarantelli, and Russell R. Dynes. New York: Springer.

Ritchie, Liesel A., Duane A. Gill, and Michael A. Long. 2018. "Mitigating Litigating: An Examination of Psychosocial Impacts of Compensation Processes Associated with the 2010 BP *Deepwater Horizon* Oil Spill." *Risk Analysis* 38: 1656–1671.

Reeves, Andrew. 2009. "Political Disaster: Unilateral Powers, Electoral Incentives, and Presidential Disaster Declarations." *The Journal of Politics* 1(1): 1–10.

Scanlon, Joseph 1988. Winners and Losers: Some Thoughts about the Political Economy of Disaster." *The International Journal of Mass Emergencies and Disasters* 6(1): 47–63.

Smith, Gavin and Dennis Wenger. 2007. "Sustainable Disaster Recovery: Operationalizing an Existing Agenda. Pp. 234–257 in *Handbook of Disaster Research*, eds. Havidan Rodriguez, Enrico L. Quarantelli, and Russell R. Dynes. New York: Springer.

Sylves, Richard. 2015. *Disaster Policy & Politics: Emergency Management and Homeland Security*, 2nd ed. Washington, DC: CQ Press.

Sylves, Richard and Zoltan L. Buzas. 2007. "Presidential Disaster Declarations Decisions, 1953–2003: What Influences Odds of Approval?" *State and Local Government Review* 39(1): 3–15.

The City of Oklahoma City. 1996. *Final Report: Alfred P. Murrah Federal Building Bombing, April 19, 1995.* Stillwater, OK: Fire Protection Publications.

The White House. 2021. "The Cabinet." Available at https://www.whitehouse.gov/administration/cabinet, last accessed June 2, 2021.

Touchberry, Ramsey. 2018. "What Is the Waffle House Index? The True Story from the Man who Created It, Craig Fugate." *Newsweek* September 14, 2018. https://www.newsweek.com/craig-fugate-explains-waffle-house-index-1120655, last accessed June 2, 2021.

Tyler, Jenna and Abdul-Akeem Sadiq. 2020. "Exploring the Benefits of Disaster Preparedness: A Study of Businesses Affected by Hurricane Irma." *International Journal of Mass Emergencies and Disasters* 38(2): 153–175.

UNDRR. 2020. *Human Cost of Disasters: An Overview of the Last 20 Years, 2000–2019.* Switzerland: U.N. Office of Disaster Risk Reduction.

U.S. Chamber of Commerce. 2009 (January 16). "Business Leaders Call for Change in Disaster Response Strategies." Available at http://www.uschamber.com/press/releases/2009/january/-business-leaders-call-change-disaster-response-strategies, last accessed June 2, 2021.

U.S. Chamber of Commerce. 2011. "U.S. Chamber Hails Success of Public-Private Partnerships in Cybersecurity Report." Available at https://www.uschamber.com/press-release/us-chamber-hails-success-public-private-partnerships-cybersecurity-report, last assessed June 2, 2021.

U.S. Chamber of Commerce. 2014. "4th National Conference on building Resilience through Public-Private Partnerships." Available at https://www.uschamber.com/event/4th-national-conference-building-resilience-through-public-private-partnerships, last accessed June 2, 2021.

U.S. Department of Homeland Security. 2019. *National Response Framework*, 4th ed. Washington, DC: U.S. Department of Homeland Security.

U.S. Department of Homeland Security. 2020. *2020 National Preparedness Report.* Washington, DC: U.S. Department of Homeland Security.

U.S. Government Accountability Office. 2008. *Hurricane Katrina: Continuing Debris Removal and Disposal Issues.* Washington, DC: U.S. Government Accountability Office.

Waugh, William. 2005. "The Disaster that Was Katrina." *Natural Hazards Observer.* Available at http://www.colorado.edu/hazards/o/archives/2005/nov05/nov05d1.html, last accessed January 25, 2011.

Waugh, William. 2006. "The Political Costs of Failure in the Katrina and Rita Disasters." *The ANNALS of the American Academy of Political and Social Science* 604(10): 10–25.

Waugh, William and Gregory Streib. 2006. "Collaboration and Leadership for Effective Emergency Management." *Public Administration Review* 66: 131–140.

Webb, Gary R., Kathleen J. Tierney, and James M. Dahlhamer. 2000. "Businesses and Disasters: Empirical Patterns and Unanswered Questions." *Natural Hazards Review* 1(2): 83–90.

Webb, Gary R., Kathleen J. Tierney, and JamesM. Dahlhamer. 2002. "Predicting Long-Term Business Recovery from Disaster: A Comparison of the Loma Prieta Earthquake and Hurricane Andrew." *Environmental Hazards* 4: 45–58.

Wendling, Cécile. 2010. "Explaining the Emergence of Different European Union Crisis and Emergency Management Structures." *Journal of Contingencies and Crisis Management* 18(-2): 74–82.

Wright, James D., Peter H. Rossi, Sonia R. Wright, and Eleanor Weber-Burdin. 1979. *After the Clean-Up: Long-Range Effects of Natural Disasters.* Beverly Hills, CA: Sage.

Zavar, E. 2019. "An Analysis of Floodplain Buyout Memorials: Four Examples from Central U.S. Floods of 1993–1998." *GeoJournal* 84(1): 157–179.

Zavar, Elyse and Ronald R. Hagelman III. 2016. "Land Use Change on U.S. Floodplain Buyout Sites, 1990–2000." *Disaster Prevention and Management* 25(3): 360–374.

Zavar, Elyse, Brendan L. Lavy, and Ronald R. Hagelman, III. 2020. "Chain Tourism in Post-Disaster Recovery." *Tourist Studies* 20(4): 429–449.

RESOURCES

- FEMA has an extensive web page with links to a wide range of documents and software to assist with business continuity planning at https://www.ready.gov/business-continuity-planning-suite.
- Small, often family owned, business often have their own preparedness needs to consider. The Small Business Administration provides information and related documents to help those with small businesses prepare, respond, clean-up, and recover during disaster. This site can be found at https://www.sba.gov/business-guide/manage-your-business/prepare-emergencies.
- Learn more about community lifelines and how to protect them, visit https://www.fema.gov/emergency-managers/practitioners/lifelines.
- To have an overview of disaster recovery and business continuity trends, the professional magazine, *Disaster Recovery Journal*, is a good place to start. You can find the information at http://www.drj.com/.

CHAPTER 11

International Humanitarian Disaster Management

Jenny Mincin

CHAPTER OBJECTIVES

Upon completing this chapter, readers should be able to:

- Define culture and understand why cultural sensitivity increases the effectiveness of international disaster relief.
- Illustrate the different kinds of disasters that affect international sectors, such as pandemics, famines, droughts, or conflict.
- Distinguish between culturally relevant and ethnocentric ways of delivering aid.
- Walk through the basic steps of humanitarian logistic delivery.
- Identify and offer alternatives to inappropriate relief efforts.
- Discuss ways to empower local stakeholders in an international relief effort.
- Understand and describe best practices for refugee assistance and resettlement.

KEY TERMS

- Community integration and resiliency models
- Cultural Diversity
- Cultural Relativism
- Disaster Assistance Response Team
- Empowerment
- Ethnocentrism
- Humanitarian Core Standards
- Humanitarian Logistics
- Integration
- Refugee, Asylee, and Displaced
- Persons
- Refugee Camps
- Refugee Resettlement
- Sphere
- UN High Commissioner on
- Refugees
- Urban Refugees
- U.S. Administration for International
- Development
- Vulnerable Populations

DOI: 10.4324/9781003021919-14

11.1 INTRODUCTION

In this chapter, we will discuss international emergency management (EM), how the humanitarian response system functions, and the different roles the U.S. plays in supporting international emergency response. As we have learned, no one and no country is immune to crises and disasters. However, in different countries, disasters can have a deeper impact and it can take longer for certain, more vulnerable communities to recover. While familiar threats such as earthquakes, volcanoes, or floods exist, different kinds of threats also appear that we do not necessarily experience in the U.S. For example, currently, the U.S. is not experiencing a violent internal conflict that has caused tens of thousands of people to flee their homes and communities. And while the U.S. is not exempt from natural and human-made disasters and conflicts, other nations may fare significantly worse when they are hit with one such as a hurricane or health emergency. The 2014 Ebola outbreak in West Africa is one example that illustrates this difference. In Western African countries, including Sierra Leone and Liberia, thousands of people died from the Ebola outbreak compared to one death in the U.S. In addition, Ebola outbreaks continued throughout parts of Africa, with most recent outbreaks (2021) in Guinea and Democratic Republic of Congo (DRC World Health Organization 2021). In the U.S., there have been no reported cases since 2014. There are several factors that contribute to the larger impact of disasters, such as Ebola. These factors include lack of resources, fragile infrastructure (including roads, schools, and health clinics), poverty, and postcolonial political systems that can be unstable and unsafe (Fordham et al, 2013). We will explore these factors in this chapter as well as understand how the international response system works.

In some regions of the world, disasters can be linked to conflict within countries and between countries, such as in South Sudan or Syria. These conflicts force people from their homes, villages, communities, and countries. Conflicts represent a different kind of disaster, one that can generate massive humanitarian crises as people flee war, conflict, and genocide. These human-caused events can significantly exacerbate other types of natural disasters such as pandemics and drought. For example, in many refugee camps in the Middle East, such as Turkey and Lebanon, displaced persons are managing the stress of loss of home and homeland as well as contending with COVID-19. Relief organizations have to manage two significant disasters at the same time and often in locations with very limited resources and infrastructure. International disaster relief organizations play an important role in responding to such events and saving lives.

11.1.1 UN High Commissioner on Refugees

In order to understand international EM, it is important to know about the UN High Commissioner on Refugees (UNHCR) and its relationship to displaced populations as humanitarian aid is coordinated through this UN organization (Mincin 2019). UNHCR was formed in 1950 after the atrocities of World War II to assist Europeans who fled or lost their homes from the war (History of UNHCR, n.d.b). The concept is based on a philosophical belief that all people deserve protection and a chance

> **BOX 11.1**
>
> ## ELEANOR ROOSEVELT AND THE UNIVERSAL DECLARATION OF HUMAN RIGHTS
>
> Current-day refugee law has its origins in the aftermath of World War II. Article 14(1) of the Universal Declaration of Human Rights (UDHR), which was adopted in 1948, guarantees the right to seek and enjoy asylum in other countries. The UDHR was and still is considered to be the fundamental framework for ensuring all basic human rights to all people regardless of age, gender, orientation, religion, political view, or disability/ability. It is the foundation in which international human rights law grew and serves as a reminder that we all deserve dignity, safety, and security, and for our most basic human needs to be met. A main architect of the UDHR was former first lady *Eleanor Roosevelt*. She was a fierce advocate for human rights in the U.S. and throughout the world fighting for women's and children's rights and the eradication of poverty. Ms. Roosevelt was appointed as a delegate to the UN General Assembly (UNGA) under Truman and later John Fitzgerald Kennedy (JFK) as well as chairing UNHCR helping to establish the first human rights frameworks (Eleanor Roosevelt Biography 2021).

for basic human dignities, including safety, a home, community, livelihood, a sense of positive well-being, opportunity, and rootedness. While states have been granting protection to individuals and groups fleeing persecution for centuries, the modern refugee system was mainly developed during the 1950s. Currently, the world is facing the biggest refugee crisis surpassing numbers seen during World War II (see box 11.1).

UNHCR is the primary international organization that coordinates, supports, and provides specific legal frameworks for the protection of people in conflict and other types of disasters. A refugee is someone who has been forced out of their country of origin because of war, genocide, conflict, climate change, and other disasters and is unable to return because of a well-founded fear of persecution (UNHCR n.d.b; Mincin 2019; Mincin, Khetarpal, and Steiner 2021). According to international law, refugees can either voluntarily repatriate if it is safe to return (returning home), integrate in a host community (staying where they initially fled to), or legally resettle in another country as a part of the refugee resettlement program (UNHCR n.d.b; Mincin 2019; Mincin et al. 2021).

An asylee meets the same general criteria as a refugee, but the individual claims asylum once outside their country of origin. Individual countries determine if the person applying for asylum will qualify or not. If the case for asylum is not approved, that person can be deported. If it is approved, they can begin the path of naturalization and remain in the new country legally (UNHCR n.d.b; Mincin 2019; Mincin et al. 2021). An internally displaced person (IDP) is defined as people who have been forced to flee and are displaced within their country of origin (or home country). Essentially, IDPs have not crossed an international border to find safety, but rather have remained inside their country seeking safety (UNHCR n.d.a, n.d.b; Mincin 2019; Mincin et al. 2021). Generally, refugees and displaced persons relocate to refugee camps or urban environments.

Through UNHCR, specific populations can be given refugee or internal displaced designation and humanitarian assistance organizations can be trained, deployed, and provide services to affected countries and populations at risk. UNHCR establishes international standard operating procedures for humanitarian organizations to deploy and provide emergency relief services to millions of people each year. It conducts advocacy on behalf of the nearly 80 million displaced people globally, ensures coordination between partnering agencies, and engages in ongoing evaluation and research in the area of emergency relief services.

11.1.2 Coordination

To be effective, international and humanitarian aid must be organized and coordinated and have resources and appropriately trained staff ready to deploy (Holguín-Veras et al., 2012; Holguín-Veras et al., 2014). In addition, prepositioning of supplies and response teams is critical during disaster response. For example, Doctors without Borders has a warehouse in Europe that can be deployed within 24–72 hours. In Yemen, a small country in the Middle East, there is an internal conflict, a civil war between the north and south that has been ongoing for six years. In addition to the civil conflict, the country is facing famine as well as being hit by the global COVID-19 pandemic. In the case of Yemen, one disaster (civil war) can lead to additional disasters (famine, lack of infrastructure, and healthcare needs) that then become compounded by global epidemics such as the COVID-19 pandemic. As a result, approximately 66% of the population in Yemen needs humanitarian assistance (UNHCR n.d.d). Although the logistics are challenging and it is not a secure location, UN agencies as well as nongovernmental organizations (NGOs), like Doctors without Borders, are providing relief, including food and basic healthcare (Holguín-Veras et al., 2012; Holguín-Veras et al., 2014). Warehouses can be filled and logistics teams can help get the supplies to Yemeni camps. Disaster response healthcare teams can be deployed to the camps to provide basic services (Kovács & Spens, 2007). As you can imagine, this effort takes a tremendous amount of coordination, communication, fundraising, and training.

In Central America, there are nearly one million refugees and displaced persons as a result of extreme violence from drug cartels, gangs, fragile economies, and severe inequality. UNHCR and partnering organizations, such as the International Rescue Committee (IRC) and Church World Service, are establishing shelters, increasing access to healthcare and education, creating safe spaces for persecuted people (such as women and girls, lesbian, gay, bisexual, transgender, and queer or questioning [LGBTQ], and people with disabilities), local integration programs to assist communities receiving refugees and displaced people, and increasing access to legal human rights services for asylum seekers.

11.1.3 Climate Change and Disaster Response

Climate change has been tracked and documented for decades and it is the type of event that is affecting every country around the world. In Miami, streets flood regularly. Along the Gulf Coast, towns are slowly disappearing because of water rise. Globally, some areas are either experiencing extreme heat and drought or torrential rain and flooding. Climate change creates political instability and can force people from their homes and communities. As the threat continues to grow, international emergency response organizations are preparing and responding to climate change disasters and crises and provide services for climate refugees. For example, more than 13 million people across the Horn of Africa (Eritrea, Somalia, Ethiopia, Kenya, Tanzania) are experiencing serious food shortages. The extreme drought and heat followed by extreme flooding is caused by climate change and is placing millions of people in danger. Organizations, such as Save the Children, are working to protect women and children from exploitations such as human trafficking and provide them with schools, shelter, and food.

In parts of Africa, the effects of climate change are immediate and deadly. In Nigeria, floods have displaced thousands of people and in Ethiopia violence from internal conflict has been exacerbated by extreme drought. Generally, these types of factors and overlapping crises create complex disaster responses. Climate change disasters and crises are not just a concern for U.S. emergency managers, but for the international community as well.

UNHCR recently released a report about the effects that climate change is having on increased extreme weather as well as impacting political unrest, increases in poverty, and driving the most vulnerable into further despair. Land that is no longer fertile, along with more frequent floods and drought, creates food shortages. Political parties and warring groups fight over limited food sources creating climate change disasters and refugees (UNHCR 2020). This is expected to increase as countries around the world fall short at implementing climate change mitigation initiatives and continue to burn fossil fuels and accelerate deforestation.

11.2 INTERNATIONAL EMERGENCY MANAGEMENT SYSTEM

Quarantelli first (1986) distinguished between two kinds of disasters that can be applied directly to international humanitarian response: disasters of consensus and disasters of conflict. To this point in the present chapter and throughout much of the book, we have discussed disasters of consensus, including natural disasters like earthquakes or wildfires. Such events typically elicit worldwide compassion and generosity in a massive and collective effort to provide relief. In addition, there are technological disasters such as chemical spills and nuclear accidents that have catastrophic effects on local communities and environments around the world (World Health Organization Chemical Incidents, n.d.a; World Health Organization Radiation Incidents, n.d.a.). Some technological events, such as the Bhopal chemical spill in India (1984), Chernobyl nuclear accident in Ukraine (1986), and the Beirut harbor explosion in Lebanon (2020) occurred because of human negligence. Technological events have lasting aftereffects including civil unrest, health and environmental destruction, and permanent loss of homes and livelihoods as was the case with Chernobyl and Lebanon. Similarly, terrorism represents a disaster of conflict where the intentional act is designed to cause great harm in support of a particular cause or ideology.

According to the Global Terrorism Database, 2019 alone saw over 8,500 terrorist attacks worldwide (Global Terrorism Database Global Terrorism START Background

Report 2020). Recent attacks on the U.S. Capital January 6, 2021, the eight coordinated attacks on hotels and churches in Sri Lanka (2019), the airport and subway attacks in Brussels, and a park in Pakistan caused horrendous loss of life, psychological trauma, devastating injuries, and economic losses. International EM is a complex and nuanced response to these types of crises and disasters. Often, humanitarian assistance is being provided in countries with little to no infrastructure and, at times, during ongoing conflicts making them unsafe and insecure (Mincin 2019). Nonetheless, these types of disasters require similar kinds of organizational responses to alleviate human suffering. Similar to the U.S. EM system, the international response system also follows structures, practices, and emergency response protocols and standard operating procedures. This includes the UN Cluster System, Interagency Cluster Coordination (established by Inter-Agency Standing Committee [IASC]), and Sphere Humanitarian Charter and Principles.

11.2.1 UN Cluster System

The UN Cluster system was established in the early 2000s with the aim of better coordinating responses and creating an accountability system for global humanitarian disasters. International NGOs are the primary partners and responding agencies in the Cluster System (United Nations n.d.a.). These include the World Health Organization (WHO), Save the Children, UN High Commissioner on Refugees (UNHCR), UN Children's Fund (UNICEF), and others. The Cluster System is divided into key areas of coordination services during response and recovery, including health, education, shelter, food security, camp management, water and sanitation, education, and logistics. Each of the cluster areas are assigned to various partnering organizations. For example, Save the Children and UNICEF play primary roles in prevention (safeguarding children) and education (access to schools during emergencies and recovery periods). UNHCR is a lead agency for establishing camps and the WHO is the primary agency for healthcare in crises (United Nations, n.d.a.). Clusters, similar to the U.S.-based Emergency Support Function (ESF) approach, include:

- Emergency Shelter
- Camp Management and Coordination
- Health
- Protection
- Food Security
- Early Recovery
- Education
- Sanitation, Water, and Hygiene
- Logistics
- Nutrition

Similar to the ESF structure you are familiar with from previous chapters, each cluster has a coordinating agency. Health, for example, is coordinated through the WHO. Sanitation, water, and hygiene are managed by UNICEF which also handles nutrition. In disaster sites, a Humanitarian Coordinator (HC) leads operations designed to be "principled, timely, effective and efficient" (see OCHA, n.d.). Coordination is considered "vital" when a disaster occurs.

The Office for the Coordination of Humanitarian Affairs (OCHA) works closely with global cluster lead agencies and NGOs to develop policies, coordinate intercluster issues, disseminate operational guidance, and organize field support. At the field level, OCHA helps ensure that the humanitarian system functions efficiently and in support of the HC's leadership. OCHA provides guidance and support to the HC and Humanitarian Country Team and facilitates intercluster coordination. OCHA also helps to ensure coordination between clusters at all phases of the response, including needs assessments, joint planning, monitoring, and evaluation. Logistical support includes:

- Prepositioned equipment between coordinating agencies and the private sector.
- Managing relationships between agencies, including airport-handling teams.
- Providing non-roof items appropriately, including materials from the UN Humanitarian Response Depot (UNHRD) (n.d.).
- Working in advance to deal with customs/entry of goods issues.
- Mapping and managing emergency stockpiles worldwide.

The UNHRD is located in various locations around the world enabling agencies to access and rapidly deliver necessary items (UNHRD n.d.a 2021).

11.2.2 Sphere

Sphere is a project that was started by several humanitarian organizations. Through the Sphere project, the humanitarian charter and humanitarian standards were established; they continue to be evaluated and updated to this day (Sphere About, n.d.). *The Sphere Handbook* is one of the most widely used book of standards for providing disaster assistance globally. Sphere established standard protocols for four core areas: water and sanitation (referred to as WASH), food security and nutrition, sheltering, and healthcare (*The Sphere Handbook* 2018). *The Sphere Handbook* is considered the gold standard for humanitarian response and recovery as well as evaluation protocols. It established client-centered services and minimum standards for all governmental and nongovernmental agencies to utilize and implement (Sphere About, n.d.). Further, *Sphere* has been tested for over 20 years in the field and is regularly reviewed and updated. Essentially, it is a "living" document for the international EM field. For additional detail on sheltering and best practices, refer back to Chapter 8 (see also Davidson et al. 2006; Raju 2013; Karunasena 2014).

11.2.3 U.S. Agency for International Development

The U.S. Agency for International Development (USAID) was established in the 1960s with a core mission of promoting democracy, political stability, and disaster assistance. A part of the USAID's framework is the concept of self-reliance. It is a concept that is echoed in other frameworks and standard operating procedures in international disaster response. The section on community integration and resiliency includes concepts of self-resiliency. The concepts of empowerment, resiliency, community integration, and self-reliance are critical aspects to rebuilding communities that foster community strength and sustainability.

International relief and development work are designed to be short term. The goal is to provide education, training, resources, and relief to communities so they can rebuild and continue the work after disaster teams leave. Self-reliance is extended to communities, families, and individuals. It is both collective and self-empowering. When communities have the resources, tools, and knowledge to recovery, heal, and rebuild, they create confidence in themselves and serve as role models in their local villages and towns. This is a core tenet of USAID and other frameworks you will learn about in this chapter (USAID's Policy Framework 2019).

The Office of Foreign Disaster Assistance (OFDA) is a unit within USAID charged with coordinating and deploying teams and supplies for international disaster response. Essentially, OFDA is the Federal Emergency Management Agency (FEMA) of global U.S. disaster response. Specifically, OFDA can provide affected areas with technical expertise and an initial assessment of the disaster in addition to assistance with logistics and supplies. OFDA has a warehouse of critical items that can be sent overseas within hours to days. In addition, OFDA oversees and deploys the Disaster Assistance Response Teams (DARTs) which are rapid disaster relief teams. OFDA has the capacity to respond to multiple disasters around the world simultaneously and can move large supplies and provide operational support to government locals efficiently and effectively.

11.3 HOW TO WORK IN INTERNATIONAL CONTEXTS

In this section, we learn about best practices and evidence-based models to working in a global world with clients from diverse backgrounds and countries.

11.3.1 Cultural Awareness and Integrating Context

International EM, at its core, is about providing relief to people around the world regardless of race, gender, orientation, economic status, disability/ability, and/or religion. In fact, people who are the most adversely affected by disasters and conflict tend to be those from the most vulnerable populations, including women and girls, people with disabilities, the aging, and the LGBTQ+ community. While we cannot be experts in all 191 UN-recognized countries and able to speak multiple languages across various dialects, we can enter countries and communities with deep empathy and compassion, humility, and an openness to learn and respect the culture of the people we are there to serve and support. Successfully engaging culturally diverse people during crises can be profoundly rewarding and satisfying work (Fordham, 2013). *And it is the most effective way to provide services.*

In addition, it is critical for all EM professionals to understand, integrate, and implement evidence-based and evidence-informed services and programs that meet the specific needs of diverse populations globally. This is not just about being the best practitioner you can be, but also about ensuring ethically sound and inclusive services that will *better benefit the community.* For example, ethnic, racial, sexual orientation, and individuals who have disabilities face unique social and psychological challenges that can result in persistent feelings of isolation, fear, anger, and even guilt or shame. When disasters occur, these feelings and experiences are magnified and intensified. When people suffer from disaster, one of the things we can do to help them feel comforted is to approach and interact with them within the context of their own, familiar and comfortable ways of living. For mental health and healthcare services, implementing evidence-based trauma and crisis care is a part of treatment protocols. To be the most effective, the services need to be provided in culturally sensitive ways (Dillard 2019).

Culturally based awareness means understanding how a design for living influences organizations, the way they are arranged, and how people behave inside those organizations. Even the way in which people choose to arrange a room, auditorium, or grassy meadow for a meeting is culturally influenced. Rules, regulations, and policies are all influenced by culture, so "doing business" in another country, including disaster relief, means understanding how and why people do things the way they do and respectfully working within their culture.

Sociologists look at specific behaviors that individuals or organizations choose when working in another culture. These two concepts, ethnocentrism and cultural relativism, depict how people may interact in other cultures. Ethnocentrism, the less useful and effective behavior model, situates you and your interactions with others within your own cultural beliefs and values. When we act out an ethnocentric frame of reference, we make judgments about other people's cultural values and norms. By turning up our nose at other people's cuisine, we offend them and implicitly tell them we do not value them, their food, or their hospitality. In many cultures, food is the way that people get to know us. You have a choice: rethink where you do your volunteer or humanitarian work or learn about the customs and food of the culture you are responding and see it as an opportunity to share and connect.

Working from a *culturally relative* perspective means that you have done your homework to understand what will work in the local disaster and you are open to learning about the people and community you will be providing support and relief. To accomplish this, it is critical to conduct research on the country and community from credible sources (see Box 11.2). In this time of misinformation and inaccurate reporting, it is important to research countries, religions, and communities from academic and official government websites. In addition, you can reach out to local community groups and religious organizations. For example, if you are deploying to Turkey to assist in one of the refugee camps, you can reach out to a local Islamic center or cultural center. Not all people who live in Turkey are Muslim, so reaching out to cultural centers is important to fully understand the context of the community. While a majority of people in Turkey are Muslim, they represent different schools of Islam, including Sufism, Sunni, and Shia. A small percentage of Turks are Yazidi, Christian, and Jewish.

If you are being deployed to the Thai/Myanmar border, you may want to research Buddhist cultural centers in your community so you can not only understand the religion and customs of the area, but also get a sense of the political tensions, especially in Myanmar. You may find them in your own community, perhaps studying at the local university, or within a community organization. It is also wise to take classes in both language and cultures to enhance your ability to enter another country in a manner

BOX 11.2

INTEGRATION AND EMPOWERMENT: WOMEN AND GIRLS AND PEOPLE WITH DISABILITIES

During disasters, certain populations are more vulnerable than others. For example, millions of women and girls worldwide suffer violence, including domestic violence, rape, and sexual assault, denial of education and employment, trafficking, and sexual violence in conflict-related situations. As a result, women and girls suffer from chronic health problems and their ability to participate fully in life is diminished. Women and girls living in refugee camps, for example, are at great risk for violence, death, and chronic health and mental health diseases. Implementing programs, such as health education, skills, and employment workshops, and safe spaces (in the case of domestic violence) are critical to protecting and empowering women and girls.

PHOTO 11.1 Safe house for domestic violence victims at a Thai refugee camp (Mincin)

PHOTO 11.2 A birthing room at the medical clinic (Mincin)

Another example is people with disabilities. Protection programs for people with disabilities often fall short resulting in millions of people not receiving assistance when it is most needed. Disability advocates can only utilize disjointed and general human rights laws and provisions to protect people with disabilities during conflict and disasters. In 2008, the UN adopted the Convention on the Rights of Persons with Disabilities extending human rights to people with disabilities globally (United Nations, n.d.b.). While a step in the right direction, the Convention does not explicitly include provisions for people with disabilities during disasters. People with disabilities do not have access to basic services in camps, including access to bathrooms and healthcare clinics (for more on this, watch Human Rights Watch's video *Refugees with Disabilities Overlooked, Underserved*: https://www.youtube.com/watch?v=O7fF0eFHn7o).

PHOTO 11.3 Children attend school for students with disabilities in Tanzania (Mincin)

that is culturally relative and likely to influence your success. Seek out electives in the social sciences, particularly sociology and anthropology, to deepen your understanding of other cultures.

11.3.2 Community Integration and Resiliency Models in International Emergency Management

Community integration and resiliency models of disaster services are the current, evidence-informed approaches being used. Community integration can be applied in just about any circumstance and environment. For example, utilizing the community integration model when DARTs are deployed to Ethiopia to assist with civil unrest and famine, team members will meet with and coordinate all services and distribution of food and healthcare with local government officials, community leaders, aid recipients, and other organizations providing emergency services. In addition, local community members are either hired or serve as volunteers with the response teams. Recruiting and hiring locals not only makes response stronger and more accurate (meeting the needs of the community), but creates resiliency and longer-term sustainability of programs and employment. When locals are trained and hired, they learn new skills, are able to contribute to their own community, and continue the work long after response teams and international relief agencies have left: the ultimate goal of international aid work (Bragin 2005, 2019; Mincin et al. 2021).

Resiliency can be found in the strengths-based approach and is less of a diagnostic medical model and more of an integrated and psychosocial model (see Box 11.3). Refugees typically have endured a lot of suffering. Understanding how they have managed to survive the suffering may give insightful clues as to how to build further resilience, to understand which evidence-based practices maybe most applicable, and to determine which programs and services may be most useful (Mincin 2012). Increasingly, the strengths-based approach (explicitly and interpretively) and psychosocial programming are being used in the refugee community (Scheinfeld, Walla and Langendorf 1997;

BOX 11.3

HIRING FORMER REFUGEES

In 2018, a US-based refugee office received funding to implement a community health promoter (CHP) program for refugees and asylees. The goals of the program were to increase health and mental health understanding among newly arrived refugees and those claiming asylum and to increase using medical and mental health services. The program was community-based, hired CHPs from the community (former refugees and asylees), and provided in homes. CHPs were trained throughout the program engaging in ongoing learning. A small program evaluation was conducted at the end of the project (Mincin et al. 2021). The evaluation found:

- Participants found the program to have a positive effect on them.
- Being a CHP enabled them to access more specialist medical services.
- Participants felt that they could access mental health support services more as well as had a better understanding of common challenges refugees/asylees had with the healthcare system.
- Participants felt a sense of satisfaction from educating their community members.
- Participants felt that the work they did was important to them, meaningful to the community, made a difference to their families, and they felt valued as a CHP worker.

Having members of the community trained and in the role of CHP made a difference in the implementation of the program. More people were reached and those who were hired as health promoters learned new skills, enhanced the ones they had, and felt a positive impact in their future career (Mincin et al. 2021). CHPs reported a sense of pride in providing critical information to refugees and asylees. Since the health promoters were refugees, they were able to fully relate to clients and help to problem solve (Mincin et al. 2021). In this small evaluation, you can see the positive impacts of a community-based, empowerment program and the effects it not only has on refugee clients, but the staff as well.

Walsh 2003; Fong 2004; Grigg-Saito et al. 2007; Halcón et al. 2007; Yohani 2008; Bragin et al. 2014; Mincin et al. 2021).

11.3.3 Guidance for Helping as Non-Aid Workers

When people are hurting and need the right items at the right time in the right place, we need to do the right thing. Though our hearts go out to those affected by disaster, we should stop first and think: what would be the most helpful? For international response, it is important to consider what humanitarian aid organizations request and need. For natural disasters, donating money to legitimate and registered organizations, such as International Federation of Red Cross and Red Crescent Societies (IFRC) and Save the Children, can enable organizations to send response teams and coordinate logistics rapidly. For example, IFRC has specific appeals to support the disaster relief teams and combat climate change. Save the Children will often request funds to support programs for children as well as local chapters coordinating drives for school supplies and children's clothes. For organizations that work with refugees and displaced populations, local goods can help feed and clothe people in crisis and support the local economy. This may include donating backpacks and school supplies, feminine sanitary kits, and coats for cold weather.

Sending the wrong kinds of donations often cause unanticipated problems making response even more difficult. Volunteers and staff must redirect their time to manage overwhelming and unnecessary items. Though people intend well, sending personal prescriptions, inappropriate clothing for a climate or culture, or items you are looking to get rid of significantly hinders response efforts. In addition, the logistics of moving items internationally for disaster response takes time and resources. It is a massive undertaking! It is critical that only what is needed is sent, as the coordination and delivery process is tremendously complex during global responses. The most important thing to do is listen to what organizations are asking for as they are based on the needs of the community and the type of crisis that is occurring.

Appropriate relief guidelines ensure that staff and volunteers in the damaged area will receive exactly what they need. More importantly, the influx of contributions will not undermine the locally struggling economy. The contributions will also be understandable as they will be written in language or symbols that are understood by all. In 2019, Albania experienced a 6.4 magnitude earthquake that killed 51 people and affected 100,000 people. The more than 350 volunteers, who responded, work with the local Albanian Red Cross. Volunteers assisted with search and rescue efforts, emergency healthcare, psychosocial support, and distribution of food, water, and relief supplies (Albania: 32,000 people still homeless three months on from devastating earthquake 2020). USAID recommends the following guidelines for material relief (www.usaid.gov):

- Send exactly what is desired with the requested characteristics, quality, and quantities.
- Package and label items specifically for the entry requirements in a particular location. Coordinate with a registered organization such as Mercy Corp or Doctors without Borders. Ensure that advance and confirmed transport and delivery plans are in place with the organization you are working with.

- Confirm with the organization they have enough staff and volunteers available to offload, sort, organize, and deliver donations.

After the 2010 Haiti earthquake, the USAID issued a set of recommendations to guide humanitarian contribution (www.usaid.gov). Summarized, they include these principles:

- Listen to what locals are asking for. Organizations should be careful to send exactly what is needed and be able to deliver the requested item in coordination with area resources and transportation arteries.
- Encourage purchase of local commodities to restart the economy and encourage recovery.
- Delivered relief supplies should be appropriate for local conditions, including climate, culture, and languages. When needed, technical training should be offered. Provided items should be sustainable through local supplies or sustained delivery of needed components.

After the 2015 Nepal earthquake, these same principles applied. In addition, USAID recommended making a monetary donation to a reputable humanitarian organization. By practicing "smart compassion," donors can generate more effective relief. USAID's Center for International Disaster Information (USAID/CIDI) provides an online toolkit toward such ends (see resources section). Also, within USAID, the OFDA sends experts and aid to over 50 countries annually. OFDA's DARTs rely on technical experts and caches of emergency relief supplies throughout the world to respond quickly and appropriately. In recent years, USAID DARTs have worked on the Syrian conflict and refugee problem, Ebola, the Nepal earthquake, a typhoon in Burma, and more.

Appropriate relief guidelines ensure that staff and volunteers in the damaged area will receive exactly what they need. More importantly, the influx of contributions will not undermine the locally struggling economy. The contributions will also be understandable as they will be written in language or symbols that are understood by all. After the Haiti earthquake, for example, starving residents threw away nutrition bars stamped with the current date. Survivors incorrectly assumed that the bars had expired and feared they might be harmful. Humanitarian aid must be effective rather than mire relief efforts or extend suffering. Typically, money is the best contribution. Money can be used locally to help the economy and to buy exactly what is needed. Donated funds can also be transferred electronically and instantaneously.

Whether compelled to migrate by natural disaster or human means, people who leave regions devastated by drought or conflict require similar kinds of support. We now turn to this aspect of international humanitarian relief.

11.4 WORKING WITH REFUGEES IN CAMPS, URBAN ENVIRONMENTS, AND RESETTLEMENT PROGRAMS

Refugees have been forced out of their homes, communities, and countries because of significant threats to their lives. They often have fled with little more than the clothes on their backs and what they could carry in bags. Within the refugee population, certain people may be especially vulnerable. These include women and girls (who are often subjected to gender-based violence and denied education in some cultures and contexts; see Rees, Pittaway, and Bartolomei 2005), people with disabilities, including physical and mental disabilities (who are often stigmatized and "forgotten"), children and youth (as they will go through major transitions as they start school in a new country and can be at an increased risk for teasing and bullying), and LGBTQ+ populations (who may have their lives threatened if "found out") (CARE, 2020).

There should be services to specifically address the needs of the most vulnerable populations as they slowly integrate and build a new life. Creating safe havens for women and girls who have had to endure violence, offering programs to refugee youth to build confidence and thwart the potential of getting involved with gangs, and empowering refugees with disabilities to learn English and gain employment will enable all refugees to increase well-being and integration. It is important to recognize the most vulnerable refugees and have staff that have expertise in these issues and programs that target these special needs. In this section, we will learn about refugee camps, urban refugees, and refugee resettlement.

11.4.1 Refugee Camps

Today, we are experiencing the highest number of refugees and displaced populations the world has seen (United Nations Hugh Commissioner for Refugees Figures at a Glance, 2021). Conflict, disasters, environmental crises, economic instability, and inequality have forced nearly 80 million people to flee (United Nations Hugh Commissioner for Refugees Figures at a Glance, 2021). Contrary to popular belief, developing countries actually shoulder the highest number of refugees, not the U.S. and Europe (United Nations Hugh Commissioner for Refugees Figures at a Glance, 2021). East African countries, such as Kenya and Tanzania, have some of the largest refugee camps in the world and Middle Eastern/Asia Minor countries, such as Turkey and Jordan, have millions of refugees living in camp environments (Hale 2020). Compare that to the U.S., which accepted 35,000 refugees in 2020.

Refugee camp environments are rough and challenging to live in on a day-to-day basis. Crime, insecurity, lack of food, boredom from lack of schools and jobs, all take a toll physically and mentally on the people forced to live there (see Box 11.4). Originally designed over a half a century ago, refugee camps were intended to be temporary locations. Today, people live in camps anywhere from 5 to 20+ years. That means babies are born in refugee camps and children grow up in a temporary environment without much structure or hope for the future. Women and men have limited access to employment and education/skills-building trainings and children have limited access to school and recreational activities.

People live in poverty, and leaving camps is either illegal (in some areas), dangerous, or both. Wildeman (2019) describes a Palestinian refugee camp in the West Bank:

These camps suffer from suffocating high population densities. For example, the 22,855 of Balata refugee camp live on less than 2 square kilometers of land. Their populations are young, with 60% less than 19 years old. Families live in square, concrete houses with just a few rooms; homes ill-equipped to deal with the extreme heat

BOX 11.4

MYANMAR COUP AND ONGOING INSTABILITY

Myanmar, also known as Burma, has been dealing with decades of military coups, authoritarian rule, and ethnic cleansing with the most recent military coup occurring in February 2021 (Maizland 2021). The homes are generally made of bamboo and refugees cannot leave the camp area. Tens of thousands of refugees live in the refugee camps, some for over 20 years. Camp services include schools, women and girl's safe spaces, skills-building workshops, and a basic hospital. With the recent military coup in Myanmar, more camps are being opened.

PHOTO 11.4 Karen refugee camp along the Thai/Myanmar border; refugee medical clinic (Mincin)

of the summer and cold of the winter. Water is limited and often unclean, plumbing very basic and sewage systems inadequate.

(Wildeman 2009)

Humanitarian aid organizations, such as Care International and Save the Children, provide specific programs and services in camp environments. For example, Save the Children has provided food and nutrition to hundreds of thousands of refugee children from South Sudan. They also provide education and protection programs for refugee children, sheltering them from labor and sex traffickers. Care International, a humanitarian aid and development organization that focuses on the needs of women and girls, provides emergency shelters, access to reproductive healthcare, and food.

11.4.2 Urban Refugees

Some refugees flee and relocate to urban environments instead of a refugee camp with the hope of employment and the possibility of integrating into the community and becoming a permanent citizen. However, often urban refugees live in shadows for fear of law enforcement and are discriminated against, making finding employment and housing difficult. In addition, it can be challenging to find the right organization that can assist with services because urban refugees tend to be dispersed throughout the cities.

11.4.3 Refugee Resettlement

Currently, some countries accept refugees and provide services to them, including the U.S., Canada, Australia, Germany, and New Zealand, among other countries. The goal of refugee resettlement, regardless of which country a refugee goes, is self-sufficiency. Self-sufficiency can include early and long-term employment, financial understanding (such as knowing financial management), the ability to advocate for oneself, self-reliance, independence from government assistance, health and wellness, and services for children and youth, women, and girls (Mincin 2012).

Key components to refugee resettlement incorporate core services such as safe and decent housing, food, general case management services, access to initial health screens, basic employment, and English language services. These services are generally offered in most programs, though programs vary greatly from county to country. Regardless, they are recognized as necessary, basic services to any refugee arriving in their new homeland and community. These are considered basic and immediate services, not long-term services. It is important to note that a goal of refugee resettlement is integration into the new country and community the refugee has newly arrived. The core services are meant to provide a "soft landing," but practitioners working with refugees should also engage in longer-term services.

When a refugee arrives in a new country, providing the necessary services to assist the refugee in settling, gaining employment, and integrating into the community will make for an overall more positive experience as they become fully participating citizens. Tangible services that can go a long way toward creating a sense of security and well-being include employment, mental health, and psychosocial support for adults and children, targeted services for more vulnerable refugees (such as women and girls, refugees with disabilities, or refugees who have serious medical conditions), secure and safe housing, and education (for adults and children and youth). However, ensuring the refugee is a part of their own healing, integration, and resettlement is arguably the most important component.

Employment plays an important role in an individual's sense of well-being, security, and self-determination (Akabas and Kurzman 2005; Carreon 2011). One main aspect to being employed as a refugee is English language proficiency (Levinson 2002; Pine and Drachman 2005; Carreon 2011). Employment not only provides refugees the opportunity to feel self-reliant, but it can expedite deeper integration into the community. However, finding employment while taking English as a Second Language (ESL) classes and adjusting to a new life in a new country can be daunting tasks; practitioners need to be aware of these competing priorities when working with newly arrived refugees. *Integration occurs on multiple pathways* (language acquisition, economic opportunity, civic participation, citizenship, health access, housing, etc.) and involves multiple sectors of a community, such as government agencies, schools, libraries, Ethnic Community Based Organizations (ECBOs), employers, faith-based organizations, advocacy groups, healthcare providers, and other organizations (Kallick & Mathema, 2016; ISED 2011).

Understanding the impact of health and mental health on the lives of refugees is also critical to resettlement (ISED 2011). Refugees are coming from different situations; some have been languishing in camps (e.g., the Somali in Dadab refugee camp or Karen in the Thailand camps), others are coming directly from combat zones (e.g., Iraqis, Syrians). With each circumstance a refugee comes from, health and mental health issues may need to be addressed. Without a sense of psychological wellness and feeling healthy, it becomes very challenging to maintain employment, provide for families, function in school, and rebound from potentially significant trauma.

Medical conditions can range from chronic diseases, such as diabetes, to life-threatening illnesses, such as cancer or kidney failure. Upon arriving at their new location, each refugee should go to an initial physical health screening. In addition, refugees should be tested for communicable diseases such as tuberculosis. Certain conditions, with proper medical treatment, can significantly improve a refugee's health and overall well-being. If a refugee has diabetes, they may have suffered in the camps. However, with medications, changes in diet, and access to education for self-improvement, diabetes can become a manageable albeit chronic illness that one can live with.

The mental health needs of refugees also vary and can include trauma-related symptoms that can alleviate over time with proper support to more chronic illnesses such as depression and anxiety. Chronic mental illness can be treated with proper medications, self-help supports, and counseling. Mental health services must be offered in a culturally appropriate manner and in the preferred language of the refugee. In addition, psychosocial programs such as community gardening and youth art classes can provide healing, support, and hope as refugees embark on their new life.

11.4.4 A Moment in the Life of a Refugee and Asylee Fleeing

It can be hard for us to imagine what it must be like to be forced out of your village, community, city, and even country because of conflict, persecution, and other types of disasters such as climate crises. There are a few websites online that give us the opportunity to get a glimpse into the treacherous and frightening journey of refugees. Here are two interactive websites you can explore and experience:

- The refugee challenge: can you break into Fortress Europe? *The Guardian*
- https://www.theguardian.com/global-development/ng-interactive/2014/jan/refugee-choices-interactive
- Syrian Journey: Choose Your Own Escape Route BBC: https://www.bbc.com/news/world-middle-east-32057601

As you walk through these websites, think about how it feels to go through the interactive journeys. Did it give you a sense as to the types of choices and perils refugees face? Did it challenge any assumptions or notions you had about refugees? Did you better understand their plight or did it bring up more questions?

11.5 DISASTER RISK REDUCTION AT THE INTERNATIONAL LEVEL

Whether a disaster of conflict or a disaster of consensus, a number of goals exist to move vulnerable people and communities toward a safer future. Since the early 1990s, efforts have been underway globally, such as the International Decade for Natural Disaster Reduction, which was followed by the International Strategy for Disaster Reduction. Such efforts have continued.

Among the more influential has been what is called the "Hyogo" Framework that arose out of a 2005 conference in Hyogo, Japan. With an eye on 2015 as a time frame to promote more global resilience against disasters, the Hyogo Framework focused on "the substantial reduction of disaster losses, in lives and in the social, economic, and environmental assets of communities and countries" (Hyogo Framework, p. 5, see resources section for link). To do so, conference attendees concentrated on integrating disaster risk reduction into development policies, with an effort to reduce vulnerability in high-risk areas. The full range of the life cycle of EM was considered as well, with efforts to focus on preparedness and mitigation across a multi-hazard context. Attendees prompted actors and agencies to build capacity at the community level – the idea of empowerment so stressed in this chapter – as a way to leverage local resources and knowledge. Within that local context, diversity should be embraced and considered, including gender, age, and other historic vulnerabilities. The desired outcome? A culture of prevention designed to reduce casualties and expedite recovery.

In March 2015, the Sendai Framework for Disaster Risk Reduction was adopted by the UN Member States at the UN World Conference on Disaster Risk Reduction in Sendai, Japan. The Sendai Framework is designed to move those involved through the year 2030. Four priorities for action undergird efforts to reduce risks. Priority 1 is to understand disaster risk, followed by Priority 2 which is to strengthen disaster risk governance and manage disaster risks. The third priority calls for investing in disaster risk reduction to promote resilience, with Priority 4 focused on disaster preparedness to enhance response and facilitate recovery (for more, visit the Resources section). Ultimately, the goal of all such efforts have been similar: to reduce losses in lives and properties, including jobs, health, and other resources, particularly within highly vulnerable communities, an effort in which we can all participate through work or volunteer effort.

11.6 WORKING AND VOLUNTEERING IN AN INTERNATIONAL SETTING

You might consider two routes to gaining experience within an NGO active in disasters. The first is paid employment while the second comes through volunteer participation. Though the challenges of NGO work may be particularly frustrating – usually need overwhelms resources – actually seeing someone lifted from poverty, able to feed their children, or move into a newly rebuilt, post-disaster structure makes all the hard work very worthwhile.

At this point, it should be clear that volunteering must be done in a manner that is sensitive to local cultures and fits in well with established customs, policies, and organizational procedures. It is therefore best to plan your future volunteer efforts carefully. First, find an organization that is experienced in disaster relief with a reputation for following the principles discussed so far. Become affiliated by filling out forms so that the organization knows where and how to contact you to help. Second, obtain appropriate training. Organizations with disaster missions usually offer training to their volunteers. The Red Cross, for example, offers specific training for shelter managers, first aid, and psychological support. Other organizations may offer on-site training and supervision such as for debris removal and construction or logistics coordination.

Further, the response period is when most people want to volunteer while the disaster is fresh in their minds. In reality, the long-term recovery period is when the majority of volunteers are needed. Be patient and know that if you volunteer it may be a year or more before you can join a volunteer site. Remember that it takes time to assess needs, set up projects, secure volunteer housing, and arrange to feed those helping. The wait will be worth it, as not only will you be able to help when and where it is most needed but you will receive benefits as well. Volunteering makes us feel good about ourselves while enriching our understanding of the people who we serve (Thoits and Hewitt 2001).

Another route might be to secure an internship which can be volunteer or paid. The USAID, for example, provides both. Work for interns can vary from conducting research and drafting documents to supporting meetings, participating in discussions with various Federal agencies, or helping with information about USAID. International career positions can vary widely from straightforward emergency response operations to the behind-the-scenes work of finances or human resources. USAID, for example, hires foreign service officers who respond to crises and humanitarian emergencies. Their work may include some of the more routine work of developing programs, creating partnerships, and engaging in planning efforts – and then transition swiftly into emergency work when disasters occur.

A good example of the diversity in EM jobs comes from the IRC. Their emergency response team may include those tasked with insuring safe water and food supplies, sanitation, medical care, or logistics. Depending on the circumstances, a staff member might work on children's issues or with those affected by sexual violence. Clearly, combining a major in EM with a minor in social services, psychology, sociology, gerontology, healthcare, and other areas could make a job applicant more attractive to a prospective employer. Other organizations, like UNICEF or OXFAM, may hire people to work full-time or for disaster-specific events. The UN includes an array of options to consider. They advertise for logisticians, for example, to manage deployment sites. Humanitarian workers coordinate critical, life-saving relief operations when disaster strikes. Others are needed in public information, conference management, internal security, and safety, and with technology, economic development, and legal assistance – yes, all these areas may be needed during humanitarian crises. Your future career in EM at the international level has a broad set of opportunities.

11.6.1 International Aid Workers: Lives on the Line

International response and relief work are rewarding but incredibly challenging. And it is also at times dangerous. According to the Aid Worker Security Database (AWSD), 483 aid workers were attacked in 2019, 42% of whom were healthcare aid workers. Of the 483 workers who were attacked, 125 were killed. Attacks happen in both disaster response like health crises and in conflict zones. For example, healthcare workers came under attack during Ebola responses. At times, the violence can be brought on because of misunderstanding about the role of humanitarian aid workers. Other times, aid workers get caught in cross fire and other violence. In recent years, the DRC has experienced an ongoing Ebola outbreak. In 2019, an armed group killed four healthcare workers in Democratic Republic of Congo (DRC). (Armed groups kill Ebola health workers in eastern DR Congo 2019.)

In 2020, Doctors without Borders lost a medical staff member to gun fire violence. The staff was caught in the cross fire of the ongoing civil war conflict in the Central African Republic. In 2018, a staff member of the IRC, Fareedullah Noori, was killed in an attack on the Ministry of Refugees and Returnees office in Jalalabad, Afghanistan. Fifteen other people were killed in the attack. In this situation, Noori and others were caught between gun fire and a car bomb while attempting to carry out their humanitarian job duties. Unfortunately, these are just a few reports of the hundreds of aid workers who have lost their lives over the last decade in the line of work.

Organizations that respond to international disasters and work in conflict zones and insecure areas must have security and safety protocols in place to save lives. It is also a reminder to not self-deploy to areas experiencing insecurity and conflict as it puts everyone, including yourself, at risk for injury and even death. Deploying through formal systems and with an affiliated and registered agency or organization in which you are trained and understand all safety protocols and security measures and you are working in a team is necessary.

***

SUMMARY

To deliver international and humanitarian aid more effectively, those who seek to help must learn about the challenges of disasters within an international context along with how to work with other cultures, governments, and partnerships to deliver appropriate aid when disasters occur. Delivering services in countries that are still developing or in conflict can be challenging and even dangerous. Best practices require respecting the people being served, implementing evidence-based and best practices, and understanding protocols and deployment policies and procedures.

We are a part of a global community. Whether conflicts and war or crises and disasters caused by climate change, we have an important role to play in alleviating pain and affecting stability. As professional emergency managers, we need to understand and respect all cultures and backgrounds in our own communities and the global community. Working with locally affected people rather than on their behalf means we are providing appropriate aid and support. Empowering those who have been affected to offer recommendations and participate in their own recovery is considered a best practice. Disasters of consensus (e.g., most natural disasters) or disasters of conflict (genocide, terrorism) can be addressed similarly in terms of how we respond to and set up aid for those affected. A higher degree of programming though may be needed for refugees driven out of familiar contexts, away from livelihoods, traumatized by events, and distanced from their social networks.

As discussed, refugees taking ownership of their own resettlement process, building upon the resilient skills they already have, and incorporating their hopes and dreams will empower them in real and tangible ways and assist them in building more skills to cope with and navigate their new life. Healing from trauma involves active participation from the client. Refugee resettlement is no exception. Refugees bring a wealth of knowledge to their own process and indeed to the community they now call home. Refugees become engaged, functioning, and positive forces in communities bring richness in culture, perspectives, and strong work ethic.

Discussion Questions

1. Distinguish between natural disasters and human-made disasters within the international context. Do you see differences in how organizations respond to each?
2. Define and give examples of cultural relativism and ethnocentrism from your own culture. How have others misunderstood or judged your way of living? How has that impacted how people think of people like you and your culture?
3. If you were going to organize a donation drive for an international area impacted by a disaster, how would you do that? What is the evidence-based best practices for doing so?
4. What key programs and efforts should be in place to receive and support refugees from disasters of conflict or disasters of consensus?
5. Organize a panel in your class and trace the history of international efforts to reduce risks and promote resilience. Why is there such a focus on development? Research the ideas of Hyogo and Sendai further (see resources section) and find out more to share on your panel.

Summary Questions

1. Distinguish and define a refugee and asylee.
2. Define and give examples of cultural relativism and ethnocentrism.
3. How is the cluster system like the ESF structure and how does it differ?
4. What are five best practices for working internationally?
5. What are three best practices for working with traumatized refugees?
6. What does a community or agency need to provide to enable effective resettlement of refugees and asylees?

7. What is it like to be a refugee or asylee? What has your experience been like why you were seeking a safe location?
8. Identify the rewards and challenges of working internationally.

REFERENCES

A&E Television Networks. 2021. *Eleanor Roosevelt Biography*. A&E Television Networks Publication. Last updated on April 9, 2021. Retrieved from https://www.biography.com/us-first-lady/eleanor-roosevelt.

Akabas Sheila and Paul Kurzman. 2005. *Work and the Workplace*. New York: Columbia University Press.

Albania: 32,000 People Still Homeless Three Months on from Devastating Earthquake. Albania IFRC 2020. Available at Albania: 32,000 people still homeless three months on from devastating earthquake - International Federation of Red Cross and Red Crescent Societies (ifrc.org). Accessed on June 4, 2021.

Bragin, Martha. 2005. "The Community Participatory Evaluation Tool for Psychosocial Programs: A Guide to Implementation. *Intervention: International Journal of Mental Health, Psychosocial Work and Counseling in Areas of Armed Conflict* 3(1): 3–24.

Bragin, Martha. (2019). "Clinical Social Work with Survivors of Disaster and Terrorism: A Social Ecological Approach." Pp. 366–401 in *Theory and Practice in Clinical Social Work*, 3rd ed., ed. J. Brandell. San Diego, CA: Cognella, Inc.

Bragin, M., Onta, K, Taaka, J., Ntacobakinvuna, D., and Eibs, T. (2014). "To Be Well at Heart: Women's Perceptions of Psychosocial Well-Being in 3 Conflict-Affected Countries – Burundi, Nepal, and Uganda." *Intervention: International Journal of Mental Health, Psychosocial Work and Counselling in Areas of Armed Conflict* 12(2): 171–186.

CARE. (2020). "Difficulties in Refugee Camp Are Intensified for Those with Disabilities, CARE International, December 2020." Retrieved from Difficulties in refugee camp are intensified for those with disabilities – CARE.

Carreon, S. (2011). Eritreans in the Big Apple: Integration of new populations of refugees in the United States. Unpublished report.

Davidson, Colin, Cassidy Johnson, Gonzalo Lizarralde, Nese Dikmen, and Alicia Sliwinski. 2006. "Truth and Myths about Community Participation in Post-Disaster Housing Projects." *Habitat International* 31(1): 100–115.

Dillard, J.V. 2019. *Cultural Diversity: A primer for the human services*, 4th Ed. Cengage Publishing Inc.: Boston, MA.

Fong, Rowena. 2004. *Culturally Competent Practice with Immigrant and Refugee Children and Families*. New York: The Guildford Press.

Fordham, Maureen, William Lovekamp, Deborah S. K. Thomas and Brenda D. Phillips. 2013. "Introduction to Social Vulnerability." Pp. 1–32 in *Social Vulnerability to Disasters*, 2nd eds. Deborah S. K. Thomas et al. Boca Raton, FL: CRC Press.

Grigg-Saito, Dorcas, Sheila Och, Sidney Liang, Robin Toof, and Linda Silka. 2007. "Building on the Strengths of a Cambodian Refugee Community through Community-based Outreach." *Health Promotion Practice* 9(4): 415–425.

Global Terrorism Database Global Terrorism Overview: Terrorism in 2019. University of Maryland. Available at https://www.start.umd.edu/gtd/global-terrorism-overview-terrorism-in-2019/, last accessed September 22, 2021.

Halcón, Linda. L., Cheryl L. Robertson, Karen A. Monsen, and Cindi C. Claypatch. (2007). "A Theoretical Framework for Using Health Realization to Reduce Stress and Improve Coping in Refugee Communities." *Journal of Holistic Nursing* 25(3): 186–194.

Hale, E. (2020). The 7 Largest Refugee Camps In The World. Refugee Council U.S.A. Accessed on October 20, 2021 from http://refugeecouncilusa.org/largest-refugee-camps/

Holguín-Veras, José, Miguel Jaller, Luk Van Wassenhove, Noel Pérez, and Tricia Wachtendorf. 2012. "On the Unique Features of Post-disaster Humanitarian Logistics." *Journal of Operations Management* 30(7–8): 494–506.

Holguín-Veras, José, Miguel Jaller, Luk Van Wassenhove, Noel Pérez, and Tricia Wachtendorf. 2014. "Material Convergence: Important and Understudied Disaster Phenomenon." *Natural Hazards Review* 15: 1–12.

Institute for Social and Economic Development (ISED). (2010). Exploring refugee integration: Experiences in four American cities. ORR Integration Report 2010. Washington, DC: ISED Solutions.

Karunasena, Gayani and Raufdeen Rameezdeen. 2014. "Post-disaster Housing Reconstruction: Comparative Study of Donor vs. Owner-Driven Approaches." *International Journal of Disaster Resilience in the Built Environment* 1(2): 173–191.

Kallick, D.D., and Mathema, S. (2016). Refugee Integration in the United States. Fiscal Policy Institute Center for Progress. Available at https://cdn.americanprogress.org/wp-content/uploads/2016/06/15112912/refugeeintegration.pdf, last accessed September 22, 2021.

Kovács, Gyöngyi and Karen M. Spens. 2007. "Humanitarian Logistics in Disaster Relief Operations." *International Journal of Physical Distribution and Logistics Management* 37(2): 99–114.

Kovács, Gyöngyi and Karen M. Spens. 2009. "Identifying Challenges in Humanitarian Logistics." *International Journal of Physical Distribution and Logistics Management* 39(6): 506–528.

Levinson, A. (2002). Immigrants and welfare use. Migration Policy Institute. Retrieved from http://www.migrationinformation.org/usfocus/display.cfm?ID=45

Maizland, L. 2021. Myanmar's Troubled History: Coups, Military Rule, and Ethnic Conflict. Council on Foreign Relations. Available at Myanmar's Troubled History: Coups, Military Rule, and Ethnic Conflict | Council on Foreign Relations (cfr.org). Accessed on June 4, 2021.

Mincin, J. 2019. *International emergency management in Encyclopedia of Security and Emergency Management*. New York: Springer Publishing.

Mincin, J. (2012). Strengths and Weaknesses of the U.S.-Based Refugee Resettlement Program: A Survey of International Rescue Committee Employee Perceptions. Available at https://www.semanticscholar.org/paper/Strengths-and-Weaknesses-of-the-U.S.-Based-Refugee-Mincin/a5cddbc9dad891c4452b4d2f89513bd38dcbb56d, last accessed September 22, 2021.

Mincin, J., K. Khetarpal, and J. Steiner (Accepted 2021). Protecting Vulnerable Populations during Health Emergencies: COVID-19 Pandemic and Displaced Populations. *Journal of Emergency Management* Special Edition: COVID-19 and Mental Health.

Office for the Coordination of Humanitarian Affairs (OCHA). n.d. "Leadership." Available at http://www.unocha.org/what-we-do/coordination/leadership/overview, last accessed April 19, 2016.

Phillips, Brenda. 2020. *Disaster Volunteers*. Oxford: Elsevier.

Phillips, Brenda and Pamela Jenkins. 2016. "Gender-based Violence and Disasters: South Asia in Comparative Perspective." in *Gender, Women and Disasters: Survival, Security and Development*, eds. Linda Racioppi and Swarna Prajnya. India: Routledge. https://doi.org/10.4324/9781315650630.

Pine, Barbara and Diane Drachman. 2005. "Effective Child Welfare Practice with Immigrant and Refugee Children and their Families." *Child Welfare League of America* 5: 537–562.

Potocky-Tripodi, Miriam. 2001. "Micro and Macro Determinants of Refugee Economic Status." *Journal of Social Service Research* 27: 33–60.

Potocky-Tripodi, Miriam. 2003. "Refugee Economic Adaptation: Theory, Evidence, and Implications for Policy and Practice." *Journal of Social Service Research* 30: 63–91.

Quarantelli, E. L. 1986. "What Should We Study? Questions and Suggestions for Researchers about the Concept of Disasters." Preliminary Paper #119, Disaster Research Center, University of Delaware. Available at http://udspace.udel.edu/handle/19716/492, last accessed April 18, 2016.

Raju, Emmanuel. 2013. "Housing Reconstruction in Disaster Recovery: A Study of Fishing Communities Post-Tsunami in Chennai, India." *PLOS Currents Disasters*. http://currents. plos.org/disasters/article/housing-reconstruction-in-disaster-recovery-a-study-of-fishing-communities-post-tsunami-in-chennai-india/, last accessed January 5, 2006.

Rees, Susan, Eileen Pittaway, and Linda Bartolomei. 2005. "Waves of Violence in Post-Tsunami Sri Lanka." *Australasian Journal of Disaster and Trauma Studies* 2, available at http:// www.massey.ac.nz/ trauma/issucs/2005-2/rees.htm, last accessed February 24, 2011.

Scheinfeld, D., Walla, L.B. & Langendorf, T. (1997). *Strengthening Refugee Families: Designing Programs for Refugee and Other Families in Need*. Lyceum Books: Chicago, IL.

Sphere About. n.d. Available at About Sphere | Sphere (spherestandards.org). Accessed on June 4, 2021.

The Sphere Handbook. 2018. Available at The Sphere Interactive Handbook (spherestandards. org). Accessed on June 4, 2021.

Thoits, P. and L. Hewitt. 2001. "Volunteer Work and Well-being." *Journal of Health and Social Behavior* 42(2): 115–121.

United Nations. n.d.a. *Universal Declaration of Human Rights*. Retrieved from Universal Declaration of Human Rights | United Nations, last accessed June 1, 2021.

United Nations. n.d.b. *Convention on the Rights of Persons with Disabilities (CRPD)*, Retrieved from https://www.un.org/development/desa/disabilities/convention-on-the-rights-of-persons-with-disabilities.html, last accessed June 1, 2021.

United Nations High Commission on Refugees. *History of UNHCR*. n.d.b. Retrieved from UNHCR – History of UNHCR, last accessed June 1, 2021.

United Nations High Commission on Refugees. n.d.c. *Who We Help*. Available at UNHCR - Who We Help. Last accessed June 1, 2021.

United Nations High Commission on Refugees. n.d.d. *Yemen Emergency*. Available at Country - Yemen (unhcr.org). Last accessed June 1, 2021.

United Nations Humanitarian Response Depot (UNHRD). n.d. Available at The United Nations Humanitarian Response Depot | UNHRD. Last accessed June 6, 2021.

United Nations Hugh Commissioner for Refugees Figures at a Glance. n.d. Available at UNHCR – Figures at a Glance. Accessed on June 6, 2021.

United States AID. 2016. Office of U.S. Foreign Disaster Assistance. Available at https:// www.usaid.gov/who-we-are/organization/bureaus/bureau-democracy-conflict-and-humanitarian-assistance/office-us, last accessed April 18, 2016.

United States Administration for International Development Policy Framework. 2019. Retrieved from WEB_PF_Full_Report_FINAL_10Apr2019.pdf (usaid.gov).

USAID's Policy Framework 2019. Available at USAID's Policy Framework | U.S. Agency for International Development. Accessed on June 4, 2021.

Walsh, Froma. 2003. *Normal Family Process: Growing Diversity and Growing Complexity*. 3rd ed. New York: The Guildford Press.

Wildeman, J. (2019). Life in a Refugee Camp Hope for the Hopeless. Alternatives International Journal. November 9, 2009. Available at https://www.alterinter.org/?Life-in-a-Refugee-Camp, last accessed September 22, 2021.

Women's Refugee Commission 2009. *Refugees with Disabilities*. Retrieved from WRC-2009-Disabilities Refugees Factsheet.pdf (miusa.org), last accessed June 1, 2021.

World Health Organization (WHO) steps up efforts to curb Ebola outbreaks in Guinea and the Democratic Republic of the Congo. 2021. Available at https://www.afro.who.int/news/who-steps-efforts-curb-ebola-outbreaks-guinea-and-democratic-republic-congo#:~:text=18%20February%202021%20Brazzaville%20%E2%80%93%20With%20efforts%20gathering,ramp%20up%20the%20response%20and%20avert%20widespread%20infections, last accessed September 22, 2021.

World Health Organization Chemical Incidents. n.d.a. Available at https://www.who.int/-health-topics/chemical-incidents#tab=tab_1, last accessed September 22, 2021.

World Health Organization Radiation Incidents. n.d.a. Available at https://www.who.int/-health-topics/radiation-emergencies#tab=tab_1, last accessed September 22, 2021.

World Health Organization Technological Incidents. n.d. Available at https://www.who.int/environmental_health_emergencies/technological_incidents/en/.

Yohani, Sophie. C. 2008. "Creating an Ecology of Hope: Arts-based Interventions with Refugee Children." *Child and Adolescent Social Work Journal* 25: 309–323.

RESOURCES

- USAID Center for International Disaster Information: Home – USAID CIDI: USAID CIDI.
- Sphere Humanitarian Core Standards: https://spherestandards.org/humanitarian-standards/core-humanitarian-standard/.
- The Global Cluster System: https://www.humanitarianresponse.info/en/coordination/clusters/what-cluster-approach.
- UNHCR website: UNHCR – The UN Refugee Agency.
- The Hyogo Framework: About the Hyogo Framework for Action (2005–2015) – Hyogo Framework – PreventionWeb.net.
- The Sendai Framework for Disaster Risk Reduction Sendai Framework for Disaster Risk Reduction 2015–2030/UNDRR.
- USAID student internships Student Internships and Recent Graduate Programs/USAID (usaid.gov).
- UNHCR Report on Climate Change: UNHCR – Data reveals impacts of climate emergency on displacement and Displaced on the frontlines of the climate emergency (arcgis.com).
- I Live in a Refugee Camp: I Live in a Refugee Camp (scholastic.com).
- Relief Web: https://reliefweb.int/.

CHAPTER 12

The Next Generation of Emergency Managers and Disaster Scientists

---

CHAPTER OBJECTIVES

Upon completing this chapter, readers should be able to:

- Discuss the value of diverse representation in the field of emergency management (EM) and the discipline of disaster science.
- Discern educational pathways through degree options and into the practical field of EM.
- Articulate reasons for why continuing professional development is essential in this field.
- Know where to look for career opportunities and job openings.

KEY TERMS

- Active Representation
- Certified Emergency Manager
- Continuing Education
- Cultural Competency
- Diversity
- Education

- Glass Ceiling
- Glass Cliff
- Inclusion
- Mentor
- Networking

12.1 INTRODUCTION

As this book started, you learned about predictions of new and larger disasters. That prediction, made decades ago by Quarantelli (1996), has come true. Global pandemics, space weather, cyberattacks, and climate change were rarely discussed at the time of the prediction, yet emergency managers contend with these disasters as today's realities. Larger disasters have happened as well, from the massive tsunami of 2004 that

DOI: 10.4324/9781003021919-15

claimed 300,000 lives worldwide to same-season, large-scale hurricanes that slam the same areas repeatedly. The impacts have been extraordinary and significant and emergency managers are needed more than ever before.

The next generation of emergency managers and disaster scientists – which includes you – will need to rise to such challenges (Cwiak et al. 2017). Evidence-based practice from disaster scientists will inform practitioners who will need to rely on science to understand natural hazards, computer courses to grapple with cyberthreats, and social science to craft effective warnings. We will need people with skills and knowledge able to assist individual households as well as entire communities in all their diversity. As part of the next generation, commit now to acquiring the knowledge you need to prepare communities and workplaces for these existing and emerging hazards and to understand, apply, and even create the science we need to strengthen the discipline further. Fully informed, you will have a better chance to mitigate hazards and save lives, properties, and economies. The work of the next generation will matter. *Your* work will matter.

The next generation will also need to be more diverse than ever, reflecting the demographic makeup of our communities and the rich knowledge bases that diversity produces. This chapter starts with an overview of why we need the next generation to be more diverse. Subsequent content then walks readers through how to select degree programs and continue needed education and training.

12.2 REFLECTING OUR COMMUNITIES

After reading this text, you know that disasters are not equal opportunity events. Historically marginalized people die, sustain injuries, and lose properties at higher rates than historically powerful groups. We need to change that reality, so that everyone has a chance to survive a disaster, respond with resilience, and recover swiftly. Clearly, work remains to be done as evidenced by the COVID-19 pandemic and disproportionate loss of life for racial and ethnic minorities, First Nations and indigenous people, and people living in impoverished regions of the world.

In 2017, experts outlined core competencies required of the next generation of professionals (see Chapter 2 to review). Across those core competencies, cultural understanding lies at the heart of how we create a safer world, reduce loss of life and injuries, safeguard properties and livelihoods, and improve resilience (Knox, Emrich, and Haupt 2019). Cultural competency requires that professionals have the knowledge, skills, abilities, and reflective depth to interact with and understand people across the diversity of our communities (Knox et al. 2019; see Box 12.1).

Yet, EM agencies have not reflected the diversity of our communities due to the historic evolution of the field from civil defense and military experience, with a higher percentage of people who are white and male. That reality has been changing, both in the practice of EM and in degree programs. The assumption is that active representation of a marginalized population makes a difference, by hiring people from historically oppressed groups, in percentages that mirror local populations (Provencio 2019).

Within EM degree programs, about 38% of U.S. students are women (Bennett 2019). We do not have solid data on the number or percentage or international

BOX 12.1

WHAT CULTURAL COMPETENCY CAN DO

Sociocultural literacy recognizes that risk is socially produced through systemic inequities, including racism, sexism, ableism, and homophobia (Webb 2016; Feldmann-Jensen et al. 2019). Why pursue cultural competency? Because it saves lives. By understanding other cultures, languages, and ways that people interact and communicate, an emergency manager can be more effective. Imagine the following:

- Writing a warning message that alerts people vacationing in Florida that a hurricane is approaching – and doing so in the languages from their countries of origin. Visitors numbered nearly 87 million people in 2020, with Canada, the U.K., Brazil, and Colombia as the countries with the most arrivals. Languages would have included (as a minimum) English, Portuguese, Spanish, and Sign Language, including words or signs (even in English) that differ in meaning from U.S.-based use. Travelers would have lacked experience with hurricanes as well as familiarity with the local area, where to find a shelter, and how to access information.

- Evacuating people requires knowing how people communicate and who they trust. In 2016, a rapid onset wildfire in Fort McMurray, Canada, led to the evacuation of 88,000 people. A large Muslim community, with limited emergency preparedness in the area, had a successful evacuation experience due to community-centered networking and established relationships among Muslim families. Sheltering then required culturally supportive arrangements suitable to gender, privacy, nutritional, clothing, and spiritual practices. Praying five times a day, for example, necessitated locations that enabled cleaning rituals, bowing, and prostrating (Mamuji and Rozdilsky 2019).

- Understanding that lesbian, gay, bisexual, transgender, and queer or questioning (LGBTQ+) people have left a home that felt safe to enter an environment fearing others might judge, bully, or harass – and creating a welcoming space where trauma ends at the door of the shelter. Families may have been separated during the disaster, and reunification will provide a healing and supportive environment. Resources and links to trusted organizations may have been disrupted as well, thus a supportive environment wherever one lands after evacuation or displacement truly makes a difference.

- Organizing post-disaster housing so that people with disabilities can leave the difficult life experienced in a shelter into housing that provides for mobility and independence. Accessible locations enable people to cook, bathe, sleep, care for families, and return to work. Journeys to work made more difficult by the disaster need to be considered, including increased accessible, affordable, and public transportation.

- Realizing well in advance that social inequities permeate people's disaster experiences, as witnessed in the COVID-19 pandemic from death and hospitalization rates to vaccine campaigns. We need to meet people where they live and work rather than expect them to come to us – disaster science has documented this and can absolutely make a life-saving difference. People died who could have lived with better mitigation by ordinary citizens, improved messaging from officials, and dedicated community outreach from trusted, credible leaders.

students, native or indigenous people, or members of LGBTQ+ communities in the field or in degree programs. One survey found that U.S. degree programs had observed a diversity increase in recent years (Bennett 2019). Some efforts have been changing the historic demographics of the field. One program, the Bill Anderson Fund (BAF), identifies promising disaster scientists and provides scholarships, mentoring, and networking. Another, called SURGE, has provided funding through the National Science Foundation to offer a diverse set of students with a first-hand research experience and mentoring (https://www.surgedisasters.com/team-leaders). The International Association of Women in Homeland Security and Emergency Management provides a similar set of connections as does the Gender and Disaster Network. The Institute for Diversity and Inclusion in Emergency Management (https://i-diem.org) trains women and people of color and works to reduce vulnerability and increase resilience. In Canada, Indigenous Services Canada partners with First Nations leadership to improve EM response.

By bringing more diverse voices and perspectives into the practice of EM, we enhance our abilities to connect with communities at risk and make the world a safer place. And, by understanding one's own history and culture as well as that of our surrounding communities, we enable everyone to practice EM more effectively. As you leave this introductory course in EM and disaster science, seek out opportunities to learn more. No matter how you identify, attend lectures, exhibits, and events, travel and learn languages from your own and other cultures and perspectives to broaden your knowledge, remembering that what you learn now may help you save lives later.

Next, let's work through some the challenges and the solutions to diversifying the next generation of EM professionals. Each section that follows includes a brief overview of what is known followed by strategies on how to increase active representation in educational programs and the practicing field.

12.2.1 Race, Ethnicity, and the Profession of Emergency Management

Research has clearly documented different disaster outcomes for people of color. Haitians, living in a situation of significant inequality, died in historic numbers during the 2010 earthquake. Even in the U.S., the percentage of people of color who died during Hurricane Katrina in 2005 was disproportionate to white residents (Sharkey 2007). To mitigate those impacts, experts have called for improved representation from those at risk, so that people hear warning messages and learn about risk from people they find credible – people like them. However, because we lack data on the number of historic minorities practicing EM, it is difficult to tell where we are and where we need to go. The Institute for Diversity and Inclusion in Emergency Management notes that while progress is being made, more hiring of people of color needs to occur (McKay 2021). Best estimates indicate that 60%–80% of emergency managers are white and concern exists that hiring practices result in people hiring new employees who look like them (McKay 2021). The Black Emergency Managers Association International embraces this approach, with a mission to:

> Provide information, networking, professional development opportunities to African-Descent homeland security and emergency management professionals. To advance the emergency management and homeland security profession within African-Descent,

and disadvantaged communities. To assist and ensure community involvement in all phases of emergency management to include funding and grant opportunities, training, preparedness, etc. with emphasis on the long-term recovery of the community.

12.2.2 Gender

Historically, the profession of EM has been a male-dominated field, although that has been changing, from firefighting to EM (Russo 2013; Parkinson, Duncan, and Archer 2019; Provencio 2019). But, again, concern exists that lack of representation has led to lack of consideration for those at highest risk. The 2015 earthquake that damaged Nepal pushed thousands of people into makeshift shelters, which quickly became dangerous for women and children. Aid agencies such as the UN funded safe spaces to reduce gender-based violence, offer female-friendly hygiene spaces, and privacy (UNFPA 2015; Phillips and Jenkins 2016). Fuller integration of women into the practice of EM can generate insights that will improve disaster response and recovery. About 33% of all students in EM programs are female, in numbers that have been slowly increasing (Cwiak 2014).

How do we increase active representation of women? An early study after the 1989 Loma Prieta earthquake looked at the experiences of women in the field of EM (Phillips 1990). Women indicated that several factors prompted their success, particularly holding credentials and experience. Yet, ten years after the Loma Prieta study, Wilson (1999) observed that little had changed to integrate women more fully into the field. Twenty years later, women have reported that one strategy is to move from one agency to another in order to move up rather than move within a single organization (Provencio 2019). Interestingly, and certainly relevant to EM, is how women may experience the glass cliff. The tendency is to promote women into difficult situations (in many kinds of businesses) where a higher failure rate occurs, thus leading women to fall off the glass cliff rather than shatter the glass ceiling that allows upward mobility (Ryan and Haslam 2005).

It was not until the 1990s under the Clinton administration that a woman reached the second-highest post in the U.S., Federal Emergency Management Agency (FEMA) Associate Director Kay Goss. Under the Obama Administration, Janet Napolitano became the highest-ranking woman in EM when she assumed directorship of the U.S. Department of Homeland Security (DHS). New Zealand promoted Sarah Stuart-Black as Director of its Civil Defence and Emergency Management agency in 2014. Seven years later, Deanne Criswell shattered FEMA's glass ceiling when President Biden elevated her from Director of New York City's Office of Emergency Management. Much can still be done to level the playing field for women in EM. Agency leadership must set the tone, by insuring that employees create and uphold a work environment that defines appropriate behavior and holds people accountable (Provencio 2017). An opportunity to secure a scholarship related to gender can be found in Box 12.2.

12.2.3 Indigenous People

Tribes and First Nations groups worldwide have struggled to become part of the EM picture and to be recognized as sovereign, self-governing entities. Yet their tribal lands

BOX 12.2

BRIDGING RESEARCH AND PRACTICE: THE LIFE OF MARY FRAN MYERS

Mary Ann Myers

The Mary Fran Myers Award, established in 2002 by the Gender and Disaster Network, recognizes that vulnerability to disasters and mass emergencies is influenced by social, cultural, and economic structures that marginalize women and girls. Research-based practice that reduces women's and girl's loss of life, injuries, and property can make a difference. The goal of the Gender and Disaster Network is to promote and encourage such an integration of research and practice.

Mary Fran Myers, Co-Director of the Natural Hazards Center at the University of Colorado at Boulder received the Award in 2002 before her untimely death in 2004. The Mary Fran Myers Award was so-named in order to recognize her sustained efforts to launch a worldwide network among disaster professionals, for advancing women's careers, and for promoting research on gender issues in disaster research in EM and higher education. A scholarship fund also exists to bring underrepresented individuals to the annual Natural Hazards Conference that she so stalwartly supported during her life.

For more information and a list of subsequent award winners, visit http://www.gd-nonline.org/mfm_award.php. For a partial list of research that her life inspired, visit http://www.colorado.edu/hazards/research/qr/. Source: Adapted from http://www.gdnonline.org/mfm_award.php, with permission.

and cultural resources sustain serious damage in disaster events. Along the U.S. Gulf Coast, for example, hurricanes, oil spills, and coastal erosion have decimated existing tribes by destroying homes, undermining abilities to engage in sustainable livelihoods, and separating families. The U.S., similar to many other nations, respects Federally *recognized* tribes as sovereign partners in EM planning and practice, although dozens of additional tribes continue to seek recognition.

The U.S. is home to 573 federally recognized tribes. FEMA has been building partnerships with tribes for some time. For example, the Cherokee Nation in Oklahoma serves as a regional warehouse for the Strategic National Stockpile used in major emergencies (Hershey 2019). Such partnerships prove incredibly vital, as influenza pandemics result in fatality rates four times as high for Native Americans (Hershey 2019). Trusted health care relationships truly matter, as found with stemming the COVID-19 pandemic that required extensive outreach among the Navajo Nation's 27,000 square miles (Close and Stone 2020; Kovich 2020). Indigenous populations may not always have such clear tribal boundaries, though, as found in New Zealand. There, the Māori may be found throughout both islands. Māori culture provided critical support after the 2011 Christchurch earthquake, particularly within urban networks that distributed resources and provided support (Phibbs, Kenney, and Solomon 2015).

Understanding people that maintain culturally distinct ways of life requires insight linked to effective practice. To improve EM and tribal relations, FEMA has launched efforts to work with Federally recognized tribes as part of ongoing planning, coordination, and collaboration. FEMA and DHS policies promote consultations, partnerships, and meaningful dialogues with American Indian and Alaska Native Tribal governments. The Tribal Emergency Management Association (iTEMA, with the "i" meaning Indian, indigenous, inter-Tribal, information, innovative, inclusive, and an "eye" to the future) in the U.S. has also formed. iTEMA pursues collaborative and multidisciplinary approaches to the life cycle of EM. The association organizes training, a conference, and support for its members (see https://itema.org, last accessed May 21, 2021).

12.2.4 An Accessible Workplace for All

Inabilities to meet disaster needs associated with disability have led to lawsuits and strong recommendations after failed mall evacuations, inaccessible shelters, and problems with temporary housing surfaced (National Council on Disability 2009; Stough, Ducy, and Kang 2017; Stough, Ducy, and Kang 2017; *Brou v. FEMA*; Chakraborty, Grineski, and Collins 2019). Similar to the argument about gendered EM practice, active representation of people with disabilities in every aspect of planning, preparedness, response, and recovery should improve outcomes for citizens with disabilities (National Council on Disability 2009).

FEMA's Office of Disability Integration and Coordination embraces the idea of the Whole Community, where emergency managers consider everyone across all phases of EM. First established in 2010, the Office has added disability integration specialists into Regional Incident Management Assistance Teams, delivered guidance about including people with disabilities in FEMA-funded initiatives, created Certified Deaf Interpreter positions, and deployed disability integration specialists to disaster sites. FEMA's Office now offers disability support via two branches. One branch, the Cadre Management and Training branch, sends Disability Integration Advisors and Disability Integration Specialists to disaster sites. Their technical expertise provides critical assistance to disaster managers. The second unit, the Program and Policy Branch, supports and strategizes with a wide array of stakeholders and offices to serve people with disabilities affected by disaster. They also publish the Disability Demographics and Program Utilization Report, which organizes data on FEMA programs. Most recently, the unit focused on providing information and resources to emergency managers and public health officials about COVID-19 vaccines and people with disabilities. Readers can get ready to help by taking courses in disability studies, gerontology, and sign language.

12.2.5 LGBTQ+

Certainly, the last decade has been extraordinary in pushing forward the rights of lesbian, gay, bisexual, transgender, and intersex (LGBTQ+) people. Though limited studies exist on the experiences and needs of LGBTQ+ populations during disasters and none on the career paths of people who are LGBTQ+, we are certainly poised at a point where such information can accumulate and have an impact. For example, studies find that lack of consideration of LGBTQ+ disaster survivors leads to loss of a safe home, familial separation, exposure and discrimination in shelters and post-disaster recovery, and trauma (Eads 2002; D'Ooge 2008; Balgos, Gaillard, and Sanz 2012; Stukes 2013; Dominey-Howes, Gorman-Murray, and McKinnon 2014; Gorman-Murray, McKinnon, and Dominey-Howes 2016; Gorman-Murray et al. 2017; Parkinson et al. 2021).

Opportunities exist for LGBTQ+ individuals to move into EM with protections under the law. The U.S., for example, supports the employment rights of all people. According to the U.S. Equal Employment Opportunity Commission, Title VII protects applicants and employees from discrimination and bias. Court decisions and Commission work have secured policy changes and money for those who have experienced discrimination such as not being hired due to being LGBTQ+, being fired after a gender transition, being denied access to a restroom because of gender identity, losing a promotion due to being LGBTQ+, or being harassed. The Executive Branch has also taken action toward greater equality for all workers. Operating from an assumption that people should be judged only from their "ability to get the job done," President Obama signed Executive Order 13672 prohibiting Federal contractors from discrimination, including sexual orientation and gender identity, which subsequent presidents continued.

How can EM students become more aware and supportive of LGBTQ+ colleagues and future disaster survivors they will serve? Campuses offer ALLY groups, where anyone can join and support LGBTQ+ students. Students who are in LGBTQ+ populations can contact campus student organizations, off-campus associations, and institutional offices that ensure rights are protected and people are respected. EM faculty also bear responsibility to ensure that classrooms are safe spaces for all students and to promote an inclusive learning environment. The same is true for emergency managers who must lead by example, mentor all members of the workforce, and exhibit "zero tolerance toward sexism and homophobia" (Parkinson et al. 2021).

12.2.6 Guidance for Everyone: Mentors and Networking

What else can you do to increase your career possibilities? Perhaps the most important relationship that you can build comes from selecting a mentor in the field. A mentor guides, advises, and encourages as you enter and move through the profession. A mentor can identify pitfalls and problems, offer solutions, and be there to listen to your questions.

Choose wisely when selecting a mentor and consider several people to provide you with good guidance. While someone with political pull or connections might lure you and should be respected, you will want a mentor with your best interests at heart – not their own career. Choose someone with a career path similar to the one that you want who has good people skills and time to spend with you. How do you find such a person? Attend conferences, join committees, serve on task forces, and get to know people. Your willingness to step up and serve will garner the attention of prospective mentors, open them up to serving in such a role, and build your resume and networks at the same time. It is likely that a mentor will emerge over time as you get to know people in the profession.

One recent effort to provide mentoring, specific to future disaster scientists, comes from the William Averette Anderson Fund (see Box 12.3). Dr. Bill Anderson, a graduate of The Ohio State University's Disaster Research Center, served as a graduate research assistant to Russell Dynes and E.L. Quarantelli. Dr. Anderson went on to work at the National Science Foundation, guiding and funding much of the disaster research in the U.S. that has informed this text. His career included serving at the World Bank and then the U.S. National Academies. His prestigious career focused on encouraging the "next generation" of scholars and practitioners, particularly historically underrepresented students and scholars. Those he mentored supported the development of a scholarship fund in his memory (https://billandersonfund.org/). Participating students benefit from a Mentor Network of professionals in the field. Mentors are matched to a mentee with similar interests and goals and have monthly meetings to assist with their professional development. Royalties from the dollars you spent on this book support the BAF and similar scholarships.

12.2.7 Fellowships and Scholarships

A number of opportunities afford you the chance to gain additional experience and even funding during your studies, for both EM students and future disaster scientists. In the U.S., The National Science Foundation has funded a number of Research Experiences for Undergraduates Sites (REUs). An REU site brings students in from across

BOX 12.3

BILL ANDERSON FELLOW: AN APPLIED LINGUIST IN EMERGENCY MANAGEMENT

There is a Japanese proverb, *jyunin toiro*, which literally means "ten people ten colors," implying that everyone has a different point of view. If I ask a question, "What does emergency management mean to you?" to ten readers of this book, I am quite sure that I will get ten different kinds of responses. This reflects the interdisciplinary characteristic of the field of hazard and disaster studies. For me, emergency management means overcoming language barriers for linguistic minorities throughout the life cycle of disasters. In what follows, I would like to highlight some key moments in my journey in the field of hazards and disasters as a graduate student with a background not traditionally associated with emergency management.

In May 2011, I earned my MA degree in Teaching English as a Second Language from Oklahoma State University (OSU). In October of the same year, I began working at Hokkaido University of Education (HUE) in Japan as a specially appointed lecturer in English as a Foreign Language. Five years later, in April 2016, massive subsequent earthquakes struck the Kyushu (southern) region of Japan. Several days after the earthquakes, a student from my English Communication class decided to volunteer as an English translator for a website being developed for English-speaking residents in Kyushu who were affected by the earthquakes. As I was giving feedback on her drafts, I realized the value for developing a language learning curriculum for university-aged volunteers in response to the growing needs for multilingual assistance in the event of an emergency in Japan.

As an American born and raised in Japan, I see a significant value in offering foreign language classes that focus on risk communication for those living in multicultural/multilingual communities. The tutoring session with my student reignited my passion for multilingual emergency assistance, an idea that I have been contemplating since the 2011 Great East Japan Earthquake. In Fall 2017, after fully completing my five-year contract with HUE, I returned to OSU to pursue a doctoral degree in Applied Linguistics and Teaching English to Speakers of Other Languages.

My dissertation project focuses on linguistic analyses of Japanese and English disaster warnings from the perspective of sociolinguistics, cross-cultural pragmatics, and multimodal communication. I have conducted several research projects within the framework of the following broad research questions: (1) *What are some cultural and situational-specific linguistic features of risk communication*? (2) *How are these features perceived by the general public*? For example, one of my current projects examines the interplay of linguistic and nonlinguistic features in framing urgency in a tsunami warning on Japanese television news.

One of the highlights of my graduate school experience is becoming a BAF Fellow in 2019. Through mentorship, regular webinars, and workshops, BAF has given me professional support and opportunities to gain deeper understanding of the field and helped me become part of a large family of hazards and disasters researchers and practitioners. My journey so far also would have not been possible without the continued support from my family and friends as well as from my dissertation committee members, Dr. Carol Moder, Dr. Dennis Preston, Dr. Stephanie Link, and Dr. Dave Neal, who believed in the value of my research.

At a first glance, emergency management may seem the preserve of those with specific academic backgrounds and trainings. However, in actuality, the field has a long history of robust interdisciplinary research and practices. I encourage the readers of this book to bring their chairs and join the conversation and work as we confront the challenges of developing more disaster-resilient communities.

~Amy Takebe, Doctoral Candidate, Oklahoma State University.

the nation to learn how to conduct disaster science research. Opportunities to apply are advertised widely at conferences, on websites, and through special announcements. Prospective REU students compete to earn a funded slot. They live at a university for the summer while being instructed on how to conduct disaster research. Students work with a mentor from their home institution to design and carry out a research project. Their funding includes opportunities to travel to and present at professional conferences. North Dakota State University, for example, offered one on cybersecurity, and encouraged women and underrepresented students to apply. Also in the U.S., the DHS has funded students as DHS-STEM (science, technology, engineering, and mathematics) Scholarship awardees. DHS awards recipients complete tuition and fees along with a monthly stipend to support their education toward a career in homeland.

12.2.8 Internships and Practical Experience

EM graduates often worry about the wording in job announcements that requires experience. Understandably, a community would not want just anyone writing emergency plans or deciding when and how to issue a warning. While courses and degrees do separate you from the pack of resumes on someone's desk, experience serves as an additional qualifier. But, how to acquire experience? Throughout this text, we have pointed out opportunities for volunteer service. Another form of volunteerism, sometimes paid, comes through internships. An intern serves in an office of EM (or similar location) and supports the professional staff. Activities can range from administrative support to operational aspects, depending on the location and need. Increasingly, agencies are offering internship opportunities for academic credit, although some may offer salary or transportation support.

Academic programs often offer structured opportunities and connections, so check with your academic advisor. You may also be able to secure an internship on your own by contacting an EM agency. Many list internships on their websites along with deadlines and requirements. Consider also reaching out to a local business or agency that could benefit from your EM knowledge and help with a mitigation assessment or business continuity plan. If you do secure an internship on your own and are still in college, though, be sure to ask for academic credit, which will look good on a transcript as well as your resume.

12.3 CONTINUING YOUR EDUCATION

Most EM positions now require a degree, particularly one in the discipline of disaster science. Securing a degree enhances your potential to pursue an EM career and also serves as a foundation for the core competencies expected of today's practitioners.

12.3.1 Undergraduate Degree Programs

Undergraduate programs typically produce students with a bachelor degree in EM, humanitarian work, or homeland security. Depending on your interests, you may want to consider adding a minor, certificate, or second major. If you are interested in helping survivors, for example, psychology and social work represent possible choices. For those interested in public service, a degree in political science or public administration may be wise. Students anticipating a future in the private sector would be smart to take business, management, health care, or hospitality courses. Criminal justice, forensics, and computer sciences allow you to map out a prospective career in homeland security and cyberthreats. Pandemic planning requires expertise in health care delivery systems along with EM. You may even wish to specialize in areas like disability studies, indigenous people, or gerontology. Preparing for and responding to hazardous materials events requires knowledge of chemical, radiological, nuclear, and biological hazards. In short, supplement EM with a strong set of general education courses, a minor and/or certificate, and a second language to enhance your abilities to communicate information, interact with other cultures, and build community partnerships. In addition to content, general education courses (sociology, English, philosophy, math) increase critical thinking, problem-solving, writing, and communication skills.

Next, determine how long the program has been in existence. Is this a well-established program or is it new? While both have merit, established programs likely have a record of their alumni on their website – look at the kinds of jobs they now hold. Next, examine the credentials of faculty members. Do they have a degree appropriate to the field? You will want faculty who have mastered the discipline, defined as a substantive body of knowledge tied to a particular profession (Phillips 2015). Increasingly, faculty hold degrees in the discipline of disaster science and view EM practice through an interdisciplinary lens. Look at their research interests. Publications listed on a curriculum vitae (CV) indicate the faculty member actively conducts research in the field and is recognized by their colleagues as an expert. Next, look at the list of courses that the faculty members teach. What will you learn from them? Then, look at the kind of service work, consulting, and practical experience they list on their CV.

The program's curriculum is important to consider too. Traditionally, EM degrees organize around the phases of disaster but may deviate or provide additional options to enhance your career path. For example, the University of Nebraska Omaha offers a classic degree model as well as a number of concentrations, including gerontology, public health, and Tribal Management. Take the time to look at course offerings too. Do the courses provide a broad range of knowledge so that you can have a wide array of knowledge and career options? Increasingly, programs are offering traditional disciplinary courses with substantive content (e.g., planning) as well as methods, theory, and a capstone (Phillips 2005, 2015). You will learn valuable analytical skills in such courses.

12.3.2 Graduate Programs

Similar concerns should drive your inquiries about a graduate degree but far more intensely. The critical feature of any graduate program should be the existence of highly qualified faculty who engage in research, know the profession, understand and contribute to informed practice, and have an established record as a successful mentor. Their CV's should demonstrate a continuing commitment to an area of expertise in which you hold an interest. Students who have graduated under their supervision should have secured employment and contributed to the field as professionals.

At the master's level, you may be able to choose between a terminal or professional degree or a more traditional graduate degree. The first results in completing your education with a master's degree in the field and moving into practice upon graduation. The program curriculum should reflect that practitioner orientation, but again should be situated in the body of disaster science, relevant policies, and established practices. Although you might not write a master's thesis, you should still graduate with skills for program assessment, community-based surveys, and an ability to read disaster studies.

The more traditional master's degree moves students into a doctorate-level program (see Box 12.4). To do so, you should have a strong background in a relevant area

BOX 12.4

PURSUING GRADUATE STUDIES

The path to my current role wasn't linear; I sort of stumbled my way into the nexus of urban planning and disaster science. In fact, it was the Hazard Reduction and Recovery Center located at Texas A&M University that initially drew my interest, and it just so happened to be located in the Department of Landscape Architecture and Urban Planning.

I am a first-generation college kid born and raised in inner city Dallas, Texas. I grew up about seven minutes outside of downtown in a neighborhood by the name of Oakcliff. The street that I grew up on specifically was a street named Stanley Smith Drive and the street perpendicular to mine was a street by the name of Prosperity Avenue. The ironic thing was that there was nothing prosperous about the neighborhood. It was a low-income Black and Latino community that was marginalized in terms of food, housing, infrastructure, economic opportunities, education, land use, you name it. A textbook example of what scholars today would deem an environmental justice community.

Growing up I didn't know that, but I did notice however that when I traveled across town to other communities, mostly white, there was a stark difference in the quality of the built environment. I also noticed the ways in which my family was impacted particularly by the environmental conditions that plagued our community from the air quality and my sister's acute and severe asthmatic episodes to poor drainage infrastructure and my family's house flooding. Those experiences and intuition led me here and have shaped my current planning research agenda. That research began in public health, but I realized once I started the PhD in planning that a lot of challenges that public health practitioners attempt to intervene on could have and should have been mitigated on the front end through good fundamental urban planning.

Within the field of urban environmental planning, my primary research interests include infrastructure planning and management, hazard mitigation, social vulnerability to disaster, environmental justice, sustainable development, public health and the built environment, and participatory action research. I use a mixed methods approach to my research that incorporates quantitative, qualitative, and applied methods such as multiple regression, cross sectional research, condition and damage assessment, spatial mapping, in-depth interviewing, participatory action research (e.g., visual inspection, photography, photo-voice, environmental sampling), and different forms of spatial and analytic epidemiology. At the intersection of my work, I use a combined social vulnerability to disaster and environmental justice framework to ensure that low income and communities of color are planned and accounted for, emphasizing participation and action in light of, for example, everyday urban stormwater management and extreme events such as urban flooding. More specifically, I investigate how the socio-spatial dynamics related to the inventory, condition, and distribution of critical infrastructures and public works, mainly water infrastructure (i.e., stormwater, wastewater, and drinking water) and green space, can modify risks of hazard exposure, resulting disaster impacts, public health outcomes, and opportunities for community resilience.

To date, I have primarily worked to understand how social processes and development patterns create hazardous human-built environments and vulnerable infrastructure and the related urban stormwater management and flood risks. I have developed and implemented participatory actions, methods, and techniques that create and advance sustainable design, planning, and development decision-making of communities to mitigate risks, achieve healthier, more equitable places and resilient natural, built, and social environments. Community engagement is the cornerstone of my research program and using socially and practical innovative approaches to address complex challenges. I believe in the importance of creating long-term change through co-learning with communities around strategic needs while supporting communities in actualizing their own resilience. I work collaboratively to increase a community's adaptive capacity through community action and "citizen science." By incorporating applied research into a rigorous academic research and teaching agenda, I facilitate a co-learning relationship between students, academic researchers, and community partners, particularly underserved and marginalized communities, to create a collaborative synergy where everyone involved understands that their contribution is important. My work has demonstrated the potential for "citizen science" to guide future conversations about what additional knowledge is necessary and what strategies are most appropriate for addressing complex issues linked to infrastructure and community resilience.

~Marccus Hendricks, Ph.D., Assistant Professor; University of Maryland; https://arch.umd.edu/people/marccus-hendricks.

Marccus Hendricks

with a degree naming that discipline (e.g., sociology, geography, psychology, and EM). Your credentials to enter a doctorate-level program should be exceptionally strong to compete for funding to pay for your education. Most people with doctorates lead agencies, work as consultants, and teach in degree programs.

A concern relevant to many students in the field stems from their personal situation. Many nontraditional or older students attempt to earn a graduate degree while working part- or full-time in the field. Doing so can be challenging as disasters do not respect the academic schedule and you do have to go to work. However, nontraditional age students often make up the majority of those matriculated in graduate programs and bring a valued sense of realism to the content and course discussion. Prospective students should look at the institution offering the degree and speak with faculty to ascertain their level of support and understanding about nontraditional students.

12.3.3 Online Degree Programs

Finally, an increasing number of institutions offer online courses or degrees. If you choose such a program, be sure to look at several aspects. First, how much experience do the faculty members have in offering distance courses? Do they hold certifications in online teaching? Have they published their approaches to distance education? Second, how do those programs offer online content? Education works most effectively when people have the chance to exchange views, ask questions, and actively interrogate the assigned reading. In short, synchronous courses usually offer a more meaningful educational experience than asynchronous courses that do not allow for much interaction. Choose a program that allows for exchange between yourself, the professor, and the other students. Features that allow you to do so foster a collaborative learning environment that benefits *you*. Look for programs that use chat rooms, online video conferencing, video instruction, e-mail, and social media. Assess the program's potential delivery of that content and desired interaction by how rapidly and *thoughtfully* your future professor responds to an e-mail inquiry. Ask for an online videoconference to see how effective they are at using the technology and how well they communicate with you – prior to spending thousands of dollars in tuition.

12.3.4 Continuing Education

Many organizations and jurisdictions offer continuing education, which is skill specific and usually occurs over a short time period like Cardiopulmonary Resuscitation (CPR) training or a longer time like pandemic planning. Options include training and badging, exercises and drills, conferences and workshops, and reading professional and scientific journals.

12.3.4.1 Training

Training is important for any professional to remain current. For example, after National Incident Management System (NIMS) became a foundation for disaster response, DHS, state EM offices, and others offered NIMS training. The same has been true to increase understanding around social vulnerability, such as how to meet the functional needs of people with disabilities. Depending on local hazards, you may be able to take a variety of classes from your EM agency (local or state) or an agency like the Red Cross or special units like the Medical Reserve Corps. Many agencies, like FEMA, sponsor independent study courses that can be taken for certification. Their sequences include a Professional Development Series that is listed in many of their job announcements (visit their site at http://training.fema.gov/IS/crslist.asp). FEMA also brings emergency managers into their campus in Emmittsburg,

Maryland, for more intensive workshops and classes (for a listing, see http://training. fema.gov/EMICourses/). International Association of Emergency Managers (IAEM) also sponsors testing to secure the Certified Emergency Management credential.

In recent years, badging has become popular. A number of institutions and agencies now offer online courses at low rates that enable students to earn badges. Those badges can be displayed digitally on job applications or social media accounts.

12.3.4.2 Exercises and Drills

Most jurisdictions plan some type of exercise or drill ranging from tabletop walk-throughs of emergency operations plans to full-scale exercises where people enact specific roles under a scripted scenario. Take these opportunities to gain insight into how partners work together to address a threat event, the challenges they encounter, and the strategies they use to overcome them.

Increasingly, we are seeing opportunities for students to participate in exercises. A recent event held in Columbus, Ohio, for example, involved hundreds of students as walk-through participants in a Point of Distribution (POD). Their efforts paid off, as seen at vaccine clinics during the COVID-19 pandemic. Participating gives you the opportunity to observe how PODs operate and exposes you to the widespread effort needed to take care of people in such an event. COVID-19 clinics relied on that rehearsal during a life-saving launch to stem the virus. Look for such opportunities to observe EM in operation.

12.3.4.3 Conferences, Workshops

People build networks by working together, typically across organizations. Another way to build networks is to attend conferences and workshops in the field. Most states have EM organizations that host annual events and often cohost special workshops or training at regular intervals. You may want to look for other relevant events, like the Ohio Safety Congress & Expo where you can find information on hazardous materials, working with construction companies and utilities, worker safety, business continuity, and more.

A number of organizations also host conferences on an annual basis, such as the Natural Hazards Workshop offered through the University of Colorado at Boulder or the National Hurricane Conference. Regional FEMA offices sponsor workshops on various topics as do FEMA, DHS, and other Federal agencies tasked with EM roles. Joining list serves helps you to keep informed on upcoming conferences. The IAEM (www.iaem.org), the Natural Hazards Center (www.colorado.edu/hazards), and others disseminate information routinely on conferences and workshops.

12.3.4.4 Professional and Scientific Journals

All professions publish various kinds of newsletters and journals, which should be reviewed for useful content and information. Most professional associations, like IAEM, also distribute information routinely and widely to benefit practitioners. Look for those sources of information and connect via list serves, subscriptions, or social media. Scientific journals should also be reviewed regularly. Numerous, outstanding journals exist in disaster science and produce helpful insights and actionable results. The value of scientific journals, like the *International Journal of Mass Emergencies*

BOX 12.5

AN INTERDISCIPLINARY JOURNEY IN HAZARDS AND DISASTERS RESEARCH

Santina L. Contreras

From an early age, I was drawn to the study of hazards and disasters. Growing up in an area exposed to a myriad of hazard risks and seeing many first-hand examples of the impacts that poor planning can have on vulnerable communities, I felt a strong drive to make an impact in this space. I started my journey motivated toward addressing issues related to earthquakes and the provision of safe and adequate housing. I studied structural engineering, obtaining a Bachelor of Science from the University of California, San Diego (2007), and a Master of Science from the University of California, Berkeley (2008). Upon graduating, an opportunity presented itself to work with a nonprofit organization on their post-disaster (2006 East Indian Ocean Tsunami) housing reconstruction program in West Sumatra, Indonesia. Through this experience and my subsequent work as an engineer, I became more conscious of the limitations of using discrete, technical approaches toward tackling hazard issues. Furthermore, I became attentive to the specific ways broader social and systematic factors contribute to the success and equitability of disaster planning initiatives and the critical role local community empowerment plays in the resilience-building process.

In an effort toward addressing these gaps, I decided to expand my training and disciplinary reach by obtaining a PhD in Planning, Policy, and Design at the University of California, Irvine (2016). I then went on to hold positions at the University of Colorado Boulder (Postdoctoral Research Associate in Environmental Design and Researcher-in-Residence at the Natural Hazards Center), Ohio State University (Assistant Professor of City and Regional Planning), and currently at the University of Southern California (Assistant Professor of Urban Planning and Spatial Analysis).

Guided by the knowledge gained throughout my journey, I now work toward making interdisciplinary contributions toward the study of hazards and disasters. My research and teaching center on the intersecting spaces of environmental hazards, international development, and community development planning. In this work, I focus on understanding relationships between local communities and external stakeholders surrounding natural hazard events, environmental planning efforts, and international development projects. I hope that my journey shows that while your path may involve a winding road, it can lead to hidden opportunities for creating new spaces and making unique contributions to the disaster field.

~Santina L. Contreras, PhD, Assistant Professor, University of Southern California; https://priceschool.usc.edu/people/santina-contreras/.

and Disasters (the oldest in the field), rely on blind, peer review to critique the contents before publication. Doing so increases confidence in the scientific community that the journal publication produces useful information and insights. The courses that you will take as an undergraduate will especially prepare you to read these journal articles, which your professors rely on, contribute to, and use in the classroom.

12.4 FINDING YOUR FIRST EMPLOYER

In 2020, the median salary in the U.S. for emergency managers was $76,250 annually (see https://www.bls.gov/ooh/management/emergency-management-directors.htmper, last accessed May 6, 2021; check for updates). Consider that the EM career median is twice that of an emergency medical technician (EMT) or paramedic ($36,650) and is higher than that of a firefighter ($52,500) or a police officer ($67,290). The EM career outlook is good, with an expected 4% growth in jobs through to 2029.

It may be that an internship or temporary job serves as your entrance to an EM position. Or, because you pursued a solid EM education and secured proper certifications, you will be offered an entry-level position. Perhaps you are moving from fire or police work into EM, or from the military into a new profession. Maybe you will find that the interdisciplinary set of studies you pursued leads you in exciting and meaningful directions (see Box 12.5).

Finding jobs starts with searching carefully and continuing to apply for the positions that suit your talents. Traditional job search sites, local or state agency websites, or social media can lead to options (e.g., search LinkedIn or join https://www.facebook.com/groups/EMJobBoard). Watch human resource pages for agencies that interest you and when disaster strikes, be ready to go where the new jobs appear.

Use your institution's resources as well. Most campuses have career offices where you can create a resume, practice interviews, and get help finding a job. Be sure to develop your resume with input from your faculty too, and highlight degrees, course

BOX 12.6

BECOMING A CERTIFIED EMERGENCY MANAGER

Susamma Chacko-Seeley

In 2007, I started a master's degree in Emergency and Disaster Management and I went to my first IAEM Annual Conference. During this conference, I was exposed to many new aspects including the CEM Program. After the conference, I became a member of IAEM. For a new member just starting a degree, pursuing the CEM designation seemed a daunting task. Once I finished my degree and spent more time in the field doing the work of an emergency manager, attaining my CEM would become extremely valuable and professionally significant. As the only nationally and internationally recognized professional certification for individual emergency managers, achieving the CEM designation indicates than one possesses a certain level of education, experience, knowledge, training, work history, and most importantly, contributions to the field.

Although I had my degree in hand, I chose to wait until 2014 to apply for the CEM in order to gain more experience in the field to understand the true impact of our work. Our field is one where we make many decisions for people and communities, and ethical decision-making is vital. Given this, I understood a degree alone was insufficient to guide ethical decisions. In fact, since the CEM program requires a certain level of experience in order to achieve the designation, it ensures that individual emergency managers are exposed to varying situations and people, including volunteer or pro bono work that furthers the profession. It is during these opportunities where I realized that working to achieve the CEM designation actually ensured the experience I gained enhanced the framework provided by the degree. For more information about this program, one can go to the IAEM website (www.iaem.com) and click on the *Certification* tab.

~Susamma Chacko-Seeley, MPA, CEM, is now a doctoral candidate at the Disaster Research Center, University of Delaware.

content, internships, class projects, volunteer work, and paid employment that demonstrates your abilities. Begin work toward securing your eventual Certified Emergency Manager (CEM) designation (see Box 12.6).

Your own journey has just begun and we wish you well as you move into the profession of EM. May you make a *difference*.

***

SUMMARY

This chapter provides an overview of opportunities for those intent on joining the next generation of EM professionals. The next generation cadre of colleagues will be more diverse than ever in the history of the field, as an appropriate reflection of the people they will serve. Becoming a professional in this field will require lifelong learning through internships, training, and more educational opportunities. Never stop learning and always commit yourself to immersing yourself in moments that will provide you with enrichment and growth. Find a mentor and learn from their guidance, wisdom, and mistakes. Pursue experience through internships, training, volunteerism, and temporary assignments. Hold fast to ethical principles and commit to earning and keeping the public trust that emergency managers need to inspire people to prepare for and be resilient to disasters and hazards they will encounter.

Discussion Questions

1. What are the three things that you should do to prepare yourself for a career in EM?
2. Where does EM need to improve in terms of active representation and why?
3. Where in your community might you find a place to secure practical experience in an internship or through a volunteer experience?
4. What additional courses should you take to be the best emergency manager or disaster scientist you can be?
5. Identify three possible mentors for you in EM and disaster science. What makes them a good mentor?
6. What fellowships or scholarships are available for you at your institution? What about in other places that pertain to EM and disaster science?

Summary Questions

1. Explain active representation. Why is it relevant to EM? What is its value?
2. Define cultural competency and why it is relevant for EM and disaster science. How does it reflect the core competency of sociocultural literacy?
3. What should you look for in a quality online program?
4. What kinds of qualities should you look for in a mentor?
5. Why should you begin working toward a certified emergency management (CEM) designation?

REFERENCES

Balgos, Benigno, J. C. Gaillard, and Kristinne Sanz. 2012. "The Warias of Indonesia in Disaster Risk Reduction: The Case of the 2010 Mt Merapi Eruption in Indonesia." *Gender & Development* 20(2): 337–348.

Bennett, DeeDee M. 2019. "Diversity in Emergency Management Scholarship." *Journal of Emergency Management* 17(2): 148–154.

Chakraborty, Jayajit, Sara E. Grineski, and Timothy W. Collins. 2019. "Hurricane Harvey and People with Disabilities: Disproportionate Exposure to Flooding in Houston, Texas." *Social Science & Medicine* 226: 176–181.

Close, Ryan M. and Myles J. Stone. 2020. "Contact Tracing for Native Americans in Rural Arizona." *New England Journal of Medicine* 383(3): e15.

Cwiak, Carol. 2014. *Emergency Management Higher Education Today: The 2014 FEMA Higher Education Program Survey.* Presented at the FEMA Higher Education Symposium, Emmittsburg, Maryland.

Cwiak, Carol L., Ronald Campbell, Matthew G. Cassavechia, Chuck Haynes, Lanita A. Lloyd, Neil Brockway, George O. Navarini, Byron E. Piatt, and Mary Senger. 2017. "Emergency Management Leadership in 2030: Shaping the Next Generation Meta-leader." *Journal of Emergency Management* 15(2): 81–97.

Dominey-Howes, Dale, Andrew Gorman-Murray, and Scott McKinnon. 2014. "Queering Disasters: On the Need to Account for LGBTI Experiences in Natural Disaster Contexts." *Gender, Place & Culture* 21(7): 905–918.

D'Ooge, Charlotte. 2008. "Queer Katrina: Gender and Sexual Orientation Matters in the Aftermath of the Disaster." Pp. 22–24 in *Katrina and the Women of New Orleans*, ed. Beth Willinger. New Orleans: Newcomb College Center for Research on Women, Tulane University.

Eads, Marci. 2002. "Marginalized Groups in Times of Crisis: Identity, Needs, and Response" Quick Response Report #152. Boulder, Colorado: Natural Hazards Research and Applications Information Center, University of Colorado. Available at http://www.colorado.edu/hazards/qr/qr152/qr152.html, last accessed May 22, 2011.

Feldmann-Jensen, Shirley, Steven J. Jensen, Sandy Maxwell Smith, and Gregory Vigneaux. 2019. "The Next Generation Core Competencies for Emergency Management." *Journal of Emergency Management* 17(1): 17–25.

Gorman-Murray, Andrew W., Sally Morris, Jessica Keppel, Scott McKinnon, and Dale Dominey-Howes. 2017. "Problems and Possibilities on the Margins: LGBT Experiences in the 2011 Queensland floods." *Gender, Place & Culture* 24(1): 37–51.

Gorman-Murray, Andrew W., Scott J. McKinnon, and Dale Dominey-Howes. 2016. "Masculinity, Sexuality and Disaster: Unpacking Gendered LGBT Experiences in the 2011 Brisbane Floods in Queensland, Australia." Pp. 128–139 in *Men, Masculinities and Disaster*, eds. E. Enarson and B. Pease. Abingdon: Routledge.

Hershey, Tina Batra. 2019. "Collaborating with Sovereign Tribal Nations to Legally Prepare for Public Health Emergencies." *The Journal of Law, Medicine & Ethics* 47(2): 55–58.

Knox, Claire Connolly, Christopher T. Emrich, and Brittani Haupt. 2019. "Advancing Emergency Management Higher Education: Importance of cultural competence scholarship." *Journal of Emergency Management* 17(2): 111–117.

Kovich, Heather. 2020. "Rural matters—Coronavirus and the Navajo nation." *New England Journal of Medicine* 383(2): 105–107.

Mamuji, Aaida A. and Jack L. Rozdilsky. 2019. "Canada's 2016 Fort McMurray Wildfire Evacuation: Experiences of the Muslim Community." *International Journal of Emergency Management* 15(2): 125–146.

McKay, Jim. 2021. "Emergency Management Profession Needs Diversity to Adapt." Available at https://www.govtech.com/em/safety/emergency-management-profession-needs-diversity-to-adapt, last accessed September 17, 2021.

National Council on Disability. 2009. *Effective Emergency Management: Making Improvements for Communities and People with Disabilities.* Washington, DC: National Council on Disability. Available at www.ncd.gov, last accessed December 21, 2010.

Parkinson, Debra, Alyssa Duncan, and Frank Archer. 2019. "Barriers and Enablers to Women in Fire and Emergency Leadership Roles." *Gender in Management: An International Journal* 34/2: 78–93.

Parkinson, D., Alyssa Duncan, William Leonard, and Frank Archer. 2021. "Lesbian and Bisexual Women's Experience of Emergency Management." *Gender Issues* 1–24. doi: 10.1007/s12147-021-09276-5

Phibbs, S., Kenney, C., and Solomon, M. 2015. Ngā Mōwaho: An Analysis of Māori Responses to the Christchurch Earthquakes. *Kōtuitui: New Zealand Journal of Social Sciences Online,* 10(2): 72–82.

Phillips, Brenda. 1990. "Gender as a Variable in Emergency Response." Pp. 84–90 in *The Loma Prieta Earthquake: Studies of Short-Term Impacts,* ed. Robert Bolin. Boulder: University of Colorado Institute of Behavioral Science.

Phillips, Brenda. 2005. "Disasters as a Discipline: The Status of Emergency Management Education in the U.S." *International Journal of Mass Emergencies and Disasters* 23(1): 85–110.

Phillips, Brenda. 2015. "Disasters by Discipline Revisited: A Ten-Year Retrospective and a Look Ahead." Keynote Speech, FEMA Higher Education Symposium, Emmittsburg, MD.

Phillips, Brenda and Pamela Jenkins. 2016/Forthcoming. "Gender-based Violence and Disasters: South Asia in Comparative Perspective." Pp. 225–250 in *Gender, Women and Disasters: Survival, Security and Development,* eds. Linda Racioppi and Swarna Prajnya. New York: Routledge.

Provencio, Alyssa L. (2017). *Gender and Representative Bureaucracy: Opportunities and Barriers in Local Emergency Management Agencies.* Stillwater, OK: Oklahoma State University.

Provencio, Alyssa L. (2019). "Gender and representative bureaucracy: A qualitative look at opportunities and barriers for women in local emergency management agencies." Pp. 285–302 in *Emerging Voices in Natural Hazards Research.* Butterworth-Heinemann.

Quarantelli, E. L. 1996. "The Future is Not the Past Repeated: Projecting Disasters in the 21st Century from Current Trends." *Journal of Contingencies and Crisis Management* 4(4): 228–240.

Russo, Barbara Rose. 2013. "Women Firefighters' Strategies for Advancement in the Fire Service: Breaking down Barriers in Gender-based occupations." PhD diss., Oklahoma State University.

Ryan, Michelle K. and S. Alexander Haslam. 2005. "The Glass Cliff: Evidence that Women Are Over-represented in Precarious Leadership Positions." *British Journal of management* 16(2): 81–90.

Sharkey, Peter. 2007. "Survival and Death in New Orleans." *Journal of Black Studies* 37(4): 482–501.

Stough, Laura M., Elizabeth McAdams Ducy, and Donghyun Kang. 2017. "Addressing the Needs of Children with Disabilities Experiencing Disaster or Terrorism." *Current Psychiatry Reports* 19(4): 24.

Stukes, Patricia. 2013. "Gay Christian Service: Exploring Social Vulnerability and Capacity Building of Lesbian, Gay, Bisexual, Transgender, and Intersex Identified Individuals and Organizational Advocacy in Two Post Katrina Disaster Environments." Doctoral Dissertation, Department of Sociology, Texas Woman's University.

UNFPA. 2015. News on the Earthquake in Nepal, Overview. Available at http://www.unfpa.org/emergencies/earthquake-nepal, last accessed January 6, 2016.

Webb, Gary R. 2016. "Emergency Management and Local Services during Disasters." Pp. 329–335 in *Guide to Urban Politics and Policy,* eds. Christine Palus and Richardson Dilworth. Los Angeles: Sage.

Wilson, Jennifer. 1999. "Professionalization and Gender in Local Emergency Management." *International Journal of Mass Emergencies and Disasters* 17(1): 111–122.

RESOURCES (ACCESSED MAY 18, 2021)

- Institute for Diversity and Inclusion in Emergency Management; https://i-diem.org/.
- Black Association of Emergency Managers International; http://www.blackemergmanag-ersassociation.org/.
- International Network of Women in Emergency Management and Homeland Security; https://www.linkedin.com/company/international-network-of-women-in-emergency-management/.
- IAEM; https://www.iaem.org/.
- FEMA Office of Disability and Inclusion; https://www.fema.gov/about/offices/disability.
- Indigenous Services Canada; https://www.sac-isc.gc.ca/eng/1309369889599/1535119888656.
- Gender and Disaster Network; https://www.gdnonline.org/.
- Disability Inclusive Disaster Risk Reduction; https://www.un.org/development/desa/disabilities/issues/disability-inclusive-disaster-risk-reduction-and-emergency-situations.html.

Index

Note: **Bold** page numbers refer to tables and *italic* page numbers refer to figures.

accidents: BP Petroleum 209; chemical 62, 70; hazardous waste 4; normal 54; nuclear 46, 72, 287; transportation 5, 24, 62, 79
accessible workplace communities 315–316
active representation 310, 312, 313, 315
aggregate research 98
Aguirre, Benigno E. 77, 171
Alaska earthquake, 1964 71
Allbaugh, Joe 8
All Hazards Approach 61, 67–70, 120, 137, 148, 150
"all risks" 69
ammonium nitrate 44
Anderson, Bill 317, 318
Anderson, William A. 92, 317
applied research 96–97
archives 103–104
Associate Emergency Manager (AEM) 29
asylee fleeing 300–301

basic research 96–97
Bettinger, Jessica 34, 35, 36
Biden, Joe 8, 313
biological hazards 45–46
blizzards 24, 39, 129, 137, 139, 144, 165
Boin, Arjen 266
bombing: Boston Marathon bombing 47; in Germany and Japan 17; of Murrah Federal Building in Oklahoma City 103, 185, 208, 270; nuclear bombs 71; radiological threats or "dirty bombs" 47; World Trade Center 103
Boston Marathon bombing 47
bridging social capital 243
Building codes 31, 69, 78, 143, 205, 239, 240, 241, 246, 248, 273
bushfires 52–54
Bush, George W. 8, 9, 13

business continuity planning 142, 143, 205, 268, 269, 270
buyout 147, 240

capability assessment 222, 223–225
careers: in emergency management (*see* professionalization of EM); in mitigation and resilience 245, 247; paths 30–31
Carter, Jimmy 7, 11, 19, 67
cascading impacts 119, 187, 275
catastrophe 62–64, 79, 174, 181
Center for Disease Control and Prevention (CDC) 10
certified emergency manager (CEM) 14, 29, 30, 67, 68, 79, 276, 328, 329
chemical hazards 44–45
Chernobyl nuclear power plant explosion 72
Chevreau, Francois-Regis 186
Christchurch earthquake 315
citizen science 323
civil defense 4, 6–7, 18, 71, 310
Clarke, L. 269
climate change 49, 52; and disaster response 286–287; heat waves and drought 52–53; wildfires and fire weather 53–54
Clinton, Bill 8, 234, 235, 260, 313
code enforcement 239, 240, 241
code of conduct 29–30
Cold War 7, 18, 19, 66, 71, 73
community-based planning 145–147, 148, 155, 225
Community Emergency Response Teams (CERTs) 30
community engagement 244–245, 323
community health promoter (CHP) program 294
community integration 293–295
community lifelines 274, 274
compounding disasters 54, 119, 187

comprehensive emergency management 67, 183–184

computer crimes 47–48

conferences 93

continuing education 92–93, 276, 324

continuum of disaster: catastrophe 63–4; disaster 63; emergency 62–63

CONVERGE facility 86–87

convergence 64, 177, 184, 189; behavior 176; framework 86–88

coordination 286

core competencies 25, 26, 94, 117, 188, 310, 320

coronavirus pandemic see COVID-19 pandemic

COVID-19 pandemic 5, 150, 154, 170; businesses 213, 265; climate change and 187; CONVERGE 87; criticisms 39; dangers of 52; death 75, 311; disaster myths and 173–174; disruptions 143; hurricanes 119; outbreak 32, 40, 141, 241; public health 38, 224; resuming operations during 266; spread of 45; in U.S. 54; vaccine distribution 140, 201, 316, 325

crisis 79; care 291; COVID-19 187; emergency managers 31; event 140; humanitarian 41; management 61; refugee 285; water 275

crisis approach 73–74

CrisMart 73

Criswell, Deanne 8, 313

critical infrastructure systems 121, 128, 274, 275, 278

cross-cutting themes in disaster science: resilience 74, 76–77; social vulnerability 74, 74–76; summary of 77

cross sectional research 97–98

crowd management: operational phase 51–52; strategic phase 51; tactical phase 51

crowds and collective behavior 49

crowdsourcing 245

cultural awareness and integrating context 290–291, 293

cultural competency 117, 118, 310, 311

cultural diversity 116

cultural relativism 291

cultural resources 13, 198, 199, 210–211, 214, 315

culture of preparedness 116, 119, 131

Cutter, Susan L. 17

cyberterrorism 5, 47–48

cyclones 4, 18, 41; Cyclone Nargis 39, 202

Dam 11

damage assessment 197–198; needs assessment 200–201; preliminary 198–200

degree programs, emergence of 14–15

Department of Homeland Security (DHS) 6, 34, 128, 146, 171, 199, 255, 260, 275, 313

derechos 24, 40

disaster(s): continuum of disaster 62–64; defining 61–62; donations 177–178; future, characteristics of 187; life cycle 68–69; political definitions 64–66; Presidential Declaration 65–66; risk reduction at international level 301; slow vs. fast-moving views 66–67; tradition 71–72

disaster myths 91, 140, 163, 172, 173, 175

disaster research: community 89; conferences and workshops 93; continuing education 92–93; funding 17; interdisciplinary journey 326; interpersonal connections 92; new media 93–94; pioneers of 16; publications 93; traditional issues 71–72; in U.S. 317; value of 8, 92–94

Disaster Research Centers (DRC) 14, 17, 90, 138, 179

disaster response: challenges of 106–107; comprehensive emergency management 183–184; flexibility in emergency management 185–186; integrated emergency management 184–185; in international context 181–183; myth-based view 172, 175–176; myths and realities 171–172; research-based view 176, 178–180; sources and limitations of community resilience 180–181; types of 180

disaster science: academic journals 96; crisis approach 73–74; cross-cutting themes in (see cross-cutting themes in disaster science); disaster tradition 71–72; evolution of 15–16; hazards tradition 70–71; history of 16–17; importance of 91, 94; in international context 18; major perspective summary 62, 74; as multidisciplinary field 85, 88, 90; research centers in U.S. 17–18; risk perspective 72–73

disaster subcultures 125

disaster warnings: characteristics of effective 169–171; disaster tradition 71-72; evacuation 167–168; public shelter usage 168–169; taking protective action 166–167; temporary sheltering 167–168; warning process 165–166, 166

displaced persons 201, 205, 284–286

diversity 29, 41, 116, 148, 211, 215, 242, 301, 302, 310, 312

dominant and social vulnerability perspectives 74

DRC Typology 179, 184

drought 52–53

dual disaster 11, 149
Durkheim, Emile 176
Dust Bowl 52
Dynes, Russell R. 4, 17, 61, 71, 162, 255, 317

earthquakes 4, 16, 24, 36, 42; in Alaska
    42, 71, 92; in California 11, 39, 125; in
    Chile 240; Christchurch earthquake 315;
    during COVID-19 40; devastating 4, 24,
    75, 182, 295; Fukushima 79; Great East
    Japan Earthquake 319; *Great ShakeOut*
    earthquake 127; Haiti earthquake 42, 63–64,
    75, 128, 182, 202, 206, 240, 296; in India
    18, 39; Japanese 39, 46; Loma Prieta 9, 11,
    71, 313; in Nepal 42, 75, 182, 296, 313;
    Northridge 206; in Pakistan 18, 42; Project
    Impact mitigation efforts 8; retrofitting **229**,
    237; 7.8 Richter Scale San Francisco 42; San
    Fernando Earthquake 7; and tsunami 10, 19,
    39, 42, 46; in Turkey 54
Ebola outbreak 10, 45, 71, 150, 284, 296, 303
education: conferences 325; disaster research
    92–93; exercises and drills 325; graduate
    programs 321, 323–324; higher 78–79;
    online degree programs 324; professional
    and scientific journals 325, 327; training
    324–325; undergraduate degree programs
    320–321; workshops 325
elevation 196, 197, 236, 237, 247
emergency: continuum of disaster 62–63; offices
    254–255
emergency management (EM) 4–5; academic
    journals 96; careers (*see* professionalization
    of EM); competencies 25–26; current and
    future challenges 5–6; evolution in U.S.
    (*see* United States (U.S.)); higher education
    78–79; planning across life cycle of (*see*
    planning process); profession of (*see*
    professionalization of EM); value of research
    92–94
Emergency Management Standard 258
emergency manager: activity phases 31–32;
    Associate 29; certified 14, 29, 30, 67, 68, 79,
    276, 328, 329; crisis 31; crowd management
    49, 50; in health care and educational
    settings 32; job of 24; local 254–255;
    mitigation plan 241–245; professional
    opportunities 37–38; role of Governor 256
emergency operations center (EOC) 24
emergency operations plans (EOPs) 142
Emergency Support Function (ESF) 4, 11–13,
    35, 137, 142, 149, 152, 153, 260, 288
emergent norm theory 60

employer, first 327, 329
empowerment 179, 289, 292, 294, 301, 326
epidemics 10, 40, 45, 150, 286
ethical standards 29–30
ethics 25, 30, 55, 105–106
ethnicity 312–313
ethnocentrism 291
EU Civil Protection Mechanism *262*
evacuation and temporary sheltering: disaster
    warnings 167–168; factors affecting 168–
    169; and public shelter usage 168–169
Event Action Plan (EAP) 51
evidence-based practice 15, 84, 91, 188, 294, 310
evolution of disaster science: brief history of
    disaster science 16–17; disaster science in
    international context 18; research centers in
    United States 17–18; what is disaster science
    15–16
explosions 4, 66; in Beirut 44, 225, 287;
    chemical plant 16, 73, 165, 225; at
    Chernobyl nuclear power plant in Ukraine
    46; Deepwater Horizon Well 209; nuclear
    10, 72; at West Fertilizer Company in Texas
    44, 176, 225
Extreme Events Reconnaissance and Research
    (EER) networks 86

Federal Emergency Management Agency
    (FEMA): challenges 9; community lifelines
    274, *274*; COVID-19 170, 187; under
    DHS 260–261; directors 8, 9, 11, 234; in
    disability support 37; disaster organizations
    10; Higher Education Project 25, 27, 78, 94,
    188; Joint Field Office (JFO) 153; mission 9;
    National Preparedness Assessment Division
    34; *2020 National Preparedness Report* 188;
    national recovery framework 199; National
    Response Coordination Center 35; National
    Threat and Hazard Identification and Risk
    Assessment 222; Office of Response and
    Recovery PA division 36; planning process
    241–242; professionalization of EM 6, 7;
    Project Impact 97; *Ready.gov* campaign
    127; regional offices 256–257; *2018–2022
    Strategic Plan* 188
federal government, public sector: congress
    261–262; executive branch 259–261
federal response plan (FRP) 9, 11, 142, 149
fellowships 317, 319–320
Fire Corps 30
Fischer, Henry W. 169, 173
flexibility 99, 101, 139, 148, 154, 163, 164, 183,
    185–186, 190, 214

floods 4–6, 24, 35–36, 40, 41–43, 46, 70, 79, 124, 128, 209, 222, 240, 284, 287
Fritz, Charles E. 16, 17, 61, 62, 63, 71, 79, 97, 105, 176, 179, 180
Fugate, Craig 8, 271
functional needs 118, 119, 202, 324

gender 46, 74–75, 77, 117, 168, 204, 208, 285, 290, 297, 313
genocide 284–285, 304
geographic information system (GIS) 28
geographic literacy 26, 94
Germany and Japan, bombing 17
glass ceiling 313
glass cliff 313
Government Accountability Report (GAO) 11
government sector EM 31–32
Great East Japan Earthquake 319
Great ShakeOut earthquake 127

Haas, Eugene J. 17, 71
hail 24, 40, 226
Haiti earthquake 42, 63–64, 75, 128, 182, 202, 206, 240, 296
Hajj 49
hardening 237
hazard identification 124, 148, 222–223, 224, 239, 258
hazards 38–40; biological hazards 45–46; chemical hazards 44–45; climate change 49–54; complexity of hazards becoming disasters 54; computer crimes and cyberterrorism 47–48; crowds and collective behavior 49; earthquakes 42; floods 42–43; high wind events 40–41; hurricanes, cyclones, and typhoons 41; identification and risk assessment 224; interdisciplinary journey 326; pandemic planning 150–152; radiological and nuclear hazards 46; space weather 48; terrorism 46–47; and threat information sources 223; volcanoes 43–44
"hazards and disaster research community" 88
hazards tradition 70–71
Hazard Reduction and Recovery Center (HRRC) 17, 322
Hazards & Vulnerability Research Institute (HVRI) 17
heat waves 52–53
high wind events 40–41
historic properties 13, 199, 210, 211, 214
household-level planning 144–145
household planning 155
humanitarian core standards 289, 290, 299

humanitarian logistics 286, 288–290, 295
hurricanes 4–6, 16, 24, 40–41, 61, 64, 70, 79; Category 5 Hurricane Iota 5; during the COVID-19 pandemic 119; hurricane Agnes 7; hurricane Andrew 9, 11, 149, 176, 202, 239, 264; hurricane Camille 7, 9; hurricane Harvey 35, 118, 176, 187, 258, 270, 312; hurricane Hugo 9, 11; hurricane Ike 14; hurricane Irma 118; hurricane Katrina 9, 37–38, 63–64, 70, 75, 79, 99, 104, 117, 139–140, 165, 168–169, 175, 181, 185–186, 197, 201, 211, 235–237, 260, 261, 270; hurricane Laura 54; hurricane Maria 11, 36, 41, 181, 187, 202; hurricane Rita 125
Hyogo Framework 301

ice storms 37, 39, 118–119, 165, 187, 206
impacts of disasters on private sector 264–265; indirect impacts 265; remote impacts 265–267
improvisation 71, 103, 138, 185, 186
inclusion 210, 312
Indian Ocean Tsunami 33, 38–39, 42, 63, 71, 75, 204, 309–310, 326
indigenous people communities 313, 315
individual-level planning 144–145
individual research 98
insurance 143; coverage 66, 228, 241; flood 165; hazard-specific 122, 267, 273; personal 203, 240; policies 240; private companies 240, 245; renter's 240
internally displaced person (IDP) 43, 66, 285
international aid workers 303
International Association of Emergency Managers (IAEM) 14, 25, 26, 29, 30, 35, 276, 325, 328
international emergency management system 287–288; and humanitarian aid 33, 36; sphere 289; UN cluster system 288–289; U.S. agency for international development 289–290
international humanitarian disaster management: climate change and disaster response 286–287; coordination 286; disaster risk reduction 301; integration and empowerment 292–293; international emergency management system 287–288; refugees, working with 296–297; UN high commissioner on refugees 284–286; volunteering in international setting 301–303; working in (*see* working internationally)
international preparedness initiatives 128–129

internships and practical experience communities 320
interviews 100–102

Joint Field Office (JFO) 153

Kennedy, John F. 285

Lagadec, Patrick 266
landslides 18, 43, 54, 64, 85, 209
land use planning 17, 239, 241, 273
Levee **229**, 236
LGBTQ+ 290, 297, 311–312, 316–317
life cycle of disasters (or four phases) 154, 161, 264, 318
life cycle of EM, private sector: mitigation 272–273; preparedness 267–269; recovery 271–272; response 269–271
Lincoln, Abraham 259
Local Emergency Planning Committee (LEPC) 44, 46
local government, public sector: accrediting 258–259; elected officials and emergency management offices 254–255; local departments 255–256
Loma Prieta earthquake 9, 11, 71, 313
longitudinal research 97–98
low-probability/high-consequence events 126

Medical Reserve Corps 30
mentors 317, 319, 321, 329
Mileti, Dennis S. 124, 235, 273
military careers 36–37
mitigation: capability assessment 223–225; careers and volunteering 245, 247; description 228; disaster, champions of 234–236; introduction 222; loss estimation 227–228; nonstructural mitigation 239–241; planning with stakeholders (see stakeholders); and resilience career examples 246–247; risk assessment 225–226; social vulnerability assessment 226–227; structural mitigation 233, 236–237, 239; threat and hazard identification 222–223
mitigation planning 31, 142, 155, 222, 227, 241–245, 246, 247, 248
mudslides 5, 43, 54
multidisciplinary approach 77–78
Murrah Federal Building in Oklahoma City, attacks on 46, 103, 185, 208, 270

NaTech 54
National Coordinating Council on Emergency Management (NCCEM) 29

National Critical Functions 275
National Governor's Association (NGA): all-hazards approach 69–70; disaster life cycle 68–69; report in U.S. 67–68
National Incident Management System (NIMS) 142, 148, 153, *153*, 154, 155, 156, 184, 185, 189, 324
national-level exercises (NLEs) 128
national-level preparedness initiatives 127–128
National Nuclear Security Administration (NNSA) 10; Office of Emergency Operations (OEO) 10
National Preparedness Assessment Division (NPAD) 34
National Response Coordination Center (NRCC) 35
National Response Framework (NRF) 11, 137, 142, 148, 149, 152, 260, 274, 275
National Science Foundation (NSF) 86; CONVERGE facility 86–87; Extreme Events Reconnaissance and Research (EER) networks 86; Social Science Extreme Events Research (SSEER) Network 88–90
National Terrorism Advisory System 171
National Voluntary Organization Active in Disasters (NVOAD) 9
natural disasters 7, 19, 39, 54, 85, 143, 181–183, 186, 284, 295–296, 304
Natural Hazard Research and Applications Information Center (NHRAIC) 17
Natural Hazards Center 70
Natural Hazards Engineering Research Infrastructure (NHERI) 86
Neal, David M. 176, 185
needs assessment 36, 198, 200–201, 204, 216, 289
Neighborhood Watch 30
networking 25, 255, 311, 312, 317
new media, disaster research 93–94
next generation of emergency managers and disaster scientists: Bill Anderson Fellow 318–319; continuing education (see education); first employer 327, 329; graduate studies 322–323; Mary Ann Myers *314*, 314–315; reflecting communities (see communities)
non-aid workers 295–296
non-governmental organization (NGO) 15, 31, 152, 184, 198, 203, 242, 246, 253, 286
non-structural mitigation 228, **231–233**, 239–241, 248
Northridge earthquake 206
nuclear hazards 46
nuclear bombs 71
Nyiragongo volcano 44

Obama, Barack 8, 128, 313, 316
observations 102–103
Office of Emergency Operations (OEO) 10
offices of homeland security 256
organizational adaptation 186

pandemics 10, 138; COVID-19 (see COVID-19 pandemic); global 91, 128, 309; planning 27–29, 32, 45, 140, 150–152, 240, 324
participatory action research 244
Peek, Lori 89
people-centered recovery 211–212; kinds of recovery planning 212–215
people with disabilities 292–293, 293
permanent housing 35, 202, 203, 204
personal protective equipment (PPE) 150
photovoice 102
planning process 186, 241, 247, 269, 270; across life cycle of EM 142–143; business continuity planning 143; community-based 145–147; incident command system 153, 153; individual-and household-level 144–145; levels of 143–144; planning and preparedness cycle 149; principles of 136–141; state and national planning guidance in U.S. 147–149, 152–154; steps in 149; types of planning 142–143; working and volunteering 154–155
points of distribution (POD) 38
preliminary damage assessment 164, 197, 198–200
preparedness: activities, types and levels of 121, 121–125; business disaster 268–269; communities 124–125; defining preparedness 120; factors influencing levels 125–126; household disaster preparedness plan 146; individuals and households 121–122; international preparedness initiatives 128–129; national-level preparedness initiatives 127–128; organizations 122, 124; previous disaster experience 125–126; prioritizing preparedness 116, 119–120; recommendations 123; risk perception 126; Sendai Framework 129; state-level preparedness initiatives 127; and whole community 119; working and volunteering in preparedness 129–130
Presidential Declaration of Disaster (PDD) 65–66
primary research 97
private sector 32; impacts of disasters 264–265; importance of 262–264; and life cycle of EM (see life cycle of EM, private sector)

professionalization of EM 6–7, 10, 19, 24–25; body of knowledge 27–28; career paths 30–31; competencies and expected behaviors 25–27; disasters change things 9, 11; ethical standards and code of conduct 29–30; leadership challenges and changes 8–9; lifelong learning 28–29; structural changes 11, 13–14; working in (see working in profession of EM)
Project Impact mitigation efforts 8
public and private partnerships 124, 254, 273–275, 277
public sector 31, 34, 124, 142, 275, 276, 277; federal government 259–262; local government 254–259; state government 256–259; see also separate entries

qualitative research 98–99
quantitative research 98–99
Quarantelli, E.L. 5, 6, 17, 61, 63, 71, 138, 175, 176, 266, 287, 309, 317
"quick response" research 17, 71–72, 99

race 312–313
radiological hazards 46
radiological threats/dirty bombs 47
Ready.gov campaign 127
Ready Oklahoma campaign 127
reconstruction 33, 137, 196, 197, 204, 235, 326
recovery: businesses 203, 205–206; damage assessment 197–198; defining 196–197; environmental concerns 209–210; historic and cultural resources 210–211; infrastructure and lifelines 206–207; people-centered 211–212; planning, kinds of 212–215; process 197; psychological impacts 207–209; shelter and housing 201–205; working and volunteering 215–216
Recovery Support Functions (RSFs) 199
refugee(s): CHP program 294; hiring former 294; Karen refugee camp 298; moment in life of 300–301; Myanmar coup and ongoing instability 298; UN high commissioner 284–286; urban 299; working with 296–301
refugee camps 284, 285, 291, 292, 297–298
refugee resettlement 285, 297, 299–300, 304
rehabilitation 196, 198
relocation 104, 122, 147, 202, 203, 205, 206, 210, 240, 241
research challenges 106–107
research methods 28, 89, 94, 99–105; archives 103–104; data collection methods 99, 99; interviews 100–102; observations 102–103; spatial tools 104–105; surveys 99–100

research process 94–96, *95*, 95–96
research types: basic and applied research 96–97; cross sectional and longitudinal research 97–98; individual and aggregate research 98; primary and secondary research 97; quantitative and qualitative research 98–99
resilience 31; careers 245–247; community integration 293–295; of critical infrastructure systems 274; culture of 241; defined 76, 120; disaster 97, 125, 211, 241, 273–274, 301; managers 143; nonstructural mitigation 239; sources and limitations 180–181; specialists 38; structural mitigation 237; and sustainability 77
response: activities 163–164; definitions 163; disaster (*see* disaster response); effective disaster warnings (*see* disaster warnings); future of 186–188; future risks *188*; phases of disaster 161–162; working and volunteering 188–189
restitution 197
restoration 197, 198, 206, 210
retrofit 31, **229**, 237, 273
retrofitting **229**, 237
Richter Scale 42
risk assessment 38, 53, 148, 222, 224, 225–228, 239
risk perception 85, 98, 125, 126, 127, 168
risk perspective 61, 72–73
Roosevelt, Eleanor 285
Roosevelt, Franklin 259
"Rs" (readiness, response, recovery, and reduction) 68
Russo, Barb 50

San Fernando Earthquake 7
scholarships 317, 319–320
scientific literacy 94, 107, 188
secondary research 97
September 11, 2001, attacks of 9, 11, 32, 148, 162, 257
severe acute respiratory syndrome (SARS) epidemic 150
social capital 140, 141, 146, 155, 182, 211, 212, 213, 216; bridging 243; cognitive 243; structural 243
social networks 130, 182, 202, 204, 207, 208, 213, 240, 243, 304
Social Science Extreme Events Research (SSEER) Network 88–90
social vulnerability 27; assessment 226–227; aware of 76; preparedness 116–118; and

resilience 74, *74*, 77, 79; spatial distribution 85; training 324
sociocultural literacy 26, 94, 117, 311
space weather 4, 5, 24, 48, 223, 309
spaghetti models 226
spatial tools 104–105
sphere 204, 288, 289
spontaneous unaffiliated volunteers (SUVs) 189
stakeholders: inclusive mitigation planning 242–244; mitigation planning basics 241–242; resilience 241; strategies for community engagement 244–245
state government, public sector: accrediting 258–259; EM and homeland security offices 256–258; role of governor 256
state-level preparedness initiatives 127
structural mitigation **229–230**, 233, 236–237, 239
subsistence living 244
Super Bowl 49
Super Outbreak of Tornadoes, 1974 71
Super Typhoon Yolanda 41
SURGE 312
surveys 99–100
sustainability 76, 77, 143, 199, 210, 212, 290, 294
Swedish Defense University 73
systems literacy 26, 188

technological disasters 7, 17, 54, 66, 181, 287
technological literacy 26, 28
temporary housing 12, 75, 196, 197, 202, 237, 315
temporary shelter 167, 202, 204, 271
terrorism 9, 16, 24, 27; assessing building vulnerability 238–239; defined 46; domestic threats 19, 46–47, 171; fear of 100; modified weapons 47; Murrah Federal Building in Oklahoma City, attacks on 46; September 11, 2001, attacks of 9, 11, 32, 148, 162, 257; Terrorist Attacks, 2001 71; warning 171
Threat and Hazard Identification and Risk Assessment (THIRA) 222
Three Mile Island (TMI) nuclear accident 72
thunderstorms 40, 53, 226
Tierney, Kathleen J. 122, 163, 175, 181, 264
TOPOFF *see* national-level exercises (NLEs)
tornadoes: annual deaths 78; destructive 4; EF1 tornado 75, 226; EF5 tornado 40, 206, 226, 237; Enhanced Fujita [EF]-4 scale tornado 261; fire 53; Fujita scale (F3) tornado 139; human responses to 16; in Missouri 237; outbreaks 49, 144; Super Outbreak of Tornadoes 71; "tornado alley" 5, 39, 125, 171

transferability 101–102

triangulation 99

tribal management 321

Truman, Harry S. 167, 285

tsunamis: Asian countries 18, 182–183; and earthquakes 10, 19, 39, 42, 46; at Fukushima nuclear power plant 10; Indian Ocean Tsunami 33, 38–39, 42, 63, 71, 75, 204, 309–310, 326; Japanese 39, 46, 128, 227

typhoons 41, 46, 296

UN cluster system 288–289

United Nations High Commissioner on Refugees 284–286

United States (U.S.): Billion-Dollar Weather Disasters 263; disaster research 317; emergence of EM degree programs 14–15; era of civil defense 6–7; evolution of disaster science (*see* disaster science); evolution of EM 6; NGA report 67–68; professionalization of (*see* professionalization of EM); research centers 17–18; state and national planning guidance 147–149, 152–154

Universal Declaration of Human Rights (UDHR) 285

urban refugees 297, 299

U.S. Agency for International Development 289–290; Disaster Assistance Response Team 36, 290, 293, 296

volcanoes 4, 24, 43–44, 85, 167, 240, 284; Nyiragongo volcano 44

voluntary organization 7, 9, 14, 30, 31, 33, 34, 35, 66, 69, 98, 164, 178, 183, 189, 198, 200, 201, 237

voluntary sector EM 33

volunteering: in international setting 301–303; in mitigation and resilience 245, 247; in planning 154–155; in preparedness 129–130;

in private sector 275–277; in recovery 215–216; in response 188–189

Volunteers in Police Service (VIPS) 30

vulnerable populations 9, 15, 37, 85, 105, 136, 140, 147, 176, 181, 290, 297

"warning fatigue" 171

warning process 165–166, 168

Webb, Gary R. 124, 185, 186, 264

White, Gilbert F. 17, 70, 234, 235, 236

whole community planning 34, 116, 117, 119, 128, 145, 148, 241, 242, 253, 260, 316

wildfires and fire weather: Australia 53–54; Canada 53; United States 53

Witt, James Lee 8, 234, 235, 236

working: in crowd settings 50–52; in planning 154–155; in preparedness 129–130; in private sector 275–277; in recovery 215–216; with refugees 296–297; in response 188–189

working in profession of EM: emergency managers, specialized opportunities for 37–38; government sector EM 31–32; international EM and humanitarian aid 33, 36; and military careers 36–37; private sector EM 32; voluntary sector EM 33

working internationally 301–303; community integration and resiliency models 293–295; cultural awareness and integrating context 290–291, 293; guidance for non-aid workers 295–296; international aid workers 303

workshops 17, 71, 92, 93, 128, 292, 298, 319, 324, 325

World Health Organization (WHO) 150, 284, 287–288

World Trade Center 32, 103, 139, 178–179, 214, 270

Yarnell fire 53

Zika virus 241